THE REFORMATION OF FAITH IN THE CONTEXT
OF LATE MEDIEVAL THEOLOGY AND PIETY

STUDIES IN THE HISTORY
OF
CHRISTIAN THOUGHT

FOUNDED BY HEIKO A. OBERMAN †

EDITED BY

ROBERT J. BAST, Knoxville, Tennessee

IN COOPERATION WITH

HENRY CHADWICK, Cambridge
SCOTT H. HENDRIX, Princeton, New Jersey
BRIAN TIERNEY, Ithaca, New York
ARJO VANDERJAGT, Groningen
JOHN VAN ENGEN, Notre Dame, Indiana

VOLUME CX

BERNDT HAMM

THE REFORMATION OF FAITH IN THE CONTEXT
OF LATE MEDIEVAL THEOLOGY AND PIETY

THE REFORMATION OF FAITH IN THE CONTEXT OF LATE MEDIEVAL THEOLOGY AND PIETY

ESSAYS BY BERNDT HAMM

EDITED BY

ROBERT J. BAST

BRILL

LEIDEN · BOSTON

2004

This book is printed on acid-free paper.

Library of Congress Cataloging-in-Publication Data

Hamm, Berndt.
  [Essays, English. Selections]
  The reformation of faith in the context of late medieval theology and piety : essays by
Berndt Hamm / [edited] by Robert J. Bast.
      p. cm. - (Studies in the history of Christian thought, ISSN 0081-8607 ; v. 110)
  Includes bibliographical references and index.
  ISBN 90-04-13191-4 (alk. paper)
    1. Reformation. 2. Theology, Doctrinal—History—Middle Ages, 600-1500. 3. Christian
life-History—Middle Ages, 600-1500. 4. Church history—Middle Ages, 600-1500. I.
Bast, Robert James. II. Title. III. Series.

  BR305.3.H36213 2003
  270.5—dc22
                                                                                        2003065215

BR
305.3
.H36213
2004

ISSN   0081-8607
ISBN   90 04 13191 4

PRINTED IN THE NETHERLANDS

CONTENTS

ACKNOWLEDGMENTS

On behalf of the author I would like to express thanks to those whose diligent labor made this collection possible. Most of the articles collected herein were translated by Ms. Helen Heron (chapters 2–9); Dr. Gotthelf Wiedermann assisted in the translation of chapter 2, which appeared in Robert J. Bast and Andrew C. Gow (eds.), *Continuity and Change. The Harvest of Late Medieval and Reformation History. Essays presented to Heiko A. Oberman on his 70th Birthday* (Brill, 2000). Chapter 1 was originally translated by Prof. Dr. John M. Frymire for publication in the *Journal of Early Modern History* III/4 (1999). Chapter 6 appeared in C. Scott Dixon (ed.), *The German Reformation. The Essential Readings.* Blackwell Essential Readings (Blackwell Publishers, 1999). For the rights to reproduce those materials we thank Brill and Blackwell Publishers; for diligently correcting the manuscript, Ms. Heidrun Munzert. Financial support was generously provided by the University of Tennessee in the form of separate grants from the Exhibit, Performance and Publication Expense fund, and from MARCO, the Medieval and Renaissance Curriculum and Outreach Project.

ABBREVIATIONS

ARCEG	*Acta reformationis catholicae ecclesiam Germaniae concernentia saeculi XVI. Die Reformverhandlungen des deutschen Episkopats von 1520 bis 1570.* Ed. G. Pfeilschifter. Regensburg, 1959–.
CAvar	*Confessio Augustana variata*
CChr	*Corpus Christianorum*
CR	*Corpus Reformatorum*
Migne, *PL*	*Patrologiea cursus completus: series latina.* Ed. J.-P. Migne. Paris, 1841–1864.
OS	*Calvini Opera Selecta.* Ed. P. Barth, W. Niesel, D. Scheuner. Munich, 1926–59.
WA	*D. Martin Luthers Werke. Kritische Gesamtausgabe. Abteilung Schriften.* Weimar, 1883–1990.
WA Br	*D. Martin Luthers Werke. Kritische Gesamtausgabe. Abteilung Briefwechsel.* Weimar, 1930–85.
WA Tr	*D. Martin Luthers Werke. Kritische Gesamtausgabe. Abteilung Tischreden.* Weimar, 1912–21.
Z	*Huldreich Zwinglis sämtliche Werke.* Ed. E. Egli. Zurich, 1905–.

EDITOR'S FOREWORD

The essays in this volume have been translated and collected in order to make more accessible to readers of English the work of Berndt Hamm, Professor of Historical Theology at the University of Erlangen, long recognized as one of the most important and original scholars at work on the religious history of Late Medieval and Early Modern Germany. As the chapters below make abundantly clear, the range and diversity of his scholarship do not easily lend themselves to summary. Nevertheless, the reader approaching his work for the first time may be helped by advance knowledge of recurring themes related to the question of continuity and change across those conceptual epochs known as the Middle Ages and the Reformation, especially (though not exclusively) as it relates to theology and religious life. Thus the title of this volume.

This is an intellectual project with which Hamm has been absorbed from the beginning of his scholarly career, and his intensive engagement with an ever-growing diversity of sources has yielded a harvest that is both rich and substantive. Two of the terms he has developed have passed into general usage in the scholarly literature, and both merit particular attention here as they serve as foundations for the rest of the collection. *Frömmigkeitstheologie* is Hamm's designation for a genre of late-medieval writing and praxis, much of it derived from and directed toward pastoral care, which was especially concerned with the pursuit of an authentic Christian life as defined by the values and institutions of the day. Literally but inadequately translated as the "theology of piety", the term appears in that form in the pages below, together with several synonyms that have been pressed into service to help carry the weight of its nuances. Thus the reader will also encounter "devotional" or "pastoral" theology and/or piety. Such are the limits of language. Why the later Middle Ages should give rise to an abundance of such literature is of course another question. Hamm has sought to answer it by identifying and analyzing a process at work in the 14th–16th centuries, which he has termed *Normative Zentrierung*: the centering or concentration of social, religious, political and cultural norms.

His work on these themes highlights one of the hallmarks of his humane and learned scholarship: the study of theology not as a static category of intellectual activity but as an intensely human expression of lived experience. Just how inadequately any sketch can suggest the breadth and vitality of that scholarship, the reader will soon discover.

Robert J. Bast
Knoxville, Tennessee
29 April 2003

CHAPTER ONE

NORMATIVE CENTERING IN THE 15TH AND 16TH CENTURIES: OBSERVATIONS ON RELIGIOSITY, THEOLOGY, AND ICONOLOGY

I. *Normative Centering: An Interpretive Category*

Categories of historical interpretation are indispensable. But when they lose their status as questions, when it is no longer apparent that they are thought constructs placed upon the past, such categories come to have fatal effects on scholarship. One forgets too easily what interpretive categories are *not*: they are neither past realities in themselves nor snapshots of them. At best they may clarify certain historical phenomena better than other heuristic tools. And nowhere is their problematic application better illustrated than in their use to characterize broad-ranging epochs, as when one takes the 15th and 16th centuries and applies to them labels like 'Late Middle Ages', 'Renaissance', 'Reformation', and 'Confessionalization' or explains them with categories such as 'rationalization' (Max Weber), 'social discipline' (Gerhard Oestreich), 'the civilizing process' (Norbert Elias), or 'christianization' (Jean Delumeau). These last four seem to me to be especially contestable, since each subject narrow bases of sources to broadly encompassing and yet highly selective models of interpretation.

In 1992 I first suggested my own interpretive category, 'normative centering' (*Normative Zentrierung*),[1] which like the others contains a relatively far-reaching, integrative heuristic claim. As an interpretive category, 'normative centering' is subject to precisely the kind of limitations described above. It, too, is nothing other than a construct placed upon the past which, so far as I can see, explains certain

---

[1] Berndt Hamm: "Reformation als normative Zentrierung von Religion und Gesellschaft", in: *Jahrbuch für Biblische Theologie* 7 (1992), pp. 241–279; idem: "Von der spätmittelalterlichen reformatio zur Reformation: der Prozeß normativer Zentrierung von Religion und Gesellschaft in Deutschland", in: *Archiv für Reformationsgeschichte* 84 (1993), pp. 7–82.

aspects of the sources (and only these) better than other such constructs.

My starting point lay in the attempt to overcome certain per-
spectival distortions in our view of the 15th and 16th centuries. It
was clear to me that "God, the World-Spirit, or Whoever" had not
packaged history "in portions of a century" any more than had the
current schools of historical interpretation.[2] For me the question was
four-fold:

1. How can one understand the so-called 'Late Middle Ages' as an
   open period which is neither determined by characteristics suggesting an 'end' or 'termination' nor forced by causal necessity
   to somehow empty into, and conclude with, the Reformation?
   Given this, how can one nevertheless describe both Reformation
   and Confessionalization as growing out of, and furthering, certain
   tendencies already seen in the 15th century?
2. How can one gain a perspective that allows him to comprehend
   the 15th and 16th centuries as a continuous, epoch-transcending
   period which, at the same time, gives the rupture of the Reformation
   from the Late Middle Ages its proper due?
3. In what way can one understand the long route from Constance
   to Trent as both magnification of tradition and, in the sense that
   old traditions were newly formulated, as innovation? Or put
   another way: as the intensification of Late Medieval trends and
   simultaneously as the dawn of the modern era?
4. How can one seriously consider the respectively singular dynamics of theology, piety, and general ecclesiastical affairs as well as
   judicial administration, politics, and the institutional aspects of
   state (in structural *and* human terms) while still taking into account,
   and accommodating for, their intensive and changing relationships to one another?

The task is thus a matter of the continuous observation and evaluation of contradictory aspects. It seems to me that the interpretive
construct 'normative centering' is particularly well suited to do justice to precisely these questions and to respect their accompanying
demands for differentiation. Defining the concept minimally: by 'nor-

---

[2] Hartmut Boockmann: "Das fünfzehnte Jahrhundert in der deutschen Geschichte",
in: *Mittelalterforschung nach der Wende 1989*, ed. Michael Borgolte (Munich, 1995)
[= Historische Zeitschrift, Beiheft 20], pp. 485–511.

mative centering' I mean the alignment of both religion and society towards a standardizing, authoritative, regulating and legitimizing focal point. Whether seen as a concentration on the redemptive power of Christ's Passion or as the reduction of authoritative theological texts to the scriptures alone (to name just a few), this point of focus can be understood as multidimensional[3] and always stands in changing relation to other dominant foci of life; e.g., the standard of the Bible and the standardizing assertions of confessional creeds in relation to the standardizing claims of political authorities. Such divergent late medieval and early modern tendencies towards a normativizing center may be indicated with terms like consolidation and concentration,[4] simplification and standardization, or as the 'reduction of complexity' – above all, however, with that designation abounding in the sources, 'reform'. What confronts us in the historical documents as the *reformatio* of church, piety, monastic orders, law, and empire, along with the polyvalent term 'humanistic reform', represents to a large extent the expectations, conceptions, and tendencies inherent in a centrifugal, standardizing course of consolidation. And they remain unthinkable outside of the context of a sharp increase in the production and use of texts and images, in printing and lay education, in rationalization and bureaucratization. Both as an intention and a reality, 'normative centering' brought these cultural innovations to a head and functioned to yield a new certainty and legitimacy, a fresh clarity and order with respect to one's life in this world and the next. It thereby provided an answer to what many contemporaries saw as unsettling patterns of differentiation, multiplicity, individualization, and concern for (and attention to) the things of this world.

---

[3] Luther, for example, differentiated between 'Law' and 'Gospel' within the standard of truth that he ascribed to God's word in the Bible. How conceptions of the role of Mary and other saints in helping to win salvation for the sinner could be bound-up with Late Medieval 'centering' upon the salvific powers of Christ's Passion within theology, piety, and art will be addressed toward the end of this article.

[4] Cf. Berndt Hamm: "Das Gewicht von Religion, Glaube, Frömmigkeit und Theologie innerhalb der Verdichtungsvorgänge des ausgehenden Mittelalters und der frühen Neuzeit", in: *Krisenbewußtsein und Krisenbewältigung in der Frühen Neuzeit – Crisis in Early Modern Europe, Festschrift für Hans-Christoph Rublack*, ed. Monika Hagenmaier and Sabine Holtz (Frankfurt a.M., 1992), pp. 163–196 (in reference to the use of the term "consolidation" or "compression" [*Verdichtung*] by Volker Press, Peter Moraw, and Heinz Schilling).

II. *The Normative Centering of Religion*

The following analysis confines itself predominantly to religious sources
which, by their nature, favor the hereafter rather than the here.
Equally relevant to my interpretative claims, however, is the assertion
that both before and after 1500, specifically extra-ecclesiastical areas
of life within the realms of politics,[5] law,[6] humanism,[7] and the visual
arts[8] also witnessed comparable courses of standardization and 'normative centering'. Further investigations must establish whether and
how these conterminous attempts toward (and realizations of) such
consolidation relate, and if they were viewed in relation to one
another by historical agents via analogy, interdependence or interaction.

The multifaceted attempts toward the 'normative centering' of religion shared, despite their variety, a common emphasis geared above
all to fulfill a need for certainty and assurance. It is well known that
contemporaries longed for guaranteed methods of obtaining grace
and salvation.[9] Behind such 'pious' quests for salvific insurance[10] lay

---

[5] Key concept: the formation of the early modern state as the intensification,
standardization, and centering of the structures of power; cf. Hamm: "Von der
spätmittelalterlichen reformatio" (as above, n. 1), pp. 59–61.
[6] Key concept: the *reformatio* of law, i.e., the centering, consolidation, and
simplification of law through the reception of Roman law; cf. ibid., pp. 46–52.
[7] Key concept: the sources of Greek and Latin antiquity as mankind's highest
authoritative standards for language, education, and way of life; cf. ibid., pp. 41–46.
[8] Here we limit ourselves to the significance of central perspective and central
layout for painting as well as for the architecture of cities, castles, and gardens from
the Renaissance into the 18th century; cf. Werner Hofmann: *Das entzweite Jahrhundert
– Kunst zwischen 1750 und 1830* (Munich, 1995). In this book Hofmann describes
the abandonment of central perspective and its monofocality in favor of a frag-
mentation of perspective, a multi-perspectival and intentional unclarity in the work
of art. As such, polyfocality became the essential signature of modern art – after,
I should like to add, the 'early modern' works of the 15th century came to be characterized by the development of a new aesthetic norm of centrality, just as city
architecture near the end of the Middle ages distanced itself from complex, angular, patchwork forms and tended toward cleaner, more simple objects and buildings and toward a new lucidity in terms of urban visual perspectives. The fascinating
and revealing question in view of the period from the 15th through the early 18th
centuries seems to be, to ask in what relation such developments stood to concurrent manifestations of 'centering' within govermental, bureaucratic, legal, educational, social, economic, cultural and religious areas, and especially in that of
confessional 'centering'.
[9] Cf. Heiko A. Oberman: "The Shape of Late Medieval Thought: The Birthpangs
of the Modern Era", in: *The Pursuit of Holiness in Late Medieval and Renaissance Religion*,
ed. Charles Trinkaus and Heiko A. Oberman (Leiden, 1974) [= Studies in Medieval
and Reformation Thought 10], pp. 3–25, esp. p. 11 ("the search for new security");
Berndt Hamm: *Frömmigkeitstheologie am Anfang des 16. Jahrhunderts. Studien zu Johannes*

a specific and shared way of interpreting experience: how one perceived his age as a time of 'crisis' with an accompanying susceptibility to feelings of ominous danger and *Angst*; how one saw himself
in the face of certain disaster, given the power of sin, the proximity of death, and the clear wrath and judgment of God; how one
looked about and in every direction sensed turbulence and discord,
the breaking down or ripping apart of the social order; and finally,
how one recognized Satan and his agents as the root of the crisis,
indeed, as the fundamental menace both to the whole of Christendom
and to each individual soul comprising the *corpus Christianum*. This
common range of fears and perceptions before *and* after 1500 accounts
for the specific types of assurance that European Christians sought:
access to God's mercy; protection from the dark and devilish powers; preservation at the hour of death; pardon before the seat of
God's judgment; an abatement of purgatorial punishments; the re-
ordering of life based on God's commandments and the counsel of
perfection found in the Gospels; the stringent regulation of morality
and discipline within the community; the recovery of concord and
order, of temporal and eternal peace.

Within a climate of uncertainty and *Angst*, these and similar goals
combined with the various programs and realizations of a reductionist, simplifying 'normative centering'. That which was considered
central, that which was necessary and helpful, was held up as the
core and key for the shaping, measuring, and determining of individual life and of social, political and economic relations. Yet the
efficacy of these fundamental principles made them especially desir-
able and vulnerable targets for the attacks of Satan and the Antichrist;
one had to purge them continually of the encroachments of the
Devil's power. Such was accomplished not only through daily com-
bat against sin, but also in the fight against those personifications of
Satan's power, those enemies of truth and order, indeed against
heretics and Epicureans, against witches, Jews, Turks, and all those
on opposing sides of the confessional divide. That is why the age of
'normative centering' was accompanied by its striking counterpart,

---

von Paltz und seinem Umkreis (Tübingen, 1982) [= Beiträge zur Historischen Theologie
65], pp. 216–303 (ch. 5, "Im Umkreis der Suche nach Gnaden- und Heilsgarantien").
    [10] Cf. Jean Delumeau: *Rassurer et protéger. Le sentiment de sécurité dans l'Occident d'autre-
fois* (Paris, 1989).

the era of an aggressive and militant preoccupation with the Devil.[11] The concentration of religiosity within a normalizing set of focal points that were interpreted to regulate all aspects of life corresponded most of all with the establishment of demarcation lines, and those deemed 'outsiders' were to be driven out, repulsed, and persecuted.[12] To be sure, a rise in the fear of the Devil and of demons, accompanied by proportionate manifestations of militancy, may be detected already in the 14th and 15th centuries. But the logic of this mentality reached its peak and (if you will) completion only in the confessional systems of the late 16th century, when a unified, uncompromising, and closed confessional creed was proclaimed within a specific territory and joined forces with the dynamics of the formation and centralization of the pre- or early-absolutist state. In terms of internal and external policy, the steps taken by territorial governments against confessional opponents powerfully demonstrate the precise parallels between their attempts to accelerate an integrating, unifying, internalizing dynamic within and their externalizing, demonizing strategies of demarcation.[13]

---

[11] Delumeau seems to me correct in his description of a metaphysical *Angst* that increased tremendously from the 14th century and reached its escalation between *circa* 1550–1650; he charactarizes such *Angst* as the feeling that the foundations of Christendom in church, state, and society were menaced by the ragings of Satan and his agents, and by the power of sin. Cf. Delumeau: *La Peur en Occident (XIVe–XVIIIe siècle). Une cité assiégée* (Paris, 1978); idem, *Le péché et la peur. La culpabilisation en Occident (XIIIe–XVIIIe siècle)* (Paris, 1983). For the importance of the Black Death for this escalation, cf. František Graus: *Pest – Geissler – Judenmorde. Das 14. Jahrhundert als Krisenzeit*, 3 ed. (Göttingen, 1994) [= Veröffentlichungen des Max-Planck-Instituts für Geschichte 86]. Luther's attacks against papists, Jews, and Turks, in whom he saw the personification of Satan's ragings, are paradigmatic; on this see Heiko A. Oberman: *Luther: Man Between God and the Devil* [German ed. 1982], trans. Eileen Walliser-Schwarzbart (New Haven, 1990); for the broader contexts of Luther's shared mentality, cf. idem: *The Roots of Antisemitism in the Age of Renaissance and Reformation* [German ed. 1981], trans. James I. Porter (Philadelphia, 1984).

[12] To be sure, there are noteworthy exceptions to this rule in which examples of 'normative centering' are characterized not by an increase, but rather a decrease in the degree of aggressiveness against ecclesiastical and religious opponents. One thinks of Johannes von Staupitz (†1524), the vicar general of the German Augustinians and Luther's teacher, spiritual guide, and pastor. Staupitz attempted to center the whole of theology, piety, and the Church upon the mercy of God (see below p. 12 with n. 32), which effected a willingness to endure – in this sense, 'tolerance' – and a reserve over and against forms of ecclesiastical militance. Cf. Heiko A. Oberman: "*Duplex misericordia*: The Devil and the Church in the Early Theology of Johann von Staupitz" (German ed. 1989), trans. Andrew C. Gow, in: Heiko A. Oberman: *The Impact of the Reformation* (Grand Rapids, 1994), pp. 35–50.

[13] Confessional 'centering' and standardization within a political unit (i.e., city,

Despite the parallels which link various aspects of the 15th and 16th centuries, one must carefully distinguish between the specific phenomena particular to the 'normative centering' of the Late Middle Ages, of the many-sided phases and courses of the Reformation, and finally that of Catholic, Lutheran, and Reformed confessionalization. The smoothing-over of contrariety represents precisely what 'normative centering', as an interpretive category, may not effect. In fact, 'normative centering' enables and impels one to seize upon the differences between diverse conceptions of re-ordering and reform and between changing levels of intensity within the 'centering' dynamic. In the broadest sense, the concept may allow us to understand the 14th through the 17th centuries as an extended period of shared fears, of similar needs for assurance, of parallel hopes for standardization, and of a comparable intensification of that phenomenon of reducing and simplifying complex systems to a manageable set of core principles.[14] 'Normative centering' is thus continuity over time and community in diversity.

The intensity with which the early modern confessional state accelerated the course of standardization or 'centering' remains unthinkable

---

territory, etc.) was accompanied by external political contact with those belonging to the same confession, such that in the end (i.e., roughly in the half-century between 1570/75 and 1625/30) international ideological systems stood antagonistically over and against one another. Just as the internal situation within the developing early modern state was characterized by confessional integration and, at the same time, hostile demarcation against confessional opponents, representing two sides of the same coin, so the phenomenon was mirrored outside of particular territories at the level of international homogenization and dualization. Cf. Heinz Schilling: "Konfessionalisierung und Formierung eines internationalen Systems während der frühen Neuzeit", in: *Die Reformation in Deutschland und Europa: Interpretationen und Debatten*, ed. Hans R. Guggisberg, Gottfried G. Krodel and Hans Füglister (Gütersloh, 1993) [= Archiv für Reformationsgeschichte, Sonderband], pp. 591–613.

[14] Nothing requires or in fact warrants an extended discussion of the chronological boundaries of the era of 'normative centering', which was an age of *reformatio* and simultaneously one of an increased preoccupation with the Devil and the demonic. For me, what remains decisive is that the core of the era, especially between the middle of the 15th century through the first decades of the 17th, was characterized by phenomena that reveal an ever-increasing intensity of 'normative centering'. In contrast to my earlier publications on the theme of 'normative centering' (as above, n. 1), I now consciously avoid the term 'process' (*Prozeß*), since it risks taking contingent and *de facto* coherent events of the past and forcing upon them the metahistorical, ideological attributes of determinism, as though things were occurring in the service of some unforeseen goal. I prefer to speak of certain phenomena, courses, sequences, or occurrences (*Vorgänge*) of 'normative centering' (*in re*), which stand in relation to specific conceptions, yearnings, hopes, and expectations of 'normative centering' (*in mente*).

without the preceding normative thrusts that characterize the early
phases of the Reformation. Concentration upon *sola*-principles – the
Holy Scriptures alone, godly law alone, faith alone, the community
of the faithful with Christ alone, the redemptive act of Christ alone,
the effectiveness of God's grace alone, and the honor of God alone
– distinguish the bellicose decisiveness with which actors on the stage
of the early Reformation attempted to reduce Christendom to a set
of core principles and to proclaim them as the defining and binding precepts for both church and society. Within the various Protestant
camps, these *sola*-principles came to function as ideologies of liberation, legitimization, and demarcation during the confessional age.[15]
The early doctrinal creeds of the Reformation played a key role in
the development of those statements of faith which, in the later 16th
century, would serve as the normativizing, basic law of the evolving
confessional state. Furthermore, such states saw the stability of their
governments as founded upon the standardized authority of creeds,
which in turn claimed their own legitimacy by asserting their conformity to the Scriptures.[16] In Catholic lands one finds a similar pattern, marked by the application of a constricted doctrinal norm (and
creed) along with the image of a 'reformed' church, which together
served as the religious buttresses in the centralization and consolidation of territorial governments.[17]

Analogous were the preceding attempts at, and perceived need of,
standardization and 'centering' during the Late Middle Ages, without
which the intensification of such phenomena during the Reformation
would be unthinkable. Here two aspects must be kept in view. On
the one hand, to consider developments during the Reformation as
the necessary and organic outgrowth of determinative late medieval

[15] Cf. Hamm: "Reformation als normative Zentrierung" (as above, n. 1), p. 277f.
[16] Cf. the paradigmatic study of Heinz Schilling: *Konfessionskonflikt und Staatsbil-
dung. Eine Fallstudie über das Verhältnis von religiösem und sozialem Wandel in der Frühneuzeit
am Beispiel der Grafschaft Lippe* (Gütersloh, 1981) [= Quellen und Forschungen zur
Reformationsgeschichte 48]; cf. also *Die reformierte Konfessionalisierung in Deutschland –
Das Problem der "Zweiten Reformation". Wissenschaft. Symposion des Vereins für Reformationsgeschichte 1985*, ed. Heinz Schilling (Gütersloh, 1986) [= Schriften des Vereins
für Reformationsgeschichte 195]; *Die lutherische Konfessionalisierung in Deutschland. Wissenschaftl. Symposion des Vereins für Reformationsgeschichte 1988*, ed. Hans-Christoph Rublack
(Gütersloh, 1992) [= Schriften des Vereins für Reformationsgeschichte 197].
[17] Cf. *Die katholische Konfessionalisierung. Wissenschaftl. Symposion der Gesellschaft zur
Herausgabe des Corpus Catholicorum und des Vereins für Reformationsgeschichte 1993*, ed.
Wolfgang Reinhard and Heinz Schilling (Gütersloh, 1995) [= Schriften des Vereins
für Reformationsgeschichte 198].

trends, like a plant emerging from its roots, represents an ahistorical projection of future events onto the past.[18] On the other, the 15th-century sources constantly confront us with the fact that the 'normative centering' of the Reformation hardly materialized out of thin air: *de facto* it assumed and drew upon a late-medieval dynamic of simplification and intensification and continued, in some ways, a regulating, normativizing sequence of standardization. An entire range of witnesses that includes theologians, church reformers and preachers, jurists, politicians, city chroniclers and scribes (*Stadtschreiber*) along with humanists and artists testifies to the concept of a simplified, reduced set of core principles identified as *the* roadmap for the pilgrimage in this world and as the guaranteed route to salvation in the next. Such statements occurred often in connection with those *sola*-formulations which held up either a concept or a person 'alone' as the sole guarantor of certainty.[19]

The phenomenon may be illustrated with a few examples from a wide spectrum of religious sources. John Wyclif occupies an uncontested primacy when one considers the radical currents of ecclesiastical and social critique. His proclamation of the Scriptures as the sole norm for religious and social relations (*sola lex*)[20] marked the

---

[18] For a much needed critique of the hazards of organic categories of historical interpretation shaped by biological metaphors, cf. Hartmut Boockmann: "Das 15. Jahrhundert und die Reformation", in: *Kirche und Gesellschaft im Heiligen Römischen Reich des 15. und 16. Jahrhunderts*, ed. Hartmut Boockmann (Göttingen, 1994), pp. 9–25, esp. p. 10f.

[19] Cf. Erich Meuthen: "Gab es ein spätes Mittelalter?", in: *Spätzeit. Studien zu den Problemen eines historischen Epochenbegriffs*, ed. Johannes Kunisch (Berlin, 1990) [= Historische Forschungen 42], pp. 91–135; here p. 115. According to Meuthen, *sola*-formulations were primarily associated with "die prinzipielle Ablösung des Komplizierten durch das Einfache, wie immer sich dieses Umschlagen vorbereitet hat [. . .] Also immer wieder: *sola, sola.* Nur ja weg von allem, was so kompliziert ist und die meisten – vielleicht sogar alle – überfordert." It must be noted that late medieval and Reformation theologians also used *sola*-formulations in the service of averting that which they considered too demanding for the majority (or perhaps everyone), but above all else in the service of their concern for spiritual concentration and meditation, for the reform-oriented purification of religion, and for greater certainty and assurance along the path to salvation. For *sola*-formulations among theologians around 1500, cf. Hamm: "Von der spätmittelalterlichen reformatio" (as above, n. 1), pp. 36–41.

[20] Cf. Meuthen: "Gab es ein spätes Mittelalter?" (as above, n. 19), p. 115; Gustav Adolf Benrath: "Traditionsbewußtsein, Schriftverständnis und Schriftprinzip bei Wyclif", in: *Antiqui und Moderni. Traditionsbewußtsein und Fortschrittsbewußtsein im späten Mittelalter*, ed. Albert Zimmermann (Berlin, 1974) [= Miscellanea mediaevalia 9], pp. 359–382.

starting-point for so-called 'late-medieval reform-biblicism'.[21] We
encounter this line, for example, among the peasants of the Upper
Rhein who swore allegiance to the *Bundschuh* and put the slogan
"God's Justice Alone!" on their flags.[22] It may be further traced to
the demand for the exclusive application of biblical precepts – "God's
Law Alone!" – as formulated in the *gravamina* and programmatic
writings of the peasants during the winter and spring of 1525, shortly
before the beginning of the Peasants' War.[23] With his sights set
particularly on the conscience-burdening accretions of canon law,
the moderate church reformer Jean Gerson (1363–1429) held up the
godly law of the biblical commandments and especially Christ's
command to love as *the* standard for the church:[24] such should be
"the originating and source-providing principle for all laws – the
form, the rule, and the model" for all of them.[25] In completely typical fashion a jurist like Ulrich Tengler, writing his famous *Laienspiegel*
one hundred years later (1509), could set forth the true justice of
God as the sole standard for decisions in all earthly courtrooms; and
yet, in a way most contrary to Gerson, he did so while referring to
the "godly dignity" of imperial (Roman) law, the ascendancy of which
he championed.[26]

---

[21] Cf. Klaus H. Lauterbach: *Geschichtsverständnis, Zeitdidaxe und Reformgedanke an der Wende zum sechzehnten Jahrhundert. Das oberrheinische "Buchli der hundert capiteln" im Kontext des spätmittelalterlichen Reformbiblizismus* (Freiburg i.Br., 1985) [= Forschungen zur ober-rheinischen Landesgeschichte 33]. One thinks, for example, of John Hus and the Hussites with their concentration on the biblical standard of the *pura lex Christi* as the norm for living.

[22] Cf. Hamm: "Von der spätmittelalterlichen reformatio" (as above, n. 1), p. 57f.

[23] Cf. Peter Bierbrauer: "Das Göttliche Recht und die naturrechtliche Tradition", in: *Bauer, Reich und Reformation, Festschrift für Günther Franz*, ed. Peter Blickle (Stuttgart, 1982), pp. 210–234; P. Blickle: "Das göttliche Recht der Bauern und die göttliche Gerechtigkeit der Reformatoren", in: *Archiv für Kulturgeschichte* 68 (1986), pp. 351–369.

[24] Cf. Christoph Burger: *Aedificatio, Fructus, Utilitas. Johannes Gerson als Professor der Theologie und Kanzler der Universität Paris* (Tübingen, 1986) [= Beiträge zur historischen Theologie 70], pp. 71–97; Hamm: "Von der spätmittelalterlichen reformatio" (as above, n. 1), pp. 53–56 and 58 (for the line Gerson-Luther).

[25] ". . . necessaria est praecipue conversio retrorsum ad ius divinum, quod est iurium omnium originale et fontale principium, forma, regula et exemplum. Fiat haec animae conversio ad Jesum." Gerson, *Conversi estis*, ed. Palémon Glorieux, in: *Jean Gerson: Oeuvres complètes*, vol. 5 (Tournai, 1963), p. 178.

[26] Cf. Hamm: "Von der spätmittelalterlichen reformatio" (as above, n. 1), pp. 47–52, with a reproduction of the woodcut from the title page of Tengler's "Der neue Laienspiegel", Augsburg, 1512 (p. 51 with further analyisis at p. 50, n. 136). This woodcut, with the mirror of "true justice" in its center, is a good example of the graphic assimilation of textual 'normative centering'. For research on didactic art during the century before the Reformation, it is most interesting just how fre-

At the same time, Gerson commenced with another dimension of 'normative centering' entirely when he sought to re-orient both the church and the Christian's life wholly around God's mercy. 'Only' through it can one weighed down by the burden of sin expect any help.[27] 'Only' the humility (*humilitas sola*) of a repentant heart is required by the sinner, who should seek refuge in God's mercy;[28] in that divine *misericordia* he should place the *fiducia tota* of his hopeful heart with complete trust.[29] By doing so, Gerson gave the following four generations of reform theologians and devotional authors an influential, fundamental outlook centered around mercy, assuagement of the conscience, and consolation. In the 15th century the weight placed both on God's mercy, and on the hope this mercy gave to mankind, became associated above all with an emphasis on the salvific function of Christ's Passion.[30] The prevalence of the Passion represented the normative polar-opposite to the traditional stress laid upon the image of God's judgment and the justice of the divine judge – which, it should be emphasized, still retained its crucial role in the religiosity of the period.[31]

---

quently graphic 'normative centering' occurred in analogy to its textual counterpart. As will be shown below, this relationship shows itself most clearly in the areas of devotion, the 'theology of piety', and 'images of piety'.

[27] For the expression *sola misericordia* as employed by Gerson, and for his corresponding conception of the Christian's assurance of hope grounded solely on God's compassion, cf. Sven Grosse: *Heilsungewißheit und Scrupulositas im späten Mittelalter* (Tübingen, 1994) [= Beiträge zur historischen Theologie 85], pp. 102–158, esp. p. 103, n. 308. Cf. also the (Pseudo?)-Gersonian *Appellatio peccatoris ad divinam misericordiam*, in: *Oeuvres complètes* (as above, n. 25), vol. 8 (Paris, 1971), pp. 536–539 (no. 20); for an accompanying woodcut with the representation of a merciful divine judgment in the form of stairs leading to salvation (with an early modern German poem below the image that refers to the text of Gerson), see below p. 37 with n. 100.

[28] Cf., e.g., Gerson: *De praeparatione ad missam*, in: *Oeuvres complètes* (as above, n. 25), vol. 9 (Paris, 1973), p. 46.

[29] Cf. ibid.: "fiduciam nostram totam in deum iactemus," and idem: *De vita spirituali animae*, in: *Oeuvres complètes* (as above, n. 25), vol. 3 (Tournai, 1962), p. 126: "desperare debeamus de viribus nostris [. . .] nec confidere in homine, sed projicere totam spem nostram in deum."

[30] For the 'normative centering' of both the late medieval 'theology of piety' and late medieval 'images of piety', centered upon the suffering and death of Christ, see below p. 18f.

[31] Religiosity around 1500 may be characterized as being held in tension by two polarized perspectives that were varyingly accented and combined with one another: on the one hand there was an emphasis on divine judgment and righteousness, a perspective that subjected the faithful to dwell on their ability – while spurring them on – to fulfill religious obligations and to perform meritorious works in order to

It was immediately *before* the Reformation when the Augustinian
hermit Johannes von Staupitz (†1524) insisted that the *sola misericor-*
dia and *sola gratia* of God, along with Christ our *only* savior (i.e., sole
rescuer), formed the core of the life of the Christian and of the
church.[32] In the works of Staupitz and other theologians around
1500, the traditional, reckoning, terror-inspiring image of Christ the
'Judge of the World' could fade completely from view when confronted by the *solus Christus* of the Passion.[33] Omnipresent at the close
of the Middle Ages was this normative image – the Christ of the
Passion[34] – which along with that other prominent figure, Mary,

---

secure their salvation; on the other there was an emphasis on mercy, a perspective
that maintained an awareness of the inadequacy of human qualities and morality.
This second perspective urged the tempted sinner to place his hope humbly and
completely in the saving protection of the proxies and intercessors Christ, Mary,
and the saints; precisely the sinner's act of placing this humble trust in them may
be considered the performance of a meritorious work. Numerous examples of authors
who wrote in the genre of devotional theology (and of artists who produced 'images
of piety') attest to a growing tendency to minimize the aspect of works and performances – in fact to minimize all aspects of mankind's spiritual capabilities – and
to maximize the aspect of divine compassion and mercy before the seat of God's
judgment. Considering just how strong a role is played by the moment of intercessional advocacy (that of Christ, of Mary, and of the saints), which stands in for
the sinner and satisfactorily fulfills the requirements of God's justice, the following
may be said: God's justice and mercy must not be understood as polar opposites
represented by severity and lenience, but may rather be seen (especially from the
perspective of Christ's Passion) to reciprocally imbue and clarify one another. That
God demands the fulfillment of expiatory acts by means of proxy and intercession
corresponds to his retributive righteousness; and yet the fact that he even allows
and accepts such intercession as the fulfillment of that which is required to save
the sinner, and that he moreover gave his only son as a sacrifice for this purpose,
corresponds to his even greater goodness and mercy. In this way God may be seen
as righteous in his merciful judgment and as merciful in his righteous judgment.
The traditional role of the righteous divine judge during the Middle Ages was
increasingly recast in the form of one who was lenient and merciful. As will be
seen in more detail below, this type of divine courtroom, characterized by an
abundance of God's grace, occupied an essential place in the 'normative centering'
of the 'theology of piety' and of 'images of piety' during the 15th and early 16th
centuries.

[32] On Staupitz's use of such *sola*-formulations cf. Hamm: "Von der spätmittelalterlichen reformatio" (as above, n. 1), p. 40f. Since he was not only the vicar general of the German Augustinians, Luther's pastor, spiritual guide, and fatherly friend
but also his theological mentor, Staupitz's pointed, radically Augustinian and biblically accentuated 'theology of grace' and Christocentrism, accompanied by their
many *sola*-formulations, lead directly to the 'normative centering' of the early
Reformation that was initiated by the young Luther's writings.

[33] See below, p. 25f.

[34] Cf., for example, *Die Passion Christi in Literatur und Kunst des Spätmittelalters*, ed.
Walter Haug and Burghart Wachinger (Tübingen, 1993) [= Fortuna vitrea 12];
Petra Seegets: *Passionstheologie und Passionsfrömmigkeit im ausgehenden Mittelalter. Der Nürn-*

became the most characteristic representation of God's mercy.[35] It was thus thoroughly typical of the times when the Nuremberg Franciscan, Stephan Fridolin (†1498), preached that in the Passion of Christ lay ". . . der punct, das centrum, das mytelst stetlein unßer hoffnung." [". . . the middle point, the center, the most central town in the region of our hope."][36] What became central in the shaping of the Christian's life was not only the notion that Christ acted on the sinner's behalf. Along with this, it was taught that in his meditations the Christian was to concentrate on the exemplary suffering of Christ and on the ideal of following his example (*imitatio Christi*); such could be accomplished according to principles similar to those formulated for the *Devotio moderna* by Thomas of Kempen and others.[37]

Within this context, the christocentric humanism of Erasmus of Rotterdam also comes to mind. Erasmus is especially relevant since so many of his younger contemporaries idolized him and were influenced heavily by his writings. Numerous 'Protestant' reformers such as Zwingli saw themselves as having been led by the Erasmian reform program to support and join up with the forces of the

---

berger *Franziskaner Stephan Fridolin (gest. 1498) zwischen Kloster und Stadt*, Spätmittelalter und Reformation, Neue Reihe 10 (Tübingen, 1998); Falk Eisermann: "*Diversae et plurimae materiae in diversis capitulis*. Der 'Stimulus amoris' als literarisches Dokument der normativen Zentrierung", in: *Frühmittelalterliche Studien* 31 (1997), pp. 214–232.

[35] Cf. Klaus Schreiner: *Maria – Jungfrau, Mutter, Herrscherin* [1994], rev. ed. (Munich, 1996).

[36] The metaphors served to place the suffering Christ within the geographical context of the middle point of a defined area and within the geometrical centrality of a city within a region. Stephan Fridolin: "Predigten über die Komplet", Munich, Bayerisches Nationalmuseum, Cod. 3801 (part 2), fol. 195r. Cf. also Johannes von Paltz, *Coelifodina* (1502), ed. Christoph Burger and Friedhelm Stasch, in: *Johannes von Paltz: Werke*, vol. 1 (Berlin, 1983) p. 13,11: "passio Christi est quasi summa totius sacrae scripturae".

[37] From the *compassio* which is brought forth through meditation and which induces the affective assimilation of Christ's suffering (which is, at the same time, the painful ruing over one's own sins for which Christ suffered), the repentant sinner will be led to *imitatio*, i.e., to an active imitation of Christ, and thereby to *conformitas*, to congruity with Christ. Cf. Martin Elze: "Das Verständnis der Passion Christi im ausgehenden Mittelalter und bei Luther", in: *Geist und Geschichte der Reformation. Festschrift für Hanns Rückert*, ed. Heinz Liebing and Klaus Scholder (Berlin, 1966) [= Arbeiten zur Kirchengeschichte 38], pp. 127–151, esp. pp. 127–134. On the *Devotio moderna* cf. most recently Nikolaus Staubach: "*Christianam sectam arripe*: Devotio moderna und Humanismus zwischen Zirkelbildung und gesellschaftlicher Integration", in: *Europäische Sozietätsbewegungen und demokratische Tradition. Die europäischen Akademien der Frühen Neuzeit zwischen Frührenaissance und Spätaufklärung*, ed. Klaus Garber, Heinz Wismann and Winfried Siebers (Tübingen, 1996), pp. 112–167 (with further bibliography).

Reformation.[38] If Erasmus was typically humanistic in his employment of classical culture for standards of education and conduct – especially *sacrae litterae* and their central text, the Holy Scriptures – then for him this meant that Christ as the instructor of virtue occupied primacy of place in the teaching of proper human behavior. "In order to take the most certain step toward salvation," Erasmus formulated as a rule, "you should hold Christ before you as your single goal and direct all of your endeavors, all of your efforts, your leisure and work toward him alone." "Keep your eyes fixed on Christ as your only and highest good, such that you neither love, nor marvel at, nor yearn for anything except Christ or that which is done for his sake."[39] For the leaders of the church and for the worldly princes – indeed for all of Christendom – Christ should become the paradigm for a life lived under the norm of *sola virtus*,[40] just as Jerome followed Christ's example as both scholar and repentant sinner.[41]

The enthusiastic reception of Jerome among, for example, the group of humanists at Nuremberg, who also took-up the slogan *sola virtus*, serves to document a particular case of 'normative centering'.[42]

---

[38] Pointed out most recently (and correctly) by Emidio Campi: *Zwingli und Maria. Eine reformationsgeschichtliche Studie* (Zurich, 1997), pp. 24–34. Cf. also Fritz Büsser: "Zwingli, ein Zeitgenosse des Erasmus", in: idem: *Die Prophezei. Humanismus und Reformation in Zürich* (Bern, 1994), pp. 13–25; idem: "Zwingli als Exeget. Ein Beitrag zum Erasmus-Gedenkjahr", in: ibid., pp. 26–46.

[39] "Sed ut certiore cursu queas ad felicitatem contendere, haec tibi quarta sit regula, ut totius vitae tuae Christum velut unicum scopum praefigas, ad quem unum omnia studia, omnia conatus, omne otium ac negotium conferas . . . [Oculus tuus] ad solum Christum tamquam ad unicum et summum bonum spectet, ut nihil ames, nihil mireris, nihil expetas nisi aut Christum aut propter Christum." Erasmus: *Enchiridion militis christiani* (1501), Canon quartus, in: *Erasmus von Rotterdam: Ausgewählte Schriften*, ed. Werner Welzig, vol. 1 (Darmstadt, 1968), pp. 168–170.

[40] Cf. the citations of Erasmus by Hamm: "Von der spätmittelalterlichen reformatio" (as above, n. 1), p. 45f. with the pointed maxim (n. 122): Christus "solus est totus imitandus." Cf. Léon E. Halkin: *Erasmus von Rotterdam. Eine Biographie* (Zurich, 1989), p. 260: "Erasmus' Theologie jedoch ist auf Christus zentriert."

[41] On the central significance of Jerome for Erasmus, cf. Eugene F. Rice, Jr.: *Saint Jerome in the Renaissance* [1985], 2 ed. (Baltimore, 1988), pp. 116–136; John C. Olin: "Erasmus and Saint Jerome: An Appraisal of the Bond", in: *Erasmus of Rotterdam, the Man and the Scholar. Proceedings of the Symposium held at the Erasmus University, Rotterdam, 9.–11. Nov. 1986*, ed. J. Sperna Weiland and W. Th. M. Frijhoff (Leiden, 1988), pp. 182–196 (with further bibliography).

[42] Cf. Berndt Hamm: "Hieronymus-Begeisterung und Augustinismus vor der Reformation. Beobachtungen zur Beziehung zwischen Humanismus und Frömmigkeitstheologie (am Beispiel Nürnbergs)", in: *Augustine, the Harvest, and Theology (1300–1650). Festschrift for Heiko A. Oberman*, ed. Kenneth Hagen (Leiden, 1990), pp. 127–235, esp. pp. 180–224. On the slogan *sola virtus* among devotional humanists in Nuremburg, cf. also Berndt Hamm: "Humanistische Ethik und reichsstädtische Ehrbarkeit

But it can also be found among devotional practices geared toward other saints such as John the Baptist, the Apostle John, Christopher, George the Dragon-Slayer, Francis of Assisi, Mary's mother Anna, Catherine or Ursula along with all of their hallowed companions. Although it varied by region and by devotional group, certain saints earned a cumulatively heightened significance through cult and liturgy, through confraternities, pilgrimages, and indulgences, through art and devotional literature, and as beloved patrons. This phenomenon may be understood as a person-oriented 'normative centering' based on mercy and protective intercession. At the same time, the example of a saint's life and martyrdom recurrently referred the devoted back to that enduring, central act of the Passion and to the believer's existential participation in Christ's suffering. This important example illustrates the fact that in the Late Middle Ages, 'normative centering' always signified plurality and multiplicity. The Passion of Christ, the effect of its grace and its power to redeem, were multiplied in the priestly sacrifice of the mass, in miracles of bleeding hosts and images, in the appearance of stigmata, in relics of the Passion etc. Above all else, however, the Passion's place as the central locus of devotion was invigorated through the intensely heightened realization that through their suffering, Mary and the martyrs fully re-enacted Christ's Passion in their own souls and with their own bodies. These material and personal manifestations all generated out from, and reflected back upon, the central christological event of the atoning sacrifice and holy blood.

The 15th-century monastic reform movement offers an example of the connections between political and religious 'centering' on the levels of intention and realization. In the movement's observant ideal, the 'normative centering' of late medieval piety toward repentance and the Passion found its culmination.[43] Like rays of light which,

---

in Nürnberg", in: *Mitteilungen des Vereins für Geschichte der Stadt Nürnberg* 76 (1989), pp. 65–147; here pp. 129–133.

[43] Cf. *Reformbemühungen und Observanzbestrebungen im spätmittelalterlichen Ordenswesen*, ed. Kaspar Elm (Berlin, 1989) [= Berliner Historische Studien 14: Ordensstudien VI]; Ralph Weinbrenner: *Klosterreform im 15. Jahrhundert zwischen Ideal und Praxis. Der Augustinereremit Andreas Proles (1429–1503) und die privilegierte Observanz*, (Tübingen, 1996) [= Spätmittelalter und Reformation, Neue Reihe 7]. Analyzing the Dominican Johannes Nider and the Augustinian Hermit Proles, Weinbrenner demonstrates how the path of repentance as formulated in the observant cloisters was understood as a repeat performance of the path of Christ's suffering; this path was to lead to a spiritual death on the cross fulfilled by the surrender of one's own will (ibid., pp.

upon passing through a magnifying glass, burn with heat, the restitution
and execution of the proper Christian life in the monastery was to
achieve the perfection of imitating Christ's suffering – a perfection
saturated with love, humility, and obedience. Monks and nuns not
only acquired the highest level of merit and assurance for themselves,[44]
but also provided the *corpus Christianum* with protection as its proxies, with guidance as its spiritual leaders, and with influential role-
models as its contemporary archetypes of the *imitatio Christi*.[45] The
faithful expected nothing less from the life of the Observants. Above
all, in the discipline of the orders they saw the guaranteed fulfillment
of those deeds which pleased God and were so conducive to one's
salvation. Thus it is completely understandable that regional princes
and city magistrates made it their business to promote *observant* monastic reform especially.[46]

This type of *cura religionis* corresponded, indeed, to the intensification
and standardization of political dominion, or to discipline and con-

---

181–197). On aspects of Nider's theology in their context within the 'theology of
piety', cf. also Werner Williams-Krapp: "Observanzbewegungen, monastische Spiri-
tualität und geistliche Literatur im 15. Jahrhundert", in: *Internationales Archiv für Sozialgeschichte der deutschen Literatur* 20 (1995), pp. 1–15.

[44] Cf. Weinbrenner: *Klosterreform im 15. Jahrhundert* (as above, n. 43), pp. 197–205
("Strukturen der Sicherheit"); Hamm: *Frömmigkeitstheologie* (as above, n. 9), pp. 291–299.

[45] Cf. the ideal representation of the Franciscan cloister at Nuremberg after its
adherence to the Observant movement by the Franciscan chronicler Nikolaus
Glassberger, written in 1508: "After the convent at Nuremberg had been reformed,
the brothers thought of nothing other than that which is Godly; some sang Psalms,
others busied themselves with books, and still others preached the Word of God.
And with the example of their life, the word of their teaching and their most
devoted intercession, they steadily led the Christian populace away from the vices
and won them over for the virtues such that anyone, were he to recall the repul-
siveness of the brothers' former depravities, upon seeing the condition and life of
the brothers as they now lived, would surely have to believe that from that profane place a most holy temple of God had burst forth like a bolt of lightning."
["Igitur reformato conventu Norimbergensi, Fratres iam nihil praeter divina cogitabant,
alii psallendo, alii libros relegendo, alii praedicando verbum Dei, et populum christianum exemplo vitae verboque doctrinae ac intercessione devotissima iugiter a vitiis
revocando et ad virtutes alliciendo, adeo quod, si quis tunc illum statum atque illam
Fratrum vitam inspiceret, qua tunc vivebant, qui prioris corruptelae fastidia mem-
inerat, existimaret, velut ex loco profano sacerrimum Dei templum subito tamquam
fulgur emicuisse."] Nikolaus Glassberger, *Chronica*, ed. Patres Collegii S. Bonaventurae,
Ad Claras Aquas, *Analecta Franciscana* 2 (Quaracchi, 1887), p. 320; cited by Seegets:
Passionstheologie und Passionsfrömmigkeit (as above, n. 34), p. 4 and n. 1.

[46] Cf. Manfred Schulze: *Fürsten und Reformation. Geistliche Reformpolitik weltlicher Fürsten
vor der Reformation* (Tübingen, 1991) [= Spätmittelalter und Reformation, Neue Reihe
2]; Dieter Stievermann: *Landesherrschaft und Klosterwesen im spätmittelalterlichen Württemberg*
(Sigmaringen, 1989).

trol, in the service of early-modern state formation.[47] That must not diminish our grasp, however, of the fundamental conviction among political authorities and subjects that a pious, disciplined life based on God's commandments laid the foundation for the well-being of an earthly state. Complementary and parallel to this tenet was the certainty that government bore responsibility for tending to the eternal salvation of its urban and rural 'children'.[48] The increased concern for sound *Policey*, understood as the strict regulation and proper ordering of the community, contained a built-in religious component during the decades before the Reformation. One witnesses a striking accumulation of government regulations aimed to keep the peace and direct the market, of sumptuary legislation, of wedding and burial ordinances, of laws pertaining to the poor, to begging, and to the setting-up and maintaining of infirmaries.[49] The establishment of preacherships and officially sponsored public forms of cult such as pilgrimages, processions, and indulgence campaigns likewise attests to the intertwining of the political and the religious spheres.

The 15th and 16th centuries belong to an age in which the dominant mentality was conditioned by a stark orientation toward the otherworldly, by attempts to make provisions for the afterlife, and thus by broad concern for ecclesiastical affairs. Thus all manifestations of 'normative centering' within its society contained, at some level of their contents, a referential correspondence to the 'centering' of piety: witness the above examples in the realms of politics, humanism, and jurisprudence. In those areas where one felt stability, certainty, and peace threatened and thus strove for reform, one sought the path of religious legitimization and regulation. Piety was not just a particular system alongside other social complexes, but the central instance of mediation among them. Indeed, piety was the lens through which all possible fears and uncertainties, all needs for

---

[47] Important and more recent studies on the emergence and development of the early modern state are provided by Harm Klueting: *Das Konfessionelle Zeitalter 1525–1648* (Stuttgart, 1989) [= UTB 1556], pp. 73–94.

[48] Cf. Hamm: "Von der spätmittelalterlichen reformatio" (as above, n. 1), pp. 65–71, where I discuss religion as the "buttress" (*Strebepfeiler*) of society.

[49] Cf. Heinz Schilling: *Die Stadt in der frühen Neuzeit* (Munich, 1993) [= Enzyklopädie deutscher Geschichte 24], pp. 38f. and 94; Werner Buchholz: "Anfänge der Sozialdisziplinierung im Mittelalter. Die Reichsstadt Nürnberg als Beispiel", in: *Zeitschrift für historische Forschung* 18 (1991), pp. 129–147; Berndt Hamm: *Bürgertum und Glaube. Konturen der städtischen Reformation* (Göttingen, 1996), p. 74f.

legitimacy and normativity, were focused: *religio est vinculum societatis*.[50]
That is why the various 'centering' impulses of the *corpus Christianum*
before and after 1500 coalesced at the level of piety and church
reform.

III. *Forms of Normative Centering: The Theology of Piety and Images of Piety*

When I speak of 'piety', I have in view an abundance of phenomena manifested in individual or communal life and expressed in internalized or externalized forms. They may all be described, however,
as the practical realization of religion – of modes of believing, proclaiming, teaching, forming ideas, conceiving and articulating values,
fears, hopes etc. – in such a way that one's life is formed and
informed by it.[51] In earlier research I concerned myself especially
with a type of late-medieval theology that I designated as the 'theology of piety' (*Frömmigkeitstheologie*),[52] a term which has since been
taken up in the field.[53] The 'theology of piety' is one which, at the

---

[50] On the origins of this familiar quotation (combined from Seneca and Lactantius)
cf. Hamm: "Von der spätmittelalterlichen reformatio" (as above, n. 1), p. 67; J. Bartier:
Légistes et gens de Finances au XVᵉ siècle. Les conseillers des ducs de Bourgogne (Brussels,
1955), p. 442 (Lactantius) and 444 (Seneca).

[51] This is how I defined and described 'piety' (*Frömmigkeit*) in my article, "Frömmigkeit
als Gegenstand theologiegeschichtlicher Forschung. Methodisch-historische Überlegungen am Beispiel von Spätmittelalter und Reformation", in: *Zeitschrift für Theologie
und Kirche* 74 (1977), pp. 464–497. I also find the latest definition of my Erlangen
colleague Walter Sparn pertinent in this context: "[Christliche] Frömmigkeit ist das
Lebensgefühl und die Lebensgestalt christlichen Glaubens." The historian encounters 'piety' in this sense either in the form of theoretical reflection (on the actual-
ization of piety) or in evidence that documents the actual practice of piety.

[52] For the first time in 1977 in the article, "Frömmigkeit als Gegenstand theologiegeschichtlicher Forschung" (as above, n. 51), p. 479, and afterwards in more
detail in my monograph (1982), *Frömmigkeitstheologie am Anfang des 16. Jahrhunderts* (as
above, n. 9), esp. pp. 132–216. Other terms such as 'pastoral theologie' (*Seelsorgerliche
Theologie*), 'spiritual theology' (*Geistliche Theologie*), 'monastic theology' (*Monastische
Theologie*), or 'catechetical theology' (*Katechetische Theologie*) can indeed explain certain
perspectives and directions meant by the term 'theology of piety', but they cannot
replace it: these other terms always intend and convey terminologically something
that is much more specialized, and thus something that cannot adequately cover
the broader type of theology represented by the literary and intentional variety of
the representatives of the 'theology of piety'. On this cf. Hamm: "Von der spätmittelalterlichen reformatio" (as above, n. 1), p. 19f. with n. 26.

[53] For example, most recently in the extensive handbook by Arnold Angenendt:
Geschichte der Religiosität im Mittelalter (Darmstadt, 1997), pp. 71–75 ("Volksfrömmigkeit

levels of both reflection and instruction, seeks to cultivate the proper, salutary form of the Christian's life; it subordinates all other matters traditional to theology in the pursuit of its primary goal of tending to the comforting and salvation of the soul. Three typical theologians of this type have already been named: their programmatic founder Jean Gerson, Thomas of Kempen, and Johannes von Staupitz. The 'theology of piety' in the 15th century was characterized by a preference to address those priests and members of monastic orders who lacked higher theological training, along with laypersons. Because their aim was to reach this heterogeneous group of *simplices*, authors discarded elaborate academic discourse in favor of more popularizing literary forms.[54] They made an effort to produce a style of writing and thinking that was elementary, edifying and that stuck closely to the contours of daily life. The pains which they took to simplify their message were bound up with their primary endeavor to reduce theology to that which served piety and was necessary for salvation; anything that did not contribute substantially toward this objective was cast aside as superfluous and dispensable. Their goal was edification, not speculation. For this reason, the 'theology of piety' saw a high degree of simplification and reduction, or 'centering', in comparison to complex scholastic theology and speculative mysticism. Theological knowledge and spiritual experience were boiled down and reduced to those elements considered primary to the didactics of 'piety'. To be sure, different authors set about the task in varying ways, some concentrating their energies on a more internalized spirituality and others directing the believers' attention toward external forms instituted by the church to ensure salvation.[55] Nevertheless, proponents

---

und Frömmigkeitstheologie" in the Late Middle Ages). For further discussion of the term cf. also Seegets: *Passionstheologie und Passionsfrömmigkeit* (as above, n. 34), p. 41f. with n. 189.

[54] Thus such authors avoided classic forms of scholastic *quaestio*-literature, for example commentaries on Lombard's *Sententiae* along with *Summae*, *Quodlibeta* or *Quaestiones disputatae*. Instead they chose more accessible forms such as biblical commentaries, thematic sermons or sermons that followed the liturgical calendar, handbooks for pastoral care, explanations of the mass and of the liturgy, meditational and devotional aids, and especially the less extensive pieces of devotional literature such as catechisms, explanations of the Ten Commandments, of the Twelve Articles of Faith, of the "Our Father" and of the "Ave Maria" along with prayer books and booklets on confession, marriage, death, and consolation, *Seelengärtlein* and *Seelenarzneien*.

[55] At the time Luther joined the Erfurt cloister of Augustinian Hermits (17 July 1505), both of these contrasting tendencies were represented under one roof by the

of the 'theology of piety' shared basic assumptions about their task and method, evident in their reduction and simplification of the material with the common aim to provide guidance which was focused almost exclusively on that which aided devotion and led to salvation.

An overview of the entire spectrum of writings characteristic of the 'theology of piety' makes it apparent that relatively few principal themes and terms, always associated with a central figure such as Christ or Mary, were treated with astounding multiplicity, repetition, and variability:[56] themes such as proper penance as contrition, confession, and satisfaction along with indulgences; Christ's saving Passion and its appropriation by mankind (i.e., coming into and shaping one's life); the protective role of Mary; rescue before the seat of God's judgment and preservation from purgatory; the art of dying well; the 'how to' of humble prayer; consolation for one plagued by temptation; the sacraments of baptism and of the Eucharist; love of God and love of mankind; the virtues and the vices as well as the enticements of Satan, of demons, and of the Antichrist. Although all such concepts were reduced at some level to the *praxis pietatis*, it is a fact that a relatively vast number of questions and themes were addressed in 15th-century devotional literature. Nor was the Reformation any different in that its theology, despite an unmistakable differentiation of themes and concepts, 'centered' and fixed upon both the scriptures and faith 'alone' and thus found cohesion and coherence within multiplicity and diversity.

Diverse representatives of the 'theology of piety' spoke stereotypically of the "simplicity of the Christian life" (*de simplicitate vitae Christianae*).[57] When they did so, these theologians characteristically emphasized specific concepts which described the 'essence' and 'core'

---

very different theologies of Johannes von Staupitz and Johannes von Paltz. Whereas Staupitz developed a highly internalized method of devotion that furthered, in ways, the mystical tradition, Paltz took the same devotional and pastoral intentions and emphasized, in contrast, the immeasurable stores of grace found in the sacraments, indulgences, and the authorized powers of ecclesiastical offices. Both perspectives recurred frequently to the 'normative center' of repentance, Christ's Passion, and God's mercy. On Paltz cf. Berndt Hamm: "Paltz, Johannes von," in: *Theologische Realenzyklopädie*, vol. 25 (Berlin, 1995), pp. 606–11, with bibliography p. 610f.; on Staupitz, cf. idem: "Staupitz, Johann[es] von", in: ibid., vol. 32 (Berlin, 2000), pp. 119–127, with bibliography p. 126f.

[56] Cf. Hamm: "Von der spätmittelalterlichen reformatio" (as above, n. 1), pp. 24–35 ("Die geistlichen Leitbegriffe und Leitbilder des 15. Jahrhunderts").

[57] Cf., for example, the treatment of this theme by Girolamo Savonarola published in 1496: *De simplicitate christianae vitae*, ed. Pier Giorgio Ricci (Rome, 1959).

of the Christian life in different but inter-referential ways. It went something like this: the Passion signifies God's compassion, which arises out of love and calls it forth; this love of God, now awoken in man, is at the same time humility, hope and true repentance; repentance shows itself in contrition and tears, prayer and confession, satisfaction and merit, whether or not it is achieved primarily through, or merely accompanied by, sacramental penance; this road to repentance is the *imitatio Christi* in the fight against the allurements of Satan; the *imitatio Christi* begins with contemplation on the Passion, with the realization of the *compassio* of the Virgin Mary, and the calling-out for her motherly compassion which, in turn, opens the door to God's compassion. The loop comes to a close: themes, concepts, and persons form a circle. Depending on the varieties of author, audience, time, circumstance, and objective, varying concepts and motifs may be employed. But they are coherent in their relation to one another. Thus one in particular can take on an accentuated function, and yet always operate in a way that lends it a complementary, *in*clusive exclusivity (*sola misericordia, sola crux, sola caritas, sola humilitas, sola spes, sola contritio*, etc.). Different concepts and motifs bring one via different entrances into the same circle. The representatives of the 'theology of piety' assiduously pursued a standardized, compressed, intensified (i.e., 'centered') formulation of the essential simplicity of the Christian life. They achieved their goal of a 'simple' theology for 'simple' people (*simplices*) precisely where we might not have expected it: in variety and multiplicity.[58]

One can therefore understand the broad currents that comprised the 'theology of piety' during the century before the Reformation as a wide-sweeping attempt toward the 'normative centering' of theology and piety – 'normative', in that it involved standards, rules, and orientation aids for leading a Christian life; 'centering', in that a reduction of themes and concepts occurred at the pivotal discursive level of what ensured salvation, a reduction that emphasized above

---

[58] Cf. Hamm: *Frömmigkeitstheologie* (as above, n. 9), pp. 144–146 (on the *sacerdotes simplices* and *simplices christiani* as the primary intended audience for the 'theology of piety') and pp. 163–175 (the goal of a *simplex theologia* for the *simplices*). On the connection between cumulative series of phenomena, variety, and multiplicity with a strong tendency towards 'centering' cf. Falk Eisermann: "Die 15 geistlichen Tode Jesu Christi", in the exhibition catalogue *Glaube Hoffnung Liebe Tod* (as below, n. 81), p. 98f.

all else the Passion of Christ and the co-redeemer Mary, the mercy of God and the repentance of man.[59]

The opening up of the content and language of theology for non-experts occurred concurrently with the phenomena of 'normative centering' outlined above. An immense number of surviving Latin and German manuscripts abundantly document the phenomenon, which in the late 15th and early 16th centuries achieved even more impact with the spread of printed books, pamphlets, and single-leaf woodcuts, many of which underwent multiple printings. As much as the 'theology of piety' was disseminated through texts, it must be understood as a multi- and mass-media event during the era 1400–1520, accompanied as it was by a flood of painted, printed, and plastic images.[60] One must understand these 'images of piety'[61] and their contemporary 'theology of piety' as different threads of a seamless garment. For we are dealing with types of images whose message can only be unravelled when one is familiar with the concrete background of certain contents and intentions of the 'theology of piety'.[62] Its impulses to popularize and to standardize were carried further through these images, which sought to lead viewers to more

---

[59] One could also say: there was a concentration on the pivotal area of religious certainties and assurances. The question then becomes: Despite certainty concerning my own state of grace and my prospects for the afterlife, how can I nevertheless obtain the maximum amount of insurance for the hereafter?, i.e., how can I on the one hand achieve the highest possible degree of sanctity and morality, and on the other, how can I obtain the highest possible degree of intercessional sanctity and expiatory services for myself from others (Jesus, Mary, the saints, family members, a confraternity etc.)? It is only from the perspective of this late medieval urgency to find guarantees of grace and salvation that one can historically appreciate and analyze the central focus of the Reformation doctrine of the unconditional promise of salvation for those who have faith.

[60] Cf. Berndt Hamm: "Die Reformation als Medienereignis", in: *Jahrbuch für Biblische Theologie* 11 (1996), pp. 137–166; here pp. 160–163.

[61] With the term 'images of piety' I mean images of varying forms and media, functions and themes whose conditions of creation, intended goals, and contexts of use are to be found primarily in the realm of 'piety' (in the sense of the realization and formation of a life based on the Christian faith). Such 'images of piety' stand in an especially close and more functional proximity to the 'theology of piety' of the 15th century when they convey intentions that are didactic and exemplary, suggestive and motivating in terms of the goal of molding and nurturing the practice of piety. On this cf. also below, n. 63.

[62] Cf. Christoph Burger: "Theologie und Laienfrömmigkeit. Transformationsversuche im Spätmittelalter", in: *Lebenslehren und Weltentwürfe im Übergang vom Mittelalter zur Neuzeit. Politik – Bildung – Naturkunde – Theologie*, ed. Hartmut Boockmann, Bernd Moeller and Karl Stackmann (Göttingen, 1989) [= Abhandlungen der Akademie der Wissenschaften in Göttingen, Philol.-Histor. Klasse, 3d. ser., 179], pp. 400–420.

devotional forms of life by shaping their thoughts, emotions, and actions. Such visual representation aimed to fashion all of its viewers in this way; and for the illiterate it served an additional role, fulfilling their need for observable, tangible explications of devotion.[63] Without wanting to discount the multi-faceted concerns addressed by art historians, and without wanting to reduce this art only to the dimension of its statements and potentially intended effects, one can nevertheless say: these are images that asked to be 'read', not only aesthetically, but also with intellectual-spiritual organs of perception.[64] That is why

---

[63] Cf. most recently Ruth Slenczka: *Lehrhafte Bildtafeln in spätmittelalterlichen Kirchen* (Cologne, 1998) [= Pictura et Poesis 10], with literature on the theme of the didactics of piety in images. Cf. also Hartmut Boockmann: "Belehrung durch Bilder? Ein unbekannter Typus spätmittelalterlicher Tafelbilder", in: *Zeitschrift für Kunstgeschichte* 57 (1994), pp. 1–22. It hardly needs to be emphasized that the discussion of 'images of piety', whose function was to teach and to remind, should not be limited to the type of panel images discussed by Boockmann and Slenczka. Many other types of images could contain contents that taught and conveyed specific elements in the service of the didactics of piety: retables, epitaphs, votive panels, devotional images, illustrations in devotional books and pamphlets etc. Since such images sought to lead the viewer to know something, remember it, reflect on it, and understand it, the affective (i.e., *in mente*) objective of attempting to motivate particular forms of piety could combine directly with the attempt to lead one to an operative *praxis pietatis* – certain prayers, for example. Also within the 'theology of piety', differences in literary form or genre were not accompanied by corresponding differences in content or objective: various texts of varying types could include didactic information, reflective prayers and meditations cast in memorizable forms, highly emotional motivational aids, and more specific orientational instruction (dogma, anamnese, pathos, ethos). In fact it is a characteristic of the 'theology of piety' to mix these elements, a characteristic that also applies to 'images of piety'. Just how diverse the functions of such images were considered may be gauged, for example, by the treatise on the lay viewing of images (1528) found in Berthold Pürstinger's (Bishop of Chiemsee) *Tewtsche Theologey*, chapters 85 and 86, ed. Wolfgang Reithmeier (Munich, 1852), pp. 589–601. Pürstinger emphasized the close connections between text and image accordingly: "Wo nu dem gemainen volckh die pild wurden entzogen, waere gleich als wo den gelerten die schrifft verpoten, nachdem kain vnderschid ist der heyling geschicht zelernen oder zedencken in schrifft oder gemael" (p. 601).

[64] That is precisely why such images could serve the illiterate by taking over the role of texts in providing informative, instructional, and emotive materials along with motivational encouragement for concrete acts of devotion, a fact that was repeatedly emphasized by late medieval theologians and the clergy. Cf. Schreiner: *Maria* (as above, n. 35), pp. 252–256, esp. p. 253: "Daß Bilder der 'layen schrift' oder der 'layen puchstaben' seien, aus denen gelernt werden könne, wie man ins 'hymelriche' komme, verfestigte sich im hohen und späten Mittelalter zu einem vielgebrauchten Topos." On the other hand, just how much such images at the close of the Middle Ages were also intended for advanced readers may be seen by the ever-increasing number of texts that accompanied them (on this see below, p. 25 and n. 67). These scrolls and borders of text underline the textual characteristic of the non-verbal language of images and the visualized meanings they produce; the texts provide an interpretive key to unlock those aspects of the images associated

they also should be interpreted in the context of the dominant themes, figures, and images that had been brought into focus by the 'normative centering' of theology. They visually represent what were held up as authoritative standards for life and death. Through their choice of themes and their specific arrangements of them, through the formal possibilities of the 'centering' of visual representation, these images emphasized precisely what the representatives of the contemporary 'theology of piety', through their devotional texts, sought to place in the center of the *vita Christiana*.

IV. *Three Exemplary Images of Piety*

Three images from the period, all pregnant with meaning and containing elements characteristic of the late-medieval 'centering' of piety, serve to illustrate the phenomenon described above.[65] The axial symmetry of all three is immediately apparent. One may say that the artists employed the possibilities of formal 'centering' available to them in the type of composition, in order to place certain iconological, devotional, and theological meanings in the interpretive center of the image. One of the objects is an altar triptych, fashioned in a way characteristic to 15th-century Europe north of the Alps.[66] Its very construction allowed the artist to place specific themes relating to 'piety' in the center of the three-part ensemble – themes which, given their cumulative repetition, seem to have been relatively few in number. In the 15th century it became fashionable to enrich images with

---

with the 'theology of piety'. Images were also produced for the spiritual development of the literate on account of the fact that, according to contemporaries, the sense of sight could significantly contribute toward piety; indeed, an image, so they thought, could produce a more suggestive effect that more directly set the devotion of the heart into motion than could that which was written or heard (cf. Berthold Pürstinger, ibid., pp. 593 and 597) – not to mention its ability to satisfy the desire for aesthetic pleasure.

[65] In terms of their iconographic aspects, the three works, especially the Ghent altar, are atypical in many ways. However, from an iconological point of view they represent, in a most typical way, those themes and ideas emphasized in the late medieval 'theology of piety' north of the Alps, especially in the urban regions of southwest Germany and Flanders.

[66] Cf. Max Hasse: *Der Flügelaltar* (Dresden, 1941); Claudia Lichte and Gerhard Weilandt: *Prachtvoll und wandelbar. Entstehung und Funktion von Flügelretabeln im Mittelalter*, ed. Württembergisches Landesmuseum Stuttgart (Stuttgart, 1994) (with further bibliography).

snippets of meaningful text,[67] a formal and didactic innovation that gave artists, their patrons, or collaborating theological experts the chance to centrally place those statements drawn from 'piety' which they found especially important. The scrolls on which text appeared in the paintings lent themselves to, and in fact made necessary, compressed and reduced statements that, in their interplay with specific images, actually intensified the 'centering' of piety. All three images considered below contain pithy statements, each of them products of the contemporary 'theology of piety', that accentuate the meaning intended to be conveyed to the viewer by the visual representation.

Let us first consider the famous Ghent altar (completed 1432) of the brothers Hubert and Jan van Eyck [plate 1].[68] In the central panel of the painting, a central axis forms along the elevated figure, robed in purple, of the reigning *pantocrator*. It is the glorified Christ, flanked by Mary and John the Baptist. Such was the traditional standard in iconographic representations of the Last Judgment. The depiction of Christ, however, reveals an unconventional theological accentuation: he is not presented as the harsh, pronouncing judge but as the kind and clement one who arbitrates and reigns with immeasurable generosity. Arched above his head on the back of the throne, a semicircular inscription reads:

> Hic est deus potentissimus propter divinam maiestatem,
> Servus omnium[69] optimus propter dulcedinis bonitatem,
> Remunerator liberalissimus propter immensam largitatem.

---

[67] On issues regarding the relation between text and image, cf. *Text und Bild, Bild und Text. DFG-Symposion 1988*, ed. Wolfgang Harms (Stuttgart, 1990) [= Germanistische Symposien-Berichtsbände 11]; *Das illustrierte Flugblatt in der Kultur der Frühen Neuzeit*, ed. idem and Michael Schilling (Frankfurt a.M., 1998) [= Mikrokosmos 50], esp. the contribution (pp. 75–99) by Sabine Griese: "'Dirigierte Kommunikation'. Beobachtungen zu xylographischen Einblattdrucken und ihren Textsorten im 15. Jahrhundert", pp. 75–99.

[68] On the triptych of Hubert and Jan van Eyck, which is displayed in the baptismal chapel of St. Bavo's cathedral, Ghent, cf. the fine introduction (with further bibliography) by Peter Schmidt: *Der Genter Altar*, trans. Achim and Eva Zacharias, photos by Paul Maeyaert (Louvain, 1995); further bibliography in Esther Gallwitz: *Ein wunderbarer Garten. Die Pflanzen des Genter Altars* (Frankfurt a.M., 1996) [= Insel Taschenbuch 1853].

[69] *Servus omnium* is taken as a title for Christ from Mark 10.44; cf. Phil. 2.7f. Despite frequent discussions to the contrary, the reigning figure is Jesus Christ and not God the Father, a point also made patently clear by the pattern of the brocade material that covers the throne: there an oft recurring ornament appears with vine leaves, grapes, and a pelican feeding its young along with the small scroll of text "IHESVS XPS." It was thoroughly typical in the medieval tradition (and

One can understand the text in terms of its Trinitarian structure and statements.[70] From this perspective, it expresses that both the lofty majesty of the Father and the giving character of the Holy Spirit are essentially made one in Christ, who made himself the servant of all "till death on the cross" (Phil. 1.2) and now reigns in full Trinitarian glory.[71]

In the lower half of the central panel, one sees how the mercy of the reigning Christ is constituted and founded in the primary act of salvation history: in the sacrifice of the Passion, which is re-enacted daily in the sacrament of the altar by the priest during the sacrifice of the mass. Out of the wounded breast of the lamb (i.e., Christ's side-wound), a stream of blood empties into the chalice of the Eucharist. The altar cloth is as red as the blood. Written on the piece of frame directly above the image are those words of John the Baptist which capture the meaning of the image and of the entire salvation mystery that it represents: *Ecce agnus Dei, qui tollit peccata mundi* (John 1.29).

One need not go into much detail with the other symbols, personages, and texts found in the painting: they underscore everything emphasized in the normative axis of the work. There, the sacrificial victim standing in for mankind – the suffering and crucified sacrificial lamb, Christ – is bound with the saving mercy of the reigning *Christus iudex*. The redness of his robes in connection with that of the altar makes it clear that his bloody, atoning act of handing himself over to be crucified was formative in shaping the generous leniency of his reign. The adoration of the lamb by the hierarchically arranged circle of angels and saints applies, at the same time, to the *immensa largitas* of the *pantocrator*. Even John the Baptist, that personification of severity in traditional images of the Last Judgment, appears as a

---

corresponded with passages in the New Testament) that the glorified Christ took on the majesterial attributes of God the Father, especially signs and symbols of the majesty of his rulership and omnipotent power (in the sense of the *deus potentissimus propter divinam maiestatem*); it would have been atypical, indeed, to assign those humble aspects of Christ's incarnation (i.e., Christ as *servus omnium*) to God the Father, especially since the 'debasement' of the incarnation was seen as a *differentia specifica* of the Son over and against the Father.

[70] I am grateful to Christel Meier-Staubach (Münster) for bringing this possibility to my attention.

[71] The designation *remunerator* admittedly applies more readily to Christ than to the specific working of the Holy Spirit, who in medieval theology was not presented as one who recompenses like Christ the 'Judge of the World', but rather as the giver of all spiritual gifts.

figure of consolation. In the open book one recognizes the opening words of the Deutero-Isaiah, "*Consolamini*" (Isaiah 40.1: "Console, console my people!").[72] In accordance with the exegetical tradition of the church, here the words are cited as a promise of the coming Christ.[73] With the gesture of his right hand, the Baptist points directly to the consolation of the world. He shows that this figure of majesty is none other than the lamb that takes away the sins of the world.

One may likewise consider the second painting as an image of mercy and consolation. It is a votive painting completed *circa* 1508 by Hans Holbein the Elder for the wealthy Augsburg wine merchant, Ulrich Schwarz,[74] who along with his immense family assumes a devout position of prayer in the lower half of the picture [plate 2]. In the heavenly sphere represented in the painting's upper region, Holbein fashioned a scene typical in its presentation of the medieval understanding of the 'individual' or 'particular' judgment (*iudicium divinum particulare*) thought to occur at the moment of death.[75] There

---

[72] Cf. Schmidt: *Der Genter Altar* (as above, n. 68), p. 48.

[73] In the four Gospels the appearance of John the Baptist, which prepares for the arrival of Christ, is commented on with the beginning of the Deutero-Isaiah. The inscription over the Baptist's head contains the words: "Hic est baptista Iohannes, // maior homine, par angelis, // legis summa, evangelii sacio, // apostolorum vox, silencium prophetarum, // lucerna mundi, [*covered up*] testis." These lines have proven untraceable in the *Analecta Hymnica*, for which information I thank Karl Schlemmer (Passau).

[74] The painting hangs in the Staatsgalerie Augsburg. Cf. the reproductions and commentary in Bruno Bushart: *Hans Holbein der Ältere*, 2 ed. (Augsburg, 1987), pp. 102–105; cf. also Hartmut Boockmann: *Die Stadt im späten Mittelalter* (Munich, 1986), p. 168f. (no. 264).

[75] According to late medieval doctrine as it had been worked out in the 13th century, the 'individual' or 'particular' judgment was God the Father's judgment of an individual's soul immediately following death, as soon as the soul had separated itself from the body. As divine judge, God the Father pronounced whether the soul went directly to Paradise, or was sent to Purgatory for punishment and purification, or fell into the damnation of Hell. On the day of the Last Judgment, the individual soul would then join its resurrected body, whereafter the two would appear together with all of the other souls before the universal judgment of Christ the 'Judge of the World'. There, Christ's verdict would ratify the preliminary decision that had been handed down at the 'individual' or 'particular' judgment. After this ratification, men and women would fully experience, through the reunion of their bodies and souls, the complete essence of either salvation or damnation for the first time; purgatory would cease to exist. On the 'individual'/'particular' judgment (*iudicium divinum particulare*), cf. Peter Jezler: "Jenseitsmodelle und Jenseitsvorsorge – eine Einführung", in: *Himmel, Hölle, Fegefeuer. Das Jenseits im Mittelalter*, ed. Peter Jezler, exhibition catalogue (Zurich, 1994), pp. 13–26, esp. p. 18f. and the literature at n. 9 (p. 26); Hamm: "Von der spätmittelalterlichen reformatio" (as above, n. 1), pp. 28–31.

the judge is not Christ, who presides over the 'universal' judgment
at the end of the world, but rather God the Father. The physical
center of the painting functions as its interpretive center, and there
the mercy of the judge is represented. He sheathes his sword, that
symbol of his justice and retaliatory wrath, and offers consolatory
words that appear in the central scroll: "Barmherzigkait will ich allen
den erzaigen, die da mit warer rew von hinnen scheiden." ["I wish
to show mercy to all those who die with truly contrite hearts."].[76]
True contrition (*ware rew*) is nothing other than the sincere pain that
one feels for his sins out of love for God. At the moment of death,
such contrition is the decisive prerequisite for determining whether
or not the sinner may pass through the open door of God's mercy.
The image draws into its center precisely those two themes which
functioned as focal points in the late-medieval 'theology of piety':
God's mercy and the sinner's true repentance.[77]

As with the van Eycks' altar painting [plate 1], God's mercy is
bound up with Christ's Passion and the figure of Mary. But Holbein
places them before God the Father as intercessors, as advocates for
sinful mankind. Christ pleads before the judge, directing attention

---

[76] Cf. the plastic representation of the same 'particular' judgment scene on a
Late Gothic clock in Munich's Frauenkirche, designed by Erasmus Grasser around
1500. Discussing the movable figures of the clock, Schreiner (citing an article by
Peter Friess) writes: "'Gottvater, der die Fürbitte [der unter ihm stehenden Figuren
Christus und Maria] erhört, steckt mechanisch bewegt das Schwert mit der rechten
Hand zurück in die Schwertscheide. Er blickt dabei geradeaus nach vorn und rollt
ebenfalls mechanisch die Augen, außerdem bewegen sich mechanisch seine Lippen.'
Hätte der Konstrukteur der Uhr Gottvater eine Stimme geben können, hätte dieser
vermutlich gesagt: 'Barmherzigkeit will ich allen denen erzeigen, die da mit wahrer
Reue von hinnen scheiden.' So stand es jedenfalls auf Spruchbändern, die
Interzessionsbilder von damals kommentierten." *Maria* (as above, n. 35), p. 185.
Schreiner fails to give any specific examples, but cf., in addition to Holbein, below
n. 79. Another possibility for iconographic representation in which the blows of
God the Father's punishing justice are warded off, and in which the victory of protective mercy over requitive righteousness is emphasized, may be seen in the so-
called "Justification" painting by Sebastian Dayg (1511) on the Marian altar in the
south side-choir of the cistercion church at Heilsbronn (Franconia). There, to the
right of his Father, the Christ of the Passion holds back the Father's drawn sword
of judgment, during which time Mary, at the Father's left, stands at the side of the
sinner in need of protection. As a Madonna draped in the cloak of protection for
the sinner, Mary shows Christ and God the Father her naked breast. On this iconographic type of 'chain of intercession', cf. below, p. 35f. with n. 99; on Dayg's intercessional painting cf. Daniela Nieden: "Untersuchungen zum Marienaltar im Münster
zu Heilsbronn", unpub. M.A. thesis, Universität Freiburg i.Br., 1995, esp. pp. 69–74.
[77] Cf. Hamm: *Frömmigkeitstheologie* (as above, n. 9), pp. 168–171.

to the wounds in his side and thus to his taking the sins of man upon himself in the Passion: "Vatter, sich an mein wunden rot! Hilf den menschen aus aller not durch meinen bittern tod!" ["Father, take a look at my red wounds! Help mankind escape affliction by remembering my bitter crucifixion!"] Mary supports the defense offered God by her Son, demonstratively holding out to the Father her right breast, symbol of the sacrifice of motherly compassion.[78] She adds, "Herr thun ein dein schwert, das du hast erzogen, und sich an die brist, die dein sun hat gesogen!" ["Lord, put away the sword that you've raised up, and put yourself up to the breast that raised your Son!"][79] As merciful redeemer and compassionate co-redeemer, Christ and Mary stand before the judging Father. Their compassion awakes his mercy. But at the same time, he remains a righteous judge: there is no sin without punishment, and God's mercy is made manifest by the acceptance of his Son's atonement for our sins, an expiation possible only through death on the cross.[80]

Our third example may also be considered a consolatory image of hope which, like the others, is characterized by a strict axial symmetry that once again makes the merciful judgment of God its focal point. This woodcut, "Das Schifflein der heiligen Ursula" [plate 3], has been attributed to Hans Suess von Kulmbach and dates from the first quarter of the 16th century.[81] Despite her status as one of the Late Middle Ages' most beloved saints, Ursula fails to occupy center-stage in this representation; she appears left-of-center at table in the lower region of the woodcut with her martyr's crown, arrow, and palm branch.[82] Instead the cross with the suffering Christ dominates

---

[78] Cf. Susan Marti and Daniela Mondini: "'Ich manen dich der brüsten min, Das du dem sünder wellest milte sin!' — Marienbrüste und Marienmilch im Heilsgeschehen", in the exhibition catalogue *Himmel, Hölle, Fegefeuer* (as above, n. 75), pp. 79–90; Schreiner: *Maria* (as above, n. 35), pp. 173–210.

[79] The same three texts that emerge from the mouths of Holbein's God the Father, Christ, and Mary were also to be found on a burial stone in the choir of the former Franciscan church in Nuremberg; see Ulrich Schmidt: *Das ehemalige Franziskanerkloster in Nürnberg* (Nuremberg, 1913), p. 18.

[80] Cf. above, n. 31.

[81] There is an exemplar in the Graphische Sammlung Albertina, Vienna, Inv.: 1960/1000, S.D. 61; cf. an illustration of the woodcut with commentary in Thomas Lentes: "Die Barke zur Ewigkeit. Der Mastbaum und die Waage des Kreuzes", in: *Glaube Hoffnung Liebe Tod — Von der Entwicklung religiöser Bildkonzepte, Ausstellungskatalog*, ed. Christoph Geissmar-Brandi and Eleonora Louis, Graphische Sammlung Albertina, Kunsthalle Vienna, 2 ed. (Vienna, 1996), pp. 194–197.

[82] Cf. ibid., p. 194: "Der . . . Holzschnitt stellt das Bild eines Schiffes vor Augen,

the scene, forming the mast of the ship. The smaller images in the left and right corners portray a priest holding up the host after its transubstantiation[83] and the devices used to torture and wound the Christ of the Passion. These support the 'centering' of the woodcut upon the salvific effect of the Passion. His side-wound presents the redeeming blood of atonement and, even more, the font of life and mercy (which also appears directly under the sacrificial altar in the van Eycks' work [plate 1]).[84] Seated at the right of the table is St. Peter, wearing the papal tiara and holding the massive key to the heavenly gates; in his right hand he bears the chalice of the Eucharist that receives the blood gushing from the holy font. The Last Judgment joins the crucified in the center of the woodcut, in that the cross-beam of the crucifix also serves as the scales of justice.[85] There, on the pan to the right of Christ, kneel humble, praying souls; to His left the pan is formed from a hellish dragon. The message, however, is clear: thanks to the salvific effect of Christ's Passion, the scales will tip in favor of salvation instead of damnation. That is why the scale is fastened to the crucifix.[86] That is why the scrolls surrounding the cross contain two verses of a hymn that begin with lines frequently employed during the period: "O crux ave spes unica!"

---

das spätmittelalterlichen Frommen als das sicherste Schiff für die Jenseitsreise galt: das *Schifflein der heiligen Ursula*. Etliche Bruderschaften wurden gegründet, um mit Gebeten ihren *Schiffslohn* zu entrichten und so im schützenden Schiff der Heiligen und ihrer elftausend Gefährtinnen die letzte Reise bestehen zu können. [. . .] Gedient hatte das Blatt zur Verbreitung der Braunauer Ursula-Bruderschaft. Ihr Gründer, der Kleriker Georg Ranshover, und ihr Schirmherr, Friedrich der Weise, laden beide entsprechend auf dem Blatt zum Einstieg in das Schiff ein: links der Kurfürst, identifiziert durch die Wappen, und rechts der Priester." Cf. also André Schnyder: *Die Ursulabruderschaften des Spätmittelalters. Ein Beitrag zur Erforschung der deutschsprachigen religiösen Literatur des 15. Jahrhunderts*, Sprache und Dichtung, neue Folge 34 (Bern, 1986).

[83] The 'T' displayed on the host is a symbol of the cross.

[84] For the image of Christ and the blood of His Passion as a 'font of grace' cf. May-Brit Wadell: *Fons Pietatis. Eine ikonographische Studie* (Göteborg, 1969).

[85] For the presentation and iconography of the 'scales of justice' and the Last Judgment cf. Leopold Kretzenbacher: *Die Seelenwaage. Zur religiösen Idee vom Jenseitsgericht auf der Schicksalswaage in Hochreligion, Bildkunst und Volksglaube* (Klagenfurt, 1958) [= Buchreihe des Landesmuseums für Kärnten 4]; Arnold Angenendt: "Theologie und Liturgie der mittelalterlichen Toten-Memoria", in: *Memoria. Der geschichtliche Zeugniswert des liturgischen Gedenkens im Mittelalter*, ed. Karl Schmid and Joachim Wollasch (Munich, 1984) [= Münstersche Mittelalter-Schriften 48], pp. 79–199; here pp. 126–128.

[86] Cf. Lentes: "Die Barke zur Ewigkeit" (as above, n. 81), p. 196: "Letztlich wird nun der Körper Christi selbst zur körperlichen Waage. Sein sühnendes Blut beschwert die Waagschale der Seelen so sehr, daß er der Hölle die Beute entreißt."

Christ stood in for mankind on the cross, and our hope should be based solely on his Passion: hope that the pious will be made more righteous, and that the guilty will be granted forgiveness.[87] The shaft of the crucifix changes at the feet of Christ into the image of Mary with the Christ-child. To her right and left are Ursula and Catharine,[88] with whom she sits in the company of other saints at the altar of the Eucharist, which presents the salvific gift of Christ's death on the cross. The merits, compassion, and intercessional prayers of Mary and other saints gathered in the ship intensify the effects of the grace unleashed by the Passion, such that the divine judge will show mercy toward those sinners who are penitent and pray for help. The ship of Ursula as a symbol of the church's *communio sanctorum* shows itself, at the same time, to be a symbol for the safe voyage of pious souls to salvation in the hereafter.[89]

---

[87] [1.] "O crux ave spes unica! // Hoc passionis tempore auge pijs // Justiciam reisque dona veniam! [2.] Beata, cuius brachijs secli // Pependit precium; statera facta // Est corporis praedamque tullit tartaris." On this see Lentes: "Die Barke zur Ewigkeit" (as above, n. 81), p. 196: "Als Ganzer ist der Hymnus nicht identifiziert. Seine zweite Strophe allerdings entstammt der Feder des Poeten Venantius Fortunatus, der diese bereits im Jahre 569 gedichtet hatte." The first strophe is taken from the Vesper hymn of Holy Week, "Vexilla regis prodeunt"; see Philipp Wackernagel: *Das deutsche Kirchenlied von der ältesten Zeit bis zu Anfang des 17. Jahrhunderts*, vol. 1 (Leipzig, 1864), p. 63 (no. 80); cf. *Lexikon für Theologie und Kirche*, 2 ed., vol. 10 (Freiburg, 1965), col. 760. For the employment of the verse "O crux ave spes unica!" during the proclamation of jubilee indulgences by the papal legate Raimund Peraudi before and after 1500, cf. Johannes von Paltz: *Supplementum Coelifodinae* (1504), ed. Berndt Hamm (Berlin, 1983) [= Spätmittelalter und Reformation. Texte und Untersuchungen 3], pp. 80, 22f. with n. 12.

[88] St. Catherine may be identified by her attributes, the sword and broken wheel. The women in the background between Ursula, Mary, and Catherine are most likely the companions of St. Ursula.

[89] In the book he kept on his St. Ursula confraternity, Georg Ranshover described the promise emphasized in the woodcut of St. Ursula's ship with the words, that "ein iglich Cristen mensch furderlich vnd bequemelich komen mag zu gnaden vnd versunung gotes vnd sicher vnd frolich schiffen durch daz wutent vnd vngestome mere dyser werlt an das gestade vnd lant des hymelischen vater lants der ewigen seylickeit"; cited by Lentes: "Die Barke zur Ewigkeit" (as above, n. 81), p. 197. Given the close interconnections between 'images of piety' and the literature of the 'theology of piety', it is characteristic that in his woodcut, Hans Suess von Kulmbach followed the essentials of the points made by Ranshover in his confraternity book (ibid., p. 194).

V. *The Centering of Piety around the Passion, Mercy, and Trust*

Above we have examined three devotional works of art from a range
of *circa* 90 years that preceded the Reformation. In them one recognized main themes and leading figures that were products of a
'normative centering'. Such motifs were emphasized concomitantly
by spokesmen for the 'theology of piety': the Passion of God's Son;
the image of Christ's suffering represented by His side wound; the
atoning powers of the blood; Mary as a guarantor of grace and
mercy; the benevolent judge, in whose justice mercy had now found
a place; the Eucharist and its sacrifice of Christ's body and blood –
its reenactment of His Passion – in the mass; trust-filled prayer; true
contrition; and the hope of the sinner.

The images provide striking evidence of how much the representation of God and Christ, as well as the understanding of the judgment of the human soul, had changed since the 12th century. Both
in the 'theology of piety' and in sacred art, the image and role of
Christ was transformed from the withdrawn dignity of the heavenly
emperor to the utter misery evoked by the very human figure of the
Passion. The severity of *Christus iudex* was displaced by compassion
on the Day of Judgment, the fear- and terror-inspiring handing down
of the verdict by a consolatory image that awoke hope and trust.

The language of 'transformation' and 'displacement', however,
should not mislead. We come closer when we speak of a certain
tendency in comparison with the Early and High Middle Ages. There
was a shift in emphasis, a thematic re-prioritizing, a change of accent.
An examination of conceptions of mercy, protection, intercession,
consolation, and hope makes it clear: innovative aspects emerged
that either had not existed or had been discernible only in traces.[90]

---

[90] Which is not to overlook the fact that, around 1500, it was not only typical
of *simplices* but could also be characteristic of theologically trained, literarily active
pastors and preachers, as well as a common feature in images, to highlight (sometimes predominantly) those elements which induced terror and produced fear. The
extremely virulent condition of living with recurring *Angst* and the feeling that one
was threatened by various religious menaces (as discussed above), the fixation upon
the hour of death, upon the balance-sheet tallied at the Final Judgment, and upon
one's own spiritual qualities and meritorious works: a wide range of witnesses attest
to how much these preoccupations left their mark on the 'theology of piety' and
on 'images of piety'; on this cf. below p. 40f. with n. 111 and n. 112 as well as
the great number of 'Last Judgment' images that convey precisely this. However,
it may be said that near the end of the Middle Ages, both theological and icono-

To be sure, the notion of a rigid judgment based on the weighing of heavenly scales calibrated to the severity of God's justice survived into the Late Middle Ages.[91] So did expectations of an enthroned *Christus iudex*, who would preside over the world on the Day of Judgment, calling some to bliss and casting others into the jaws of Hell. The reception of both traditions is well attested in texts and images.[92]

However, given the influence of especially Bernard of Clairvaux (†1153), one detects the prerequisites for a shift in conception and representation. Once the emphasis on the humbled figure of the human, suffering Christ and on the salvific effect of His Passion gained more currency, the presentation of the Last Judgment changed drastically. French cathedrals attest to this alteration with portals that depict the theme between the 12th and 13th centuries, during the transition from the Romanesque and early Gothic to the high Gothic styles.[93] There, the human Christ of the Passion, half-naked and

---

graphic changes in an opposite direction demonstrate just how notions of the effects of God's lenience and human intercession were brought to bear over and against the traditional severity of the *dies irae, dies illa* mentality (cf. above, n. 31). To this extent one can speak of a shift in accent, a change in emphasis, and a tendency to 'center' upon pity and compassion. As regards iconography, reference should be made only to new or increasingly popular images of representation, for example: God's court as the seat of clemency, the pitiable and suffering Christ of the Passion, 'Christ in the Wine Press', the Mount of Olives, the Vera Icon (Veronica's cloth), St. Gregory masses, pietà, the Madonna wearing protective robes, Mary displaying her breast and offering the gift of her milk, images of the rosary, the 'steps to salvation' involving a 'chain of intercession', and God the Father as a merciful judge (cf. the following text).

[91] Cf. the concept of the 'scales of justice' on which the sinner would be placed at the time of judgment, which remained as valid as ever (on which see above, n. 85). On the other hand, in light of the logic of exoneration prevalent in late medieval theology and piety, it must be kept in mind just how much the 'weighing' of the sinner by the heavenly judge was influenced by the sacrifice of Christ, who served as the sinner's proxy. Similarly, if the church's system of threatened purgatorial punishments approached a type of dreamt up Divine bookkeeping system, then the effects of the grace earned from indulgences and intercession could reduce those punishments to nil. This mix – a fixation upon performance-justice-reward/punishment and upon hope for total exoneration – was characteristic at the close of the Middle Ages (cf. above, n. 31).

[92] Cf. Reinhard Schwarz: "Die spätmittelalterliche Vorstellung vom richtenden Christus – ein Ausdruck religiöser Mentalität", in: *Geschichte in Wissenschaft und Unterricht* 32 (1981), pp. 526–553.

[93] Cf. Willibald Sauerländer: *Gotische Skulptur in Frankreich 1140–1270*, with photographs by Max Hirmer (Munich, 1970), pp. 24–29. The change is clearly evidenced by a direct comparison between the representations of the Last Judgment on the middle west Portal (1145–55) and the middle south Portal (1210–15) of the

showing his wounds while angels displayed the instruments of His suffering, superseded the God-Christ who, flanked by His apostles, had sat enthroned in majesty as the heavenly judge.[94] Following earlier Byzantine examples, John the Baptist joined Mary as an intercessor at Christ's side in the deesis, replacing John the Evangelist.[95] The apostles, on the other hand, were moved frequently to the portal arches, where instead of holding books as they once had, now exhibited the instruments of their martyrdom.

All of these alterations mirrored an intention clearly formulated by monastic and scholastic theologians before and after 1200.[96] They sought to give the courtroom of God's justice the character of a tribunal of grace and clemency; there, they hoped, God's redeeming love, the recognition of Christ's Passion as the sinner's proxy, and the power of holy intercessors (especially Mary) to effect forgiveness, would become the order of the day.[97] The composition and arrange-

---

Notre-Dame cathedral at Chartres; ibid., p. 25 (plate I) and illustrations nos. 107–113. Cf. also Adolf Reinle: "Der Christus am Strassburger Engelspfeiler. Ein frühes franziskanisches Denkmal", in: *Neue Zürcher Zeitung* (international ed.), 11–12 April 1998 (no. 84), p. 53.

[94] The change in representations of Christ in images of the Last Judgment was admittedly long underway. Already during the Romanesque art of the 11th century, the judging Christ could be represented with his wounds. Along with this, from the first half of the 11th century to the beginning of the 13th, one observes a continual expansion and intensification of the passion in the representations: early on Christ appears only with the cross of His Passion, followed in time by the marks of the wounds on His hands and feet, then by the appearance of angels bearing the devices used to inflict His wounds, until finally He loses His imperious robes and sits half-naked, displaying his side-wound. On this development, cf. Beat Brenk: *Tradition und Neuerung in der christlichen Kunst des ersten Jahrtausends. Studien zur Geschichte des Weltgerichtsbildes* (Vienna, 1966) [= Wiener byzantinische Studien 3], pp. 133–142 and pp. 238–242.

[95] Cf. ibid., p. 141.

[96] Cf. the citations taken from Bernard of Clairvaux, Thomas Aquinas, and Bonaventure in: Angenendt: "Theologie und Liturgie" (as above, n. 85), p. 129f., and idem: *Geschichte der Religiosität im Mittelalter* (as above, n. 53), p. 136f., including the important sentence from Thomas: *Summa theologiae*, suppl. q. 90 art. 1 resp.: "Conveniens est, ut ipse Christus secundum humanam naturam, cuius redemptionis beneficio ad regnum admittimur, illi iudicio praesideat." Just as in the Late Middle Ages, already in the 13th century one finds the idea that the figure of the Christ of the Passion, along with the display of His wounds, increases the terror among Christ's enemies since the magnitude of His suffering holds up the dimensions of their guilt and the dread of their punishments before their very eyes.

[97] Cf. Sauerländer: *Gotische Skulptur* (as above, n. 93), p. 28: "Hatten die Gerichtsportale des 12. Jahrhunderts den Nachdruck auf die Warnung vor der Verdammnis und vor den Schrecken der Hölle gelegt, so sprechen hier die Hoffnung auf Erlösung durch den Heiland und das Vertrauen in die Fürbitter und in die Apostel, welche im Martyrium den irdischen Tod überwanden."

ment of images in the Ghent altar [plate 1] combined an earlier Byzantine and Romanesque style of presentation – the exalted *majestas Domini* – with a new iconography of the merciful judge based on the Passion and saintly intercession.

Especially noteworthy in the Late Middle Ages, both before and after the Ghent altar, is how these tendencies in theology and art could enable a completely new conception of judgment to emerge alongside of the conventional scenario of the *iudicium mundi*. This corresponded to a principally new yet varied iconography of God's judgment in the 'images of piety' of the 14th, 15th, and early 16th centuries. What separated these images from their traditional counterparts may be seen especially in Holbein's painting [plate 2]: in the proceedings against sinful man, Christ appears not as the judge but as the advocate, usually with his mother, Mary.[98] The Christ of the Passion displays to the judging Father the marks of His suffering, especially the side-wound. As one saw with Holbein, Mary can appear to the Father's left on the same horizontal plane as Christ, for with her exposed breast she also appeals directly to God as the advocate of the sinner. A triangle of persons arises that corresponds to the structure of the Last Judgment but, compared to traditional representations, alters the arrangement of the deesis. God the Father replaces the Son as judge; Christ takes the spot formerly held by Mary; and she in turn occupies the place of John the Baptist (or John the Evangelist). Together the two intercessional advocates obtain pardon for mankind from the judge, God. Mercy becomes the sole criteria on which the court's decision is based.

As we have pointed out, however, this new iconography of God's judgment varied. One finds an alternate structure, for example, in

---

[98] On this new type of representation since the early 14th century, cf. the examples of images and texts (with further bibliography) in Dieter Koepplin: "Interzession", in: *Lexikon der christlichen Ikonographie*, vol. 2 (Freiburg, 1970), cols. 346–352; idem: "Reformation der Glaubensbilder: Das Erlösungswerk Christi auf Bildern des Spätmittelalters und der Reformationszeit", in: *Martin Luther und die Reformation in Deutschland*, exhibition catalogue Nuremberg, Germanisches Nationalmuseum (Frankfurt a.M., 1983), pp. 333–378; here pp. 334–352 ("Spätmittelalterliche Glaubensbilder"); *Christus und Maria. Auslegungen christlicher Gemälde der Spätgotik und Frührenaissance aus der Karlsruher Kunsthalle*, exhibition catalogue (Karlsruhe, 1992), pp. 49–59; Marti and Mondini: "'Ich manen dich der brüsten mein" (as above, n. 78), pp. 79–90 and 198–201 (nos. 21–23), p. 282f. (no. 91); Schreiner: *Maria* (as above, n. 35), pp. 183–188; cf. also above, n. 76 (painting by Sebastian Dayg).

what may be called the 'chain of intercession' or 'graduated intercession', a type of iconographic representation that occurs more frequently than (and probably pre-dates) the triangular God-Christ-Mary
image described above. Appealing to the first link in the chain, the
sinner offers prayers to Mary, who then forwards his entreaty to
the next instance of authority, Christ. He in turn appeals to God the
judge, displaying the wounds of His Passion. Occasionally John the
Evangelist, who had stood with Mary under the redeeming crucifix
(John 19.25–27), appears in order to support her in supplication.[99]
The effect on the judge, however, is the same as that seen in tri-

---

[99] Koepplin ("Interzession", as above, n. 98, col. 347) employs the term "combined
intercession" (*kombinierte Interzession*) for the various types of compositions that display
God the Father with the intercessional pleadings of Christ and Mary. Here I distinguish between two types of intercession, depending on whether the breast-displaying
Mary, just like the wound-displaying Christ, appeals directly to God (Type I) or
whether she displays her breast and makes her plea through Christ (Type II). In
the exhibition catalogue *Himmel, Hölle, Fegefeuer* (as above, n. 75), there are two
examples from the first half of the 14th century: p. 81, plate 49 (glass window from
the Freiburg cathedral) and p. 199, cat. no. 22 (*initiale* of a choir psalter ms.). These
early representations of the combined intercession of Jesus and Mary cannot be
decisively placed in either category, although to me Type II seems the more likely
choice. There are good reasons to argue that Type II forms of representation began
to be applied earlier than those of Type I; foremost among them is the fact that
this graduated sequence had found literary representation already in the 12th century, in the form of a 'chain of intercession' (the sinner turns to Mary, who turns
to Christ, who then appeals to God the Father), through the highly influential work
De laudibus Beatae Mariae Virginis by Arnold of Chartres, abbot of Bonneval and friend
of Bernard. Under Bernard's name this work had a wide reception (see Migne *PL*
189, col. 1726). At the beginning of the graphic assimilation of Bernard's thought
stood representations of Mary/Christ and Christ/God the Father in two different
scenes, a split made patently obvious for the first time in a devotional book of text
and images, *Speculum humanae salvationis* (written before 1324), which was distributed
widely throughout Europe and proved groundbreaking for the development of an
iconography of 'particular' judgment; cf., for example, *Himmel, Hölle, Fegefeuer* (as
above, n. 75) p. 80 plate 48 (taken from an ms. of the *Speculum humanae salvationis*
around 1330). If the intercessors (with or without a sinful, pleading human) are
combined in an image, then those arranged in order beneath God (Type II) can
either be lined up along the same plane or graduated in the form of actual 'stairs
of salvation'. This provided graphic representation of the juridically based theological concept in which the road to clemency was graduated along progressive instances
of authority. For the occasional appearance of the third figure of intercession, John
the Apostle/Evangelist (in the graduated order: the dying human crying from his
deathbed for rescue – John – Mary – Christ – God the Father), cf. the exhibition
catalogue *Martin Luther und die Reformation in Deutschland* (as above, n. 98), p. 337f.
(no. 447); *Ludwigs Lust. Die Sammlung Irene und Peter Ludwig*, exhibition catalogue,
Germanisches Nationalmuseum Nuremberg (Nuremberg, 1993), p. 110 (text) and
112 (image), no. 86: "Ars bene moriendi".

angular representation: God allows Himself to be swayed in favor of mercy by the intercessional advocacy (*intercessio*) of Christ and Mary. The judge, it turns out, is an indulgent father. On a scroll of text in a woodcut from 1495 He answers: "Oh Son, I just can't say 'no' to you and your mother."[100]

Such representations of a mercifully predisposed God occasionally referred to preservation during temporal crises such as plague, war, and famine.[101] Looking at the scholarly literature, however, one notes an astounding unawareness that the majority of examples concern the 'individual' judgment at the moment of death, which determines the fate of a particular soul in the next world.[102] These images betray a close relation to late medieval *ars moriendi* literature, primers in the art of dying well. They are images of hope conceived evidently for pastoral purposes 'from below', from the perspective of sinners in need of help who appeal to God's grace; before the sinners' eyes

---

[100] "Abnuere o tibi nate nihil matrique valemus." Woodcut "Von der gnaden-richen Furbitt vor got dem Vater fur die armen sunder" (see above, n. 27); reproduction with commentary in the exhibition catalogue *Himmel, Hölle, Fegefeuer* (as above, n. 75), p. 200f. (no. 23); cf. another image of the 'stairs of salvation' in *Martin Luther und die Reformation in Deutschland* (as above, n. 98) p. 336f. (no. 446) with the scroll of text coming from the mouth of God the Father: "Queque petita dabo, fili, tibi; nulla negabo." On the 'inability' of God, who cannot refuse the intercessional pleading of Christ and Mary (which gives the sinner a high degree of assurance in his expectations and certainty in his hope), cf. Arnold of Bonneval's (as above, n. 99) formulation: "Christus nudato latere patri ostendit latus et vulnera, Maria Christo pectus et ubera, nec potest ullo modo esse repulsa, ubi concurrunt et orant omni lingua disertius haec clementiae monumenta et charitatis insignia." To the freely chosen, merciful, self-imposed obligation of God in which this 'inability' is grounded, cf. Berndt Hamm: *Promissio, pactum, ordinatio. Freiheit und Selbstbindung Gottes in der scholastischen Gnadenlehre* (Tübingen, 1977) [= Beiträge zur historischen Theologie 54].

[101] Cf. the examples in the exhibition catalogue *Himmel, Hölle, Fegefeuer* (as above, n. 75), p. 84, illus. 53; and in Schreiner: *Maria* (as above, n. 35), pp. 183 and 185; there is an example of a plague-altar (by Martin Schaffer, between 1513–15) with a 'chain of intercession' linking St. Sebastian and St. Rochus to Mary, who in turn stands in front of Christ, who faces God the Father, in Kurt Löcher: *Germanisches Nationalmuseum Nürnberg: Die Gemälde des 16. Jahrhunderts* (Stuttgart, 1997), pp. 443–446.

[102] Even in the woodcut "Von der gnadenrichen Furbitt" (as above, n. 27 and n. 100), which includes God the Father not only wielding the sword of His wrath but also holding the arrows of earthly plagues, the textual passages refer (among other things) to the situation of the sinner at the end of his life. On 'individual' or 'particular' judgment, cf. above n. 75. These images of Divine judgment thus iconologically connect the idea of combined intercession before God the Father, a concept that arose in the 12th century and was especially propagated in Cistercian circles (cf. above, n. 99), with the scholastic theory of 'particular' judgment that spread widely in the 13th century.

appear images of a merciful judge in a clement courtroom.[103] In
short, they presented concepts similar to the van Eycks' portrayal
[plate 1] of the merciful judge and Suess's image [plate 3] of the
benevolent judgment. The van Eycks and Suess did so, however, in
a completely different way that, if iconographically unusual, was typical of contemporary theological developments.

In late-medieval images of the *iudicium mundi*, it was characteristic
to represent both sides: salvation *and* damnation. From one side of
Christ's mouth came a bough of blooming lilies; from the other, the
sword of judgment.[104] Such bifurcated presentation disappeared, how-

---

[103] Gerson, in his influential *Appellatio peccatoris ad divinam misericordiam*, speaks of
the "tribunal clementiae, bonitatis et misericordiae" or simply of the "tribunal misericordiae" in which mercy overpowers requitive justice and its sentence (quoted
from the ed. cited above, n. 27, p. 538f.) The influence of this text may be seen
in the woodcut mentioned above (n. 102).

[104] This is the Christ of the Last Judgment (and for that matter, only His severe
side, without any mention of the merciful aspects found in contemporary images
of the judgment) that Luther had in mind when, in retrospect, he wrote in 1533:
"Denn ich kandte Christum nicht mehr denn [= anders] als einen gestrengen richter,
fur dem ich fliehen wolt und doch nicht entfliehen kundte." *WA* 38,148,11f. Cf.,
for example, his statement from 1537 as well: "Also machen sie [i.e., die Papisten]
aus Christo nichts denn einen strengen, zornigen Richter, fur dem man sich furchten
musse, als der uns wolle inn die helle stossen, wie man in gemalet hat auff dem
Regenbogen zu gericht sitzend und seine Mutter Maria und Johannes den Teuffer
zu beiden seiten als furbitter gegen seinem schrecklichen zorn. Das heisst ja Christum
fein, rein weggenomen und nicht allein ungekennet, sondern schlecht [= schlichtweg,
einfach] gar zugedeckt, begraben und verschorren, das ich nicht mehr also in sehe,
das er fur mich geboren, gelidden, gestorben und aufferstanden sey (wie die kinder
im Glawben [= Glaubensbekenntnis] sprechen), sondern allein also, das er mich
richten wolle nach meinem leben und wercken, ob ich fur die sunde bezalet und
gnug gethan habe oder nicht." *WA* 46,8,32–9,4. For further statements of this kind
by Luther cf. Otto Scheel (ed.): *Dokumente zu Luthers Entwicklung*, 2nd ed. (Tübingen,
1929), nos. 182, 194, 312, 346, 381, 383. Such comments by Luther say a great
deal about the mentality of *Angst* among the faithful around 1500, and about Luther's
own sense of being in a state of spiritual crisis: he was tempted to flee Christ. Such
comments say precious little, however, about the character of the many witnesses
documentable from the late medieval 'theology of piety' and its associated images.
Indeed, were one to evaluate matters on the basis of Luther's understanding, he
would never come upon the idea that the large majority of these witnesses did not
hold up the Christ of the Last Judgment before the faithful's eyes, but rather the
compassionate Christ of the Passion – that Christ (even when appearing at one's
'particular' or 'individual' judgment) who stood in for mankind through His suffering,
who presided over a clement courtroom, and who interceded for the poor sinner.
In Luther's retrospective presentation, the late medieval figure of compassion – the
Christus pro nobis – disappears completely behind the looming shadow of the pitiless
Christus iudex. Perhaps this is to be explained on the basis of the intense pressures
inherent to the necessary conditions for salvation that, on his part, man must fulfill
conditions which continued to be demanded and remained continually present in

ever, where God's courtroom came to be portrayed as bathed in the light of compassion and presided over by a fatherly judge swayed by the benevolent Christ who, along with *tota dulcis Maria*, served as the sinner's advocate. There, the side of damnation fell completely away despite the fact that, in the theological conception of 'individual' judgment, salvation and damnation always stood face-to-face.

One could extend these iconographic findings through an examination of the spiritual drama of the Late Middle Ages. "The Munich Drama of the Dying Man" (1510), for example, offered a type of verbalized and dramatized chain of intercession. There, exposing her breast, Mary appealed to Christ, who in turn pointed to His wounds while entreating the Father. In the end, the chain of intercessors persuaded the heavenly judge. He could not deny His Son's request for compassion. "God" explained that He would desist in His wrath and stand by the sinner in grace, provided that he give himself over to a life of repentance and obedience.[105]

The new conceptions and representations of God's judgment in these examples give expression to the widespread 'centering' of late-medieval religiosity around the Passion, mercy, and trust. An emphasis not on daunting severity, but on inviting compassion characterized a noticeable degree of the theological literature before and after 1500

---

late medieval theology and devotional practices (see further below). This pressure to meet such conditions aroused bitter feelings in the young monk Luther, from which he lost sight of the 'sweet' Christ of the Passion and fixed his gaze steadily on that day in which that other Christ would sit before him and demand an account and explanation as to why His Passion had not changed Luther into a God-loving man. For that reason, his spiritual guide and pastor Staupitz, pointing to the wounds of Christ, could not help Luther either.

[105] Cf. Johannes Bolte (ed.): *Drei Schauspiele vom sterbenden Menschen* (Leipzig, 1927) [= Bibliothek des Literarischen Vereins in Stuttgart 269–70], pp. V–VIII, 5–9 (vv. 103–244); on which cf. Theo Meier: *Die Gestalt Mariens im geistlichen Schauspiel des deutschen Mittelalters* (Berlin, 1959) [= Philologische Studien und Quellen 4], p. 131f. Cf., on the other hand, the very different situation, also found in the spiritual drama of the 15th century, in which the Last Judgment is portrayed and Mary, despite her intercession, is unable to change the mind of the judging Christ; examples of such dramas may be found in Schreiner: *Maria* (as above, n. 35), pp. 207–209. That Mary (together with Christ) appears before the judge, God the Father, and succeeds in her intercession and yet cannot further influence the judging Christ, conforms to the theological logic of the relation between 'individual' and 'universal' (i.e. final) judgment. The final decision over the otherwordly fate of a person occurred already at the moment of 'individual' judgment, such that at the Last Judgment the sentence may not be changed whatsoever (cf. above, n. 75). What the intercessory pleas of Mary and John during scenes of the Last Judgment emphasize, therefore, is the enduring compassion applied to those who are saved.

that concerned itself with the care of souls and preaching.[106] The creators of innumerable images of the Passion, of Mary, and of the saints set their sights above all else on mercy and comfort, on the promise of help for contrite sinners, on the articulation of the flock's plea for compassion.[107] The Passion of Christ gained an increasingly significant place in theology, piety, liturgy, poetry, and the visual arts from the 11th and 12th centuries through the end of the 15th.

Because the elements of the Passion became normative focal points of religiosity near the end of the Middle Ages, they were subject to undergo an even more discriminating sequence of consolidation, reduction, and compression – a 'centering within centering', so to speak. Thus the faithful's view could be re-directed especially toward the side wound and the heart of Christ[108] to the point where, in some images, the entire representation of the Passion-narrative and of Christ's body was reduced to a wounded, bleeding heart.[109] Here was contained, like a consecrated host exhibited for the viewing of the devout,[110] the most conspicuous concentration of the salvific powers of the Passion, where Christ willingly substituted Himself for sinful mankind.

The Late Middle Ages witnessed heightened anxieties over sin, the Devil, and God's judgment. A variety of religious and historical

---

[106] It remains a task of future scholarship to evaluate how large this group was, and to establish whether or not perhaps even the predominating tone of the 'theology of piety' around 1500 was defined by this intention and through this type of 'centering' (this despite the comments in the first part of n. 90 above).

[107] Cf. above, n. 90. On the quantitative dimensions cf. Hamm: "Von der spätmittelalterlichen reformatio" (as above, n. 1), p. 25f., n. 51.

[108] Examples in the exhibition catalogue *Glaube Hoffnung Liebe Tod* (as above, n. 81), passim; cf., for example, Henk van Os: *The Art of Devotion in the Late Middle Ages in Europe 1300–1500*, exhibition catalogue, Rijksmuseum (Amsterdam, 1994), p. 116f. and plate 36 (an isolated heart of Christ in the center of the cross).

[109] Examples in the exhibition catalogue *Glaube Hoffnung Liebe Tod* (as above, n. 81), pp. 140–155, with excellent analysis by Thomas Lentes, pp. 144–147 ("Die Vermessung des Christus-Körpers") and pp. 152–155 ("Nur der geöffnete Körper schafft Heil. Das Bild als Verdoppelung des Körpers").

[110] On the cult of the host during the Late Middle Ages (and related delusions regarding Jewish host desecration), cf. Angenendt: *Geschichte der Religiosität im Mittelalter* (as above, n. 53), pp. 503–508 (with further bibliography). The increase in passional devotion since the 11th and 12th centuries (i.e., since the era of the crusades) betrays close connections with a new dimension of anti-Judaism and Jewish pogroms: the Jews were simultaneously persecuted as the initiators *and* as the enemies of Christ's Passion and charged with ritual murder and host desecration; cf. Michael Toch: *Die Juden im mittelalterlichen Reich* (Munich, 1998) [= Enzyklopädie deutscher Geschichte 44], pp. 111–120 (with further bibliography).

factors had increased the amount of cumulative needs for assurance and of necessary meritorious works. Relief from these burdens was offered whenever devotional artists in some way emphasized purity and suffering, sacrifice and atonement, or agency and intercession. Their representations of Christ, Mary, and the saints pointed again and again to the immeasurable treasures of God's grace: such riches could help the spiritual weakness of even the worst sinner, if he would only allow himself to be helped.

To be sure, presentations of atonement, intercession, compassion, and protection always aimed toward the heart's contrition and the sinner's performance of satisfactory or meritorious works; they sought to change his life to one of increasing obedience to God's commandments and counsels. Over against God, what the sinner might actually accomplish may have been recognized as minimal. But an appeal to the satisfaction of those requirements, without which no one could be saved, always accompanied the offer of deliverance from hell and purgatory. Through their devotions, sinners were to appropriate the Passion affectively *and* operatively, in their hearts and in their actions. On the highway to salvation, God's mercy always made up only one lane. The other consisted of true repentance, a certain quality and morality on the sinner's part that satisfied the requirements of heavenly justice.[111] God's mercy remits and protects, but it still must strike a compromising balance with God's righteousness. Thus the type of sermon that celebrated God's comforting mercy went hand-in-hand with one that warned of His terrifying judgment and called for repentance.[112] For many preachers, in fact, it was common to proclaim both central messages – dread and solace – in the same sermon.

Noteworthy in the interplay of 'dread' and 'solace' is the fact that, near the end of the Middle Ages, recognizable 'centering' in theology and in the visual arts yielded a strong shift in emphasis toward the message of mercy. This trend extended as far as the mottoes *sola misericordia Dei* and *solus Christus*.[113] Even the indulgence sermon around 1500 attests to the shift. The Augustinian hermit Johannes

---

[111] Cf. above, p. 28 with n. 77 and p. 11 with n. 31.

[112] Compare, for example, Staupitz's sermon on mercy (*Barmherzigkeitspredigt*) in Nuremberg 1516/17 with Savonarola's *terrifica praedicatio* in Florence during the 1490s. On Staupitz, cf. Hamm: "Humanistische Ethik" (as above, n. 42), pp. 133–143; on Savonarola cf. Pierre Antonetti: *Savonarola: Ketzer oder Prophet? Eine Biographie* [French ed. 1991] (Zurich, 1992), esp. pp. 71–73 ("Die *terrifica praedicatio*").

[113] Cf. above, pp. 11–13; for displacement and shifts in accent cf. above, p. 32f.

von Paltz (†1511),[114] for example, extolled the indulgences for the papal jubilee not in traditional terms, but as special allocations of God's grace that far excelled all previously known aids for obtaining it. Now, exclaimed Paltz, even "the worst of sinners" could obtain "the most effective help" since an unparalleled influx of grace (*singularis influentia*) was flooding from heaven into the church.[115] Admittedly, a critic like Staupitz (also an Augustinian hermit) could emphasize that indulgences were wholly unnecessary, because God lavishes the effects of the Passion, nothing less than the total annulment of guilt and punishment, upon any contrite sinner.[116] Two preachers within the same order, who shared the same tradition, could also share intentions and an emphasis on mercy while articulating them in two very different ways.

We risk a tremendous misunderstanding, however, should we suppose that an emphasis on divine compassion and man's resulting hope in some way contradicted the perceived need among early-modern elites, and many of their 'simpler' contemporaries, for increased discipline, order, and regulation within society. The case is exactly the opposite. According to the representatives of the 'theology of piety' around 1500, spiritual and social life had its basis in faith, hope, and love. Precisely this basis led them straight from an emphasis on protective guarantees of grace and salvation to an insistence on a life lived in spiritual discipline, seriousness of purpose, sanctity,

---

with n. 90. In this context it is most telling, how preachers around 1500 could warn against praising the mercy of God too strongly. That is what the Strasbourg cathedral preacher, Johannes Geiler von Kaysersberg, meant when near the end of the 15th century he asserted that, given the current state of the world, it was very dangerous to preach on the mercy of God since for every one person troubled by religious doubts, there would spring up "hundert, ja tausend und zehnmal hunderttausend anmaßende Menschen"; cited by E. J. Dempsey Douglass: *Justification in Late Medieval Preaching. A Study of John Geiler of Keisersberg* (Leiden, 1966) [= Studies in Medieval and Reformation Thought 1], p. 174 with n. 4. On the phenomenon of "easy grace," about which Geiler warned, cf. the jubilee preaching from 1500 discussed below.

[114] On Paltz, cf. above, n. 55; on the support of Paltz by Elector Frederick the Wise and his brother Johann (see below) cf. Hamm: *Frömmigkeitstheologie* (as above, n. 9), Index of Names.

[115] This material is further summarized, analyzed, and documented in ibid., pp. 289–291.

[116] See ibid., p. 240 with n. 127; on Staupitz's connections to Frederick the Wise and to the Nuremberg city council (see below) cf. Theodor Kolde: *Die deutsche Augustiner-Congregation und Johann von Staupitz. Ein Beitrag zur Ordens- und Reformationsgeschichte* (Gotha, 1879), pp. 209–328.

and fulfillment of the law. The prospects for shaping a Christian society and for maintaining social stability, they asserted, were far better served by grace and trust than by the strategy of dread and *Angst*. It was thus perfectly consistent that not only Paltz but also Staupitz enjoyed enormous support from the Saxon Elector Frederick the Wise and his brother Johann, from the city council at Nuremberg and other governments. Here 'normative centering' occurred quite typically, both in a polar concentration on God's mercy and Christ's law and in the interplay between religious and political 'centering'.

VI. *From the Centering of the Late Middle Ages to the Centering of the Reformation: Continuity and Upheaval*

This analysis has established, I hope, how strongly religiosity around 1500 could emphasize God's compassion, the salvific effect of Christ's Passion, and mankind's humble trust in them both. Within the late-medieval 'theology of piety' and its accompanying 'images of piety', one recognizes the impetus to reduce and to focus that the Reformation took up in its theology – one that was christocentric, oriented around the Passion, and centered upon trust in God's promise and grace. From the 'theology of the Passion' of a Johannes von Staupitz ran a direct line to Luther's 'theology of the cross'.[117]

As an interpretive category, however, 'normative centering' also directs our attention toward the break between the Late Middle Ages and the Reformation. What reformers reduced to a single focal point during the 16th century – *solus Christus, sola gratia, sola scriptura* etc. – had always remained in a state of open plurality during the Late Middle Ages. Such was part and parcel of late-medieval religiosity. They considered not only the Passion as beneficial to the soul after

---

[117] On Staupitz cf. above, p. 12 with n. 32. On the theological ties between Staupitz and Luther, cf. Heiko A. Oberman: *Masters of the Reformation. The Emergence of a New Intellectual Climate in Europe* [rev. and abridg. trans. of 1st German ed., 1977], trans. Dennis Martin (Cambridge, 1981), pp. 75–91; David C. Steinmetz: *Luther and Staupitz. An Essay in the Intellectual Origins of the Protestant Reformation* (Durham, North Carolina, 1980) [= Duke Monographs in Medieval and Renaissance Studies 4]; Lothar Graf zu Dohna: "Staupitz und Luther: Kontinuität und Umbruch in den Anfängen der Reformation", in: *Pastoraltheologie* 74 (1985), pp. 452–465; Richard Wetzel: "Staupitz und Luther. Annäherung an eine Vorläufer-Figur", *Blätter für pfälzische Kirchengeschichte* 58 (1991), pp. 369–395 [= *Ebernburg-Hefte* 25 (1991), pp. 41–67].

death, but also the intercession of Mary, the saints, and others. At
some level, on the other hand, intercession was always conceived in
relation to Christ's suffering and death on the cross. Late-medieval
religion was a religion of mercy. It could concentrate its energies on
the saving agency of the suffering figure Christ and, at the same
time, on the protective help of the figure Mary standing under the
crucified. Passional and Marian devotion reciprocally reinforced one
another: Mary protects all those who honor the Passion; the Passion
stands all those who honor Mary in good stead. As one reads in the
sources, Christ's cross was denoted as our "sole hope."[118] This was
completely consistent with, for example, a painting of 1517 in which
a pious patron appealed to Mary as an intercessor who should be
our "only hope" after God:[119] "Mediatrix nostra, que es post deum
spes sola, tuo filio me representa!"[120]

Given its compulsory impetus to reduce and compress, 'normative
centering' had isolated and employed several *sola*-formulations well
in advance of the Reformation.[121] This *sola*, however, always repre-

---

[118] See above, p. 31 with n. 87: "O crux ave spes unica!"

[119] On calling out to Mary in prayer with the words "Tu es unica spes nostra"
and "O dulcissima mater nostra Maria, unica spes et refugium animae nostrae",
cf. Dempsey Douglass: *Justification in Late Medieval Preaching* (as above, n. 113), p. 195.

[120] Jan Gossaert, diptych of the Chancellor of Besançon, Jean Carondelet, 1517;
Paris, Musée National du Louvre; reproduction in Max J. Friedländer: *Die frühen
niederländischen Maler von van Eyck bis Bruegel* (Cologne, 1956), plates 219/220. That
the prayers of the patron, Carondelet, were intended primarily for the situation of
his death, is also evidenced by the back side of the panel containing Mary: above
a skull a scroll of text reads "Corde contemnit omnia, qui se semper cogitat mori-
turum. hieronimus." In their two-sidedness, the diptyches of the century preceding
the Reformation are, on the one hand, evidence of individualization in that they
allow the praying countenance of an individual patron to come to the fore; on the
other, however, they provide evidence for religious 'centering' in that they make
either the pitiable, wretched Christ of the Passion or Mary holding the Christ-child
the privileged addressee; in so doing, they appeal to the *pro me* aspect of divine
compassion. Cf., for example, the diptyches in Mary's honor executed for patrons
in van Os: *The Art of Devotion* (as above, n. 108), p. 116f., plate 36: diptych for
Willem van Bibaut (anon. 1523); also Dirk de Vos: *Hans Memling. Das Gesamtwerk*
(Stuttgart, 1994), pp. 278–283: diptych of Martin von Nieuwenhove (Memling, 1487).
A diptych executed for a patron featuring the pitiable, wretched Christ may be
seen in the exhibition catalogue, *Martin Luther und die deutsche Reformation* (as above,
n. 98), p. 343f. (no. 458): diptych executed for Count Georg von Löwenstein (by
Hans Pleydenwurff, around 1456). Cf. ibid., p. 368 (no. 490) on how far this *pro
me* aspect of the gift of salvation could go in the Late Middle Ages: there, an image
of a praying cleric before the cross (anon. 1519) is accompanied by the text: "O
iesu sis mihi iesus" (cf. Matth. 1.21)!

[121] Cf. above, p. 8 with n. 19.

sented complementary exclusivity; it always contained a sort of plural elongation, a wide spectrum of distinct focal points that corresponded to Catholic 'gradualism', to man's ascent to God, and to the graduation between man and God.[122] The centrifugal thrust of the Reformation, in which 'centering' further reduced those principles to a concentration on the singular and one-sided efficacy of God's role in man's salvation, broke with this plural and gradualist system.

I am inclined, therefore, to speak of 'normative centering' during the Late Middle Ages with great caution and always with qualification. There were traces and tendencies that pointed in this direction. Perhaps only upon reaching the age of the Reformation and the era of Lutheran, Reformed, and Catholic confessionalization, however, may one actually refer to 'normative centering' in terms of *dominant* conceptions and phenomena. There is a break or change over and against the 15th century that transverses the various confessions and reveals a new type and quality of 'normative centering'. At the same time, I am also convinced that one can adequately grasp the religious, juridical, political, and cultural 'centering' underway in the 16th century *only* when one recognizes its relation to the dynamics of expectations, ideas, and structures found already in the 15th and before. When viewed from the perspective of the 16th century, one finds a significant precursor in tendencies to normativize, to compress, to fix upon – to 'center' – before 1500. Seen in religious terms, this late medieval precursive tendency possessed an inherent polarity: an intense concentration on regularization, obedience to the law, the quest for virtue, and the sanctification of one's life on the one side; on the other an increasingly focused emphasis on mercy, intercession, and grace that sought to relieve the burden of the conscience, to protect the sinner via the agency of Christ, Mary, and the saints, and to fortify the soul. The strictness of spiritual rigor and the relief of gratuitous compassion made up the two sides of late medieval and early modern 'normative centering'. During the 16th century, both aspects were at work among all confessions and, at the same time, were interpreted, manipulated and employed in confessionally specific ways. During recent years, historians of early

---

[122] Cf. Hamm: "Reformation als normative Zentrierung" (as above, n. 1), p. 252f. On the phrase "complementary exclusivity" (*komplementäre Alleinigkeit*) cf. above p. 21.

modern Europe have devoted much of their efforts to the categories of 'social discipline' and of governmentally regimented 'Policey'. Such categories, it must be remembered, formed only *one* side of 'normative centering'. Put more precisely: they formed *one* aspect of *one* side, i.e., the social-political aspect of the side that tended toward a regularizing, insistent stringency.

As an interpretive category and term of research, with 'normative centering' we have not hit on a major vista that takes us high and wide through the 16th century. Instead it offers nothing more – and nothing less – than a possible path through the dense undergrowth of the past. Other historians will find neither 'centering' nor a normative reduction of diversity. And rightly so, since the age may also be characterized as one of increasing differentiation, complexity, and individualization at all reaches of life.[123] Especially during the 16th century, rife with opposition among and between the various Protestant camps and Catholicism, it was in fact 'normative centering' that, through its simplifying and demarcating dynamic, contributed to the intensification of tendencies toward particularization in the rivalry ridden competition between notions of the 'best' (and thus *only*) way of life, efforts toward reform, religious confessions, and confessional states.

---

[123] On the association between 'normative centering' and individualization cf. above, n. 120 (diptych examples); on the association between differentiation and 'centering' cf. above, n. 58.

Plate 1.

Plate 2.

Plate 3.

CHAPTER TWO

BETWEEN SEVERITY AND MERCY. THREE MODELS OF PRE-REFORMATION URBAN REFORM PREACHING: SAVONAROLA – STAUPITZ – GEILER

I. *Urban* 'dirigenti religiosi' *of the Reformation and Late Middle Ages*[1]

1. The success of the Reformation in the cities of Germany and Switzerland is generally considered to be inconceivable apart from the key role played by urban preachers. It was through such preachers, their compelling and stirring sermons, not least also through the pamphlets they composed, that the teaching of the Reformation received its decisive popular impetus among urban communities and the peasant population of the surrounding countryside. At the same time, these preachers influenced the religious politics of civic, noble and princely authorities in a normative way.

Yet the influence which the urban preachers exercised on the introduction and implementation of local or territorial reformations after about 1522, can be properly understood only in the context of late medieval developments. My *first thesis* is this: the principal reason why the preachers of the Reformation were able to acquire such enormous authority in their cities and beyond, was that before and after 1500, learned and respected urban preachers, pastors and devotional writers had already gained a high level of spiritual leadership among the urban public, especially where influential elements of that public were already striving for spiritual reform.

The offices held by such spiritual leaders were diverse. Some were secular priests in endowed preaching positions in cathedrals or other city churches; others, more commonly, were preachers at mendicant

---

[1] This essay is an expanded form of a lecture given at the international Savonarola-Conference in Ferrara, Italy, in Spring 1998. The main focus of this conference was the significance and the influence of religious leaders (*dirigenti religiosi*) in European cities during the 15th and 16th centuries. – I shall restrict myself in the bibliographical references in the footnotes mostly to lists of sources. More extensive material on urban piety and preaching in the 15th and 16th centuries can be found in my book *Bürgertum und Glaube. Konturen der städtischen Reformation*, Göttingen 1996.

churches. Additionally, there were the itinerant penitential and indul-gence preachers who visited the towns and cities for a period of days or weeks only, such as during Lent, and who drew the crowds with their eloquence. Compared to the preachers of the early Reformation the urban preachers of the late middle-ages may appear less spec-tacular, because they operated within the framework of the approved doctrine of the church and did not challenge the ecclesiastical hier-archy, but they already fulfilled to a degree the function of urban *dirigenti religiosi* in the full sense of the word "*dirigere*": guidance, ori-entation, regulation, direction, standardisation, control, criticism and correction. The preachers of the urban pulpit were prominent and, at times, controversial figures among the civic communities. Their drive for an ecclesiastical and ethical reform of the community was often frustrated by obstacles, in particular those posed by the polit-ical authorities, and yet their influence on the formation of a com-munity's norms and conscience should not be underestimated. The new ideas of the Reformation's preaching could therefore slip into an existing, tried and tested form.

2. Even in terms of their message there is a certain continuity between the preachers of the Reformation and the spiritual objec-tives of the late medieval *dirigenti religiosi*. The stirring effect of urban Reformation preaching derived directly from the special nature of its message. By declaring Scripture an exclusive norm for the life of the church and the individual believer, that preaching met two essen-tial needs: the longing for the liberating experience of forgiveness and peace of conscience on the one hand, and the need for a bind-ing communal order and discipline on the other. Reformation preach-ers, the *dirigenti religiosi* of the cities, seized this dual opportunity of guidance by interpreting the Bible on the one hand as the com-forting message of God's mercy, liberating believers from the need to justify themselves through religious works as well as from the demands of church imposed obligations, and on the other hand by interpreting it as the binding message of a holy God, who wishes to sanctify his liberated congregation in the spirit of love and remove the leaven of vice from it.

It is worth emphasizing that the auditors of these urban sermons were not only attracted by the promise of God's unheard-of grace, but also by the proclamation of a new severity in the fight against sin and vice. With regard to the latter, the various classes of the communities had differing views of a Christian order of love and discipline. While the governing elite were mainly concerned with securing their subjects' obedience and willingness to bear burdens, the less well-to-do wished to see the greed, extravagance and indulgence of the rich checked, economic pressures relieved and social misery alleviated. Thus the polarity of grace and severity, mercy and justice, Gospel and Law, freedom and discipline, comfort and admonition, promise and menace determined the message of Reformation preaching as well as the expectations of the believers. Christ reigns over the city as the crucified saviour, but also as law-giver and judge. Between these poles range the various types of *dirigenti religiosi* and of urban Reformations.

3. The theological dialectic of the inviting mercy of the reconciled God and the impelling severity of the divine law-giver, so central to the character of the diverse types of Reformation, is incomprehensible apart from an awareness of the tensions within late medieval theology. It presupposes a polarity which is at the same time different from and analogous to that of the preachers and pastors of the late medieval cities. In this respect, too – and this is my *second thesis* – the influence and attraction of urban Reformation preaching can be adequately grasped only if note is taken of the way in which the various positions of the pre-Reformation *dirigenti religiosi* were continued and, at the same time, changed. A closer look at the urban reform preachers before and after 1500 reveals that they, too, find their individual positions within a field of tension between the poles of God's infinite mercy for the sake of Jesus Christ, and of his relentless strictness as the heavenly law-giver, judge and avenger. The comforting call to throw oneself completely on God's saving mercy stands alongside the menacing warning that only those will reach salvation who truly repent of all their sins, make satisfaction for their transgressions and follow God's law.

The sermons and devotional writings of these spiritual leaders therefore demonstrate in an exemplary way how the spirituality of the late Middle Ages was caught between two dominating perspectives and, depending on the individual author, tended to the one or the other direction. One perspective stresses the strictly judging, rewarding and punishing justice of God which through encouragements, warnings or terrifying threats compells the believer – who is considered capable of religious achievements and merits – to earn his salvation with good intentions and works. On the other hand there is the perspective of mercy: it conveys an awareness of human weakness and of the insufficiency of good works, directing the believer to the saving mercy of God the Father, Christ, Mary and the saints. It is to their compassion, mediation and intercession that weak and afflicted sinners are encouraged to entrust themselves with full hope. In the following I shall attempt to investigate how these two perspectives are accentuated and combined, for it is this that determines the character of the theology and spirituality preached in each case. How does the respective preacher relate to each other the strictness of the Law and the leniency of the Gospel? How does he define justice (or righteousness) and mercy, and what kind of compromise determines their relationship? Is the category of retributive justice the prevailing norm dominating his discourses on mercy, or is divine mercy his point of departure, seeing even the retributive justice of God in the light of his saving grace? Such questions indicate how diverse, even contradictory, the spiritual orientation of the late medieval urban *dirigenti religiosi* was. The components of threats, warnings, encouragement and consolation are mixed in all possible proportions.

4. On the basis of such criteria the urban *dirigenti religiosi* before and after 1500 may be divided into three main types: first, we note the type of preachers who strike predominantly a menacing key, terrifying their listeners by preaching the wrath of a punishing God, the relentless severity of a *deus iudex*. The objectives of a complete change of life-style, of Christian perfection and of the spiritual purification of the individual as well as the community are central to their sermons. Second, we encounter a contrasting type of preaching, in which the leniency and comfort of God's mercy dominate over all the terrifying aspects of his justice and punishment. Such preaching unfolds before the listener above all the boundless treasures of divine mercy, in particular of Christ's suffering and its vicarious atonement. Such preachers of the *misericordia Dei* tend to play down the demands made on the spiritual capabilities of the believer and the notion of the sinner's indispensable co-operation for his salvation, maximizing instead the believer's hope in the manifold forms of assistance offered by God and the Church. Finally, a third type of preachers displays no clear prevalence of either menacing severity or comforting mercy. These are the preachers who attempt to strike a balance between retributive justice and generous mercy, between threat and comfort, between moral exertion and trust. Depending on circumstances and audience they may emphasize more strongly the seriousness of divine judgement, the urgency of penitence

and the necessity of good conduct for salvation; at other times their
sermons will highlight the saving power of grace based on vicarious
atonement or merits, of intercessions, sacraments and indulgences,
which compensate for the believer's moral failures and spiritual
weakness.

In the following I intend to illustrate these three main types of
spiritual counselling by reference to the examples of three prominent
dirigenti religiosi in cities of the late middle-ages: Girolamo Savonarola
(1452–1498) in Florence, Johannes von Staupitz (ca. 1468–1524) in
Nuremberg and Johannes Geiler von Kaysersberg (1445–1510) in
Strasbourg. As preachers and spiritual writers all three made an
extraordinary impact. All of them provoked a lively response in the
cities mentioned and enjoyed enormous respect and veneration among
the political elite. All of them subjected the prevailing secular circumstances to a focused spiritual perspective. All of them aimed at
reform and at the spiritual renewal of the believer, monastic life and
the church, in particular at true penitence and a love of God which
radiates throughout the whole life of a Christian; and all of them
had in view the urban community which they wanted to provide
with religious guidance.

5. There is a close connection between the preachers' attitude and
the political, social, cultural and religious climate of the cities in
which they operated. Of course, their attitudes were also influenced
to a large degree by their respective ecclesiastical status: as prior of
a Dominican convent closely connected with the rule of the Medici
(Savonarola), as head (Vicar-General) of a congregation of observant
monasteries of the Augustinian order in Germany and the Netherlands
(Staupitz), and as someone commissioned by the Chapter to serve
as Cathedral Preacher (Geiler von Kaysersberg). Yet, whatever differences there are in their manner of preaching and in the specific
character of their spirituality, these cannot be explained adequately
by reference to their ecclesiastical status or to the differing urban
situations alone.

Admittedly, Savonarola's style of preaching is inconceivable apart
from the particular social and political context of upper Italy and
the city republic of Florence with its highly developed Renaissance
culture; and Geiler's and Staupitz' very different styles of delivery
are, no doubt, also determined by the fact that they did not preach
from a pulpit in the heated and polarized atmosphere of the city on
the Arno, but in the more moderate, peaceful and conservative cli-

mates of Strasbourg and Nuremberg. But it would be wrong to see these contexts as inevitably determinative: In Savonarola's Florence there were other preachers who did not share the menacing tone of his sermons, just as one should not necessarily deduce Geiler's individual style of preaching at Strasbourg or Staupitz' at Nuremberg from the peculiar characters of these cities. No doubt the Dominican Savonarola was heavily influenced by the Thomist teaching of his order, but at the same time he stood in the tradition of the penitential preachers from various orders of northern Italy. Staupitz, the Augustinian friar, was naturally loyal to the theology of the (alleged) founder of his order, yet his interpretation of St. Augustine was also considerably influenced by medieval theological traditions outside his order. Conversely, Geiler adopted as his model Jean Gerson, a secular cleric like himself, but at the same time felt drawn to the monastic ideal of withdrawal from the world.

Each of the three therefore displays his own dynamic of theology, spirituality and personal character, which transcends his local and social context and his form of ecclesiastical life – just as the way that the writings of each found reception beyond the boundaries of local circumstances or theological traditions. We are therefore dealing with three individually conditioned, yet quite exemplary types of urban *dirigenti religiosi*, who may be compared in spite of their geographical distance. I view their individual originality as an accentuation or illustration of the generally typical. A comparison thus affords us an impression of the variety of type and the range of message in reform preaching before the Reformation.

II. *Girolamo Savonarola: Preacher of God's Severity*

1. With his stirring sermons Girolamo Savonarola, prior of the Dominican convent of San Marco in Florence from 1491, represents the menacing and terrifying type of penitential preaching which announces the relentless strictness of God's punishing justice. In the same way that Savonarola himself in his pulpit felt an enormous pressure which, as he declared, almost burst the arteries in his breast,[2]

---

[2] Savonarola: 3rd sermon on the Psalms, 13th January 1495, in: *Prediche sopra i Salmi*, ed. Vincenzo Romano, vol. 1 (Rome, 1969) [Edizione nazionale delle opere

so he subjected his listeners to a shocking eschatological and moral
pressure. Long before he appeared in public with his claim of a
prophetic vision of future terrors and a prophetic interpretation of
political events, his preaching style already possessed the character
of a *terrifica praedicatio* (terrifying preaching). This is how he himself
described one of his sermons which he delivered in the Florentine
cathedral of S. Maria del Fiore on 27 April 1491.[3] In it he harshly
chastised the greed, extravagance and vanity of the clergy, the hard-
heartedness of the rich and powerful who imposed unbearable taxes
on the poor, and the sexual vices of the licentious. Throughout the
nineties he continued with an untiring, pounding monotony to crit-
icise the superficiality of monastic life, the excessive finery of women,
the pernicious preference for pagan books by humanist scholars, and
above all the unholiness of gamblers and blasphemers, of the indifferent
and of sceptics, the so-called "lukewarm", condemning again and
again the secularisation of the clergy, the exploitation of the poor
and the perversity of the "sodomites" (i.e. homosexuals). God's wrath,
Savonarola threatened in his sermon of 1491, will visit all such people of vice with terrible plagues; a new flood of retribution will come
over them and only a small number, he himself and those faithful
chosen by God, will escape the horrifying destruction.

This terrifying tone, alarming the listeners in a partly fascinating,
partly shocking way, was maintained by Savonarola throughout the
following years: the wrath of God at the Florentines' disobedience,
his approaching punishment in the shape of natural catastrophes,
the imminent flood and eternal condemnation in hell, the call to
conversion and penitence, the promise of salvation for the few who
repent in time and serve God in holy simplicity and pure love,
renouncing all worldly affluence.[4] After 1492 Savonarola intensified

---

di Girolamo Savonarola], p. 56.12–15. Cf. also Savonarola's testimony: "I should
like to say nothing and be silent but I can not; for the Word of God is like a fire
in my heart, and if I did not beat out the flames they would consume me entirely."
Cf. Jer. 20.9; 1st sermon on Amos and Zechariah from 17th February 1496, in:
Prediche sopra Amos et Zaccaria, ed. Paolo Ghiglieri, vol. I, Rome 1971, pp. 20.28–21.1.

[3] Savonarola: *Compendium revelationum* (October 1495), in: *Compendio di rivelazioni*
[. . .], ed. Angela Crucitti (Rome, 1974), p. 136.5f.: "Quamobrem eodem mane
terrificam praedicationem egi"; cf. the earlier Italian version (August 1495), ibid.
p. 10.9f.: "feci una spaventosa predicazione".

[4] On the subject of 'simplicity' cf. Savonarola's treatise of August 1496: *De simplicitate christianae vitae*, ed. Pier Giorgio Ricci (Rome, 1959) [Edizione nazionale delle
opere di Girolamo Savonarola]. Gundolf Gieraths (*Savonarola: Ketzer oder Heiliger?*,

the menacing and terrifying character of his penitential sermons through new types of prophetic visions. The most important of these was the vision of the sword, to which he returned again and again:[5] He saw a hand in heaven holding a sword with the inscription: "The sword of the Lord will come over the earth shortly and swiftly" (*Gladius Domini super terram cito et velociter*),[6] while above the hand it read: "True and just are the judgements of the Lord" (*Vera et iusta sunt iudicia Domini*; Revelation 19.2). A loud voice sounded over the whole earth: "Hear ye, all dwellers of the earth, thus speaks the Lord: I, the Lord, speak in my holy wrath. Behold, the days are approaching when I will wield my sword over you. Return to me, before my wrath blazes up; for then misery will come over you; you will seek peace and not find it." Following this, angels floated down to earth to offer a white garment and a cross to every human being. The repentant accepted this gift of grace and cleansing; most, however, rejected it full of scorn. But then God's sword turned against the earth: The sky filled with dark clouds and thunder, swords, hail, arrows and fire all at once rained down, plagues, famines and innumerable afflictions erupted on earth. Only those dressed in the white garments and carrying the crosses in their hands were rescued by the angels. The vision ended with an appeal to the Florentines: "Therefore heed the word of God: The Lord desires to have mercy on you. Return to the Lord, for he is merciful and compassionate and shows righteousness to all who call on him. But if you refuse, I will avert my eyes from you for ever." Soon, it will be "too late":

Freiburg – Basel – Vienna, 1961, p. 181) aptly summarises the content of the five books: . . . back to simplicity, back to the original love. Savonarola addresses the individual ranks and professions and shows that Christian love does not consist in wealth, external acts, parroted prayers, magnificent church buildings, gold-embroidered robes and splendid vessels, nor in indulgences, pilgrimages and the veneration of relics, but in purity of heart, in sincerity of attitude and in authentic love. Genuine Christians trust in God's providence and expect the highest bliss in the hereafter.

[5] Savonarola only later described the vision he had in 1492 ("in the night before my last Advent sermon") in his *Compendio di rivelazioni/Compendium revelationum* (Aug./Oct. 1495), ed. Crucitti (as in n. 3): report of the vision pp. 12.10–14.15 (Italian) and pp. 138.7–140.14 (Latin).

[6] In this famous statement about the Sword, Savonarola combines the Vulgate terminology "gladius Domini" (cf. Isaiah 34.6) with the phrase "cito et velociter" (Joshua 23.16 and Joel 3.4). In his 1st sermon on Haggai (1st Nov. 1494) Savonarola states that it is not quite two years since he prophesied to Florence: "The Sword of the Lord will come over the earth soon and speedily!" Cf. below, p. 58 with n. 7.

Then the sinners will ask for an opportunity to repent but receive none.

For the prophetic visionary Savonarola this terrible moment of judgement in which the sword of divine wrath would strike arrived in the autumn of 1494. The French King Charles VIII, whom Savonarola saw as the Lord's instrument of punishment against godless Italy, stood at the borders of Tuscany with his army, ready to move against Florence. On 1 November Savonarola announced to his anxious listeners that events were proving him right. Less than two years ago he had announced to them for the first time that the sword of the Lord would come shortly and swiftly over them. Not he, but the Lord had predicted it to them. Now this prophecy has come true: The sword has arrived![7] And yet there still is a chance to turn to God. In this politically desperate situation, in which the city's government is confused and without sense of direction, Savonarola's preaching becomes an impassioned entreaty to repent: "I speak to you, Florence, and have but one desire: to shout to you with a loud voice: Repent!"[8] "Repentance is the only remedy."[9] "You sinners, you obstinate and lukewarm people, all you who always delay your repentance: Repent now, do not delay any further – the Lord is still waiting for you and calls you to himself."[10]

2. Even though this sermon contains massive threats by identifying current events as the sword of God and by announcing to his listeners that, not least for spatial reasons, they are already much closer to hell, which is at the centre of the earth, than to the much more distant heavenly paradise,[11] one cannot fail to notice how powerfully Savonarola can combine such a message with an element of comfort and with a reference to God's welcoming mercy. He woos the Florentines by calling to them: "Repent! See how good and merciful the Lord is; he wants to lead you to the ark and save you. Come therefore, you sinners, come, for God is calling you."[12] Even though the flood will come, the saving ark has been built. This is

---

[7] Savonarola: 1st sermon on Haggai, 1st Nov. 1494, in: *Prediche sopra Aggeo*, ed. Luigi Firpo (Rome, 1965) [Edizione nazionale delle opere di Girolamo Savonarola], p. 12.13–17.

[8] *Prediche sopra Aggeo*, ibid., p. 11.19–21.

[9] Ibid. p. 11.4.

[10] Ibid. p. 4.21–25.

[11] Ibid. p. 2.6–11.

[12] Ibid. p. 4.27–30.

the image to which Savonarola returns again and again. The sword of the Lord and infernal condemnation are, indeed, imminent; but "the heavenly kingdom is close at hand" as well. To enter into the ark of divine mercy, all that is required is a sincerely penitent heart.[13]

From November 1494 Savonarola accentuates the theme of mercy more strongly than in previous sermons. His own words reveal that he is fully aware of this shift, as we see for example in a sermon in which he addresses God: "Lord, I did indeed consider you to be the greatest good and your mercy to be boundless. But the true greatness of your mercy was beyond my powers of comprehension."[14] Previously, he had directed his attention above all to the hard-heartedness of the sinners and their impending doom, expecting "that the earth would certainly open up to devour the godless and obstinate, seeing that no more mercy was to be expected from you",[15] but now God let him know that in his abundant mercy he is still inviting sinners to turn to him,[16] that the door of the ark is still open. It may not stay open for much longer, and few only will turn to God while the great majority will be consigned to hell; but thanks and praise are due to God's boundless mercy, that a small part of humanity at least will be saved.[17] Savonarola explains to his disturbed listeners: "We should not marvel at the small number of the righteous, for we must not forget that it is no little thing when God raises human beings, who had fallen so low, to such lofty heights."[18] After all, only a small number of sinners are capable of showing a genuine penitence which flows from an attitude of true love; the majority can only muster an inferior, pretended penitence.[19]

This last statement already indicates where Savonarola sees the limits of God's mercy. The Dominican prior and preacher of penitence is an impressive example of the way in which the infinite mercy of God could be exalted even by those late-medieval preachers of penitence who terrified their listeners out of their wits with their prophecies of doom. The entire preaching activity of Savonarola,

---

[13] Ibid. p. 3.6–8.
[14] Ibid. pp. 3.30–4.3.
[15] Ibid. p. 4.12–15.
[16] Cf. ibid. p. 18.12f.: "See, my beloved, how great is the love of God . . .!"
[17] *Prediche sopra Aggeo*, ibid. p. 2.20–27.
[18] Ibid. p. 2.27–30.
[19] Ibid. pp. 2.30–3.3. On the characteristics of true repentance cf. ibid. p. 3.8–22.

especially after the end of 1494, could be presented as a mission in the name of divine mercy; he himself characterises his mission occasionally as such, and in 1496, evaluating his own preaching, he judged that he had kept "to the side of mercy".[20] There is a pronounced trend in more recent Savonarola research to interpret the caesura of the year 1494 in this way: the gloomy prophet of doom, who announced his city's destruction, became instead a prophet of salvation, a herald of divine mercy and the harbinger of a time of blessing in this world. Florence, it is maintained, now came to represent not the Babylon of Rome but a heavenly Jerusalem on earth.[21] We may, indeed, register a change in Savonarola: To the same degree that he turned into a political prophet and saw the first fruits of the realization of his ideas of political, social and religious change in Florence – through a *rapprochement* with the French king, the expulsion of the Medici, the introduction of a republican constitution and the reform of public morality – to the same degree, therefore, to which he was politically and socially successful, allowing himself to be drawn into the reform of urban society, there took shape before his visionary eye the possibility of a purified and holy community on earth, a new Jerusalem. It is for this hoped-for Florence that he predicted a bright future, a millenium of good fortune as it were, of fame and wealth based on its ethical renewal, its existing virtues and a pure, divine love that would unite all citizens. This is the vision of a theocracy in which Christ is king of Florence, in which everyone lives in accordance with Christ's law and in which Savonarola, as the authorised prophet of the divine will, guides this republic of Christ through the dangers of this world.

3. Savonarola arrived at his theocratic vision of a holy Florence in effect as late as November 1494, during Charles VIII's Italian campaign. In my view, however, the change in the Dominican is misrepresented if we focus exclusively on this shift from prophecy of doom to one of salvation, of his preaching of wrath and the flood

---

[20] Savonarola: 1st sermon on Amos and Zechariah, 17th Febr. 1496, in: Prediche sopra Amos et Zaccaria (as in n. 2), p. 17.14: "alla parte della misericordia".

[21] This interpretation of Savonarola is particularly represented by Donald Weinstein: *Savonarola and Florence. Prophecy and Patriotism in the Renaissance* (Princeton, 1970), especially Chapter IV: Florence, the New Jerusalem (pp. 138–158), e.g. p. 145: "It was a fundamental transformation of Savonarola's eschatology. [...] The preacher of repentance had become a prophet of the millenium, exchanging his earlier radical pessimism for an even more radical optimism."

to one of mercy and the ark. Careful reading of his sermons between 1494 and 1498, the year of his execution, reveals how the themes of menace and terror continue to prevail without interruption; by the same token his preaching before 1494 had already contained announcements of divine mercy. Savonarola's way of preaching remains a *praedicatio terrifica* (terrifying preaching) – the difference is that he has changed the aim of his threatening: Whereas he previously wanted to save a small number from the general corruption in church and society, he now sees the chance of a city cleansed from the wicked, which will become a centre of church renewal (*renovatio ecclesiae*) radiating throughout Italy and Europe, and of mission among the heathens throughout the world. That the Florentines have been offered this unique opportunity in spite of the continuing immorality of their private and public lives, is for him evidence of God's incomprehensible mercy. But the way in which he presents the chance of repentance and self-cleansing is imbedded in an undiminished barrage of threats predicting the most horrendous plagues as well as individual and political ruin.

An example of this can be seen in a sermon delivered by Savonarola on 13th January 1495. Here he combines the possibility of a renewal of the Church spreading out from Florence with the proclamation of terrible divine sanctions if the Florentines do not mend their ways. He takes up his earlier vision of the Sword and adjures his listeners: "Believe, then, and change your ways! Do not think that the punishment has passed you by; for I observe how the Sword is turning back."[22] "Its point is not yet turned down. God is still waiting for you to do penance."[23] The wrath of God is still enflamed, his Sword will shortly be drawn.[24] "Do penance while the Sword is still sheathed and not yet dipped in blood!"[25] God's punishment, his scourge and chastisement is near; if they do not change their ways soon, it will be too late. This tenor runs through the whole sermon. It gives the passages where Savonarola speaks of God's offer of mercy[26] the character of an urgent, sombre ultimatum. This is true

---

[22] Savonarola: 3rd Sermon on the Psalms, 13th January 1495, in: *Prediche sopra i Salmi* (as in n. 2), p. 42.7–9.
[23] *Prediche sopra i Salmi*, ibid. p. 54.8–10.
[24] Ibid. p. 56.24–27.
[25] Ibid. p. 62.10–12.
[26] E.g. ibid. p. 52.10–13.

even in Savonarola's well-known comparison of the offer of salvation with an apple: "Do not forget, Florence, that I told you I had
given you an apple, as a mother gives a crying child an apple to
soothe it. But if the child continues crying and does not quiet down,
she takes the apple away and gives it to another of her children.
Therefore I tell you, Florence, God has given you the apple – i.e.
he has chosen you as his own. If you will not repent and return to
God, he will take the apple from you and give it to others. This
will happen as surely as I stand here in the pulpit."[27]

4. The character of this sermon is typical of Savonarola's style of
preaching and his political and moral proposals for reform in the
following years. His view of the possibility of renewal and salvation
is always determined by the perspective of the avenging righteousness and punitive militancy of the wrathful God. This change in the
city to which he aspires and which he partially achieves is also characterised by a spirit of unrelenting strictness, cleansing militancy and
punitive severity. Among his favourite biblical passages are Jesus'
words in Matthew 10.34: "I have not come to bring peace but a
sword." For him this means that God's righteousness will and must
extirpate the wicked from the city and send them to hell.[28] Savonarola
repeatedly challenges the political leadership of the city to tighten
policing measures, practise a relentless criminal justice, track down
the depraved and sentence them to physical punishment and even
execution. God desires a devout Florence, cleansed of the irrespon-
sible ungodly. Only in this way can his wrath be appeased.[29] God's
true righteousness and true mercy are, in Savonarola's eyes, complementary in that they are uncompromising, even cruel, in their deal-
ings with the depraved and political enemies. Consequently in May
1495 he demanded vigilance against adversaries within the city walls,
justifying this with the claim that "[m]ercilessness has meantime
become a great mercy."[30] In the same sense two months later he

---

[27] Ibid. p. 58.4–12.
[28] Savonarola: 1st Sermon on Haggai, 1st Nov. 1494, in: *Prediche sopra Aggeo* (as
in n. 7), pp. 9.29–10.5.
[29] Cf. Pierre Antonetti: *Savonarola: Ketzer oder Prophet? Eine Biographie* (Zürich, 1992)
[Original French edition: Savonarole. Le prophète désarmé, Paris 1991], p. 196.
Among the many biographies of Savonarola, Antonetti's stands out because it remains
close to the sources and is soberly objective in its analysis, avoiding both the hagio-
graphic and apologetic tendencies of Savonarola-enthusiasts and the opposite tendencies of his critics.
[30] Cf. Antonetti (as in n. 29), p. 147, on a sermon delivered by Savonarola on

can describe a lenient sentence as a particular kind of ruthlessness: "for an indulgent justice is *de facto* a 'ruthless compassion' when it tolerates violation of the divine Law".[31] Hence: One must simply be ruthless in the proper – i.e. radically severe – way to convey God's true compassion, his aim to save and renew the Church. Anyone who is compassionate in the wrong way by being lenient to iniquity is in reality bringing God's dreadful avenging righteousness into play. Hence Savonarola's intention to purify Florence is the project of a terrifying, judgmental and where necessary, devastating compassion, a *terrifica misericordia*.

It is not *that* Savonarola – like all preachers of repentance in the Middle Ages – talks of God's mercy but *how* he does so that is definitive for the character of his preaching. The fact that God elects people at all and is prepared to save them is a sign of mercy. But this mercy is discharged according to the yardstick of punishing and rewarding justice. It exalts to salvation only those who have put on the "white robe" – i.e. those who in loving devotion to God have done penance and cleansed themselves from sin "till their conscience is completely clean and white".[32] A mercy like this must simultaneously be relentless because it must destroy the unclean, remove them even now from the sanctified community within the city. Savonarola

---

8th May 1495: On 8th May he again prophesied the *renovatio Ecclesiae* at a time unspecified, but unavoidable since it is desired by God. This will take place violently ("with the Sword" he says); he also prophesies the conversion of the unbelievers and the expansion of Florentine territory through the recovery of lost cities. He pleads for vigilance against internal enemies, against the lukewarm, and against those who oppose the republican constitution; the latter he desires to be punished as an example to others, for "Mercilessness has meantime become a great mercy" and even Jesus Christ was not sent "to bring peace, but the sword" into the world.

[31] Cf. Antonetti (as in n. 29), p. 161, summarising Savonarola's sermon of 12th July 1495 impressively: On 12th July a further attack on the lukewarm whom God abhors, for "it is better to be a prostitute, a soldier or a boor than a lukewarm person". He also battles with those who are "cold" i.e. content with a religion reduced to ceremonial, hymns and music. Florence must awaken and weed out its sinners, the city must live with a pure heart, for God will give them wealth and power, even at the price of "two or three plagues" and an inexorable justice which must forget any tolerance; this too is shown in the Old Testament. As an example he mentions the punishment of the Israelites for their whoring with the daughters of the Moabites (Numbers 25.1–13) and the penalty for desecrating the Sabbath (Numbers 15.32–36). The new political order must be supported by a "strict dispensation of justice", for an indulgent justice is *de facto* a "ruthless compassion" if it tolerates violation of the divine Law.

[32] Savonarola: 3rd Sermon on the Psalms, 13th January 1495, in: *Prediche sopra i Salmi* (as in n. 2), p. 53.25–27.

demonstrated this kind of mercy and purification when, on Palm Sunday 1496, he sent a procession led by a thousand white-robed children through the streets of Florence crying "Long live Christ the King and Queen Mary!"[33]

5. In the last days of his life, when the eloquent preacher of repentance was in prison awaiting his execution he wrote the famous interpretation of and meditation on Psalm 51 (Vulgate 50) "Be merciful to me, O God, a Sinner",[34] which was printed and widely distributed after his death. The text is full of the self-abasement of the supplicant who cries for God's saving mercy and puts his hope in it. There is no trace of fear and threat because the central theme is exclusively the personal relationship between the penitent and his God. But even in this prayer the main concern is the cleansing of the penitent. It is the tears of repentance that cleanse the heart of the sinner.[35] Since it is God's mercy which makes this loving repentance possible, Savonarola can pray: "Wash me, I beseech you, with the water of your mercy!" as well as "Wash me with the water of my tears!"[36] This cleansing comes about through the intensity of union with Christ: "If you pour over me the power of his blood, if Christ dwells in me through faith, if I am united with him through

---

[33] Cf. Antonetti (as in n. 29), p. 200. For a precise description of the procession (in which, after the children, came all the orders in the city, the secular priests with the suffragan bishop, the civil authorities and a incalculable number of adults, likewise in white robes) see Joseph Schnitzer: *Savonarola. Ein Kulturbild aus der Zeit der Renaissance*, vol. I (Munich, 1924), pp. 332–334.

[34] Savonarola: Expositio in psalmum *Miserere mei Deus*; critical edition of the Latin original in: *Operette spirituali*, ed. Mario Ferrara, vol. 2 (Rome, 1976) [Edizione nazionale delle opere di Girolamo Savonarola], pp. 195–234. On the reception in the first decades cf. Josef Nolte: "Evangelicae doctrinae purum exemplum. Savonarolas Gefängnismeditationen im Hinblick auf Luthers theologische Anfänge", in: J. Nolte, Hella Tompert, Christof Windhorst (eds.): *Kontinuität und Umbruch. Theologie und Frömmigkeit in Flugschriften und Kleinliteratur an der Wende vom 15. zum 16. Jahrhundert* (Stuttgart, 1978) [= Spätmittelalter und Frühe Neuzeit 2], pp. 59–92.

[35] Savonarola already set forth these ideas, for example, in his 1st sermon on Haggai on 1st November 1494, in: *Prediche sopra Aggeo* (as in n. 7), p. 9.4–11 (in an exegesis of Vulgate Psalm 136.1: "By the rivers of Babylon we sat down and wept"): "O Florence, sit down, too, by the rivers of your sins. Weep so that your tears turn into rivers to wash them away. Think of your heavenly Fatherland, the source of your soul. Endeavour to return there through repentance as the Israelites did. In a foreign country one cannot sing but merely weep – i.e. you in yourself, where you have distanced yourself from God through your sins."

[36] Savonarola: Expositio in psalmum *Miserere mei Deus* (as in n. 34), Latin edition p. 202.12f.: "Lava me, inquam, aqua gratiarum tuarum"; p. 202.15f.: "Lava me aqua lacrimarum mearum", with the continuation: "lava me aqua Scripturarum tuarum".

love and emulate him in humility and suffering, I shall be cleansed of all my sinfulness and you will wash me with the tears I weep through love of Christ."[37] In this way, on the day of his execution, Savonarola (as he prays at the end of the document) will become, through conformity to the suffering Christ of Golgotha, a pure offering which God will accept for salvation: "Take me as a sacrifice of right-eousness, as an offering of devout purity, as a burnt offering from the life of my order and as a sacrificial beast on the altar of your Cross!"[38]

Thus Savonarola remains true to his principles to the end. He appeals to a divine mercy that is at the same time righteousness in that it accepts as a spotless offering the human life purified by pen-itence and modelled on Christ. The category of righteousness which demands purity and rewards purity is the higher criterion which determines Savonarola's discourse on and supplication for mercy.

III. *Johannes von Staupitz: Preacher of God's Mercy*

1. Without exaggerating the contrast, one can say that the direct antithesis to Savonarola's prophetic, apocalyptic and threatening preaching and to his correlation of God's mercy and righteousness can be seen in the sermons delivered by Johannes von Staupitz, Vicar-General of the German Observant order of Augustinians, in Advent 1516[39] and in Lent 1517[40] to a Nuremberg public.[41] Luther's

---

[37] Ibid. pp. 210.29–211.5: "[. . .] quando virtutem sanguinis eius effundes super me, quando per fidem habitabit Christus in me, quando per dilectionem ei coni-unctus fuero, quando humilitatem eius et passionem imitabor, tunc mundabor ab omnibus immunditiis meis, tunc lavabis me lacrimis meis a Christi amore fluentibus."

[38] Ibid. p. 234.16–18: "[. . .] suscipias me in sacrificium iustitiae, in oblationem sanctimoniae, in holocaustum religiosae vitae et in vitulum crucis tuae", with the continuation: "per quam transire merear ab hac valle miseriae ad gloriam illam, quam praeparasti diligentibus te. Amen." The preceding final section of the docu-ment is determined by the thought that the people freed of guilt by being totally consumed by the fire of love of God bring God an "offering of righteousness" (sacrificium iustitiae); ibid. pp. 233.18–234.14.

[39] Staupitz immediately translated the Nuremberg Advent sermons of 1516, deliv-ered in the vernacular, into a Latin tract which appeared at the beginning of 1517: *Libellus De exsecutione aeternae praedestinationis*, ed. Lothar Graf zu Dohna, Richard Wetzel (Berlin – New York, 1979) [= *Johann von Staupitz: Sämtliche Schriften* 2 = Spätmittelalter und Reformation 14].

[40] Staupitz' German Nuremberg Lenten sermons in 1517 have been preserved in the form of the so-called *Nürnberger Predigtstücke*. This is a selection of high-quality

superior, teacher, father confessor and fatherly friend fascinated his listeners both male and female by the vividness with which – looking at Christ's vicarious expiatory suffering – he proclaimed the greatness and omnipotence of God's mercy. In these sermons there is no trace of a threatening or terrifying note. Only very marginally is there a suggestion of the possibility of damnation and the torments of hell. The whole focus of these sermons is on love and faith, not on intimidation and fear. Where he speaks of the righteousness of the Judge, it is depicted as the leniency of the merciful Father: "Hence we should love God as the most benevolent, most merciful Father, and fear him as a righteous, mild judge – not as a slave fears his master but as a child his father."[42] This childlike fear of God, as Staupitz repeatedly explains, has nothing to do with a transgressor's fear of the executioner but is humble reverence and loving faith in God's infinite, paternal loving-kindness.[43] Hence the pain of a true repentance for one's own sins is not to be likened to a shabby "gallows repentance" which is only thinking fearfully of avoiding punishment.[44] A person who is truly repentant regrets far more that he has violated the Commandments of God, his beloved Father, and thereby offended and angered him.[45]

2. Admittedly there are in Staupitz, too – very restrained and cautious – echoes of the wrath of God, but that wrath does not, as

---

transcripts from the pen of Nuremberg humanist Lazarus Spengler, who served as secretary to the city council. He had the writing ability and theological training necessary to convey Staupitz' thoughts and words adequately so that we may quote the transcripts as Staupitz' text filtered through Spengler's sympathetic reception. Compared with the documents written and published by Staupitz himself (especially in comparison with the temporally close *Libellus De exsecutione aeternae praedestinationis*) there are no noticeable differences, but throughout there is a high level of theological and terminological correspondence. Edition of the *Nürnberger Predigtstücke* in: Joachim Karl Friedrich Knaake (ed.): *Johann von Staupitzens sämmtliche Werke, vol. 1: Deutsche Schriften* (Potsdam, 1867), pp. 15–42.

[41] My planned edition of Staupitz' letters will give detailed information on Staupitz' many contacts with Nuremberg before 1516/17, his sojourns in the Free City and his followers there. Cf. for the present Berndt Hamm: "Humanistische Ethik und reichsstädtische Ehrbarkeit in Nürnberg", in: *Mitteilungen des Vereins für Geschichte der Stadt Nürnberg*, 76 (1989), pp. 65–147, here 133–143.

[42] "Dorumb sollen wir Got lieben als den allerfreuntlichsten, parmherzigsten vater und forchten als einen gerechten, milten richter, nicht mit ainer knechtlichen, sonder ainer kindtlichen forcht." Staupitz: *Nürnberger Predigtstücke*, ed. Knaake (as in n. 40), p. 26.

[43] Cf. e.g. ibid. p. 44.

[44] Ibid. p. 16.

[45] Ibid. p. 17.

in Savonarola, become a theme in its own right. The Augustinian monk does not wish to proclaim to his Nuremberg congregation that God rages against them and threatens them with afflictions, but that God ever and again pardons them if they confess their sins and call on him full of trust for merciful forgiveness: "For his mercy is boundless and infinite and of such a kind that it cannot be denied to one who craves it sincerely and reverently."[46] Hence God is not only the one who graciously effects all that is good in mankind, prompting human hearts and stirring them to good works. He is also the gracious God who accepts them by grace, particularly at the end of their earthly existence, even when their devotion is fragile and the quality of their repentance imperfect.[47] With the boundless worth of his Passion, Christ acts vicariously for sinners everywhere where their own sanctity remains a pitiful fragment. Staupitz' theme is not the purity and perfection of a pious life, a renewed Church, a reformed Order or a converted community, important though the serious sanctifying of life in the spirit of love is for him. What he is chiefly concerned about is God's mercy to those who are elect yet unclean, loving yet imperfect, those who have been showered with blessings yet are still needy, those sanctified but not yet unambiguously saints.

Staupitz returns again and again to this ambivalence, even at table in the Augustinian monastery, when dining with distinguished citizens of Nuremberg, proclaiming his sometimes serious, sometimes humorous thoughts about everything under the sun.[48] It is difficult and problematical, he says, to pass judgement on man's devoutness and spiritual nature, for holiness is something hidden: "No one knows where God the Almighty lives or on whom He desires to work the

---

[46] "Dann sein parmherzigkait ist unmessig und unendtlich und der aigenschafft, wan der mensch die hertzlich begert, das die keinem rechtbegerenden kan versagt werden." Ibid. p. 24.

[47] On the deficits of human repentance, which are compensated for by the merit of Christ's Passion cf. ibid. pp. 16–19.

[48] These so-called *Nürnberger Tischreden*, delivered by Staupitz, are also handed down in the records of city council secretary Lazarus Spengler (cf. n. 40). They date from Advent and Lent 1516/17 (perhaps only from Lent) when Staupitz preached in Nuremberg and occasionally invited some patricians and reputable burghers to communal repasts in the Augustinian monastery. On the people who belonged to Staupitz' circle of friends – among them the leading city councillors – cf. Hamm (as in n. 41), pp. 133–135; Edition of the German *Nürnberger Tischreden* in: Knaake (as in n. 40), pp. 42–49. Like the *Predigtstücke*, the *Tischreden* reproduce the Augustinian cleric's particular body of thought in a remarkably authentic way.

greatest grace",[49] and it often happens that there is more virtue, devotion and divine influence hidden under the robe of a middle-class woman than under the habit of monks or nuns.[50] In God's eyes a reverent Christian soul is one moment sick and leprous, the next clean and pure.[51] In statements such as these the Augustinian expresses his reserve with regard to extreme ideals of sanctity and purity and human appraisals of the sanctity and purity of others. He cautions the people of Nuremberg against judging the depths of the human heart, which cannot be seen from the outside but can only be known by God.[52] When someone told him while dining that he had heard that the Emperor Maximilian had expressed the hope that one day after his death people would pray to him: "Holy Maximilian, inter-cede for us!" Staupitz answered: I would not object if his Majesty were to be sanctified – but I should dearly like to know what sort of nature and essence one must have to become sanctified (i.e. to enter Paradise).[53] This idea of not knowing and not being able to judge, so characteristic of Staupitz, is strikingly different from the attitude of Savonarola who asserts an exact knowledge of what holiness is and which people in Florence and Rome are candidates for hell.

3. We see exactly the same contrast in the way in which Savonarola and Staupitz react to the political events and radical changes taking place in their time. Savonarola, convinced of his own prophetic authority, claims that he has an unequivocal, apocalyptic divinely-revealed knowledge of certain future earth-shaking events and of the hidden meaning of the current political situation. He lays open and interprets history. Thus, for example, he knows that the French king Charles VIII carries the prophesied Sword of God[54] and that he as a new Cyrus is bringing about the renascence of the Church and

---

[49] "Nymandt wais, wo Got der almechtig wonen, bey welchem er auch am hochsten gnad wurcken will." Staupitz: *Nürnberger Predigtstücke*, ed. Knaake (as in n. 40), p. 33 (under the title: "Do not judge others").

[50] Ibid.: "[. . .] und beschicht gar zu vil malen, das undter ainer samaten schauben mere tugent, beschwerlikait [perhaps better improved by 'beschawlikait' than Knaake's suggested 'bestendigkait'] unnd gots wurckung dann unter der kutten verporgen ligt."

[51] Staupitz: *Nürnberger Tischreden*, ed. Knaake (as in n. 48), p. 45.

[52] Ibid.

[53] Ibid. p. 47: "Ich mocht gar wol leiden, das sein mjt. heilig wurd, allain das ich doch wist, was schicklikait und wesens ainer sein must, der doch heilig wurd."

[54] Cf. above p. 58 with n. 7. Cf. Savonarola: 3rd Sermon on the Psalms, 13th January 1495, in: *Prediche sopra i Salmi* (as in n. 2), pp. 55.12–56.27.

the perdition of the ungodly.[55] Staupitz, too, declares to his hearers in Nuremberg his firm belief that all earthly events occur within God's administration and rule (*verwaltung und regirung*).[56] But he believes that this all happens contrary to any human conjecture or calculation – to the great astonishment of people who time after time are amazed at how rapidly events unfold quite differently from their expectations. God does not show his hand. His wisdom is awesome and awe-inspiring. While Savonarola's prophetic knowledge uncovers things alarming and threatening, Staupitz' deliberations on the impossibility of foreknowing the future work towards the reassuring advice to see God's merciful omnipotence – *sein macht, sein krafft und parmherzigkait* (his might, his power and mercy) – in everything that may happen unexpectedly or inexplicably.[57] The hidden God is the amazingly loving God.

It is the same basic attitude of trust in God which will also lead us in troubled times not – as with Savonarola – to fear the wrath of God but to feel the rod of a loving Father and love him in return.[58] For God "desires to be loved rather than feared by us, his creatures, therefore humankind should love him more than fear him."[59] Whatever happens apparently to our detriment, we can firmly believe that it happens by the will of God for our benefit.[60] As Christians, says Staupitz, we have the assurance that nothing can separate us from the love of God (Rom. 8.39) – not even the sword, "because we are anointed with the oil of mercy".[61] Here Staupitz's use of the sword as metaphor follows the manner not of Savonarola, but of St. Paul; it is not intended to conjure images of divine retribution, but rather to stand as shorthand for the afflictions, temptations and persecutions which, though they must come, cannot shake the Christian's faith in God's loving care.

---

[55] Cf. e.g. Savonarola: *Compendio di rivelazioni/Compendium revelationum*, ed. Crucitti (as in n. 3), pp. 14.28–15.8 (Italian) and pp. 140.29–141.9 (Latin).

[56] Staupitz: *Nürnberger Predigtstücke*, ed. Knaake (as in n. 40), p. 29.

[57] Ibid. p. 29f.

[58] Ibid. p. 25f.

[59] "Also wil auch Got von unns, seinen creaturen, mer geliebt dann geforcht werden, dorumb ine der mensch mer lieben dann forchten soll." Ibid. p. 25.

[60] Staupitz: *De exsecutione aeternae praedestinationis*, ed. Dohna, Wetzel (as in n. 39), §195: "[. . .] quaecumque contra se facta pro se facta firmiter credit" (allusion to Rom. 8.28,31); cf. ibid. §93, §174 and §237f.

[61] Ibid. §240: "[. . .] an gladius? non, quia uncti sumus oleo misericordiae" (cf. James 5.14f.).

4. The Augustinian preacher's attitude to individual and collective crises corresponds to the kind of political instruction that he dis-
penses from the pulpit and at the tables of the ruling classes of the
Free City. The nucleus of his political ethics lies in the maxim: A
ruler should behave in such a way that he is more loved than feared
by his subjects; for love and trusting affection serve far more than
fear, harshness and cruelty to uphold a system of government.[62] How
rulers deal with the opprobrious weaknesses and transgressions of
their subjects should also be determined on this principle. Staupitz
challenges a fanaticism of purification: "*Man kann die posen von den
guten nit ganz sondern*" (One cannot completely separate the evil from
the good). A god-fearing, righteous and prudent regime will rather,
by its own honourable conduct, cover up the defects and disgrace
of the *reudigen Schafe* (mangy sheep).[63] In principle, even in the case
of wrongdoers in prison, far more can be achieved in a city through
friendliness and a manner that inspires confidence than through cruel,
terrifying stringency.[64] Those who commit public misdemeanours
ought to be subject to public punishment, but this should be under-
taken sensitively, "on a just scale, at a suitable time and without
harming the public good".[65]

5. While Savonarola pursues a very inflexible, consistent theocratic
vision, what Staupitz expects from the members of his order, the
faithful in the Church and the political community is certainly determined by a fundamental spiritual perspective. At the same time it
is modified by a certain tolerance, equanimity and spiritual and cler-
ical self-restraint. This goes so far that he can say: "I would be hap-
pier and less worried to be ruled by a clever, shrewd rogue than by

---

[62] Staupitz: *Nürnberger Predigtstücke*, ed. Knaake (as in n. 40), pp. 38f. and 25. On
the maxim that a ruler should so behave towards his subjects that they love him
more than fear him (also ibid. p. 36f.) cf. Cicero: *De officiis* 2.23: "omnium autem
rerum nec aptius est quicquam ad opes tuendas ac tenendas quam diligi nec alie-
nius quam timeri". On the contrary maxim of the Nuremberg Humanists e.g.
Konrad Celtis, cf. Hamm (as in n. 41), p. 139 n. 297.
[63] Staupitz: ibid. p. 37 with the central statement: "Ein fromer, erlicher regirer
und oberer ist allain ein schandtfleck- oder schandendecker, dann ein vernunfftiger,
frommer regent bedeckt die schandt der underthanen." (A pious, honest ruler or
authority only covers over blemishes or disgraces, for a rational, pious regent compensates for the disgraceful acts of his subjects.)
[64] Ibid. p. 38f.
[65] "[. . .] mit ainer rechten mass, zu bequemer zeit und on zurruttung gemains
nutz." Ibid. p. 42; on Staupitz' ideas of a consistent criminal justice (which is in
no way lax) cf. also p. 35.

a pious fool."[66] For Staupitz human piety, religiosity and saintliness are, in any case, surrounded by many question marks, as we have seen. It is very difficult to assess spiritual quality and morality. There is the danger of self-confident arrogance or apprehensive despair with regard to one's own situation. Decisive here, as Staupitz tirelessly preaches, is that we put our whole trust solely in God's mercy and love, run to him again and again in order "to crave a new mercy and grace every time."[67]

Mercy and trust are the key concepts in his preaching. He gives clear expression to this pastoral conception when he comes out energetically against the intimidating preachers of his time who are driving sinners to despair and sets up against them his picture of consolation.[68] It is much easier to throw someone into water than to pull him out:[69] "Therefore every preacher, as a guide appointed by God, should direct his teaching toward showing the sinners a comforting right path so that, liberated from the burden of their consciences and scrupulous feelings and freed from sin, they may be receptive to God's grace and mercy and the merit of his Passion."[70] Staupitz instructs those who are free from sin (or who think they are) to confess their need before God in like manner and to seek the mercy and help of the Crucified. God derives little pleasure from one who commits no sin and consequently no longer cries to him for mercy

---

[66] "Ich will dannocht lieber und mit mynder beschwert regirt werden von ainem geschickten, vernunfftigen puben dann ainem fromen narren." Staupitz: *Nürnberger Tischreden*, ed. Knaake (as in n. 48), p. 49 (end of the text).

[67] "[. . .] allemal ain newe parmherzigkait und gnaden zu begern." Staupitz: *Nürnberger Predigtstücke*, ed. Knaake (as in n. 40), p. 23, under the title (p. 22): "Wie der mensch durch ain vertrewlich gemute und hoffen Got dem almechtigen verainigt werden und aus menig seiner sunden an Gotes parmherzigkait nit verzweiffeln sol." (How man will be united with God the Almighty through a confident disposition and hope and should not doubt in God's mercy because of the great number of his sins).

[68] Ibid. p. 27f.

[69] Ibid.: "Es ist nit schwer, ainen in ain wasser zu werffen; das ist aber nit gering und vil grosser, ainen im wasser lebendig zu behalten und dovon zu entledigen." (It is not difficult to throw someone into water, but it is no small task, and indeed a much greater thing, to keep a person alive in water and to remove him from it.)

[70] "Deshalb auch ain yder prediger als von Got aingesetzter weglaiter seine leer dohin ergrunden solt, den sundern ainen trostlichen rechten wege anzuzaigen, dodurch sie von beschwerung ires gewissens und ainem scrupulosischen gemute entledigt, von sunden entpunden, auch gots gnad und parmherzigkait und der verdienstnus seins leidens vehig sein mocht(en)." Ibid. p. 27.

and compassion.[71] Thus the whole preaching style of the Augustinian flows into the praise of the *summa misericordia* (supreme mercy) of God which meets the *summa miseria* (supreme misery) of humanity.[72]

6. Staupitz recognizes the vulnerability of his position. He expressly deals with the accusation that he speaks "too mildly and too familiarly" (*zu milt und vil vertrewlich*) about God's mercy. That, one might allege, would reduce God's wisdom and righteousness to nothing.[73] Then God would react to the continually new insult of a sinner's misdeeds with continually new pardon; he would behave like a foolish man who is constantly slapped in the face and who constantly allows himself to be persuaded to react good-naturedly.[74] Staupitz answers: God does behave in just such a foolish way – according to earthly standards – as we can see in the innocent, submissive suffering of Christ: Christ allowed himself, without resisting, to be mocked by Herod and his followers as the "greatest fool".[75] Staupitz continues: "By enduring such foolishness Christ made the fountain of mercy so vast and plentiful for us that he will always give man a share in his mercy if he heartily sighs and begs, so often as he comes when he has fallen, yes even if he came thus a thousand times a day."[76]

Certainly God is just and wise, but there, in Christ's Passion, "justice and wisdom are made to obey and serve mercy", as Staupitz says, echoing Psalm 144.9 in the Vulgate: "God's mercy surpasses all his other works."[77] This clearly demonstrates how for Staupitz the relationship between God's righteousness and mercy is the reverse of what Savonarola preached. In Savonarola's sermons mercy and

---

[71] Ibid. p. 24.

[72] Staupitz: *De exsecutione aeternae praedestinationis*, ed. Dohna, Wetzel (as in n. 39), §64: "Admirantur theologi unionem hypostaticam divinae naturae cum humana, immortalitatis cum morte, impassibilitatis cum dolore. Ego admiror coniunctionem summae misericordiae cum summa miseria."

[73] Staupitz: *Nürnberger Predigtstücke*, ed. Knaake (as in n. 40), p. 24.

[74] Ibid. p. 24f.

[75] Cf. Luke 23.11.

[76] "Mit solcher geliten thorhait hat er unns den prunnen der parmherzigkait so weit und reichlich gemacht, das er dem menschen uff ain hertzlich erseuffzen und bitten, so offt er komet und gefallen ist, ja ob er den tag tausent mal der gestalt keme, seiner parmherzigkait allweg tailhafftig machen will." Staupitz: *Nürnberger Predigtstücke*, ed. Knaake (as in n. 40), p. 25.

[77] "[. . .] ist gerechtigkait und weishait der parmherzigkait gehorsam und underthenig worden; und nach den worten des propheten <übertrifft> die parmherzigkait Gotes alle andere seine werck." Ibid. Cf. Vulgate Psalm 144.9: "[. . .] miserationes eius super omnia opera eius"; instead of using the verb "surpasses" (übertrifft) we could amend the text by using "is above" or "is greater than".

salvation are spoken of solely in the framework of a severe avenging justice which demands purity and pursues the path of threat,
fear and harshness. Staupitz, however, shows God's righteousness –
even in its punitive aspect – totally in the light of a mercy that show-
ers blessings upon impure, imperfect sinners. Hence he preaches a
confidence in God's mercy which is at the same time a love of his
justice.

IV. *Johannes Geiler von Kaysersberg: Preacher between Severity and Mercy*

1. In the manner of their preaching Savonarola and Staupitz represent opposite extremes on the scale of late medieval options for
giving spiritual guidance from an urban pulpit. Their exceedingly
emphatic emphases on God's punitive, purifying strictness or on his
inviting mercy were breathtaking and intriguing – though Savonarola
polarised while Staupitz integrated, with no sign of turbulent excite-
ment and division among his listeners. Even where they were seriously endeavouring to reform the life of the individual, Church and
city, both before and after 1500 the pastoral of the urban *dirigenti
religiosi* was characterised by the attempt to forge a "moderate" *via
media* between the foci of the strict justice of the judgmental God
and the gentle compassion of the merciful God, between threat and
solace, between fear and hope. This attempt was apparent already
at the beginning of fifteenth century in Jean Gerson who had insisted
on both mankind's capacity and ability for meritorious works, and
on the necessity for humble readiness to trust unreservedly in the
mercy of God, Christ, Mary and the saints. One of the best-known
preachers before the Reformation who adopted Gerson's pastoral
conception was Johannes Geiler von Kaysersberg. From 1478 to
1510 he enthralled the people of Strasbourg with his sermons as
official preacher in the cathedral as well as in other churches and
particularly in the nuns' convents of the city.
    2. If we want to define his type of preaching and pastoral care,
his medial position as a secular priest between the Dominican
Savonarola and the Augustinian recluse Staupitz, we must take account
of two points in particular: first, his theological mould; and second,
the pastoral problem he saw facing him. The shape of his understanding of justification, grace, penitence and merit is striking. In his
teaching on mankind's way to salvation he inclines decidedly to the

later Franciscan direction as it was represented by William of Ockham, handed down by Gerson and, towards the end of the fifteenth century, exemplified particularly by the Tübingen professor (and one-time Cathedral preacher in Mainz) Gabriel Biel.[78] This gives his whole style of preaching from the outset a cast totally different from that of a "theology of grace" Augustinianism such as is characteristic of Staupitz. We shall return to this later.

From a pastoral point of view Geiler, as preacher and pastor of Strasbourg, sees the main problem as spiritual presumption: people fail to take God's Commandments seriously, they sin heedlessly and then put their trust in God's mercy, Christ's vicarious suffering and their own Baptism.[79] The devil whispers to them: "God has made a covenant with us. Come then, the devil says, sin bravely, for however great your sins may be, God's mercy is still greater!"[80] Geiler describes his difficulty as a preacher in the following manner: "The whole world in our time is so corrupt that it is quite dangerous to preach about God's mercy. For where there is one who despairs there are 100, nay 1,000 and ten times 100,000 overconfident people; and yet they are all mistaken."[81]

This quotation, very characteristic of Geiler, shows that he defined the main spiritual problem of the citizens differently from Savonarola and Staupitz in their urban contexts. Savonarola disapproves particularly of the attitude of the – as he sees it – godless "lukewarm", i.e. the indifferent, the sceptical and frivolous who practise a blend of values from church piety and from secular culture, and who abhor him as a sinister, fanatical zealot. Staupitz is concerned about the easily swayed weaklings but particularly about the earnestly pious –

---

[78] On Geiler's personal and theological attachment to Gabriel Biel cf. E. Jane Dempsey Douglass: *Justification in Late Medieval Preaching. A Study of John Geiler of Keisersberg* (Leiden, 1966) [= Studies in Medieval and Reformation Thought 1], pp. 7 and 37.

[79] Cf. the quotation from Geiler in Dempsey Douglass, ibid. p. 173, n. 6.

[80] "[diabolus . . .] dicit deum pactum nobiscum fecisse. Eya, inquit, pecca audacter, quia quantumcunque magna sint peccata tua, maior est misericordia sua." Geiler von Kaysersberg: *De xii fructibus spiritus sancti*; cited by Dempsey Douglass, ibid. p. 174, n. 3.

[81] "Sic infectus est hac tempestate mundus totus, ut periculosum admodum sit de misericordia dei predicare. Ubi unus enim reperitur desperans, centum inveniuntur, immo mille et decies centena milia presumptuosi; et tamen omnes decipiuntur. Dominus enim etsi misericors, iustus tamen iudex nemini facit igitur iniuriam per sententiam, sibi quod eius est auferendo." From the same work, following the quotation in n. 80; cited by Dempsey Douglass, ibid. p. 174, n. 4.

i.e. on the one hand the spiritually proud and on the other those with an over-anxious, timorous, fainthearted conscience. Geiler's particular complaint, however, is about an ethos of cheap grace, the attitude of the lax who rely too much on God's mercy without being willing to take up the hard work of a life of penitence.

When considering these differing attitudes of the three preachers we must not forget that they are dealing with different cities and people; but at the same time the way they perceive the urban population is characteristically different. Savonarola's outlook is considerably influenced by the confrontation of the Dominican, set on reform and oriented above all to the ideal of poverty, with the glittering Renaissance culture of Florence. Staupitz, frequently although only for short periods in Nuremberg, sees the city with the eyes of an outsider, the Superior of a monastic order who is more used to dealing with the pastoral problems of monks and nuns than with those of burghers and their wives. Geiler on the other hand, who served for decades as chief preacher in the city Cathedral, is directly bound up with the life of Strasbourg's citizens. But he does not set his sights only on the worldly (to his mind, all too worldly) citizenry. He also has his eye on the reformed nunneries, particularly the 'Reuerinnen' (Penitents) to whom he also preaches and who present him with other pastoral challenges than the worldly, challenges requiring more consolation than strictness.

3. Geiler's view of the spiritual carelessness and credulity of the men and women of Strasbourg moves him to put strong emphasis on the importance of keeping God's Commandments, on the severity of the divine Judgement and on the relentlessness of God's righteousness, which judges according to works. Typical, for example, is the admonitory, even threatening tone in which he tells the story of two monks: After one of them died he appeared to the other in a lamentable state and with distressed expression. When the other asked him why he appeared to him in such a state the dead monk answered three times with the words: "No one believes, no one believes, no one believes." When the living monk asked what it was that no one believed, the other replied, "how strictly God judges and how severely he punishes". Having uttered those words he vanished and left the living brother in a state of fear and trembling.[82] Again and again

---

[82] "[...] Respondit defunctus tribus vicibus: 'Nemo credit, nemo credit, nemo

Geiler points to the impending eternal death of damnation and the tribunal "of the stern judge, where we must account for everything even to the last farthing" (cf. Mt. 5.26).[83]

It is interesting to see how Geiler, as compared to Savonarola, speaks in this connection about God's punitive sword of judgement. Geiler admonishes those who are unwilling to forsake the house of their sins for fear of the contempt, ridicule and defamation of their fellows. They should disregard such gossip as the gabbling of geese and be less intimidated by the *rauschenden laub* (rustling leaves) than by the *außgezognen schwert Gottes* (unsheathed sword of God).[84] In contrast to the prophetic and apocalyptic Savonarola, who expected the coming of an historical apocalyptic cataclysm with the sword of God, in Geiler's conventional eschatology the sword symbolises God's judgmental action immediately after death, when God the Father assigns the soul, separated from the body,[85] its place either in Hell, Purgatory or Paradise – as so many pictures from the late Middle Ages depict this individual judgement, showing God the Father with his sword of judgement unsheathed.[86]

It is in keeping with this pastoral style of admonitory strictness

---

credit.' Quaesivit vivus, quid esset, quod nemo credit. Respondit defunctus: 'quam districte iudicat deus et quam severe punit'. His dictis disparuit et viventem fratrem magno timore concussum dereliquit, ut dicitur in speculo exemplorum." Geiler von Kaysersberg: *Navicula poenitentiae*, cited by Dempsey Douglass, ibid. p. 172, n. 2.

[83] "[. . .] des strengen richters, da wir muessen rechnung tuon biß auf den lesten quadranten." Geiler von Kaysersberg: *18 Eigenschaften eines guten Christenpilgers* = Deutsche Predigten 1508, Nr. II, in: Gerhard Bauer (ed.): *Johannes Geiler von Kaysersberg: Sämtliche Werke, Teil 1: Die deutschen Schriften, Abt 1: Die zu Geilers Lebzeiten erschienenen Schriften, vol. 2* (Berlin – New York, 1991), p. 151.20–22.

[84] Ibid. p. 149.17–150.1. Cf. Geiler von Kaysersberg: *Der Pilger mit seinen Eigenschaften*, in: *Sämtliche Werke* (as in n. 83), vol. 1 (Berlin – New York, 1989), p. 63.24–29: "[. . .] sunder fürcht mer das schwert Gottes des herrn, des dir leib und sel wirt von ain ander teilen in ewige verdamnuß, und das schwert und den man fürcht mer, den das yederman iber dich spottet!" (Be more afraid of the sword of God the Lord that will separate body and soul into eternal damnation, and fear the sword and man more than that someone mocks!)

[85] Cf. the quotation in n. 84. In the so-called particular or individual judgement immediately after death where God the Father is the judge, the soul is judged separate from the body, while in the universal or Last Judgement Jesus Christ judges the soul reunited with the body, together with all mankind.

[86] Cf. e.g. the votive picture of Ulrich Schwarz painted by Hans Holbein the Elder (ca. 1508) in the National Gallery in Augsburg; illustrations and commentary in Bruno Bushart: *Hans Holbein d. Ä.*, 2nd edition Augsburg, 1987 pp. 102–105; cf. also Hartmut Boockmann: *Die Stadt im späten Mittelalter* (Munich, 1986), p. 168f., Nr. 264.

that Geiler continuously calls attention to the standard against which
every person is to be measured in the divine Judgement. The first
and foremost requirement for the Christian pilgrim in order that he
may ultimately reach the goal of his earthly pilgrimage, eternal life,
is a pure love with which he loves God above all else for his own
sake. As a ship is closed below to the water and open to heaven
above, so must the heart of the Christian, in love and yearning for
its heavenly home, shut itself off from all earthly desires and plea-
sures.[87] For "strait is the gate and narrow is the way" (Mt. 7.14).[88]
While for Staupitz (and also for the Thomistic speculation of
Savonarola) Christian love of God and of one's neighbour is a gift
of the electing grace moving the heart of the elect, Geiler, in accordance with his Ockhamist approach, sees in love the supreme principle of human achievement. The sinner must, on the basis of his
own natural rational capacity, spur himself on to virtue, extract what
there is in his native abilities (*facere quod in se est*) and in this way
attain to a true love of God and his neighbour. Like his contemporary
Gabriel Biel, Geiler also believes that people can and must, by virtue
of their own innate, reasoned morality, bring forth even the pain of
true contrition from their love of God. Geiler's guidance for the soul
achieves its particular character of strictness against the background
of an anthropology of the moral freedom, sensibility and potentiality of the individual, still persisting after the Fall. The ethical standard is no higher than that of Staupitz, for the Augustinian is even
more radical and consistent in making love of God the sole criterion of Christian spirituality and ethics. But Geiler appeals to man's
ability and obligation to acquire salvation through his own efforts.
It is true that the sinner can only have a claim to eternal life and
make amends for the punishment for sin because God has conferred
on him justifying grace. But it is the person himself, the human as
a moral character who – with the contribution of his own free will –
brings forth acceptable and commendable works of pure love of God
and his neighbour in order to withstand the Judgement. It is true
that salvation is impossible without the fundamental contribution of

---

[87] Geiler von Kayserberg: *Navicula poenitentiae*; cited by Dempsey Douglass (as in
n. 78), p. 39 column 2.
[88] "Der weg ist schmal unnd das thor ist eng." Geiler von Kaysersberg: *18
Eigenschaften* (as in n. 83), p. 142.5f. with the context on Christian virtue which one
must acquire "with strict practice" (p. 142.1).

Christ's Passion or without Christ's subsequent acceptance of the sinner for Justification and Redemption. However, it is characteristic
of Geiler's theological outlook and pastoral aspirations that he com-
mences from this principle: Neither for the transmission of justifying grace nor for the opening of the Kingdom of Heaven and
admission to the heavenly glory is the Passion of Christ the sole and
complete ground of merit (*"Numquam tamen est sola et totalis causa meritoria"*).[89] God desires that we gain eternal life through our own free
actions – i.e. we receive it not simply as a gift but as something
purchased – and consequently we take possession of it with a kind
of legal right (*"quasi iustitiae titulo"*).[90] The admonitory and urgent
insistence with which Geiler impresses the fulfilling of God's Commandments upon the people of Strasbourg is always directed at this eschatological obligation and opportunity, at the necessity and possibility
of gaining Heaven as Christian "purchasers".[91]

4. However this is only the one side of Geiler's pastoral goals, the
judgmental aspect which I spoke of earlier.[92] Other than for Savonarola
the aspect of mercy achieves a significance of its own in Geiler's
preaching and devotional writings. The *misericordia Dei* as the focus
of consolation and exhortation confronts the focus of the awe-inspiring
righteousness of the Judge. On the one hand, when he shows the
misericordia Dei to advantage Geiler von Kaysersberg has an eye on
the despondent sinners who apprehensively doubt their own religious
efficacy – indeed, who tend to despair. Here he is probably thinking, as we have seen, less of the lay citizens than of those in religious orders, particularly nuns.[93] On the other hand God's mercy
must be magnified to those who presumptuously put their trust in

---

[89] "Respondeo breviter, quod, licet passio Christi sit principale meritum, propter
quod confertur gratia, apertio regni et gloria, numquam tamen est sola et totalis
causa meritoria." Geiler von Kaysersberg: *Navicula poenitentiae*; cited by Dempsey
Douglass (as in n. 78), p. 183, n. 2 (with a reference to a verbatim passage in
Gabriel Biel's 'Collectorium', ibid. n. 3).

[90] "Vult nos Dominus vitam aeternam mereri et propriis actibus quasi iustitiae
titulo possidere pro soluto, titulo honorabili et pro empto et non solum pro donato."
Ibid. (Geiler von Kaysersberg: *Navicula poenitentiae*), p. 183, n. 2.

[91] Cf. e.g. a letter written around 1500 by the Nuremberg provost Sixtus Tucher
in which he describes the Christian life as a "blissful business" through which one
may "win eternal profit and gain with temporal possessions"; quoted in Hamm (as
in n. 41), p. 129.

[92] Cf. above under I/3.

[93] Cf. above p. 00, n. 81 with the following text.

their own spiritual superiority and probity. The first group must be encouraged to hope by being shown the boundlessness of God's mercy and forgiveness, the second must be educated in humility by being made aware that in God's verdict, even their best deeds would merely be sewage if God in his limitless mercy did not descend to their level and accept their works as meritorious.

As pastoral advice Geiler formulated the maxim: "Before the Fall (into sin) mankind should reflect on the divine righteousness, but after the Fall he should always pay heed to the divine mercy. For God's mercy is so great that it would never condemn a person laden with all the sins of the world who felt pain that he had, in committing them, arrogantly offended so good a lord, his God, and who firmly resolved to refrain [from such sins] in the future."[94] To those who are worried, frightened and overzealous, Geiler characteristically stresses: God is not as strict as you think. You have a God who is lenient and generous.[95] In this sense Geiler asks for compassionate ("süße") father confessors;[96] and with this compassion he ministers to the Christian pilgrim who feels himself deprived of the spiritual virtues – patience, hope and love.[97] He invites the pilgrim to turn like a beggar full of trust, in beseeching prayer, to God, to all the good angels and saints and "to crave from them spiritual alms and ask with an assured hope for all that he needs".[98] The steadfast hope of the tempted Christian should be focused on the promised fact that in the judgement after death, he will have powerful advocates:

---

[94] "Ante casum igitur cogitet divinam iustitiam, sed post casum divinam misericordiam semper attendat. Misericordia enim Dei tanta est, ut, si homo haberet omnia peccata mundi super se et doleret, quod cum eis tam bonum dominum Deum suum superbe offendisset, et firmiter proponeret amplius abstinere, Deus talem nunquam damnaret." Geiler von Kaysersberg: *Navicula poenitentiae*; cited by Dempsey Douglass (as in n. 78), p. 175f., n. 4.

[95] About the Christian pilgrim who takes on too heavy a burden of spiritual discipline he writes: "Er entzücht Got sein glorij, wann es scheynett vor andern menschen, als ob Got so streng sey, das sich der mensch also eroeßen mueß. Du hast ainen milten, reilichen Got." (He takes away God's glory, for it makes it seem to others, as if God were so strict that man must exhaust himself to an extreme degree. You have a lenient, generous God.) Geiler von Kaysersberg: *18 Eigenschaften* (as in n. 83), p. 155.14–17.

[96] "Ipse [sacerdos] erit tibi dulcis, sicut et debet." Geiler von Kaysersberg: *Navicula poenitentiae*; cited by Dempsey Douglass (as in n. 78), p. 154, n. 1.

[97] Geiler von Kaysersberg: *18 Eigenschaften* (as in n. 83), p. 159.23–31.

[98] "[. . .] von inen tzů begeren der gaystlichen allmůßen und alles, das er nottürfftig ist, mit ainer unzweifelichen hoffnung da haischen." Ibid. p. 160.3–8.

Christ will show his Father the wounds of his Passion and Mary will show her son the breasts with which she devotedly nursed him. Thus emerges an effective stairway of salvation.[99] Sinners should place their hope above all on Mary who, herself human, is closest to them.[100] Neither the Son nor the Father can or will deny her loving advocacy.[101] Mary's pure compassion, her special position before God and the certainty that she will hear them gives human hope a kind of personal assurance of salvation.[102]

With his comforting pastoral advice Geiler forges ahead to the point where – exactly like Gerson – he commends even despair and despondency as a means of salvation to the faithful who have uneasy consciences. He advises anyone who doubts whether his virtuous deeds are well pleasing to God "that you despair and lose trust in all your good works and count them worthless."[103] He should not despair of God's mercy but of the efficacy of his own emotions and deeds.[104] If the sinner is troubled as to whether he has made sufficient confession or is adequately prepared to receive the Eucharist, he should humbly despair of his pious endeavours, turn his gaze from them and put all his trust in God's mercy alone.[105] He may joyfully "have complete confidence and trust that through the merit of our

---

[99] Cf. Dempsey Douglass (as in n. 78), p. 191.

[100] Cf. ibid. pp. 191–195.

[101] Cf. the quotation from Geiler's *Navicula poenitentiae* in Dempsey Douglass, p. 193, n. 3.

[102] On the characteristic conception of the Christian certainty of hope (which, to be sure, can be based on different ideas – e.g. more mystic, christological or mariological) of Jean Gerson and those 'Frömmigkeitstheologen' who come from his tradition cf. Sven Grosse: *Heilsungewißheit und Scrupulositas im späten Mittelalter* (Tübingen, 1994) [= Beiträge zur historischen Theologie 85]; Berndt Hamm: "Warum wurde der Glaube für Luther zum Zentralbegriff des christlichen Lebens?", in: Stephen E. Buckwalter, Bernd Moeller (eds.): *Die frühe Reformation in Deutschland als Umbruch* (Gütersloh, 1998) [= Schriften des Vereins für Reformationsgeschichte 199], pp. 103–127, here 107–113; English translation in chapter 5, below (here pp. 157–163).

[103] "[. . .] daz du verzwifelst und verzagst an allen dinen gůten wercken und nit dovon haltest." Geiler von Kaysersberg: *Von den zwölf schefflin*, ed. Luzian Pfleger, in: *Archiv für elsässische Kirchengeschichte* 6 (1931), pp. 206–216, here 212; cf. ibid.: "daz du gantz uff din eigenen fliß verzwiffelst" (that you despair totally of your own diligence).

[104] "Pridie desperationem de Dei misericordia vituperavi; hodie autem desperationem de propriis meritis laudo. Et sic non est contradictio." Geiler von Kaysersberg: *De dispositione ad felicem mortem*; cited by Dempsey Douglass (as in n. 78), p. 171f., n. 5.

[105] Cf. the texts quoted in Dempsey Douglass, pp. 168–170 with their punch-line "sola misericordia Dei" (e.g. p. 169 n. 1 and 169f. n. 4).

dear Lord he will be blessed and possess the joy of eternal life".[106] In the same sermon he goes on to say that God did not 'make the Kingdom of Heaven for geese': "He did not suffer in vain. It is his desire that we be blessed."[107] Thus for Geiler, Christ's Passion can become the supporting foundation of hope and trust. Because all of this is particularly relevant for the dying, Geiler formulated guidelines to teach how one should behave in the hour of death: "Bend and abase yourself humbly in total despair of your own merits and strengths. Beware in the hour of your death of arrogance, presumption and proud satisfaction in your good works, but put all your hope and trust in the suffering, death and merit of our dear Lord Jesus Christ. For all our righteousness is false and like a stained, filthy rag in the eyes of God." (cf. Isa. 64.6 Vulgate.).[108]

5. In the same context, however, at the end of a sermon in which Geiler advises his female audience[109] to put their whole trust in the vicarious agency of Jesus Christ, he urges them to continue *"mit allem fliß"* (with all diligence) to employ their spiritual powers and emotions so that Christ's bitter suffering and death may bring forth fruit, and that they may in this way become blessed.[110] The advice to humbly doubt their own capabilities and not to rely on them leads into the exhortation to harness their own spiritual virtue with all diligence (*facere quod in se est*).[111] It is precisely this humble turning away from oneself, precisely this total trust in Christ, Mary and the saints, which is the highest achievement of one who loves God. For

---

[106] "[. . .] ein gantz hoffen und vertruwen haben, daz er durch daz verdienen unsers lieben herren selig sol werden und die freid des ewigen lebens besitzen." Geiler von Kaysersberg: *Von den zwölf schefflin* (as in n. 103), p. 216.

[107] "Er het nit vergebens gelitten. Sin will ist, daz wir selig werden." Ibid.

[108] "Tucken und sich demuetecklichen trucken durch ein gantze verzwyfelung an synen verdiensten und krefften. Hůt dich in der stund dynes sterbens vor hochfart, vermessenheit und üppigem wolgefallen dyner gůten werck, sunder all din hoffnung und vertrüwen setz in das lyden, sterben und verdienst unsers lieben herren Jesu Christi. Wann alle unser gerechtikeiten falsch sind und vor der angesicht gottes als eyn befleckt, unrein tůch (Isa. 64.6 Vulgate)." Geiler von Kaysersberg: *Sterbe-ABC*, in: *Sämtliche Werke, vol. 1* (as in n. 84), p. 107.12–20 (19th Rule).

[109] According to Pfleger (as in n. 103, p. 206) Geiler's sermon *Von den zwölf schefflin* which we have already quoted three times (cf. n. 103, 106 and 107) was apparently delivered in a Strasbourg nunnery (probably St. Margaret and Agnes) on 21st January 1500.

[110] Geiler von Kaysersberg: *Von den zwölf schefflin* (as in n. 103), p. 216.

[111] On 'facere quod in se est' (i.e. the maximum exertion of one's own spiritual capacities as a provision for grace and salvation) in Geiler von Kaysersberg cf. Dempsey Douglass (as in n. 78), Index p. 236 column 2.

love reaches its highest intensity and real meritoriousness when it has become so humble that it no longer thinks about its own merit. At the same time this is a warning to those who incline to spiritual pride: Strive for the Kingdom of Heaven in such a way that you do not expect anything from your own achievements but everything from God's mercy! As Geiler sees it only so will they be meritorious. When Geiler encourages them to humility, to despair of self and to total faith in God's mercy, he is thinking of the maximum development of a human being's religious capacity.

Hence in Geiler the perspective of mercy does not nullify the perspective of justice; it is simply another method the preacher uses to motivate those in need of orientation to develop their moral excellence to the full. Of course it is not simply a pastoral method; it is also a dogmatic position, for in Geiler's theology of piety, God's avenging justice stands in a balanced relationship with his mercy, which is based on vicarious atonement and intercession. This gives Geiler's sermons and devotional writings as a whole a character of moderate balance and sound sense. It would be hard to imagine him making the sort of statements Staupitz makes, stating for example that the merciful God behaves like a 'naive fool' with regard to sinners.[112] God's mercy as described by Geiler always takes account of man's free will and his diligent efforts to show honour and obedience to God's Commandments. But the preacher must constantly encourage the people energetically to these efforts. That, according to Geiler's self-understanding, is his primary duty. In this respect ethical strictness is the Alpha and Omega of his spiritual guidance in the city.

6. This may be confirmed by considering how Geiler von Kaysersberg behaved as the religious and political conscience of the city council of the Free City of Strasbourg – with all the independence which the office of Cathedral preacher (appointed by the cathedral chapter, not by the city council) bestowed on him. Savonarola's apocalyptic rigorism was foreign to him. He had no desire to change the city's constitution or to set up a theocracy under the control of the clergy. He, like Staupitz, took as a matter of course the pragmatic juxtaposition of spiritual and secular areas of authority, of ardent otherworldly piety and sober political and commercial calculation,

---

[112] Cf. above under III/6.

and he did nothing to shake it. But unlike Staupitz he could make vigorous attack on the city authorities when he thought it was a matter of the validity of God's Commandments as the highest legal norm in the city. When in 1481 there was a substantial increase in the price of grain and provision for the poor was endangered, he encouraged the poor, should the need arise, to break open the granaries of the rich with axes and take what they needed. He did, however, add the reservation that the time had not yet come; when it did, he would tell them. As a result the council requested that in future he refrain in his sermons from *"solicher swerer rede"* (such ominous talk).[113] Several years later, towards the end of the century, he challenged his listeners from the pulpit to depose their rulers if they did not take measures against blasphemy: "If they refuse to do it, one should elect others who do love God."[114]

In 1500 Geiler's displeasure at the behaviour of the city council reached such a pitch that in a sermon he said of the councillors, "they are all on the devil's side, like their ancestors and progeny". A council delegation asked Geiler why he had said this, assuring the preacher that the council did not want to do anything improper. Geiler promised the council a written catalogue of charges that he himself would present at the town hall. This took place in January 1501.[115] In these "21 Articles of Complaint"[116] Geiler lists a series of civic practices and regulations which in his view transgressed "against Christian Law and God's Commandments".[117] He warned that the city might suffer serious damage because of this blatant spiritual disobedience – perhaps not in temporal matters but certainly in spiritual.[118] The souls of the magistrates and the community would

---

[113] Uwe Israel: *Johannes Geiler von Kaysersberg (1445–1510): der Straßburger Münsterprediger als Rechtsreformer* (Berlin, 1997) [= Berliner historische Studien 27], p. 240f.

[114] "Wolten sie es aber nit thůn, so sol man von allem volck andere erwelen, die got lieb hetten." Ibid. p. 262 and 289.

[115] "[. . .] sye weren alle des teüfels, und ir vorfahren und ir nachkomen." Cf. the report Geiler gives in his prologue to the '21 Articles'. It is edited together with the 'Articles' in L. Dacheux: *Die ältesten Schriften Geilers von Kayserberg* (Freiburg i. Br., 1882; reprinted Amsterdam 1965), p. 1f. (prologue), 3–42 (21 Articles) and 43–76 (notes).

[116] On the formation, transmission, construction and content of the '21 Articles' cf. the judicious account in Israel (as in n. 113), pp. 178–267.

[117] "[. . .] wider christeliche gäsatz und Gottes gebotte." Introductory comment of Geiler to the '21 Articles', ed. Dacheux (as in n. 115), p. 3.

[118] Geiler's postscript to the '21 Articles', ibid. p. 40.

fall into God's disfavour and consequently become eternally corrupt.[119] Here Geiler is revealed as the threatening herald of God's
strict justice. His recommendations for reform are admittedly on the
whole moderate, and fit in principle into the existing legal structure
so that in the following years the council did indeed take up some
of these proposals.

Corresponding to the balance between justice and mercy as depicted
above, Geiler sometimes advocates greater strictness, sometimes greater
leniency and care in his Articles. Thus he demands that the city
impose harsher penalties for killing a stranger, blasphemy and violation of virgins.[120] Homicide calls for punishment by hanging or
beheading: the existing legislation, which provides merely for a fine,
is not sufficient deterrent – indeed may be said to be an invitation
to capital offences. The council should also take stronger measures
against games of chance[121] and heathen or secular behaviour in the
Cathedral that profanes the sacred place.[122] On the other hand Geiler
advocates that the council should be more restrained in the use of
torture, in particular that they should not without sufficient suspi-
cion *aufziehen* (strappado) or *marteren* (torment) and consequently damage the person and reputation of the accused.[123] In the preceding
years Geiler had continually tried – finally with success – to abol-
ish the practice of refusing those condemned to death confession,
last communion and Christian burial.[124] It is also remarkable how
emphatically Geiler desires in his Articles to see that the right of
asylum of ecclesiastical institutions is respected[125] and the care of the
sick, homeless[126] and poor[127] assured. By his standards of social ethics

---

[119] Introductory comment of Geiler to the '21 Articles', ibid. p. 3: "fallen in
ungenoden Gottes und ewige irer selen verdamnisz" (fall into God's disfavour and
the eternal damnation of their souls).

[120] Geiler treats the three cases ("schlecht ein burger ein fremden zu tod" [if a
citizen beats a stranger to death], "gotslesterung" [blasphemy] and "geschendung
der jungkfrouwen" [violation of a virgin]) in Article 18, ed. Dacheux (as in n. 115),
p. 36. Cf. Israel (as in n. 113), pp. 261–267.

[121] Cf. Article 7, 8 and 9 (ed. Dacheux, pp. 21–25) and Israel, pp. 218–221.

[122] Cf. Article 16 and 14 (ed. Dacheux, pp. 31f. 33–35) and Israel, pp.
232–235.241–247.

[123] Cf. Article 16 and 14 (ed. Dacheux, pp. 31f. 33–35) and Israel, pp.
232–235.241–247.

[124] Cf. Israel (as in n. 113), pp. 264–267.

[125] Cf. Article 15 (ed. Dacheux, p. 32) and Israel, p. 250.

[126] Cf. Article 12 on the Hospice (ed. Dacheux, pp. 26–30) and Israel, pp. 238–241.

[127] Cf. Article 13 (ed. Dacheux, p. 30f.) and Israel, pp. 227–231.

this is a fundamental public responsibility of sharing the mercy demanded by God.[128] In this context he also strives for tax relief for those with smaller incomes and for the destitute. It is not acceptable for the poor to be more heavily encumbered than the rich; rather that the principle of justice should be in force: "Those who have much should give a lot, those with little should give little and thus they are equal, each according to his state."[129] At the end of his 21st Article which he wrote to 'warn' those who ruled the city Geiler sets as a maxim the Vulgate quotation from Ecclesiastes 12.13: "'Fear God and keep his Commandments; that is every man' – i.e. each person is created for this purpose."[130]

7. Shortly after Geiler's death in 1510 his friend the Humanist Jacob Wimpfeling wrote an obituary in which he praised the moderate position of the Cathedral preacher, neither too strict nor too lenient: "He made sins neither too small nor too great."[131] As we have seen, this is a fitting characterisation of Geiler's preaching and pastoral work. Like Gerson and Biel[132] he strove for a balance between consolation and warning and for a balance in the proclamation of the strict justice and gracious mercy of God. Hence he represents a third kind of urban preacher, located between a style of preaching which predominantly threatens and inculcates God's retributory justice and one which predominantly comforts and extols God's omnipotent mercy. As we have seen, Savonarola fit his statements about mercy into the pattern of divine justice which demands purity and punishes impurity; Staupitz held that both rewarding and punishing justice derive from God's overriding mercy. In Geiler we find the

---

[128] On the norm of mercy cf. Article 12 (ed. Dacheux, p. 29f.); cf. also the norm of "mönschlicheit" (humanitas) in Article 13 (ed. Dacheux, p. 31 with p. 67, n. 2).

[129] "Wer viil gutz hat, sol viil geben, wer wenig hat, soll wenig geben und also die burger glich sin, ieder nach syner macht." Article 20 (ed. Dacheux, p. 38) and Israel (as in n. 113), p. 256.

[130] Geiler's postscript to the '21 Articles', ed. Dacheux, p. 41: "'Time Deum et mandata eius observa: hoc est omnis homo', id est ad hoc factus est omnis homo."

[131] "Nulli blandus adulator, non peccata nimium attenuans nec plus aequo exaggerans, in dicenda veritate nullius timens potentiam." Cited by Israel (as in n. 113), p. 284.

[132] On Gabriel Biel as cathedral preacher in Mainz cf. the recent publication of Wilfrid Werbeck: "Gabriel Biels fünfter Predigtjahrgang (1463/64). Ein Bericht über die Gießener Hs. 838", in: Ulrich Köpf, Sönke Lorenz (eds.): *Gabriel Biel und die Brüder vom gemeinsamen Leben. Beiträge aus Anlaß des 500. Todestages des Tübinger Theologen* (Stuttgart, 1998), pp. 93–135.

attempt to see the features of God's gracious mercy in the process
of his justice, and the features of his avenging justice in the workings of his mercy.

V. *Looking on to the Reformation*

The contrast between the extremes of Savonarola and Staupitz gives
an impression of the breadth of the religious spectrum that was
shaped by the preaching of the urban *dirigenti religiosi* of the late
Middle Ages. Geiler von Kaysersberg on the other hand shows the
potentiality of the nuances and hybrid forms that determined the
middle area of the spectrum. This moderate, accommodating, bal-
ancing mediation of God's severity and mercy, of threat and consolation was presumably typical of everyday pastoral life in the
majority of European towns around 1500.

   At the beginning of this article I drew attention to the relationship
between the preaching of the late Middle Ages and that of the
Reformation. I should like to take up that thread again at the conclusion. The Reformation would in fact substantially alter the coordinates in that it made a structural break with the conceptual
framework of ideas of the late Middle Ages – affirmed even by theologians such as Staupitz – that viewed human merit, satisfaction, and
morality as relevant to salvation. Reformation theology would go on
to assign what is in principle a new kind of autonomous efficacy
and dominance to divine grace and mercy. But as I have already
stressed, the work of the reforming *dirigenti religiosi*, their commitment
to preaching, spiritual welfare, instruction, church order and urban
discipline in the face of rulers and local authorities, were kept in
motion by the tension between compassion and strictness, between
liberating Gospel and commanding Law. The *foci* of mercy and justice would permit ideas of consolation and severity, tolerance and
rigor, freedom and control to emerge again in Reformation preaching, ideas that in many respects call to mind late medieval models.
Again and again we can see how contemporary the theological and
pastoral alternatives of Savonarola, Staupitz and Geiler remain.

   On a new level – shunted, so to speak, by a religious kind of tec-
tonic fault – we can detect three analogous types of *dirigenti religiosi*
in the Reformation: 1. The apocalyptic type of Girolamo Savonarola
with his vision of the imminent sword and an Italy cleansed of god-

lessness can be found again, for example, in the work of Thomas Müntzer from Zwickau to Mühlhausen or in the leaders of the so-called "Anabaptist Kingdom of Münster". 2. In contrast, the model typified by Johannes von Staupitz is brought to mind by the way in which Luther and – deriving from him (although also contested by him) – the Antinomianism of Johann Agricola no longer regard the life of the justified Christian in the positive leading perspective of divine Law. The mercy of Jesus Christ received through the Gospel becomes the fully sufficient principle of the new ethics of the Christian life. 3. The mediating type of a Johannes Geiler von Kaysersberg, with his balance between mercy and strictness, has its Reformation analogy in urban *dirigenti religiosi* such as Ulrich Zwingli, Johannes Oekolampad, Ambrosius Blarer, Martin Bucer or John Calvin – i.e. in the typical "Reformed" (sometimes called the "Upper German/ Swiss") incorporation of the directing divine Law and strict ecclesiastical discipline in the field newly ordered by the Gospel.[133]

Thus in certain respects the Reformation shifts back into the context of the late Middle Ages – or should we say: The tensions of the late Middle Ages transmute themselves into the new context of the Reformation?

---

[133] Cf. Heiko A. Oberman: *Masters of the Reformation* (Cambridge, 1981), pp. 277–78: "In the struggle against the unbearable burden of church law, Summenhart aimed not to liberate the Christian conscience from the law but rather to trim to a theologically valid compass a body of legislation bloated by canonists and their canons. The urban reformers restricted that scope of validity even more narrowly, identifying it with the canon of scripture. But like Summenhart they had no intention of abolishing the law entirely; rather they endeavoured to proclaim, to preach for the first time an authentic law – making it all the more binding on the individual and, in view of the threat of divine penalty, upon the community. At the same time they introduced a major difference, teaching that, although obedience to God might indeed often turn away divine wrath, God's loving attention no longer came in response to human merit.
The process is thus better described as a 'reorientation of church law toward the word of God and a whetting of Christian consciences', than with the image of liberation at the hands of [. . .] 'freedom fighters'. The believer's conscience, that formerly left the confessional burdened by innumerable stipulations of the church's canon law, now merely exchanged that load in the south German urban Reformation for a new and absolute obligation to observe God's law recorded in the canon of scripture."

CHAPTER THREE

VOLITION AND INADEQUACY AS A TOPIC IN LATE MEDIEVAL PASTORAL CARE OF PENITENTS

I. *The Harrowing Question at the End of the Middle Ages*

How did late-medieval pastoral theology deal with the problem of the spiritual inadequacy of Christians? How did it evaluate the views of the afterlife held by those monks and nuns, priests and laity whose way of life betrayed an alarming lack of piety, either in their own eyes or in those of their pastors? And what standards, solutions and advice did that theology give on the one hand to the pastors and on the other to those who had, or were believed to have had, too little reverence? How might the scrupulous best deal with their own weak and timorous souls? In what follows I shall apply myself to this cluster of questions. It should immediately be clear that here we are addressing exactly that set of problems which subsequently gave rise to the Lutheran Reformation: the struggles of Martin Luther, as a young Augustinian monk, with his pervasive sense of inadequacy before God, and the attempts of his pastor, Johann von Staupitz, to give him comforting guidance. Staupitz is representative of that type of theology so typical of the century before the Reformation upon which I should like to especially concentrate. An outgrowth of experience gained in pastoral counseling, this 'Theology of Piety' was channeled into spiritual care. It aimed to articulate the proper and salutary art of holy living; consequently, it particularly addressed the problem of how to give people motivation, consolation, support and protection in their spiritual weakness, their discouragement, or their hardening of heart.[1]

---

[1] On the term 'Theology of Piety' cf. the balance drawn in my article: "Was ist Frömmigkeitstheologie? Überlegungen zum 14. bis 16. Jahrhundert", in: *Praxis Pietatis, Festschrift für Wolfgang Sommer*, ed. Hans-Jörg und Marcel Nieden, Stuttgart, 1999, pp. 9–45; on Staupitz (ca. 1468–1524) cf. Berndt Hamm: Staupitz, Johann[es] von (ca. 1468–1524)", in: *Theologische Realenzyklopädie* 32 (2000), pp. 119–127 (with bibliography); idem: "Johann von Staupitz (ca. 1468–1524) – spätmittelalterlicher

This intensive confrontation with spiritual insufficiency is best understood in the context of a common characteristic of late-medieval spirituality: fervent striving for religious perfection and efficiency on the road to salvation. The ecclesiastical and in particular, the monastic movement for reform in the 15th century was, as we know, motivated by popular ideals of austerity and observance, of regularization and perfection in the area of conflict between fear of judgment, hope of reward and the mentality of merit. The ideals of spiritual ascent once cultivated exclusively by Christian mystics were transformed into a more mundane and less elitist, meditative piety of passion and penitence for ordinary men and women, shorn of their ecstatic and visionary components. And yet throughout the sources we still encounter the idea of a series of stages which has as its aim the improvement and perfection of *devotio*, love, humility, hope, patience and obedience. Virtually all of the late-medieval guidelines for piety reflect this gradualistic thinking about an intensifiable devotion to God. The Christian is expected to ascend to heaven on the ladder of virtue. And the sources convey the common conviction that no-one can be saved without his or her own volition and ability. A salutary Christian death was an *ars*, a capability and virtue which had to be achieved, and with which – like a merchant – one purchased the benefits of heaven.[2] In order not to fall victim to eternal damnation, the dying person must at least be in a condition of true repentance, or *vera contritio*: a completely voluntary regret for his own sins, arising spontaneously from a pure love of God, and a corresponding faith in God's divine mercy. After the 12th century, under the influence of Bernard of Clairvaux, the Augustinian ideals of perfect love and willing devotion blended with the new emotional culture of a 'passion

---

Reformer und 'Vater' der Reformation", in: *Archiv für Reformationsgeschichte* 92 (2001), pp. 4–24. On the relation between the two Augustinians in particular see Richard Wetzel: "'Meine Liebe zu Dir ist beständiger als Frauenliebe'. Johannes von Staupitz (†1524) und Martin Luther", in: *Luther und seine Freunde*, edited by the Evangelisches Predigerseminar Wittenberg, Wittenberg 1998, pp. 105–124.

[2] On the metaphor of "spiritual Kaufmannschaft" ("commercialism") so characteristic of the religious mentality of the age, cf. Berndt Hamm: "Humanistische Ethik und reichsstädtische Ehrbarkeit in Nürnberg", in: *Mitteilungen des Vereins für Geschichte der Stadt Nürnberg* 76 (1989), pp. 65–147, here p. 129. On the use of the metaphors of acquisition and purchase in the context of the *ars moriendi* cf. Johannes von Paltz: *Die himmlische Fundgrube* [1490], ed. Horst Laubner et al., in: J.v.P.: *Opuscula* = Paltz: *Werke 3*, Berlin – New York, 1989, pp. 241,18–242,10; 243,1–11 (with reference to the parable of the merchant and the pearl of great price in Mt. 13.45f.); 248,10–12.19–23.

mysticism', which stressed the soul's need for the cultivation of compassionate suffering (*compassio*) and elevating, comforting tenderness (*dulcedo*).[3] The Christian goals of true repentance, satisfaction and merit were thereafter embedded in this demanding culture of volition, love, pain and tenderness which plumbed the deepest depths of the emotional life of the soul.

The result of this internalization and intensification of the criteria of piety was a sharper diagnosis of human spiritual inadequacy.[4] This intensification of spiritual demands increased peoples' feelings of inadequacy and their anxiety over it. Pastors and theologians recognized that the intensification of spiritual demands correspondingly raised people's feelings of anxiety and spiritual deficiency. Behind cognitive weaknesses in the knowledge of faith, behind a shortage of effective good works, pastoral theologians diagnosed serious psychic and emotional deficits as the root of such peoples' problems. What can be done to help, they asked, if a sinner recognizes what is salvific but cannot actually desire it? If he cannot love God, or suffer with the suffering Christ, or feel genuine pangs of regret for his sins? And if, in consequence, he cannot make an honest confession in preparation for the Sacrament, or go to Communion with the devotion of a heart which loves and desires God, and ultimately cannot feel the sweetness of union with Christ?

Such questions occur increasingly in the 15th century. The late-medieval theology of piety developed in response to what appeared to be an increasingly pervasive spiritual malady, the weakness of the human heart to *feel* what it should. (It is an open question whether such a growing tendency might have been fostered by the epochal crisis of the Great Plague, or by the failure of the Councils of Constance

---

[3] See Peter Dinzelbacher: "Über die Entdeckung der Liebe im Hochmittelalter", in: *Saeculum* 32 (1981), pp. 185–208 (with bibliography); Berndt Hamm: "Von der Gottesliebe des Mittelalters zum Glauben Luthers. Ein Beitrag zur Bußgeschichte", in: *Lutherjahrbuch* 65 (1998), pp. 19–44; English translation in chapter 4, below p. 128f.

[4] Cf. Adolar Zumkeller: "Das Ungenügen der menschlichen Werke bei den deutschen Predigern des Spätmittelalters", in: *Zeitschrift für Katholische Theologie* 81 (1959), pp. 265–305. The fact that the spiritual capacity of the sinner, especially his repentance and confession, became such a problem in the later Middle Ages is seen by Martin Ohst as directly connected to the increasing legal refinement of ecclesiastical norms, making them correspondingly less transparent for laypeople. The opacity of sin makes spontaneous, direct repentance impossible. Cf. Ohst: *Pflichtbeichte. Untersuchungen zum Bußwesen im Hohen und Späten Mittelalter* (Tübingen, 1995) [= Beiträge zur historischen Theologie 89], pp. 117–138.

and Basle). On the one hand, pastoral theologians defended the firm principle that when life draws to a close, what is decisive is the ability to love God and feel the pain of contrition – i.e. the internal, affective closeness of the sinner to God. On the other, the age is marked by a sense of a spiritual disillusionment, a critical observation of how widespread, even among those in monastic orders, is the inability to love and feel regret – let alone to experience the blissful sensation of sweet proximity to God. Simultaneously, however, proponents of the theology of piety demonstrate a widespread conviction that God desires the salvation of this great number of emotionally handicapped sinners, both male and female. Consequently, pastoral theologians sought ways and means to help them.

II. *The Typical Solution provided by Johannes von Paltz (†1511): Where there is Inadequacy, a Good Will Suffices*

A passage from Johannes von Paltz' *Coelifodina* of 1502 – a manual of practical guidelines for pastoral care[5] – can serve as a most instructive example of such a way of looking at the problem and its solution – indeed as an example of no small significance, for when Martin Luther was accepted as a novice into the Augustinian monastery at Erfurt three years later, Paltz was one of his brother monks. For Paltz as for all Scholastic theologians, the essential qualitative leap in the life of the Christian is to be found when God pours into his soul the *habitus* of justifying grace, the so-called *gratia gratum faciens*. According to Paltz it is only through this gift of grace, raising a person to a new level of willingness and capability, that the soul is made capable of true love of God and thereby capable of a genuine contrition, one born of childlike reverence rather than from

---

[5] Critical edition: *Coelifodina*, ed. Christoph Burger, Friedhelm Stasch = *Johannes von Paltz: Werke 1* (Berlin – New York, 1983); cf. also the second volume, first published in 1504, of Paltz' Handbook for Spiritual Counselors: *Supplementum Coelifodinae*, ed. Berndt Hamm = *Paltz: Werke 2* (Berlin – New York, 1983). On these two chief works, which were intended by Paltz to be crowned by a major third volume, "Summa divinorum beneficiorum" (apparently never realised), and on the person of the author see Berndt Hamm: *Frömmigkeitstheologie am Anfang des 16. Jahrhunderts. Studien zu Johannes von Paltz und seinem Umkreis* (Tübingen, 1982) [= Beiträge zur historischen Theologie 65], pp. 119–128 and 131; idem: "Paltz, Johannes von", in: *Theologische Realenzyklopädie* 25 (1995), pp. 606–611.

fear of threatened punishment.[6] Admittedly the problem of affective
weakness and religious incapacity is not solved by the reference to
the transformation of the soul wrought by infused grace and
justification. The fundamental question of the soul's ability or inability remains in two perspectives: looking back from justification and
looking towards the future. Since not everyone attains the influx of
justifying grace, the key question that arises is this: Is there a kind
of ability through which a person who has committed a deadly sin
can prepare himself to receive the *gratia gratum faciens* so that his
capacity and susceptibility are the decisive factor? How much inability is pardonable? Secondly, with regard to the future, the question
arises: what kind of satisfactory, sin-erasing and meritorious effect
does the achieved state of grace have? How much ability is necessary to wipe out all the sins deserving Purgatory? How serious here
is the deficiency of a sense of 'sweetness', the absence of blessed feelings of reverence, the inability to grasp a mystic foretaste of union
with God?

As to the first question, Paltz replies in the spirit of the late Franciscan – i.e. Scotist and Ockhamist – understanding of justification:
the sinner is required to freely choose to prepare himself, with his
own innate powers, to receive justifying grace.[7] In Paltz's view an
exemplary paradigm of the positive possibility of human ability is
the famous precedent of the thief crucified on Jesus' right (Lk.
23.39–43). In a lengthy section of the *Coelifodina* on the *ars bene
moriendi* Paltz explains how the thief employed his innate abilities
and consequently attained Christ's grace.[8] He turned to God's Commandments with good intent (*bonum propositum*) and in so doing
entrusted himself, full of hope, to God's pardoning mercy.[9] Following
Augustine, Paltz phrases it thus: He fled from the wrathful to the
reconciling God,[10] and has thereby shown how one can achieve grace
through hope even at the end of one's life.

---

[6] Cf. Hamm: *Frömmigkeitstheologie* (as in n. 5), pp. 275–277.
[7] Cf. op. cit. pp. 254–259: on the connection between preparation for grace,
and the formulations *facere quod in se est, liberum arbitrium, ex puris naturalibus* and *meritum de congruo.*
[8] Johannes von Paltz: *Coelifodina* (as in n. 5), pp. 210,20–228,2: De arte bene
moriendi.
[9] Op. cit. pp. 218,7–219,22.
[10] "[. . .] consulit beatus Augustinus, quod fugere debemus a deo 'irato' ad ipsum
'placatum'. Et si quis dicat: Quomodo inveniam ipsum placatum?, respondet
Augustinus: 'Placabis eum, si speras in misericordia eius.'" Op. cit. pp. 218,11–14;

To be sure, Paltz continues, in view of its numerous mortal sins and the proximity of death, a troubled conscience might well have doubts that it can follow the way of the thief and be made alive through Christ's grace. The vision of guilt and incapacity can lead to paralysis and despair. Paltz counters this danger with a clarifying quotation from his esteemed teacher, Johannes von Dorsten (†1481) – like Paltz, an Augustinian monk and professor at the University of Erfurt: "Trusting in Christ's mercy I preach to such a person that he should contemplate Christ's mercy. Christ does not ask for long periods (of piety) and he does not demand multifarious efforts. A good intention is sufficient. To reveal this the angels at Christ's birth proclaimed the peace of present grace and eternal, future glory for 'people of good will' (*hominibus bonae voluntatis*)".[11] Hence the admission of the sinner to grace and salvation does not depend crucially upon good works achieved physically – just as the thief, nailed to the cross, could not perform any good works with his hands and feet and yet entered Paradise immediately after his death – but upon the fundamental internal direction of the emotion and will.[12] A few pages later, where he specifically chooses as a central theme the inexpressible compassion of Christ,[13] Paltz expresses this sum and substance of his comforting reflections in the words: "Why do we fear we shall be damned by him who, so that we should not be damned, was willing to be damned himself by the most shameful death, and as the true Lamb of God bore the punishment which we had earned? (. . .) Hence offer to the one who was offered for you, because he

---

Quotation from Augustine: *Enarrationes in Psalmos*, in Ps. 146, n. 20 (Migne, *PL* 37,1913; *CChr* 40,2137,18f.).

[11] "Forte nec adhuc quiescit tremula conscientia dicetque: [. . .] Qualiter gratia Christi vivificabit me, qui pluribus peccatis mortalibus gravor et naturae mortem in foribus exspecto? Hic respondet mecum institutor meus, magister Ioannes de Dorsten, dicens: Huic ego de pietate Christi confisus pietatem Christi considerandam praedico. Hic non quaerit multa temporis spatia, non requirit multos labores, dumtaxat bona sufficit voluntas, in signum cuius eo nato angeli nuntiaverunt pacem gratiae praesentialiter et gloriae futurae aeternaliter *hominibus bonae voluntatis* [Lk. 2.14]." *Coelifodina* (as in n. 5), pp. 219,27–220,1.

[12] "Si igitur non vales iam currere pedibus corporis nec operari corporis manibus, curre ad Christum pedibus affectus et voluntatis, extende ad ipsum brachia cordis. Sic fecit latro ille, qui pedes et manus cruci alligatos habuit et statim audire meruit: *Hodie mecum eris in paradiso* [Lk. 23.43]. Et sic patet, quomodo iste latro spem habuit." Op. cit. p. 220,3–7.

[13] Op. cit., Heading for the section pp. 230,19–232,18: "Secundum confortativum peccatoris, ne desperet in extremis, est ineffabilis Christi pietas."

so willed it, as much as you have: at least a good will (*bonam saltem voluntatem*) and, by virtue of his sacrifice, have confidence that you will be saved! (. . .) He does not weigh the magnitude of the work but the soul of the giver. The one who examines the heart sees and seeks the heart rather than the hand, the feet of the emotion rather than those of the body. Hence endeavor to give him your heart! Hasten to him with the feet of your heart!"[14] – just as the thief on the cross stretched out the arms of his heart to him.[15]

Hence Christ's vicarious Passion makes it possible for Christ to ask from the sinner a mere minimum of ability in preparation for the grace which justifies. This minimum is a good will and the corresponding good intention to become better. The merciful God is satisfied with this minimum, provided that the sinner achieves the most that he can in his desperate situation: that he does "all that is in his power". As with other late-medieval theologians of piety, Paltz's appeal to the Scholastic formula *facere quod in se est*[16] stands in his works in a pastoral, comforting context.[17] Within the frame of reference of divine intercession and mercy, this defines only a minimum of active human participation: The sinner must be able to have the will, be it ever so exiguous. At the same time the passages quoted show the extent to which Paltz clearly stands in the tradition of internalization, under the influence of the turn inwards which goes behind the external dimension of physical deeds to the soul's intent, its desire, love and grief.[18] But typical of the changed situation

---

[14] "Quomodo damnari timemus ab eo, qui, ne damnaremur, morte turpissima damnari voluit et poenam, quam nos meruimus, ipse verus agnus dei tulit? *Iniquitates* profecto *omnium nostrum* deus pater *posuit super eum*, Isaiae 53 [6.5]. Illi ergo, qui pro te *oblatus est, quia voluit* [Jes. 53,7], hoc offeras, quod habes, bonam saltem voluntatem, et vigore oblationis ipsius confide, quia salvus eris! Quia secundum beatum Hieronymum non attendit in oblatione quantum, sed ex quanto; non pensat magnitudinem muneris, sed animam donantis. *Cordis scrutator* [Sap. 1.9] plus cor respicit et quaerit quam manum, plus pedes affectus quam corporis. Cor igitur tuum illi dare studeas! Cordis pedibus ad ipsum festines!" *Coelifodina* (as in n. 5), pp. 232,6–15.

[15] Op. cit. p. 220,4f. (brachia cordis), quoted above n. 12.

[16] Cf. Heiko A. Oberman: "Facientibus quod in se est deus non denegat gratiam. Robert Holcot, O.P. and the beginnings of Luther's theology", in: *Harvard Theological Review* 55 (1962), pp. 317–342; Wilfrid Werbeck: *Indices zu Gabrielis Biel Collectorium circa quattuor libros Sententiarum* (Tübingen, 1992), p. 160, entry 'facere quod in se est'.

[17] Cf. Hamm: *Frömmigkeitstheologie* (as in n. 5), subject index p. 371, entry 'facere quod in se est'.

[18] This Augustinian tradition clearly comes to the fore in the early theology of Luther, as for example in his lectures on Romans: "Quia qui sic operatur, ut per

in the 15th century is how in Paltz, such introspective plumbing of the depths of the emotions is not intended to increase the demands on the soul, but rather to exonerate. If Christ has done everything necessary for you, then in the end it is no longer a matter of your deeds. Simply follow his invitation and accept his atonement, hope for his loving-kindness and feel regret for your sins. You need do no more. To be able to desire this is enough.

III. *The Further Lowering of the Minimal Requirement: If there is no Good Will, then Desiring to Desire is Enough*

The purpose behind minimalizing the human requirement and maximizing the divine mercy becomes even clearer if we look more closely at how Paltz analyzes even the requirement of *bona voluntas*. He deals with the situation of sinners who say "I cannot feel any good intention or genuine disapproval of my sins."[19] To these weak souls who lack the desire to feel regret Paltz replies: "If you do not have this, then grieve that you do not have it. And yearn to have such possessions!"[20] But if a person cannot feel such a yearning, Paltz continues, then he should at least yearn to be able to yearn. Under such emotional conditions, this is at least *facere quod in se est* – to do the best that one can – and God will then through his grace make up the missing desire and pangs of regret. The appropriate path to take is to be found in the sacraments. If you are trapped in your inability and cannot grieve for your sins out of childlike reverence, then, Paltz advises, at least grieve for them imperfectly out of fear of damnation and flee to the sacraments of Christ. They will transform your anxious regret (*attritio*) into a genuine, loving regret (*contritio*).[21]

---

ea ad gratiam iustificationis se disponat, iam aliquo modo iustus est. Quia magna pars iustitiae velle esse iustum." *WA*, 56.254,23–25. Cf. Augustine: Epist. 127,5 (Migne, *PL* 33,485): "Iusta vero vita, cum volumus, adest, quia eam ipsam plene velle iustitia est; nec plus aliquid perficienda iustitia quam perfectam voluntatem requirit."

[19] "Ego non possum habere bonam voluntatem et displicentiam veram peccatorum." *Coelifodina* (as in n. 5), p. 221,7f.

[20] "Dico: Si non habes, doleas te non habere. Si non perfecte odis peccata tua, doleas te non odire. Si non habes devotionem, doleas te non habere. Et desidera talia bona habere iuxta illud: *Concupivit anima mea desiderare iustificationes tuas*" [Vulg.-Ps. 118.20]. Op. cit. p. 221,8–11.

[21] Continuation of the quotation from n. 20: "Sensit enim David se non semper

Paltz reinforces both his doctrine of the emotionally transforming power of Confession and the Eucharist, and his minimalizing pastoral strategy, by appending an exemplary tale from the life of Bernard of Clairvaux. Paltz took over this story from his teacher, Dorsten; there are no traces of it in the various "Lives" of St. Bernard.[22] Yet it is very typical of the late medieval way of thinking: Bernard came to a city where a nobleman had lived in great sin with a blood-relation. When he fell ill the priest came to him with the elements of the Eucharist and asked him whether he felt grief that he had sinned with his blood-relation. The nobleman answered that he felt no grief, and still took pleasure in her. Thereupon the priest replied that he could not give him absolution or dare to administer the sacrament, and departed. But when Bernard learned of this incident from the priest he went back with him to the nobleman and likewise asked him whether he was not sorry for such a great offence. When he again replied in the negative and said that he felt joy in it, Bernard said: "Do you not feel any grief that you cannot feel grief for such a sin?" The nobleman replied: "To be sure it grieves me that I feel no grief." Then Bernard instructed the priest to give him absolution and administer the sacrament "because he did as much as he could do" (*quia fecit quod in se fuit*); and Bernard trusted that the Sacraments would compensate for what was lacking. And this indeed happened, Paltz concludes: "after he had tasted Christ's Sacraments he felt such a remorse and abhorrence of his sin that he could never again look upon that person."[23]

---

aeque bene dispositum, et quando non desideravit iustificationes dei, tunc desideravit, quod possit desiderare; et sic fecit quod in se fuit, et tunc dominus deus residuum supplevit. Sic etiam si non doles pro peccatis tuis ex timore filiali, id est ex amore dei, tunc saltem doleas pro eis ex timore servili, id est ex timore inferni vel mortis, et fugias ad sacramenta Christi, et iuvaberis per ipsa. ut ad veram contritionem pervenias, ut postea patebit" [Reference on pp. 260,7–263,12]. Also p. 221,11–17.

[22] Cf. Adolar Zumkeller: "Die Lehre des Erfurter Augustinertheologen Johannes von Dorsten (†1481) über Gnade, Rechtfertigung und Verdienst", in: *Theologie und Philosophie* 53 (1978), pp. 27–64 and 179–219: here p. 61f. with the exemplary story as related by Dorsten in a sermon in n. 167 and Zumkeller's remark: "Eine Quelle für diesen Bericht, den wir in den authentischen Viten des hl. Bernhard (Migne, *PL* 185,221ff.) nicht nachweisen konnten, gibt D. nicht an."

[23] Continuation of the quotation from n. 21: "Ista profunde novit sanctus Bernhardus, quando venit ad quandam civitatem, ubi quidam vir nobilis infirmabatur, qui cum quadam consanguinea sua, quam secum habuit, graviter peccavit. Ad quem cum sacerdos cum venerabili veniens sacramento interrogaret, an doleret, quod cum

What we encounter here and in many comparable passages in Paltz makes the interpretation of *facere quod in se est* totally flexible. The axiom "if I do the best I can God inevitably grants me his grace" is no longer to be seen as a rigid standard of divine and ecclesiastical law; instead it makes possible a flexible reduction of the requirements according to the respective capabilities of a particular person. If he does not wish to renounce his sins, then he should at least wish that he did so desire. A desire to desire is enough – and a minimum of desire will always be possible. If he can feel no grief, he should at least grieve that he has no grief – as expressed by the axiom "*doleas, quod non doleas!*" And if he cannot desire what God demands, then he should at least desire that he may be able to desire it.[24]

Paltz repeats his well-loved term 'at least' (*saltem*, less frequently *solummodo*)[25] when addressing any potentially problematical areas of

---

propinqua sua peccaverat, respondit: Non doleo, sed beneplacitum in ea habeo. Respondit sacerdos: Tunc vos absolvere non possum nec communicare audeo. Et abscessit. Cui sanctus Bernhardus obvians causamque intelligens reduxit sacerdotem ad nobilistam et eo praesente interrogavit similiter eum, an doleret de tanto crimine. Respondit iterum, quod non, sed gauderet. Dixit sanctus Bernhardus: Non doles, quod non potes dolere de tanto peccato? Respondit: Certe doleo, quod non possum dolere. Tunc sanctus Bernhardus iussit eum absolvi et communicari, quia fecit quod in se fuit; et sperabat, quod sacramenta residuum deberent supplere. Quod factum est, nam postquam perceperat Christi sacramenta, tantam contritionem et detestationem peccati in se sensit, quod nec istam personam de cetero videre poterat." *Coelifodina* (as in n. 5), pp. 221,18–222,5. The decisive passage with the intervention of Bernhard reads as follows in Dorsten: "Tunc beatus Bernhardus interrogavit ipsum, an ne desideraret, quod posset eam odire et a se dimittere et dolere de peccatis. Qui respondens dixit: Immo multum desidero, quod possem. Mox beatus Bernhardus dixit sacerdoti: Absolvite eum et communicate! Quod ut factum fuit, statim virtute venerabilis sacramenti mox in tantam contritionem et amaritudinem cordis de suis peccatis cecidit, ut etiam, quam intime diligebat, de cetero videre non poterat." Quoted by Zumkeller op. cit. p. 61f. n. 167. Comparison of the Paltz version with Dorsten's account shows that Paltz patently set special value on the equation of *doleo quod non doleo* with *facere quod in se est* and on God's making good by the power of the sacraments whatever is missing of the true pain of repentance.

[24] Cf. below n. 25, 31 and 34.

[25] Cf. the following occurrences of *saltem* in the *Coelifodina* (as in n. 5): pp. 62,14; 64,4; 102,24 (saltem affectu devoto); 108,15; 109,12f.; 200,3; 211,3 (saltem timorem servilem); 221,15 (saltem dolere ex timore servili); 232,10 (bonam saltem voluntatem); in the *Supplementum Coelifodinae* (as in n. 5): pp. 55,12; 56,3; 98,6 (saltem in proposito); 103,2; 115,2; 120,4 (saltem desiderare castitatem); 181,12; 205,12; 206,6f.; 243,22 (saltem attritionem); 244,35; 252,19; 254,22; 258,24; 285,29 (saltem attritus); 401,26. For the corresponding use of *solummodo* cf. e.g. *Coelifodina* pp. 126,16 (solummodo peccator faciat, quod faciendum est).

Christian life, above all when dealing with the preparation for death, and the benefits then to be found in the sacraments, indulgences and a simplified program of meditation on Christ's Passion in which, if I interpret it correctly, the burden is shifted away from the *compassio* of the penitent to the saving *compassio* of Christ.[26] Typical of this is the way Paltz differentiates within imperfect regret (*attritio*) three further stages of anxious grief in order to plumb the greatest crises of insufficiency and promise help to those afflicted by it.[27] The lowest degree of intensity of *attritio* which is still sufficient for a valid reception of the Sacraments is reserved for the seriously ill since God demands less from the sick than from the healthy. One could call this a 'calibration downwards', in the sense in which Petra Seegets has spoken of the teaching and instruction of the Franciscan theologian, Stephan Fridolin: for those who are troubled, "the stages of the religious requirements laid upon humanity proceed progressively downwards and finally stand at the absolute minimum".[28]

Another example of this pastoral method of minimalization[29] is how Paltz deals with the helplessness of those members of monastic orders who complain that it is impossible for them to keep their vow of chastity. It goes against their nature and is thus foolish; perhaps it was even a trick of Satan that prompted them to make such a vow. Paltz answers: Not the vow but the doubting of the vow comes from the devil. In order to keep it, one must desire chastity and request it from God.[30] To the objection: "I am so weak that I do not even desire it", follows the typical solution: "If you do not desire chastity then you must nevertheless desire that you can desire it."[31]

---

[26] Cf. the passages on meditation on the Passion in Paltz: *Die himmlische Fundgrube* (as in n. 2), pp. 228,1–236,8, especially pp. 234,12–235,7, and *Coelifodina* (as in n. 5), pp. 106,7–137,15, especially p. 126,8–17.

[27] Cf. Hamm: *Frömmigkeitstheologie* (as in n. 5), p. 279f.

[28] Petra Seegets: *Passionstheologie und Passionsfrömmigkeit im ausgehenden Mittelalter. Der Nürnberger Franziskaner Stephan Fridolin (gest. 1498) zwischen Kloster und Stadt* (Tübingen, 1998) [= Spätmittelalter und Reformation. Neue Reihe 10], p. 133 n. 51. Cf. Fridolin's tract: *Lehre für angefochtene und kleinmütige Menschen*, edited by Seegets in Berndt Hamm/Thomas Lentes (eds.): *Spätmittelalterliche Frömmigkeit zwischen Ideal und Praxis* (Tübingen, 2001) [= Spätmittelalter und Reformation. Neue Reihe 15], pp. 189–195.

[29] "Minimalisierungsprogramm" is Seegets' (op. cit.) appropriate modification of my term "Minimalprogramm" to bring out more clearly the processive character of Stephan Fridolin's pastoral strategy, which closely approximates to Paltz' intentions.

[30] *Supplementum Coelifodinae* (as in n. 5), p. 119,23–33.

[31] "Sed forte dicis: Ego sum ita tepidus vel tepida, quod etiam non desidero casti-

One should beseech Christ, Mary and the saints for chastity, or at least for the *desiderium castitatis*.[32] If it is not granted then at least one has done what one can; in the end, God will perhaps accept the will for the deed (*voluntatem pro facto*)[33] and the emotion for the effect (*affectum pro effectu*).[34] With this daring minimalization of the *facere quod in se est* Paltz remains firmly within traditional categories of internalization: the will, the emotions, the yearning and pain of the spirit. Yet in view of the vicarious work of Christ, the intercession of the saints and the means of grace available through the Church, he consistently offers relief for the emotionally encumbered. He reduces the requisite human participation to a minimal remnant of will, desire and regret with the stated aim that the great multitude of *maximi peccatores*, with their weaknesses and fear, can also be saved.[35] One might say that what then follows in the theology of Martin Luther, his fellow monk at Erfurt,[36] is the elimination of this minimal requirement and the proclamation of the completely unconditional justification and salvation of the sinner. But here Luther does not lower the standard farther in Paltz' sense; his is not a further pastoral reduction on the human level of *facere quod in se est*.[37] On the contrary: Luther

---

tatem. Dico tibi: Si non desideras castitatem, tamen debes desiderare, quod possis eam desiderare, iuxta illud Psalmistae: *Concupivit anima mea desiderare iustificationes tuas* [Vulg.-Ps. 118.20]. Debes igitur cotidie orare pro desiderio castitatis, quousque sentias te desiderare [. . .]" Op. cit. p. 119,33–38. On this allusion to Psalm 118 cf. above n. 20 and 21.

[32] *Supplementum Coelifodinae* (as in n. 5), pp. 119,38–120,15.

[33] "[. . .] tamen forte dominus recipit voluntatem pro facto, cum non consentias turpitudini. Quia saepius contingit, quod quis magnum habet conatum pro virtute et instanter petit pro ea et redditur domino deo ita gratus, sicut qui sine labore videtur eam habere de facto." Op. cit. p. 120,16–20.

[34] "[. . .] saltem desidera, quod possis desiderare potius mori quam consentire [scil. turpitudini]. Et continua hanc petitionem per totum tempus vitae tuae; et tunc in fine forte dominus recipiet affectum pro effectu." Op. cit. p. 177,14–17.

[35] Cf. Hamm: *Frömmigkeitstheologie* (as in n. 5), pp. 146–156 (Die seelsorgerliche Grundintention: Gnade und Heil für die multitudo peccatorum).

[36] Following his entrance to the Erfurt convent on 17th July 1505 the novice Luther probably would have found little opportunity for close personal contact with Paltz, as the latter left the Augustinian monastery in Erfurt between the end of August 1505 and January 1506 in order to assume the office of prior in Mülheim near Koblenz. Cf. Hamm, op. cit. pp. 78f. and 332. However Luther would have come to know the two main extensive Latin works of his prominent brother in the order as well as his German book of edification 'Die himmlische Fundgrube', which with its 21 printed editions between 1490 and 1520 was nothing less than a bestseller among the literature of late medieval theology of piety; cf. the edition of the work in: Johannes von Paltz: *Opuscula* = Paltz: *Werke 3* (as in n. 2), pp. 155–284.

[37] Cf. however the treatment of 'facere quod in se est' in Luther's first Lectures

separates the sinners' pardon completely from the category of the
minimally adequate emotional repentance necessary for salvation,
and links it solely to God's promise '*extra nos*', because all humans
are totally inadequate before God.[38]

IV. *Exoneration – a Trend of the Late Middle Ages*

The minimalization of the willingness and ability required for salvation,
as we have examined it in the work of Johannes von Paltz, is a
highly significant example of a conspicuous trend in pre-Reformation
pastoral care and the theology of piety – although he perhaps goes
farther than almost all his contemporaries. It is characteristic that
Paltz was also an active preacher and defender of the papal Jubilee
Indulgence.[39] The Jubilee campaigns with their noisy marketing of
special grace belong in this context which we must describe in more
detail. The way out of the dilemma of the notorious inability of the
majority of believers revealed by Paltz is, I believe, a kind of final
stage in numerous late medieval attempts to give a religious dispensation to weak, anxious and fainthearted people who were plagued
by their inability, irrespective of whether their incapacity was real
or only imaginary.[40] In one way or another pastorally-oriented theologians offered them emotional relief by reducing the religious demands
and correspondingly enlarging the effect of the means of grace. Hence
Sven Grosse fittingly described the means of consolation employed
by Johannes Gerson and the numerous theologians of piety influenced

---

on the Psalms, 1513–1515, which is clearly to be seen in the setting of the late
medieval tradition; on this Berndt Hamm: *Promissio, pactum, ordinatio. Freiheit und
Selbstbindung Gottes in der scholastischen Gnadenlehre* (Tübingen, 1977) [= Beiträge zur
historischen Theologie 54], pp. 377–385.

[38] Cf. Oswald Bayer: *Promissio. Geschichte der reformatorischen Wende in Luthers Theologie*,
Göttingen, 1971 (= Forschungen zur Kirchen- und Dogmengeschichte 24); see below,
pp. 147–152.

[39] Cf. Hamm: *Frömmigkeitstheologie* (as in n. 5), pp. 84–91 und 284–291.

[40] On this complex of problems see Sven Grosse: *Heilsungewißheit und Scrupulositas
im späten Mittelalter. Studien zu Johannes Gerson und Gattungen der Frömmigkeitstheologie seiner
Zeit* (Tübingen, 1994) [= Beiträge zur historischen Theologie 85], also the tract of
the Franciscan Stephan Fridolin: *Lehre für angefochtene und kleinmütige Menschen* (as in
n. 28), and on this Seegets (as in n. 28), pp. 123–141.

by him in dealing with scrupulous, overtaxed people as a "strategy of minimal requirement".[41]

Behind such a pastoral method and strategy there is a real theological dynamism, with certain variable conceptions of God and humanity, justice and mercy, judgment and grace. Related to this is the noteworthy emphasis on "unburdening" arising from a particular theological anthropology. It applies to the outer dimension of physical activity, to the inner dimension of the sensibilities of the soul and their expression through the body, and to higher spiritual nature of the soul itself. A typical example may be seen in the recurring insistence of pastoral theologians that when one truly repents, it is not absolutely necessary to weep tears as Peter did; what is decisive and sufficient is the inner weeping of the heart.[42] Also typical is their tendency to distinguish between the pain of the senses and the spiritual pain of the will, emphasizing that what is decisive and sufficient is the spiritual inclination of the will, even if one's emotions are so conflicted that one feels unable to hate sin, or to suffer with the suffering Christ, or with the fellow man whom one should love. As for the sinful, it is not the weaknesses of sensuality and lust (*sensualitas* and *concupiscentia*) which are determinative but the part played by reason and volition (*ratio* and *voluntas*). Hence in turning away from sin and turning toward Christ the intention of the higher soul suffices – even if this is only rudimentary and stuck in its elementary stages.[43] Such differentiations are intended to point a way

---

[41] Grosse op. cit. pp. 93–96 and throughout.

[42] The scholastic doctrine of penance took its direction from the identification of penitence with weeping over sin in Peter Lombard (*Sententiae* IV, dist. 14, cap. 1–2), quoting here from Gregory the Great. Also of importance for the later Middle Ages was the interpretation by Thomas Aquinas in his Commentary on the *Sentences* (IV, dist. 14, q. 1, art. 1, qcl. 6, ad 2), which Paltz, like his teacher Johannes von Dorsten, quotes with the following words: "Sed diceret quis: Ego vellem libenter deflere peccata mea, sed lacrimas habere non possum. Respondet beatus Thomas Super quarto, distinctione 14, quod flere seu plangere in descriptione poenitentiae non dicit fletum sensibilem exteriorem, sed fletum mentis interiorem, qui non est aliud quam detestatio peccati seu dolor cordis de peccato." *Supplementum Coelifodinae* (as in n. 5), p. 209,20–24 (reference there to Paltz' source in Dorsten's text).

[43] Cf. Johannes von Paltz: *Supplementum Coelifodinae* (as in n. 5), pp. 213,19–214,24 and 217,18–218,6, in each case using Thomas' Commentary on the *Sentences*. See also Johannes Geiler von Kaysersberg: "18 Eigenschaften eines guten Christenpilgers", 1.Eigenschaft: "[. . .] Und nach dem willen deiner vernu<n>ft soltu ym [scil. deinem Nächsten] gutes wollen und sol dir laid sein, das dein sinnlichait darwider ist." J.G.v.K.: *Sämtliche Werke*, ed. Gerhard Bauer, Teil 1, Abt. 1, vol. 2 (Berlin – New

out of physical and spiritual incapacity and to counteract any over-
burdening. Here two principles play an important part:

1. Stress is laid upon the fact that God himself does not overtax
those who are weakened by their sins and the consequences thereof –
in accordance with the stock Latin quotation which can be traced
back to Jerome: God does not require from man anything which
exceeds his capability (*"Ultra posse viri/ non vult Deus ulla requiri"*).[44] (In
Early High German: "Got fordert nit mer von unß, dann wir ver-
mugen.")[45]

2. Combined with this is the directly connected idea that only
something that is within his power (*potestas*) can be demanded from
a person – i.e. which lies within the scope of his rational freedom
of will – and that the whole area of affective and emotional sensa-
tions eludes the sovereign control of the thinking, willing subject.[46]
Hence a pious desire of the soul led by rational faith and corresponding physical acts can be demanded as a minimal ability on the
part of the sinner. A *desire* to feel regret, a determined directing of
the desire for regret must be possible even if the affective nature
refuses, and the tears will not flow.

York, 1991), p. 138,27–29. Stephan Fridolin: *Lehre für angefochtene und kleinmütige
Menschen*, (as in n. 28), p. 119,11–15.

[44] This *dictum commune* which was particularly widely received in the late Franciscan
(Scotist and Occamist) tradition is listed by Hans Walther: *Lateinische Sprichwörter und
Sentenzen des Mittelalters*, vol. 5, Göttingen 1967, Nr. 32 and 105; on its use in the
circles inspired by Gerson cf. Grosse (as in n. 40), p. 49 with n. 21.

[45] Stephan Fridolin: *Lehre für angefochtene und kleinmütige Menschen*, (as in n. 28),
p. 191,22f.

[46] The Dominican Johannes Diemer (†late 15th century) expresses himself in precisely this sense in a sermon for the nuns of St. Catherine's cloister in Nuremberg,
where he answers the question of the necessity of tears in repentance by referring,
like Paltz, to Thomas Aquinas (n. 42 above): "verantwort sant Thomas und spricht,
das die zeher nit standen in des menschen gewalt, das er die hab, wen er wol.
Darumb ist es nit not; wol es ist gut, wer sye hat; darumb ist es genunck, das er
das im willen hab." Andrew Lee: *Materialien zum geistigen Leben des späten fünfzehnten
Jahrhunderts im Sankt Katharinenkloster zu Nürnberg*, Diss. phil. in typescript, Heidelberg,
1969, p. 166. On Biel's standpoint, which allows him to affirm both principles, see
Wilfrid Werbeck: "Gabriel Biels fünfter Predigtjahrgang (1463/64). Ein Bericht über
die Gießener Hs. 838", in: Ulrich Köpf/Sönke Lorenz (eds.): *Gabriel Biel und die
Brüder vom gemeinsamen Leben. Beiträge aus Anlaß des 500. Todestages des Tübinger Theologen*
(Stuttgart, 1998) [= Contubernium 47], pp. 93–135, here p. 111 n. 78 ("nihil enim
praecipitur nobis nisi quod est in facultate liberi arbitrii") and p. 112 (on the distinction between the *appetitus animalis* resp. *sensitivus* which is born of necessity and
the *appetitus rationalis* resp. *intellectivus* oriented on independent judgment, following
Thomas Aquinas: *Summa theologiae* I/II, q. 26, art. 1 corpus).

The minimal program of a pious life which Paltz so consistently thinks through to its end has many spiritual fathers in the 14th and 15th centuries. While their work reveals a strong dynamic development of the themes of exoneration and comfort, at the same time it could convey and even amplify traditional models of horrendous severity and rigid discipline. It is often the same theologians who put a strong emphasis on the comforting means of grace of God and the Church who also want to keep alive in the conscience of the ordinary man the *Dies irae, dies illa*, the fearful scenario of deadly sin, divine judgment, the account demanded from man, the torments of Purgatory and eternal damnation.[47] Paltz, too, can speak as a theologian of judgment, although the theme of the severity of Christ, the justly judging arbiter of the world, is only a secondary motif in the Erfurt Augustinian's dominant theology of mercy.[48] Paltz belongs to the pastoral theologians of the Late Middle Ages who in the anticipation of the divine Judgment see the urgency of a special task: impressing upon spiritually weak Christians (or those who feel themselves to be weak) the remedy of divine mercy, so that they may find a way out of their dilemma, not closing themselves off from proffered grace, nor remaining mired in impenitence or despair, but in the end might be saved. In this sense the prospect of the Last Judgment can strengthen the prospect of mercy and the efforts to exonerate; but at the same time it can also make clear to us how little the late medieval offer of a comforting means of grace embodies any antithesis in principle to the widespread ideals of spiritual austerity and perfection on the way to salvation. Such ideals were propagated particularly by members and associates of monastic orders. Minimalization downwards did not exclude an increased endeavor to strive harder and aim higher, since in current notions of the afterlife, the graduated span between being merely saved from Hell and the highest grace of heavenly bliss was very great.

Hence just as in the 15th and early 16th centuries, even among

---

[47] Cf. Christoph Burger: "Die Erwartung des richtenden Christus als Motiv für katechetisches Wirken", in: Norbert Richard Wolf (ed.): *Wissensorganisierende und wissensvermittelnde Literatur im Mittelalter. Perspektiven ihrer Erforschung* (Wiesbaden, 1987), pp. 103–122.

[48] Paltz speaks as a theologian of judgment in a sermon entitled *De adventu domini ad iudicium* (1487), only extant in fragments, ed. Christoph Burger, in: Paltz: *Opuscula* (as in n. 2), pp. 381–408; cf. also the passage 'De reddenda ratione de misericordia dei' in Paltz: *Supplementum Coelifodinae* (as in n. 5), pp. 379,7–384,29.

representatives of an emphatic theology of consolation we find the
dimension of the judgment, justice and severity of God, so there
emerges in view of human insufficiency and uncertainty a clear late
medieval tendency to place greater weight upon God's exonerating
guarantees of salvation and the *communio sanctorum*, particularly in the
field of Christ's Passion. At least the most important theological and
iconographic innovations of the late Middle Ages,[49] insofar as they
are relevant for piety, point in exactly this direction. Their distinc-
tive quality consists particularly in that in contrast to the preaching
of threat and terror[50] and in the midst of a climate of fear,[51] the
emphasis shifts more firmly to God's abundant mercy. Thus the possibility of grace, mediation, intercession and salvation is revealed to
the weak or faint-hearted. In the following section I will trace only
four important lines of tradition which played a significant part in
this respect in the century before the Reformation.

---

[49] On the iconographic innovations or pictorial inventions of the late Middle
Ages, which in various ways emphasize the merciful mildness of God, the saving
power of the Passion of Christ and the protective intercession of Mary and the
saints, see above pp. 22–43, especially p. 32 with n. 90.

[50] For example the penitential sermons of the upper Italian mendicant preachers of the 15th century, especially Girolamo Savonarola with his *terrifica praedicatio*
in Florence in the 'nineties'; cf. Pierre Antonetti: *Savonarola: Ketzer oder Prophet? Eine
Biographie* (Zürich, 1992) (French first edition, Paris, 1991: *Le prophète désarmé*), especially pp. 71–73; see also above pp. 55–65.

[51] Cf. Jean Delumeau: *La Peur en Occident (XIVe–XVIIIe siècle). Une cité assiégée*, Paris
1978; German: *Angst im Abendland. Die Geschichte kollektiver Ängste im Europa des 14. bis
18. Jahrhunderts*, 2 vols., Reinbek 1985, new edition in one volume: Reinbek 1985/1989;
idem: *Le péché et la peur. La culpabilisation en Occident (XIIIe–XVIIIe siècle)*, Paris 1983;
Peter Dinzelbacher: *Angst im Mittelalter. Teufels-, Todes- und Gotteserfahrung: Mentalitätsgeschichte
und Ikonographie*, Paderborn, 1996, in particular on the late medieval and modern
periods pp. 135–260. Overall Dinzelbacher comes to the conclusion that in the
period he investigated there was a "Dominanz des Schrecklichen" and the religious
use of threats as opposed to the witness of hope, trust and consolation, a quantitative and qualitative priority of the "negativen, angstbesetzten Aspekte der Religion"
over the "positiven, schenkenden Vorstellungen" (p. 264). In the present state of
research I would not wish to contest that priority, but with an eye on the textual
and pictorial materials I have studied would draw attention to the – apparently
swelling – stream of a hope-strengthening counter-current in the period from 1480
to 1520. This side of the late Middle Ages – the proclamation of mercy within a
climate of fear – has up to now been too little regarded in research, resulting in
an overdrawn contrast between the late Middle Ages and the Reformation.

V. *Four Lines of the Theological Tradition of Comforting Exoneration for the Weak and Troubled*

1. The Franciscan, John Duns Scotus (†1308) and the Scotists with their doctrine of attrition[52] had a significant influence on the doctrine of confession reflected in all of the monastic orders. Starting from their master's position and expanding upon it, the Scotists took the view that normally the sinner is only capable of imperfect *attritio* without the aid of the Sacraments. Herein lies his *facere quod in se est*. In the sacrament of confession the priest's power to give absolution by virtue of Christ's Passion compensates for the penitent's incapacity and transforms the *attritio* into fully valid *contritio*. Consequently the way through the sacrament is recommended to the weak as an easier and more certain way. Only a few could attain the true repentance of the justified by the more difficult extra-sacramental path. God's exonerating mercy and beneficence reaches its intensified effect through the sacral-institutional mediation of the priest.

The strength of this theory lay in the fact that it took seriously and pastorally the unsettling, troubling feelings of deficiency experienced by people of the time and connected them with the offer of assurance contained in the sacraments. The extent to which the Scotists influenced other theologians outside their own special Franciscan school with their teaching on repentance can be seen on the one hand in the Augustinians Johannes von Dorsten[53] and Johannes von Paltz[54] who are, so to speak, more Scotist than the majority of Scotists. Under the impression that humanity is hardened by sin, they identify the *attritio* sufficient to receive the sacrament of confession with a kind of terrified gallows repentance arising from the 'servile fear' (*timor servilis*) of the punishments of Hell and Purgatory. Among the Scotists, however, it was customary to attribute even the pangs of the imperfect repentance of *attritio* to the love of God.[55] On

---

[52] On the doctrine of repentance in the late medieval Scotist school see above all the works of Valens Heynck, e.g. Heynck: "Zur Lehre von der unvollkommenen Reue in der Skotistenschule des ausgehenden 15. Jahrhunderts", in: *Franziskanische Studien* 24 (1937), pp. 18–58; cf. also Hamm: *Frömmigkeitstheologie* (as in n. 5), pp. 276f. and 280f.

[53] Cf. Zumkeller (as in n. 22), pp. 60–62.

[54] Cf. Hamm: *Frömmigkeitstheologie* (as in n. 5), pp. 276–284.

[55] An exception is the Scotist Stephan Brulefer, a Franciscan, who, like Dorsten and Paltz, understands *attritio* as regret born out of fear and also sees in the transition

the other hand the secular priest Gabriel Biel (†1495), cathedral preacher at Mainz and later professor at Tübingen, also stands under the spell of the Scotist teaching in his understanding of repentance.[56] Already in one of his first sermons at Mainz on 1st January 1458 (at the Feast of Christ's Circumcision) he says that the sacraments of baptism and confession impart grace through the consummation of the sacrament, since no positive emotional impulse in the sense of a congruent contribution (*de congruo*) is required to bring about the infusion of grace. It is sufficient that the recipient is not in a state of unbelief and has not consented to a mortal sin. Such a preparation is not only possible for those who are proficient in spiritual matters; it is also possible for imperfect sinners who still have carnal dispositions. "Behold: Every one who is aware of his own weakness will come to know abundantly how great and precious is the efficacy which lies in the Sacraments."[57]

The Scotist sphere of influence consequently reveals how not only weak flickers of love but also apprehensive dread can be rated positively without any desire to fan the flames of anxiety or to hold people captive in their fear. Such anxieties are integrated into a program of consolation which says to sinful people who do not yet sense any love of God, but only fear of punishment in eternity: Your anx-

---

from *attritio* to *contritio* in justification the shifting of the motive for repentance from fear of punishment to love for God. Cf. Hamm, op. cit. p. 278.

[56] Cf. Wilfrid Werbeck: "Gabriel Biel als spätmittelalterlicher Theologe", in: Ulrich Köpf/Sönke Lorenz (eds.): *Gabriel Biel und die Brüder vom gemeinsamen Leben. Beiträge aus Anlaß des 500. Todestages des Tübinger Theologen* (Stuttgart, 1998) [= Contubernium 47], pp. 25–34; on Biel's activity as cathedral preacher in Mainz (from Christmas 1457 to the end of the church year 1563/64) cf. also Werbeck: *Gabriel Biels fünfter Predigtjahrgang 1463/64. Ein Bericht über die Gießener Hs. 838*, pp. 93–135. On Biel's later scholastic dispute with the attritionism of Duns Scotus see Heiko A. Oberman: *Der Herbst der mittelalterlichen Theologie* (Zürich, 1965) [= Spätscholastik und Reformation, vol. 1], pp. 139–152.

[57] "Sic autem [baptismus et paenitentia] conferunt gratiam ex opere operato, quia ad consequendaum gratiam per ea non requiritur motus bonus interior de congruo sufficiens ad gratiae infusionem, sed sufficit, quod suscipiens ea non ponat obicem infidelitatis, contrariae voluntatis aut consensus in mortale peccatum commissum vel committendum [a little higher on the left margin: secundum Scotum 2.]." "Haec dispositio omnium est, infantium et adultorum, non solum in spiritualibus exercitatorum, verum etiam carnalium adhuc et imperfectorum. Ecce: quanta et quam appretiata sit haec [the last five words on the right margin] utilitas in sacramentis, quisquis propriae infirmitatis conscius satis noscit." 1. Predigtjahrgang Biels, In circumcisione Domini, 1.1.1458: Gießen UB, Hs 827, fol. 18v/19r (I owe the transcript of this text to Wilfrid Werbeck).

iety is a first step towards salvation. It is a good beginning because God can make something positive out of it in the sacraments.

2. A highly-esteemed authority within the circles of pre-Reformation theology of piety was the Dominican mystic Heinrich Seuse (†1366), particularly with the widespread Latin and vernacular circulation of his *Horologium Sapientiae*.[58] In Book I, Chapter 14 he deals in depth with the problem of affective weakness in meditation on the Passion. Here we must remember how intensely the *compassio* of contemplation of Christ's Passion and the sinner's pangs of contrition were seen together in the Late Middle Ages. If you cannot attain the *affectus compassionis*, if you cannot "weep with those who weep" (Rom. 12.15) and "feel pain with the One who suffers (Christ)", then, Seuse advises, you should at least (*saltem*) rejoice and give thanks for the favors shown to you freely through Christ's Passion. But if you cannot do even this and your heart remains emotionally barren and hardened, then entrust yourself with your inability to God's hands, exercise your spirit in concentrated contemplation of the Passion and your body in the physical gestures of piety: stretching out your hands and lifting your eyes to the Crucified One, beating your breast, kneeling, and comparable pious observances. In this way you practice virtue even when the sweetness of the affect is lacking. Seuse praises and recommends this method of intense spiritual exercise, which focuses not on the pleasure of the practitioner, but on what is pleasing to God. His graduated minimal program would be a model for the future: If you lack the feeling of regret then at least have the *intentio*! His solution would also be a touchstone: In the life of a Christian what matters is not the sweetness and exhilaration enjoyed at the present moment but the movement towards future bliss gained by practicing obedience.[59] What is important is not the achieving,

---

[58] On the history of the transmission of Seuses' writings cf. Alois M. Haas/Kurt Ruh: "Seuse, Heinrich OP", in: *Die deutsche Literatur des Mittelalters. Verfasserlexikon*, vol. 8 (Berlin – New York, 1992), cols. 1109–1129: here 1113–1117, on *Horologium Sapientiae* 1116f.

[59] "Quod et si quidem *flere cum flente* aut dolere cum dolente non potes, saltem affectu devoto de tantis beneficiis tibi per eam [scil. passionem] gratuito exhibitis gaudere debes et gratias agere. Quod si nec affectu compassionis nec gratulationis desiderio moveris, sed dura quadam affectione te in eius recordatione deprimi sentis, nihilominus in duritia cordis tui ad laudem dei memoriam huius salutiferae passionis qualitercumque percurre et, quod a te habere non potes, ipsius manibus piissimis committas. Verumtamen persevera petendo, pulsando, quaerendo, donec accipias. *Percute bis silicem* [Num. 20.11], interiori videlicet recordatione et corporali nihilominus

nor the possessing, but the existential movement, the intent – the stretching out, right up to and including the physical gesture.

3. The similarly well-accepted pastoral recommendations of the Franciscan mystic theologian Marquard von Lindau (†1392)[60] go in a parallel direction when he speaks on the question of the correct preparation for receiving the Eucharist. We can recognize in him, too, the characteristic emphases of the Franciscan Scotist doctrine of attrition[61] (even if he himself is no disciple of this doctrine with his demanding scheme of mystical ascent). Particularly noticeable is the marked pastoral concern with its threefold application: (1) the indigence of the poor sinner, (2) the abundance of grace in the sacraments which compensates for all human deficiency and (3) the *facere quod in se est*, the ability to wish and desire on the part of the sinful soul. To the faint-hearted person who feels that he is totally unworthy, Marquard (with reference to Duns Scotus) says that in the Sacrament of the Eucharist God does not look at what the person was or is, but at what he would like to be and what he craves from God. What is important is the *begird*, the sinful soul's yearning for grace and salvation, not its capacity – according to the rule: "(. . .) nach der begird empfechst du got und get got zu dir" ("According to your yearning you receive God and God goes to you"). "Wie selig dann der mensch gern wer, nach der begird und seligkeyt enpfecht er got."[62] "Wer da vil begert, dem wirt ouch vil gege-

---

labore, *te ipsum exercens ad pietatem* [1. Tim. 4.7] per extensionem manuum seu oculorum ad crucifixum sublevationem vel pectoris tunsionem aut genuflexiones devotas vel cetera similia pietatis officia, continuando, donec egrediantur aquae lacrimarum largissime, ut et ratio bibat devotionis aquas et corpus animale eius ex praesentia accensum ad gratiam habilitetur. Quod si forsan causaris te affectum hunc delectabilem et *dulciorem super mel et favum* [Ps. 18.11] rarius experiri, nimirum quia forsitan tentationibus interim exercitaris, multo to virilius agis, si virtutem ipsam non pro delectatione quam experiaris, sed pro virtutibus ipsis et solo beneplacito dei tota intentione, etsi non affectione sectaris. Affectus enim beatitudinis est, exercitium vero virtutis." Heinrich Seuse: *Horologium Sapientiae*, ed. Pius Künzle (Freiburg/ Schweiz, 1977), p. 495,4–24.
   [60] On the history of transmission of Marquard's writings cf. Nigel F. Palmer's article: "Marquard von Lindau OFM", in: *Die deutsche Literatur des Mittelalters. Verfasserlexikon*, vol. 6 (Berlin – New York, 1987), col. 81–126.
   [61] See above p. 105 at n. 52.
   [62] "Das vierd czeichen ist, das der mensch durch sein verloren czeitt willen furcht gottes rach. [. . .] Das nu der mensch in diszem jamer aber nit verczweyfel, so hat sich got dem menschen geben in dem sacrament also, das der mensch mit dem sacrament hat gepusset alle seine verlorene czeitt und hat in dem, das er das sacra-

ben"[63] ("To those who yearn much, much will be given"). People who feel that they are poor without the riches of spiritual virtues, barren without the tears of true repentance and cold without the warmth of love and consequently do not venture to go to the Eucharist may be likened, in his opinion, to one who could approach a treasure only if he brought money with him, or a well only with a pitcher full of water, or a fire only if he were already warm.[64]

---

ment wirdiglich empfangen hat, ein als gut werck gewurcket, das er nit pessers in der czeitt gethun mocht. Und also ist und wirt dem menschen sein jamer gepessert in dem sacrament. Und das das war sey, das bewert uns der Schott [= Duns Scotus]: Als er enpfangen wirt von dem menschen, nit an sicht als er was oder als er ist, mer er sicht jn an nach allen genaden als der mensch gern wer. Als wie got vergiszet aller deiner sunden, die du ye getest, und sicht dich nit an, als du warst ein sunder noch als du zu mol in sunden pist, mer er sicht dein synne an und dein begird. Und als gut, als du geren werest und an got begerest, das du sich geren peszerst, also nach der begird enpfechst du got und get got zu dir und wirt auch also enpfangen, als du geren werst. Und darumb, so sol ein mensch sich nit furchten noch forcht halben das sacrament nit lassen, sunderlichen so dem mensch sein sund leyt sein und geren sich pessert. Wie selig dann der mensch gern wer, nach der begird und seligkeyt enpfecht er got." Marquard von Lindau: Predigt *De corpore Christi*, Nürnberg Stadtbibliothek, Cod. Cent. VI, 60, fol. 79r–106v: here 94r–95r (from Part III,4); on this sermon cf. Palmer (as in n. 60), col. 98f. No. A.6: Part III names "sechs menschliche Schwächen, auf welche Gott durch die Eucharistie mit sechs Zeichen der Minne antwortet" (six human weaknesses, to which God answers through the Eucharist with six signs of love)". I owe the transcription of the text to Antje Willing/Erlangen; cf. also her dissertation: *Literatur und Ordensreform im 15.Jahrhundert. Deutsche Abendmahlsschriften im Nürnberger Katharinenkloster. Mit textkritischer Ausgabe der Sakramentspredigten des Gerhard Comitis OP (Nürnberg, Stadtbibliothek: Cod. Cent. VI, 52, fol. 277r–314v)*, Diss. phil. typescript (Erlangen, 2000), on Marquard von Lindau pp. 261–361.

[63] Marquard von Lindau: *Eucharistie-Traktat*, ed. Annelies Julia Hofmann (Tübingen, 1960) [= Hermaea 7], p. 303,10f.; cf. p. 301,16–20: In the sacrament of the eucharist "der milt herre" will not "mit dem menschen umb sin schuld rechnen, ob [= falls] er kumet mit waren ruwen. Noch will er in nit ansehen, als er ist gewesen, mer als er gern were, ob er echt kumt mit vollkomner gantzer begird." On this tract, which reworked the sermon cited in n. 62 and contributed to its very widespread reception in southern Germany cf. Palmer, op. cit., col. 99–103 No. A. 7.

[64] Op. cit. (ed. Hofmann), pp. 303,16–304,11, e.g. the closing passage: "Die tůnd ze glicher wise, als ein kalter mensch wer, der hitze begerte und er ein heisses fur [= Feuer] wussete, zů dem er doch nit gan wollte, er wurd denn vor warm und enzundet. Sich, diese lute wussent nit, das sich der riche kung [= König] so uss grosser minne hat gesetzet in das edel sacrament mit allem sinem schatz und richeit und begerte anders nit, denn dz der mensch sines schatzes kouffte mit minne und begirden. Owe dar umb alle armen hertzen an [= ohne] tugenden, alle turre hertzen an heissen trehen, alle laewe hertzen an goetlicher minne, kerend zů dirre edelen spise, gant zů disem richen kramer und begerend allein, so wirt uch geben! Minnent allein von gantzem hertzen sinen schatz, so wirt uch nit verseit alles des, dz ir begerent!" The final sentence reformulates the scholastic axiom: "Facientibus quod in se est deus non denegat gratiam."

The effects and further development of Marquard's ideas and metaphors can be seen, for example, in a sermon on the sacrament of the altar, delivered by a Father Sigmund of whom no further details are known.[65] He too was a Franciscan, and his sermon, which has been handed down in a manuscript from the mid-15th century, was probably addressed to nuns. Where he writes of the doubts of people whose sense of spiritual inadequacy makes them shrink from receiving the Eucharist, his words call to mind Marquard's way of looking at the problem. Yet the way in which he describes the plight of the female sinners who feel totally incapable and insensitive is even more intensely dramatic. They feel and lament not only their deficiencies in the virtues, in repentance and in love, but also an utter absence of sincere, reverent yearning for the Eucharist; totally despondent, they shrink from the sacrament: "Oh, woe! I dare not go to it, for I am cold, I am no more than lukewarm, I am empty, without any grace, I am cold. Woe! There is no warmth in me, nor devotion. Woe! There is no longing nor love in me, nor any desire for the eucharistic food. I am so barren of grace, I can neither pray, nor meditate, nor do any good thing; I am incapable of any good, I dare not go, I can find in myself neither repentance nor sorrow for my sin."[66]

In the theological and pastoral therapy of encouragement he delivers in his sermon, Sigmund (like Marquard) uses the metaphors of treasure, well and fire, augmenting them with two others equally vivid: the table richly set for the hungry, and the doctor by whom the patient is healed.[67] The decisive point is always that the person

---

[65] The title reads: "Diese predige det uns der wirdig vater Sygmund der barfüss in der pfingswuchen und seit von dem heiligen sacrament, wie man sich vor und noch halten sol. 'Parasti in conspectu meo mensam' [Vulg.-Ps. 22.5] etc." Edited in: Kurt Ruh, Dagmar Ladisch-Grube, Josef Brecht (eds.): *Franziskanisches Schrifttum im deutschen Mittelalter, vol. II: Texte* (München – Zürich, 1985), pp. 100–116; cf. also Ruh's article "Vater Siegmund OFM", in: *Die deutsche Literatur des Mittelalters. Verfasserlexikon*, vol. 8 (Berlin – New York, 1992), col. 1206f.

[66] "Owe, ich dar nit dar gon, ich bin also kalt und also lew und also treg, an allen genoden bin ich kalt. Owe, es ist kein hitz in mir noch andacht. Owe, es ist weder minn noch liebe in mir, noch kein begird zü der spis. Ich bin also dürr an genoden, ich mag weder beten noch betrachten noch nütz gütes tün, ich bin ungeschickt zü allem güten, ich getar nit dar gon, ich fund weder rüw noch leid in mir über min sund." Edition (as in n. 65), p. 109,293–298 with context in lines 283–307.

[67] Op. cit. pp. 110,308–112,369.

does not have to bring any aptitude, virtue or ability to the sacrament but simply his need, his yearning for healing and heavenly riches, after which he receives everything freely given in the gift of the eucharistic body. "So go to the most worthy sacrament! There will I show you the doctor who can heal you body and soul. This doctor can make all your illnesses well. He can heal all your wounds, because he comes to all who desire him. He brings the dead soul to life. If the soul is leprous, he cleanses it of every stain and blemish. If you are blind, he is the light. If you dwell in the darkness of sin, he is the day. If you are dead, he is life. If you are mute and deaf, he is the truth. If you have strayed, he is the path that can and will guide you. You need not travel far to buy this medicine. Thus turn back to him (. . .) Receive the precious treasure of the most worthy sacrament. If you are poor in virtues, it is the treasure and the chest in which everything good is contained; in it you will find whatever your heart desires".[68]

It is clear from the advice Sigmund gives that he stands in the Franciscan tradition of Marquard. Like the latter he too emphasizes that with the sacramental gift of grace God does not respond to an individual's particular spiritual capabilities, but to his wishes and desires, his reaching out and yearning. The longing to be pardoned and the craving for salvation are central concepts for him too – even when he addresses people who think they no longer have any yearning (*begird*) for the sacrament of the altar. Consequently he counsels the faint-hearted to appeal to God from the depths of their desire for salvation, forgetting their own spiritual poverty: "Ask him what you will, and he will hear you according to your wish and desire".[69]

---

[68] "So gang zü dem hochwürdigen sacrament, do will ich dir den artzet zöigen, der dich gesund kan machen an lip und an sel. Der arztet kan alle siechdagen [= Krankheiten] gesund machen. Er kan alle wunden heilen, wenn [= denn] alle, die sin begerent, zü denen kunt [= kommt] er. Die toten selen macht er lebendig. Ist die sel ussetzig, er macht sy rein von allen flecken vnd von allen mosen [= makeln]. Bistu blind, er ist daz liecht. Bistu vinster in den sunden, er ist der dag. Bistu tot, er ist daz leben. Bist ein stum und horstu nit, so ist er die worheit. Bistu irrig, er ist der weg, der dih furen kan und wil [. . .] Du bedarfft nit verr [= fern] gon köffen die arztenig. Dorumb so ker dich zü im [. . .] Enpfach den edlen schatz in dem hochwirdigen sacrament. Bistu arm an tugenden, so ist er der richtûm vnd der schatz, in dem alles güt beschlossen ist, in dem du vindest waz din hertz begeren mag." Op. cit. p. 111,347–363.
[69] "Bit in, waz du wilt, und er erhört dich noch dinem willen und begirden." Op. cit. p. 112,2f.

At the same time, however, it seems to me that the comparison of the two Franciscan preachers shows clearly that the high standard demanded by Marquard, even as he encourages frightened consciences in preparation for communion, is lowered by Sigmund. Marquard speaks of a "true repentance",[70] a "whole-hearted love"[71] and a "perfect, complete yearning"[72] with which a sinner should approach the Eucharist, there to purchase Christ's riches "with love and yearning".[73] In Sigmund there is no longer any mention of such a provision, but simply of yearning and pleading. It is typical of his approach that in the course of the sermon he later discusses the spiritual plight of those sisters who experience no feelings of grace, sweetness, reverence and love, even *after* receiving the sacrament. To such he gives the same advice: not to despair, but "with yearning hearts" to beseech God in prayer for grace and love.[74]

The differences between Marquard and Sigmund are perhaps characteristic of the change between the latter half of the 14th and the middle of the 15th centuries. In contrast to a highly mystical understanding of the union of the soul with God, its submissive devotion to Jesus and its feelings of a blissful sweetness, Sigmund takes the experiences of spiritual inadequacy which beset his time and integrates them in an understanding of spiritual existence altered 'downwards' – an existence which has a spiritual quality even without any mystical experience of ardour, sweetness or regeneration. He sees as its foundation the rudimentary desires, aspirations and prayers to God of the soul, standing before him poor and empty-handed, craving from him all the riches of his grace and salvation. This is the basis of the late Franciscan theology of poverty forged by Duns Scotus and his school out of which, towards the end of the 15th and the beginning of the 16th centuries, theologians such as Stephan Fridolin and Johannes von Paltz were able to develop their minimal program for the weak or faint-hearted.[75] The language of this tra-

---

[70] Cf. above n. 63 and in the eucharistic tract quoted there also p. 300,20–23.

[71] Cf. above n. 64: "minnet allein von gantzem hertzen".

[72] Cf. above n. 63; also in the eucharistic tract p. 303,14f: "Won [= Denn] hand sie volkomen begird, jn wirt ouch volkomenlich gegeben."

[73] Cf. above n. 64; also in the eucharistic tract p. 303,9f: "Won [= Denn] in dem wirdigen sacrament hat er all sin gaben veil und verkouffet si umb minne."

[74] Vater Sigmund: Eucharistie-Predigt (as in n. 65), pp. 114,443–116,539; "mit begirlichen hertzen", p. 114,444.

[75] Cf. above p. 98 at n. 28.

dition lingers on in Luther's words in 1520: "Therefore no one can or should reap any benefit from the mass unless he grieves and yearns for the grace of God, and longs to be free of his sin and comes to desire this testament [of grace]".[76]

4. Finally let us mention the strand of tradition found in the writings of Jean Gerson (†1429), Chancellor of the University of Paris, who more than any other set the agenda and provided the inspiration for the theology of piety in the 15th century.[77] In his works it is particularly noteworthy how he places the doubts about one's own ability at the center of a spirituality for troubled souls. Gerson, too, formulates a comforting program of minimal human desire and ability on the basis of *facere quod in se est*.[78] Admittedly, he sees as a higher stage the way of a mystical theology, when a person is no longer in the least fixated upon his own ability or inability but, consistently and humbly doubting his own spiritual adequacy, flies to God's compassion and finds certainty of hope solely in the promises of this mercy.[79] For Gerson, to transcend the question of one's own

---

[76] "Derhalben sol unnd kan auch niemant fruchtparlich bey der messe sein, er sey dan in betrubnisz und begirden gotlicher gnaden und seiner sund gerne losz were odder, sol ehr yhe in bosem fursatz ist, das er doch unter der mesz sich wandele und vorlangen gewinne disses testamentes." Martin Luther: "Von den guten Werken", *WA* 6,230,34–231,2; quoted from: *Martin Luther Studienausgabe*, Hans-Ulrich Delius (ed.) vol. 2 (Berlin – Ost, 1982), p. 44,3–7.

[77] Cf. Christoph Burger's article: "Gerson, Johannes (1363–1429)", in *Theologische Realenzyklopädie* 12 (1984), pp. 532–538; on reception of Gerson cf. Herbert Kraume's article: "Gerson, Johannes (Jean Charlier de Gerson)", in: *Die deutsche Literatur des Mittelalters. Verfasserlexikon*, vol. 2 (Berlin – New York, 1980), col. 1266–1274. On Gerson as advocate, representative and pioneer of the theology of piety cf. Burger: *Aedificatio, Fructus, Utilitas. Johannes Gerson als Professor der Theologie und Kanzler der Universität Paris* (Tübingen, 1986) [= Beiträge zur historischen Theologie 70]; Grosse (as in n. 40); Hamm: *Frömmigkeitstheologie* (as in n. 5), especially pp. 136–175.

[78] On Gerson's "Strategie der Mindestforderung" (Grosse) see above p. 101 with n. 41.

[79] On the two stages in Gerson's comforting of the conscience, i.e. the dimension of minimal demand and the dimension of sure and certain hope quite apart from all human virtue, cf. the study by Grosse (as in n. 40), pp. 75–131 and elsewhere. On Gerson's characterization of human spiritual humility as 'Verzweiflung an sich selbst' cf. below p. 159 with n. 20. The question would be worth clarifying whether and in what context this theologically pointed expression of Gerson's is to be found in theologians before or alongside him.

ability is, so to speak, an ability of a higher order. Someone who commits himself to divine mercy and from his own subjective view-point stands empty-handed before God, reveals with this attitude the real, objective riches of religious merit and worthiness before God.[80] But it is characteristic of the changed situation in the 15th century that the peak of spiritual ability is expressed in this precise way and not otherwise: as total resignation and doubt in one's own ability and as praise of God's infinite mercy, the *sola misericordia dei*. Here Gerson was a pioneer.[81]

VI. *A Vigorous Theology of Mercy, circa 1500: Johannes von Staupitz in comparison with the Late Franciscan Tradition*

Two theologians who around 1500 emphatically endorsed Gerson's understanding of self-resignation and the flight to God's mercy were Johannes Geiler von Kayserberg (1445–1510), the preacher at the Cathedral Church in Strasbourg, and the Augustinian monk, Johannes von Staupitz, head of the German Observant Augustinian Congrega-tion. Staupitz, it must be said, represents an essentially different type of theological-pastoral exoneration which I have not yet touched upon. Geiler (like Stephan Fridolin and Johannes von Paltz in their different ways) stands with Gerson on the foundations of the late Franciscan doctrine of free will, for which the individual – even as a mortal sinner – is in principle master of his own will, able to turn it either to God or to the Devil.[82] Staupitz, however, is one of the

---

[80] On the fundamental distinction, arising from the study of the medieval theo-logical and religious sources, between a "verobjektivierenden und verallgemeinern-den Aussageebene" (of belief) and a more "subjektiv-existentiellen Aussageebene" (of love, humility and hope), between a reflective form of doctrinal speech and an immediate form of speech in prayer, see below pp. 158–163.

[81] On Gerson's *sola misericordia* dei in the context of the 15th century, see above p. 11 n. 27.

[82] On this late Franciscan position of Geiler, in which the Scotist and Occamist ingredients can hardly be separated, see E. Jane Dempsey Douglass: *Justification in Late Medieval Preaching. A Study of John Geiler of Keisersberg* (Leiden, 1966) [= Studies in Medieval and Reformation Thought 1], with the problematic assertion of Geiler's nominalism; on the aspects of *sola misericordia dei* and *totalis de se desperatio* see there pp. 162–176, especially p. 168 n. 4, p. 169f. n. 1 and 4, p. 171 n. 5, also above pp. 73–86. Cf. Geiler's "Sterbe-ABC" (1497), 19. Regel, in: *Sämtliche Werke* (as in n. 43), vol. 1 (Berlin – New York, 1989), p. 107,13–20: "Tucken [= sich ducken] und sich demuteclichen trucken [= niederdrücken] durch ein gantze verzwyfelung

rare late-medieval proponents of a radical Augustinian doctrine of the bondage of the will.[83] This means that for Staupitz there is no trace of any religious ability prior to the influx of justifying grace; consequently, there can be no emotional preparation for the reception of grace, not even the slightest inclination, desire or regret. Grace itself kindles a spiritual capacity in the person, and with it the heartfelt emotions of a true remorse for sin rising out of a love of God which is worthy to be called 'repentance'.[84] It is interesting that Staupitz, too, develops a graduated minimal program of the pangs of regret – not, however, like Paltz, Dorsten and the Scotists, during the stage before the reception of justifying grace, but thereafter, in the life of one born again through justification. In general, Staupitz does not place much value on feelings of terror or anxiety. The gradations which he makes denote stages *within* the new, trusting relationship of the soul to God.

In one of his Lenten sermons at Nuremberg in the spring of 1517 (preserved in the transcript of Lazarus Spengler, secretary to the city council), [85] Staupitz mentions four aspects of the inadequacy of human repentance. At the same time he shows four ways out of the dilemma

---

an synen verdiensten und krefften. Hůt dich in der stund dynes sterbens vor hochfart, vermessenheit und üppigem wolgefallen dyner gůten werck, sunder all din hoffnung und vertrüwen setz in das lyden, sterben und verdienst unsers lieben herren Jesu Christi. Wann [= denn] alle unser gerechtikeiten falsch sind und vor der angesicht gottes als eyn befleckt, unrein tuch [Jes 64.6 Vulg.]."

[83] On Staupitz cf. above n. 1; here see especially David Curtis Steinmetz: *Misericordia Dei. The Theology of Johannes von Staupitz in its Late Medieval Setting* (Leiden, 1968) [= Studies in Medieval and Reformation Thought 4]; Heiko A. Oberman: *Werden und Wertung der Reformtion. Vom Wegestreit zum Glaubenskampf* (Tübingen, 1977], pp. 82–140 (ch. 6: Augustinrenaissance im späten Mittelalter), on Staupitz pp. 97–118.

[84] On Staupitz' understanding of penitence cf. Lothar Graf zu Dohna, Richard Wetzel: "Die Reue Christi: zum theologischen Ort der Buße bei Johann von Staupitz", in: *Studien und Mitteilungen zur Geschichte des Benediktiner-Ordens und seiner Zweige* 94 (1983), pp. 457–482; see below pp. 142–146.

[85] Staupitz: Nürnberger Predigtstücke, in: Joachim Karl Friedrich Knaake (ed.): *Johann von Staupitzens sämmtliche Werke, vol. 1: Deutsche Schriften* (Potsdam, 1867), pp. 15–42; the sermon on penitence cited below is on pp. 15–19. – Spengler's records of Staupitz' sermons are of high quality and in the case of the sermon on penitence particularly detailed (whereas with other sermons often only a short excerpt is recorded). The city clerk of Nuremberg had both the necessary writing skill and the theological competence to reproduce Staupitz's words and thoughts adequately, so that his accounts can be taken as authentic evidence for Staupitz' preaching style. A comparison with work that Staupitz himself wrote and published, particularly with the contemporary leaflet *De exsecutione aeternae praedestinationis*, reveals no kind of difference, rather a high degree of theological and terminological agreement.

caused by the sinner's inability to produce what is required of him: a "satisfactory" repentance, sufficient "zu abtilgung der sunden und erlangung gotlicher barmherzigkait" ("to wipe out his sins and attain divine mercy"):[86]

1. Because it is merely a *human* remorse, even the authentic, love-inspired sorrow which God kindles through grace in the heart of the sinner is so pitifully small that it can in no way achieve the forgiveness of sins by its own emotional quality. It is only the immeasurably precious grief for the sins of the world that Christ vicariously offered in Gethsemane, together with the spiritual sufferings of his Passion, that compensate for all the shortcomings of our human repentance and, as it were, raise them up to God; only then can our remorse merit the divine forgiveness of all our guilt and punishment. Consequently, says Staupitz, if we are truly sorry for our sins we should pray humbly to God to "unser rew unvolkomenhait mit seiner rew und schmerzlichen traurigkait erfullen" ("supplement our inadequate repentance with his repentance and aching sadness").[87]

2. In examining the spiritual deficiencies of repentance Staupitz admittedly goes beyond establishing its inadequacy in principle *coram deo* when he turns to the degree of human repentance and lowers the sights on what is humanly possible. In fact the pain of genuine, sincere repentance required to wipe out all punishment for sin should be as great as the "wollust" (pleasure) which was enjoyed in perpetrating the sin. But since it is difficult "zu einer solchen hohen rew zu komen" ("to reach such a high degree of remorse") God in his merciful forbearance contents himself with a lesser degree of ability to repent on the part of the sinner if the latter does the best he can – *facit quod in se est* – with real pangs of regret and entrusts himself to the saving efficacy of Christ's Passion. Here once again ("abermals") Staupitz refers to the christological compensation which supplements the shortcomings of human penitence.[88]

---

[86] Ed. Knaake op. cit. p. 18.

[87] Op. cit. p. 16f. with the words cited on p. 17.

[88] Op. cit. p. 17f. with the decisive passage: "Wiewol nun gar beschwerlich ist, zu ainer solchen hohen rew zu komen, will doch got der almechtig als ein parmherziger vater, wo wir durch ein geordente rew hierin unnser vermogen thun [= facimus quod in nobis est] und uns der mitwurcklichen krafft und erfullung [= Ausfüllung, Ergänzung] des pluts Christi underwerffen, abermals gedult tragen, uns auch nit verlassen, sonder unser purg [= Bürge] und selbhelfer [= in eigener Person unser Helfer] sein, also was auff moglichen ankerten vleis [= auf allen uns möglichen

3. In a further step Staupitz looks at the need of such people who are truly and sincerely penitent but doubt whether this is "genu(n)gsam" (sufficient) to wipe out the debt and punishment for their sin. The typical late-medieval question of qualitatively and quantitatively sufficient penitence is here sharpened to the haunting question of the mandatory quota of remorse. The Augustinian preacher can encourage "burdened souls" with "good Christian consolation" that the cumulative way of repeated acts of repentance is open for them: "Even if a person is not able to repent enough at one time and all at once as necessity demands, he should frequently feel displeasure for his sins and experience a passionate penitence, the more often the better and more fruitful. The pain will also be amplified through this manifold remorse since 'a little, often, makes a lot'; thus the number of pains and regrets will become sufficient to wipe out the sins and to obtain divine mercy and grace."[89] This third aspect of deficiency and 'becoming sufficient' is, in comparison to the other three, more of a secondary aspect.

4. As we have noted, the sinner was expected to be frequently and "passionately" penitent. Yet Staupitz finally comes to the disillusioned conclusion that things usually happen differently in confession, and that there is a discrepancy between what is said and what is felt. Customarily, penitents assure the father confessor that they repent from the bottom of the heart ("von grundt seins herzens") the sins they name and any that may have been forgotten, and they claim that these cause real regret. But this confession of the mouth very rarely corresponds to a true repentance of the heart which is based on love of God. In view of this fundamental crisis of repentance which relates to the "rechten grundt" (genuine basis) of penitence,

---

daran gekehrten Eifer hin] an unns erwindet [= an uns fehlt, uns ermangelt], das solchs an ime als unserm erloser und purgen zugee und erstatet werd [= zu seinen Lasten gehe und von ihm ergänzt werde]. Und ob wol [= wenn auch] in berewung unser sunden der schmertz des herzens so gross und reichlich nit ist, das er sich mit dem wollust [der] begangen[en] sunden mag vergleichen, so will sich doch der almechtig abermaln an menschlichem vermogen begnugen lassen [. . .]"

[89] "Ob wol ein mensch uff einzeit und einmal so genungsam rew, wie die nothurfft erfordert, nit haben mag, sol er doch den misfal seiner sunden und ein hitzige berewung zu offtermalen, und ye offter ye pesser und fruchtbarer, furnemen. Durch diese gemanigfaltige rew wirdet auch der schmertz gemert, dann offt wenig macht einmal vil, also das dodurch die menig des schmerzens und berewens zu abtilgung der sunden und erlangung gotlicher barmherzigkait und gnad genugsam wirdet." Op. cit. p. 18.

Staupitz, too, takes up the advice common at the time, which was also so highly respected by Paltz: "*doleas, quod non doleas!*"[90] Characteristic of his solution, however, is that, unlike Paltz, Dorsten and the Scotists, Staupitz does not find the compensation for insufficient penitence in the transforming power of the sacrament, or in the priest's power of absolution, but rather in the direct relationship of prayer between the sinner, God, and the crucified Christ. In so doing Staupitz once again ("abermaln") gives a variation of the christological constant of his preaching, in that the person as penitent is always dependant on the compensation Christ's suffering provides for his human insufficiency. Thus he gives a new turn to the challenge to feel pain for absent pain, or repentance for insufficient repentance, which leads us back again to the first and second aspects of insufficiency, even to the appearance of individual formulations: "Ob er wol kain volkomene rew erlangen mag, so sol er doch uber das einen hertzlichen schmerzen und rewen nemen und haben, das ime uber sein moglichen vleis[91] an genungsamer rew mangelt [marginal note: *doleo quod non doleo*], und got den almechtigen abermaln ermanen, diesen mangel durch sein pitters leiden und plutvergisen zu erfullen und neben seiner geprechenlichen rew ain parmherziger mitwurcker zu sein. Bedarff es nit zweiffels: Got wil sich an vermogen ains menschen setigen lassen und diesem rewer sein gnad nit entziehen" ("If the person cannot achieve perfect penitence, he should have and hold a heart-felt pain and penitence for the fact that it is beyond his ability to have sufficient penitence [marginal note: 'I grieve that I do not grieve'], and implore the almighty God to supplement this deficiency through his bitter sufferings and the shedding of his blood, asking that God become a merciful partner in the sinner's weak repentance. Have no doubt: God will be satisfied by what one is capable of doing and will not withdraw his grace from this penitent").[92] As a theologian and pastor, Staupitz is not an Attritionist; rather, he sees the beginnings of repentance in a heartfelt love of God and grief over the offense one's sins give to God.[93] Nevertheless, in his expla-

---

[90] On Paltz see above p. 97 at n. 24.

[91] The meaning is: above and beyond his 'facere quod in se est', in spite of his efforts according to his ability.

[92] Staupitz: Nürnberger Predigtstücke (as in n. 85), p. 18f. The closing sentence is once again an adaptation of the scholastic axiom: "*Facientibus quod in se est deus non denegat gratiam.*" Cf. above n. 64.

[93] Cf. Luthers emphatic reference to the fact that it was Staupitz who instructed

nation of a 'sufficient' *contritio* he lowers the minimum expected from the repentant sinner and his *facere quod in se est*. The graded movement of his preaching leads from the "greatest pain" ("hochsten schmerz") of one who is totally overcome by Christ's sufferings[94] through the lesser remorse of one who is still genuinely penitent, to the pain felt for the lack of penitential pain. He tells both the weak and the anxious that the love of God makes it possible for human repentance to consist simply of running to God's mercy with earnest plea, and placing complete trust in the protective effect of Christ's Passion.[95]

I think it significant that Staupitz, the Augustinian Professor at Wittenberg stands together with Paltz, his fellow-Augustinian and Erfurt colleague, at a final stage of the late-medieval endeavor to transfer the weight of salvation from the side of the spiritual quality and activity of mankind to the side of God's gracious, saving mercy. Hence in the 15th and the early years of the 16th centuries, the four influential strands of an exonerating pastoral theology which I have sketched experienced a kind of impetus and sharpening. Paltz shows how far one could go in such endeavors on the basis of a late Franciscan doctrine of free will, following the consequences of this position to a minimum of personal will and ability. Staupitz, on the other hand, shows how one could go still further on the basis of an Augustinian doctrine of the bondage of the will and of predestination, in the tradition of mystical theology,[96] through a very intense interpretation of the vicarious and communicative support of Christ's sufferings. In his theology not only does any trace of ethical goodness in humanity before and apart from the working of God's justifying grace vanish; Staupitz also emphasizes man's total incapacity to obtain sufficient or deserved remission or reward from God through his own heartfelt emotions and works of love even *within*

---

him that love for God and his righteousness is not the end but the beginning of repentance: Luther to Staupitz, 30th May 1518: *WA* 1,525–527. On the interpretation, see below pp. 143–152. On the aspect of giving offence to God cf. Staupitz: Nürnberger Predigtstücke (as in n. 85), p. 16f.

[94] Staupitz: Nürnberger Predigtstücke (as in n. 85), p. 16f.

[95] Cf. esp. op. cit. pp. 22–25 the Predigtstück entitled: "Wie der mensch durch ain vertrewlich gemute und hoffen got dem almechtigen verainigt werden und aus menig seiner sunden an gotes parmherzigkait nit verzweiffeln sol".

[96] Staupitz' view of the immediacy of the soul to God/Christ ("den edeln gespons unser selen", op. cit. p. 16f.) and the mystical union with him is clearly echoed in the sermon title just quoted (n. 95).

the effective field of infused grace. The satisfaction and merit of Christ's Passion must always coalesce with our insufficiency and compensate for it, for only then is a satisfaction and merit on the human side possible. Even if a person were to feel the greatest, most heartfelt and love-inspired penitence that one can have, if it were not embedded in the penitence of Christ it would be incapable of wiping out the guilt and punishment of even a single mortal sin.[97] In this theological context Gerson's idea of self-doubt[98] also takes on a new significance. It is not simply a subjective gesture of humility but corresponds to the actual objective situation of the justified sinner before God. He really has every reason to doubt his own capabilities – including his spiritual ability – and to put his hope exclusively on that mercy of God which chose him before the beginning of time and to which God remains true.[99]

VII. *The Insufficiency of Human Satisfaction and the Infinite Value of the Satisfaction of Jesus Christ*

The aspects of human inability and minimal capacity discussed in the previous paragraphs related particularly to the first stage of repentance, prior to the reception of the sacraments of confession and the Eucharist. I pass over another problem era recognized by contemporaries, the "scrupulous" confession – which was likewise weighed down by the dilemma of what one should yet cannot do,[100] and gave rise to corresponding attempts by father confessors to relieve fears[101] –

---

[97] Staupitz op. cit. p. 16: "so gros kann des menschen nit rew sein [. . .], das sie ain ainige begangne todsundt ablesch."

[98] Cf. above p. 113 with n. 79.

[99] On despairing of oneself in Staupitz cf. Hamm: *Frömmigkeitstheologie* (as in n. 5), p. 222 with n. 34.

[100] Cf. Hamm op. cit. p. 218f. On compulsive features of fixation on a perfect confession in the late Middle Ages see also Johan Huizinga: *Herbst des Mittelalters. Studien über Lebens- und Geistesformen des 14. und 15. Jahrhunderts in Frankreich und in den Niederlanden*, 11th edition of the German translation, edited by Kurt Köster (Stuttgart, 1975), pp. 258–260.

[101] In this case too Johannes von Paltz is typical of a particular late medieval tendency when in the case of the gravely ill he comes to the solution that it is not the performance of confession but the will to confess that counts: "si non possunt confiteri et libenter vellent, tunc nihilominus virtute sacramenti extremae unctionis eorum attritio fit contritio". *Supplementum Coelifodinae* (as in n. 5), p. 244,15–17.

and turn at least briefly to the final part of penitence, namely expiation (*satisfactio*).

The work of Staupitz demonstrates particularly well how closely the problems of genuine repentance are bound up with the question of a fully valid satisfaction in the late-medieval pastoral care of penitents. In his Lenten sermons in Nuremberg, we see the expiatory dimension of (lifelong) penitence particularly where he relates the question of "genu(n)gsamen rew" (sufficient repentance) to liberation, both from the everlasting punishments for sin in hell and from the temporary punishments of purgatory.[102] Here Staupitz stands solidly within a common late-medieval tradition: In the 15th century theology of piety, repentance was held in principle to be expiatory with regard to temporal punishments for sin. It is, as it were, an inner expiation of the soul, rather than the canceling of disciplinary punishments meted out by the Church in the form of physical acts or voluntary suffering. Confession too should be seen in this light insofar as it can also be understood as a kind of expiation, a verbal expiation corresponding to the fact that one has not only sinned in thoughts and deeds but also in words.[103]

But the matter of expiation for sin gives rise to precisely those basic questions which we have already encountered, particularly with regard to repentance and regret: How much or how little is man capable of before God? Can he not at least desire what is good, or desire to desire it? Can God accept the desire for the deed, particularly in the case of weakness and mortal anguish, if the person can do no more? How much desire is necessary, how much unwillingness and inability is pardonable? How much vicarious compensation is achieved by Christ's Passion, and the intercession of Mary and the saints? How much can the living help the dead by prayers, indulgences, and votive masses? The answers we have already found can be corroborated and further developed. Above all we could show that the same development can be observed in dealing with the topic of expiation which leapt to the eye with the problem of remorse.

---

[102] Cf. Staupitz: Nürnberger Predigtstücke (as in n. 85), e.g. p. 17; on this see Hamm: *Frömmigkeitstheologie* (as in n. 5), p. 240.

[103] On the understanding of repentance and confession as satisfaction cf. e.g. one of the sermons of the Dominican Johannes Diemar: in Lee (as in n. 46), p. 231. In regard to the satisfactory effectiveness of confession he formulates the rule: "so vil eins diemutigerlicher und unterscheidlicher sagt, so vil mer legt er die sund ab".

Late-medieval pastoral theology is particularly innovative in shifting emphasis from human ability and action to the vicarious, exonerating activity of divine mercy and mediation.[104] It should be noted that, even in this theology of intensified grace and mercy, the axiom of the equity remains unquestioned: The heavenly Judge with his avenging righteousness leaves no sin unpunished.[105] Since God remains true to his just nature, the equivalent satisfaction for sins is necessary. Yet at all stages of human life – including the distressing problem of sufficient expiation – the principle of representation and intercession counters this unbending principle of justice. God is just, but to an even higher degree he is merciful; thus he himself provides for the expiation. Christ takes the punishment upon himself on the cross and provides satisfaction for sinners, though they themselves must take some active part in the expiation, however minimal. Original sin can be forgiven them for Christ's sake alone without expiation on their part since they took no active, deliberate part in it. Sins of commission, however, demand an expiatory participation since sinners themselves subjectively committed their transgressions. Because they now willingly and actively furnish a minimum expiation of their own – e.g. by a meditative and emotional contemplation on Christ's Passion – the whole work of salvation in that expiatory Passion comes to benefit them. The minimal contribution of their own reverence is as it were the key to open the immeasurable riches of the vicarious expiation of the Son of God.

Heinrich Seuse expresses the astonishing liberating effect of the Passion in an exemplary way when, contemplating the long and fearsome punishments of purgatory, he cries: Oh long and terrible agony![106] "But see how each person could compensate for (*compensare*)

---

[104] Cf. above p. 104 at n. 49.

[105] Cf. Arnold Angenendt: "Deus, qui nullum peccatum impunitum dimittit. Ein 'Grundsatz' der mittelalterlichen Bußgeschichte", in: Matthias Lutz-Bachmann (ed.): *Und dennoch ist von Gott zu reden, Festschrift für Herbert Vorgrimler* (Freiburg i.Br. – Basel – Wien, 1994), pp. 142–156. Cf. also the following footnote.

[106] In the context of the question of the satisfactory effect of meditation on the Passion in respect of the punishments of purgatory Seuse says: "Qualiter autem haec utilissima meditatio poenam purgatorii relaxare habeat, tibi indicabo. En autor naturae nil inordinatum in sua natura relinquit; sed nec divina iustitia quidquam mali impunitum dimittit, quod non aut hic aut in futuro debitae subiciat correctioni. [...] O nimis longa miserae animae exspectatio! O diutina et acerba nimium cruciatio! Dolor perseverans et immensus! Paenitentia gravior omni terrestri cruciatu!" Seuse: Horologium Sapientiae, lib. 1,14 (as in n. 59), p. 496,9–19.

these punishments by the easiest and briefest expiation if he knew how to take it from the riches of the Passion of the spotless Lamb. These riches, of the greatest value because they come from the greatest love, the worthiest person and the most immense agony, are always available in sufficient, overflowing abundance. Thus one could receive them in such a way, and with a reverent attitude gain for himself so much of their merit and expiation that, even if he deserved to be cleansed (in Purgatory) for a thousand years, he would be freed from all punishment in one moment (*in brevi de toto liberaretur*)."[107] "The merest drop of my most precious blood" says Christ "is sufficient for the redemption and expiation of the whole world."[108] The greatest burdens of punishment which God's righteousness lays upon sinners become through Christ's vicarious mediation a bare residuum of punishment which can easily be wiped out in the brief span of this life.[109]

In these statements, expressed in the framework of the intensified Passion-piety of his time, Seuse formulated the fundamental solution of the dilemma caused by the necessity to make expiation and the inability to make expiation – even if the details concerning the nature of the individual's contribution and the role indulgences might play remained controversial. Around 1500 a tract – clearly Franciscan – entitled "On Divine Love"[110] connected the obligation and ability of the justified sinner with the fundamental or supplementary expiation and merit of Christ's Passion by means of two principles grounded

---

[107] "Sed vide, quod hanc poenam levissima et brevissima satisfactione compensare posset, quicumque ipsam de thesauro passionis agni immaculati sciret recipere. Hic namque thesaurus pretiosissimus propter caritatem maximam personamque dignissimam ac dolorem immensissimum sufficiens et superabundans exstat; et ideo taliter posset se homo ad hunc applicare et de eius merito et satisfactione tam devote ad se trahere, ut si mille annis deberet purgari, in brevi de toto liberaretur." Op. cit. p. 496,19–26.

[108] "Postea meritum passionis meae debes summo cum affectu extollere et magnificare cogitando, quoniam *apud me copiosissima est redemptio* [Vulg.-Ps. 129.7] et quod minima gutta pretiosissimi sanguinis, qui per omnes partes corporis mei vulneribus repleti largiter effluxit, pro redemptione et satisfactione totius mundi suffecisset." Op. cit. p. 497,20–24.

[109] On the terms 'brief' (brevis) and 'easy' (levis) cf. op. cit. p. 497,5f.

[110] Title: "Von der gotlichen lieb etliche gütte stucklen zu mercken"; edited in: Ruh, Ladisch-Grube, Brecht (eds.): *Franziskanisches Schrifttum* (as in n. 65), pp. 232–247 (at the end the date: 1508). According to the editors' information the manuscript collection containing this tract and preserved in the Bamberg Staatsbibliothek came from the convent of the Clares in either Bamberg or Nuremberg.

on a fundamental axiom: it is by virtue of Christ's suffering and
only in the context of its effectiveness that a person has the possibility of making satisfaction for all that he owes God ("das er gott
mag genüg thün für alles, das er gott schüldig ist").[111] First, it is certain that: "Was der mensch nit hat oder vermag auß seinem verdienst, das vermag er auß dem verdienst des leidens Ihesu" ("What
one does not possess or cannot do out of one's own merit, one can
accomplish through the merit of the suffering of Jesus").[112] The second principle is: "So der mensch ym das leiden Cristi inniklicher
einpild und sich mer damit bekummert, so er mer verdient die krafft
und das verdienst des leidens Ihesu" ("The more one meditates deeply
upon Christ's Passion and compassionately takes it to heart, the more
one obtains the power and merit of the suffering of Jesus").[113]

The author of the Bamberg Tract, representing a late Franciscan
way of thinking, puts much greater emphasis than many other theologians around 1500 on the religious capabilities of one who has
been redeemed, assigning a key role to the free will (indeed, liken-
ing it to an all-powerful queen).[114] Yet the polarity in principle between human will and capability on the one side, and the redemptive
mediation of Christ on the other, generally holds true for the theological and pastoral situation before the Reformation: it is between
these two poles that a force-field of cooperation should emerge. Even
Staupitz kept a firm hold on the human *facere quod in se est* and the
necessity of one's own expiation and merit.[115] As the individual was
accountable for his own mortal sin, so must he, with his powers of
intellect and volition, become a co-operating subject in his movement toward salvation. The way to salvation must of necessity be
the way of his own volition and capability, redeemed by grace. By
around 1500, it makes no difference whether one holds a perfectionist

---

[111] Op. cit. p. 238f., lines 196–199 (with the explanation: "darum ist Cristus
Ihesus unser teglich opfer für unser sund und fur alle gütter und gaben, die wir
haben entpfangen und teglich entpfahen von gott").
[112] Op. cit. p. 239,200f.
[113] Op. cit. p. 239,207–209.
[114] "Man mag [= kann] auch dem willen die lieb nit nemen mit gewalt, wen
[= denn] der frey willen ist die kunigin im reich des menschen und hat vollen
gewalt und will ungezwungen sein. Und darum ist die lieb der gancz schacz des
menschen und das allerpest, das edelist, das liebst; und das wil der herr von uns
haben [. . .]" Op. cit. p. 237,144–147.
[115] Cf. Adolar Zumkeller: *Johannes von Staupitz und seine christliche Heilslehre* (Würzburg,
1994) [= Cassiciacum 45], Sachregister s.v. 'Facienti quod in se est Deus non
denegat gratiam' (p. 253), 'Genugtuung' (p. 254) und 'Verdienst' (p. 264).

and optimistic view of this human capacity, or one more disillusioned and minimalist: all sides affirm that the human subject must take a role in the work of salvation, which is then incorporated into the greater soteriological work of Jesus Christ.[116] In this respect the Reformation which commenced with Luther provides a fundamentally different understanding of the position of humanity before God.[117]

VIII. *The Reformation in the Context of the Late Middle Ages*

In closing what must be emphatically stressed is the direct connection between the dynamic of the late medieval theology of piety outlined above, and the impetus of the Reformation. In numerous theological studies of the 14th and particularly the 15th centuries a man's inability before God, the insufficiency of both his inward and outward acts, and his need of protection as "a poor little worm"[118] is defined in a different and more pointed way from earlier centuries, and the phenomenon of the scrupulous or timorous conscience also gains a new importance. Directly corresponding to this there emerges a theological way of thinking which intensifies ideas about God's "infinite love and mercy"[119] assigning new functions of liberation, protection and consolation to Christ's vicarious pain and suffering, expiation and merit. This is the most important conclusion of my essay, validated and reinforced by the iconographic innovations in the works of art from the 14th and 15th centuries.[120] In contact with and in contrast to the fears, terrible visions and threatening sermons

---

[116] On the soteriological role of the human subject in Staupitz' understanding see Johannn v. Staupitz: *Libellus de exsecutione aeternae praedestinationis*, ed. Lothar Graf zu Dohna, Richard Wetzel (Berlin – New York, 1979) [= Staupitz: Sämtliche Schriften 2], p. 124, 40 with n. 50.

[117] Cf. Wilfrid Joest: *Ontologie der Person bei Luther* (Göttingen, 1967).

[118] On the image of the poor, miserable, unclean "Wurm" or "Würmlein" (based on Vulg.-Ps. 21.7 and Job 5.6) cf. e.g. Heinrich Seuse: Horologium Sapientiae, lib. 1,14 (as in n. 59), p. 497,15; Vater Sigmund: Eucharistie-Predigt (as in n. 65), p. 103,72; Stephan Fridolin: Lehre für angefochtene und kleinmütige Menschen, in: Berndt Hamm, Thomas Lentes (eds.): Spätmittelalterliche Frömmigkeit Zwischen, Ideal und Praxis (Tübingen, 2001) [= Spätmittelalter und Reformation. Neue Reihe 15), p. 191,30 and 193,25.

[119] Cf. the tract 'Von der göttlichen Liebe' (as in n. 110), p. 238,176–178: "Und darum so hat got der hymlisch vater in dem werck gegen menschen erzaigt sein unentliche lieb und barmherzikait, wen [= denn] das was wider des menschen verdienst."

[120] Cf. above p. 104 with n. 49.

of that period, a significant line of pastorally-oriented theology tended
to stress *sola misericordia, sola gratia* and *solus Christus* as they were frequently expressed, even before the Reformation.[121] In this respect
the Reformation brings a late-medieval dynamic to a conclusion:
The minimization of human capability so common around 1500
becomes a total incapacity *coram deo*, while the late-medieval maxi-
mization of God's mercy is radicalized to the doctrine of the soteriological efficacy of God alone.

This way of looking at things does not disqualify my oft-repeated
thesis that the Reformation was a break with the system, a fundamental change.[122] The Reformers' understanding of justification, however diversely expressed, really does represent a break with the
late-medieval conception of the human path to salvation and also
with the forced theological conceptions of mercy and release as we
have encountered them.

What I have said above about the late-medieval understanding of
the subjective moral role of the individual journeying towards salvation
gives us an inkling of the immensity of this break. At the same time,
however, it gives us a better understanding of the Reformation, especially of its beginnings: seen in the context of the innovative dynamic
of late-medieval piety, it was logical for many.[123] From this perspective the Late Middle Ages and the Reformation together constitute the era of a religious transformation.[124] The years between
1300 and 1550 constitute the comprehensive age of a new understanding of mercy, mediation and exoneration. Clearly, important
aspects of this new orientation might be traced back to earlier decades

---

[121] On the multiplication of 'sola' formulations in the decades before the Reformation
(formulated as a research hypothesis) cf. Berndt Hamm: "Von der spätmittelalterlichen reformatio zur Reformation: der Prozeß normativer Zentrierung von Religion
und Gesellschaft in Deutschland", in: *Archiv für Reformationsgeschichte* 84 (1993), pp.
7–82: here 37–41.

[122] Cf. especially Berndt Hamm: "Einheit und Vielfalt der Reformation – oder:
was die Reformation zur Reformation machte", in: Hamm, Bernd Moeller, Dorothea
Wendebourg: *Reformationstheorien. Ein kirchenhistorischer Disput über Einheit und Vielfalt der
Reformation* (Göttingen, 1995), pp. 57–127.

[123] Cf. Bernd Moeller: "Die Rezeption Luthers in der frühen Reformation", in:
Reformationstheorien (as in n. 122), pp. 9–29.

[124] On this application of the concept of 'transformation' cf. Thomas Lentes:
"'Andacht' und 'Gebärde'. Das religiöse Ausdrucksverhalten", in: Bernhard Jussen,
Craig Koslofsky (eds.): *Kulturelle Reformation. Sinnformationen im Umbruch 1400–1600*
(Göttingen, 1999) [= Veröffentlichungen des Max-Planck-Instituts für Geschichte
145], pp. 29–67.

and centuries, particularly to the radical change of the 12th century.[125]
I am not so much concerned with making a rigid demarcation of
the period as with emphasizing how clearly we can detect a coherent religious accentuation of the problem and a similarly sharpened
coherent dynamic of solution *within* the 14th to the 16th centuries.

There is much more to the coherence of this age of transformation than the dynamic of mercy. In this same era we find increasing trends toward social regulation and discipline, forceful models of
government, new emphases on order, obedience and sanctification
over against the 'satanic powers' of unrestrained and undisciplined
libertinism. In its drive for regulation and control the era is also
innovative.[126] Yet the Late Middle Ages and the Reformation are
also bound together by complex combinations of theological, pastoral, social and political trends which produced both a culture of
mercy and release and a culture of regulation and discipline.[127]

---

[125] Think, for example, how much the theology of piety towards the end of the
Middle Ages with its interpretation of the Passion of Christ took its bearings from
Bernard of Clairvaux and his school; on the caesura of the 12th century cf. above
p. 89f. with n. 3.

[126] This must be underlined even if, as stressed above, in theology and the imagery
of piety, the innovation and dynamic of change consisted particularly in an increased
emphasis on mercy, protection and assurance for needy humanity.

[127] Cf. above p. 86f.

CHAPTER FOUR

FROM THE MEDIEVAL "LOVE OF GOD"
TO THE "FAITH" OF LUTHER – A CONTRIBUTION
TO THE HISTORY OF PENITENCE

I. *The Twelfth-Century Turn to the Inner Feeling of the Love of God*

To the criteria of a genuinely historical research project on the
Reformation belongs the principle that one can only understand the
Reformation in the light of the Middle Ages – not simply from its
last decades but by looking back at the forms of theology, piety and
mentality as they developed over centuries. In so doing we must take
account of the diversity in the Middle Ages, of its innovations and
continuities. Only these can show us how far the Reformation is
embedded in the Middle Ages and in what sense it can be understood as a radical change. To illustrate this by the example of the
two biblical concepts of love and faith, which are cardinal for western religiosity, I shall trace these themes in a broad arc extending
from the 12th century to first quarter of the 16th century and the
earliest writings of Martin Luther.

   Any analysis of love in the Middle Ages, be it the erotic love
between the sexes or the love of Christ experienced by mystics, would
do well to begin with the time of transition in the 12th century.[1]
Before this the historical record is relatively silent about the significance
of love – and by this I mean in particular love as an emotional element of life, as a central driving-force and motivation of existence.
This might seem surprising since both in pagan and Christian antiquity there already existed an emotional culture of love – sensuous
after the fashion of Catullus or Ovid or transcending all sensuous-
ness to the purely spiritual like Augustine's love of God, and between
these every possible nuance of physical and spiritual affection: parental

---

[1] Cf. Peter Dinzelbacher, "Liebe II. Mentalitäts- und literaturgeschichtlich", in:
Lexikon des Mittelalters, vol. 5 (Munich/Zürich, 1991), Cols. 1965–1968; idem: "Über
die Entdeckung der Liebe im Hochmittelalter", in: *Saeculum* 32 (1981), pp. 185–208
(with literature).

love, brotherly love, love of a friend and love of one's neighbor.[2] Yet in western Europe, by about 500 A.D. – above all in the Kingdom of the Franks after the time of Chlodwig – totally different conditions had developed which eroded the foundations that had supported a culture of refined feelings. In place of the urban, highly literate culture of antiquity a predominantly uncivilized, agrarian world emerged, with very primal, 'archaic', not to say primitive ways of acting and thinking.[3] This change in mentality can be seen, for example, in the way that emphasis shifts, in the realms of both law and religion, to the plane of the external act. In weighing either crime or sin, the decisive question is what actually happened – e.g. whether someone did or did not kill another. The question of the emotional feelings and personal intentions – whether the person deliberately intended to kill or whether he killed unintentionally through an unfortunate chain of circumstances – is pushed completely into the background. Misconduct and sin are defined one-sidedly on the basis of the deed, and in correspondingly heavy fashion the ecclesiastical penitential system of the period made pivotal the external work of contrition – i.e. the satisfaction (*satisfactio*), not the soul's inner pangs of remorse for its transgression. The Irish penitential manuals, which greatly influenced the development of the penitential process throughout the west from the 7th century onwards, regard fasting as the most important form of penance. The duration of the fast is graduated according to the seriousness of the sin; only when the sinner has completed the corresponding period of fasting or a substitute compensation – i.e. has "done enough" – can he be granted reintegration into the Church community of salvation.[4]

---

[2] Cf. Leo Pollmann: *Die Liebe in der hochmittelalterlichen Literatur Frankreichs. Versuch einer historischen Phänomenologie* (Frankfurt am Main, 1966) [= Analecta Romanica 18], pp. 11–32 ('Love' in Greek and Roman literature). On the relationship of the religious love of God, self and neighbor (in this order) in Augustine, cf. his writing "De moribus ecclesiae catholicae et de moribus Manichaeorum" (388–390), ed. by John Kevin Coyle: *Augustine's "De moribus ecclesiae catholicae". A study of the work, its composition and its sources*, Fribourg 1978, pp. 267–302; cf. also Augustine: "De doctrina christiana" I, cap. 26f., *CChr.* SL 32, p. 21f.

[3] Cf. Arnold Angenendt: *Das Frühmittelalter. Die abendländische Christenheit von 400–900*, 2nd edition, Stuttgart/Berlin/Cologne, 1995.

[4] Cf. ibid. pp. 210–212 and 334f.; idem, *Geschichte der Religiosität im Mittelalter* (Darmstadt, 1997), pp. 630–639, especially p. 635, with the claim that for certain types of religion, emphasis on deeds is normative. Cf. also Cyril Vogel: Article "Busse (liturgisch-theologisch), D. Westkirche, I. Bußdisziplin und Bußriten", in: Lexikon des Mittelalters, vol. 2 (Munich/Zürich, 1983), Cols. 1132–1135 (with literature).

Consideration of the nature of penance in the early Middle Ages is informative for our theme insofar as it reveals how dominant was the fixation upon compensatory action and proper ritual in relation to a central and exemplary element of religious practice. Apparently it was not felt necessary to take into account the inner motives of mental pain and love of God. This relationship of external and internal, of doing and feeling, was reversed, however, during the 12th century in an almost breathtaking way. In the wake of an ethically refined, chivalrous culture, the breakthrough of reform in monastic life, rapidly expanding cities and a blossoming urban culture there emerged quite new manifestations of internalization and individualization.[5] This means: Love was now discovered as a central feeling in human existence – or rather, rediscovered.[6] For the new awareness of sensuous and spiritual love was closely related to the intensive renaissance of Ovid and Augustine which took place in the 12th century.[7] It is the same 12th century in which on the one side the earthly ideal of chivalrous, courtly love was cultivated in the courts of the nobility[8] and a subject such as the story of Tristan and Isolde was transformed into the shape of a courtly romance[9] and in which

---

[5] Colin Morris: *The Discovery of the Individual 1050–1200* (London, 1972) [= Church History Outlines 5]; Dinzelbacher (as below, n. 10), pp. 243–250 (with literature); John F. Benton: "Consciousness of Self and Perceptions of Individuality", in: Robert L. Benson/Giles Constable (eds.): *Renaissance and Renewal in the Twelfth Century* (Cambridge, Mass., 1982), pp. 263–295.

[6] Cf. the programmatic title of Dinzelbacher's article in n. 1.

[7] On the Ovid renaissance cf. Franco Munari: *Ovid im Mittelalter* (Zürich/Stuttgart, 1960); on the continuing effect of Augustine cf. also Grete Lüers: "Die Auffassung der Liebe bei mittelalterlichen Mystikern", in: *Eine heilige Kirche* 22 (1940), pp. 110–118, with the beautiful but inaccurate sentence at the beginning: "Since Augustine, to whom Christian art assigned as emblem a burning heart in true recognition of his being, the question of the essence of love never let go of the medieval philosophers and the pious." It did, in fact, let go of thinking and pious Christians in the early Middle Ages for centuries, so that in the 12th century there really was a re-*naissance* of the Augustinian *caritas*. On the concept of the "Renaissance of the 12th century" cf. the standard text by Charles Homer Haskins: *The Renaissance of the Twelfth Century* (Cambridge, Mass., 1927) and the bibliography in Hermann Jakobs: *Kirchenreform und Hochmittelalter* 1046–1215, 2nd edition (Munich, 1988) [= Oldenbourg Grundriß der Geschichte 7] p. 123f.

[8] On the original Provençal conception of aesthetic, courtly love (*fins amours*, *fin amour*) cf. Leslie T. Topsfield: *Troubadours and Love* (Cambridge, 1975); F. X. Newman (ed.): *The Meaning of Courtly Love* (Albany, 1968); Herbert Kolb: *Der Begriff der Minne und das Entstehen der höfischen Lyrik* (Tübingen, 1958) [= Hermaea NS 4]. On 'courtly love' in general cf. also the survey by Joachim Bumke: *Höfische Kultur. Literatur und Gesellschaft im hohen Mittelalter*, vol. 2, 3rd edition (Munich, 1986), pp. 503–582.

[9] Cf. Francoise Barteau: *Les Romans de Tristan et Iseut* (Paris, 1972); Gerhard

on the other side, the mystical way of an intimately close love of Jesus was first experienced and described.[10] Solomon's Song of Songs, which previously, in accordance with the interpretation prevalent in the early Middle Ages, had been understood as an allegory of the relationship between the bridegroom, Christ and the Church as the bride, was now dramatically re-interpreted.[11] Between 1135 and 1153 the Cistercian abbot, Bernard of Clairvaux (1090–1153) wrote his famous sermons on the Song of Songs which set a precedent for the later Middle Ages. In these cloistered sermons written in Latin he substitutes the role of the individual soul for that of the Church.[12] The soul is the bride who embraces her divine bridegroom with a tempestuous, ardent passion which sets aside all reason.[13] This love of God pays no heed to honour and privilege, profit and recompense but is its own fulfilment: "To savour it", writes Bernard, "is its own reward. I love because I love; I love in order to love".[14] The way to salvation is that of the ascent of the loving soul, beginning with the meditative remembrance of the suffering Christ, to the mystic union with the divine Spirit, a *unio* which Bernard – like so many mystics after him – pictured as an embrace and kiss.[15] With

Schindele: *Tristan, Metamorphose und Tradition* (Stuttgart, 1971) [= Studien zur Poetik und Geschichte der Literatur 12]. Cf. also Denis de Rougemont: *L'amour et l'occident*, 1939.

[10] Cf. Peter Dinzelbacher: *Vision und Visionsliteratur im Mittelalter* (Stuttgart, 1981) [= Monographien zur Geschichte des Mittelalters 23], pp. 150–155.

[11] For information on the medieval interpretation of the Song of Songs cf. Friedrich Ohly: *Hohelied-Studien. Grundzüge einer Geschichte der Hoheliedauslegung des Abendlandes bis um 1200* (Wiesbaden, 1958); Riedlinger: *Die Makellosigkeit der Kirche in den lateinischen Hohenliedkommentaren des Mittelalters* (Münster, 1958) [= Beiträge zur Geschichte der Philosophie und Theologie des Mittelalters 38/3].

[12] According to Ohly (ibid. p. 147) this signifies "a transfer of the Church's Heilsgeschichte to the sphere of spiritual experience".

[13] The relevant passages from Bernard's interpretation of the Song of Songs are cited in Kurt Ruh: *Geschichte der abendländischen Mystik*, vol. 1: *Die Grundlegung durch die Kirchenväter und die Mönchstheologie des 12. Jahrhunderts* (Munich, 1990), p. 258f.

[14] "Fructus eius usus eius. Amo quia amo; amo, ut amem." *Sermones super Cantica Canticorum*, Sermo 83,2 (4); *Sancti Bernardi opera*, ed. by Jean Leclercq, vol. 2 (Rome, 1958), p. 300,25f.

[15] Cf. Ruh (as n. 13) p. 258 and p. 265. As one of the first – before the time of Bernard – the Benedictine Rupert von Deutz (1070–1129) described the experience of the embrace and kiss of Christ; cf. Dinzelbacher: *Über die Entdeckung der Liebe* (as n. 1) p. 197: "Again and again as he contemplates the Cross the crucified Christ turns his eyes upon him and benevolently accepts his salutation: 'But that was not enough for me: I wanted to touch him, embrace and kiss him [. . .] I sensed that he desired it [. . .] I held him, embraced him, kissed him for a long time. I sensed how hesitantly he permitted these caresses – then he himself opened

this – initially typically monastic – theology of spiritual experience[16] Bernard of Clairvaux became the great pioneer in making love (*amor dei, dilectio, caritas*) central in the theology and piety of the following centuries. The arc extends from his fundamental treatise *De diligendo Deo* (Concerning the love of God)[17] to the tract written in 1517 by Johannes von Staupitz, '*Von der lieb Gottes*' (On the love of God).[18]

Bernard was in this respect a pioneer, a modern man in his century. On the other hand with his theology of emotionally-based love he resisted the contemporaneous intellectual awakening in the French cathedral schools and seminaries. The 12th century has two theological faces: one is the kind of pious, humble, worshipful theology represented by Bernard,[19] the other the contrasting type of scholastic theology then developing, a penetrating dialectic methodology as embodied in the Breton, Peter Abelard (1079–1142), so bitterly hounded by Bernard.[20] Abelard stands for the new type of theological intellectual,[21] for a new rational desire for knowledge and understanding. Certainly one cannot understand the intellectual awakening of thought simply as a diametrically opposed counterpart to the emotional outburst of love: It must also be seen as a complementary

---

his mouth so that I might kiss more deeply.' Naturally Rupert then interprets his experience allegorically on the basis of the Song of Songs; but what he described was what he experienced: French kisses with God. And in the event he is driven by a loving yearning such as no one had evinced in *this* way to the best of our knowledge for the Son of God who in the early Middle Ages was far more the '*Rex tremendae maiestatis*', the awful avenger who lives on a plane far above humanity." On the mystic kissing cf. also below, n. 37.

[16] Cf. Ulrich Köpf: *Religiöse Erfahrung in der Theologie Bernhards von Clairvaux* (Tübingen, 1980) [= Beiträge zur historischen Theologie 61].

[17] The treatise is typical of the new program of independent thematic examinations of Christian love; edited in the edition by Leclercq et al. (as n. 14), Vol. 3, (Rome, 1963), pp. 109–154, bilingual in the edition edited by Gerhard B. Winkler: *Bernhard von Clairvaux: Sämtliche Werke lateinisch/deutsch*, Vol. 1 (Innsbruck, 1990), pp. 57–151. From the same period cf. e.g. Hugo von St. Viktor (†1141): *De laude caritatis*, Migne *PL* 176, 969–976.

[18] Edited in: *Johann von Staupitzens sämmtliche Werke*, ed. by Joachim Karl Friedrich Knaake, vol. 1: *Deutsche Schriften* (Potsdam, 1867), pp. 88–119. Staupitz dedicated the tract for the new year 1518, which grew out of his Advent sermons in 1517, to Kunigunde, widow of the Duke of Bavaria. It then also appeared in printed form in 1518.

[19] Cf. Jean Leclercq: *L'amour des lettres et le désir de Dieu*, 1957.

[20] Cf. the colloquium papers: *Petrus Abaelardus (1079–1142). Person, Werk und Wirkung*, ed. by Rudolf Thomas (Trier, 1980) [= Trierer theologische Studien 38].

[21] Cf. Jacques Le Goff: *Die Intellektuellen im Mittelalter* (Stuttgart, 1986) [French edition: *Les intellectuells au Moyen Age*, 1957/1985]; on Abelard: pp. 40–54 ("the first great modern intellectual").

expression of the new kind of internalization and individualization which developed in the 12th century. Like the pressing desire for love, the pressing rational desire to know the grounds is the expression of an inner unease which is not satisfied simply with taking over the contents of faith without question but wants to venture behind the façade of what exists to the dimension of motives and reasons. This also explains why such a rational, philosophical intellectual like Abelard was not only a renowned lover – Heloise and Abelard are certainly the most famous lovers in Church history – but as a systematic philosopher established love as the decisive motivating impulse for the entire redemptive event in early Scholastic theology.

Abelard and Bernard, unlike Anselm of Canterbury a few decades earlier, no longer see the essential reason for the Incarnation and for Christ's Passion in the offended majesty of God which demands satisfaction (*satisfactio*),[22] but in the love of God which gives itself freely to humankind. The experience of this divine love fires the human heart to a reciprocal love.[23] In this way the sinner comes to a true repentance for his transgressions, an inner ache, a sighing and weeping of the heart which does not arise from fear of punishment but from grateful love of God and loving compassion for the suffering Christ.[24] Abelard no longer understands sin – as in the early Middle Ages – in the sense of its outward form but solely from the inner

---

[22] Anselm of Canterbury (†1109) in his *Cur deus homo* completed in 1098 in the Latin/German edition edited by Franciscus Salesius Schmitt (Darmstadt, 1965) (following the text of Schmitt's critical edition).

[23] On Abelard's teaching on reconciliation cf. especially his commentary on the Epistle to the Romans: Migne *PL* 178,833D–836D; also Reinhold Seeberg: *Lehrbuch der Dogmengeschichte*, vol. 3, 6th Edition (Darmstadt, 1959), pp. 239–243. On the doctrine of reconciliation in Bernard of Clairvaux cf. particularly his *Sermones super Cantica Canticorum*, Sermo 43,1–3, ed. by Leclercq et al. (as n. 14) vol. 2, pp. 41–43; and Dinzelbacher: *Über die Entdeckung der Liebe* (as n. 1), pp. 193f., 195.

[24] On Abelard's teaching on repentance and remorse cf. in particular *Ethica* ('*Scito te ipsum*'), chs. 17–25, Migne *PL* 178,660–673, ed. by David E. Luscombe: *Peter Abelard's Ethics* (Oxford, 1971), pp. 76–111; and Martin Ohst: *Pflichtbeichte. Untersuchungen zum Bußwesen im Hohen und Späten Mittelalter* (Tübingen, 1995) [= Beiträge zur historischen Theologie 89], pp. 56–59. On the relationship to Christ's Passion of human love of God cf. Abelard's Commentary on Romans: Migne *PL* 178,836B. Admittedly, in the understanding of penitence in the first half of the 12th century we can only see initial approaches to the whole imaginative field of the pangs of repentance motivated by Christ's Passion and, in imitation thereof, entering into it (according to Bernard's saying in *Super Cant.* 20.8: "qui Christo passo compatitur, compungitur") it was increasingly widely explored up to the end of the 15th century; cf. Ruh (as n. 13) pp. 242–244 and below, pp. 137–139.

involvement of the will and intent: It is not whether I have actually
killed which is of prime importance but whether I intended to kill
and could have avoided the killing. The question of blame (*culpa*) is
now posed in a different form, depending solely on the intention of
the perpetrator and his awareness of what he does.[25] Correspondingly
in the understanding of penitence the whole weight now falls on the
change of direction of the inner will, on the intention to love and
the pangs of remorse, not, as in earlier days, on the acts of penance.
As in the explanation for the Incarnation and for Christ's Passion,
in the theological analysis of the process of penitence the aspect of
satisfaction now retreats completely behind the motif of love. From
this example we see how closely the mystic, affective theology of a
Bernard is related to the intellectual, scholastic theology of an Abelard,
how forcefully the central motif of love in the one theology also predominates in the doctrinal system of the other. Where Bernard as
a monastic theologian meditates on the experience of love, Abelard
as a dialectical theologian reflects on the logic of love.

We must remember that with this internalizing understanding of
penitence Abelard concurs completely with the early Scholastic trend
of his age. Even before him, in the first decades of the 12th century, the school of Anselm of Laon had so firmly transferred the
emphasis to the inner penitential emotion of remorse that for the
succeeding generations and schools of scholastic theology the complex problem arose of what could then be achieved by the external
penitence (*poenitentia exterior*), i.e. the act of confession to a priest, the
priestly absolution from sins and the satisfaction through the penitential acts imposed by the priest.[26] The assumption seemed obvious
– and was held by many around 1200 – that all guilt and punishment was wiped out by the penitence of love, so that both the earthly

[25] Cf. Benton (as n. 5), pp. 271–274 ("Guilt, shame and intention") with literature; Arnold Angenendt: Deus qui nullum peccatum impunitum dimittit. Ein 'Grundsatz' der mittelalterlichen Bußgeschichte", in: *Und dennoch ist von Gott zu reden. Festschrift
für Herbert Vorgrimler*, ed. by Matthias Lutz-Bachmann (Freiburg i.Br./Basle/Vienna,
1994), pp. 142–156; 153f.; Seeberg (as n. 23), p. 238f.
[26] On the doctrine of penitence of the school of Anselm of Laon (†1117) cf.
Ludwig Hödl: *Die Geschichte der scholastischen Literatur und der Theologie der Schlüsselgewalt*,
Part I: *Die scholastische Literatur und die Theologie der Schlüsselgewalt von ihren Anfängen an
bis zur Summa Aurea des Wilhelm von Auxerre* (Münster, 1960) [= Beiträge zur Geschichte
der Philosophie und Theologie des Mittelalters, vol. 38 H.4], pp. 6–45 (especially
pp. 26; 28f.; 38f.; 44f.) and the summary in pp. 376–380.

acts of satisfaction and the other-worldly purifying punishments in Purgatory were no longer necessary.[27]

Among the majority of early Scholastic theologians of the 12th and early 13th centuries there arose the following consensus: What is decisive in penitence occurs in the true repentance of love which the Holy Spirit effects in the heart of the sinner. As soon as the sinner feels this acute pain of love – like Peter after his threefold betrayal – he immediately receives from God forgiveness for his sins i.e. from their guilt and the eternal infernal punishments for sin.[28] Hence the conclusive justification of the sinner is already given with the loving motif of repentance. A person who experiences such pangs of repentance, such a *vera contritio*, always also humbly desires to receive the priestly sacrament of confession and absolution and to commit himself to the Church's discipline of penance. To this extent every true repentance is related to the Church's power of the keys. But if the sinner should die in this spiritual state of *contritio* before contact with the priest takes place, he is saved on the basis of the inner reconciliation with God that has already taken place. Hence from the 12th century the decisive weight in the event of penitence no longer lies on the level of *satisfactio* but on the emotional level of the wounded, mourning love. This is where salvation or damnation is decided. Did not Jesus say of the great sinner (thus characterizing penitential love) as we read in Luke 7.47: "Her sins, which were many, have been forgiven, for she has shown great love"?[29] This transfer of emphasis from satisfaction to loving repentance corresponds to the contemporaneous change in the Church's penitential practice. The priestly forgiveness of sin is now moved forward. Normally now, unlike in the previous centuries, it no longer presupposes the whole process

---

[27] Cf. ibid. p. 281 and p. 293f.

[28] The 'as soon as' is based on an earlier aphorism derived from a combination of Ezekiel 33.12 and 18.21f.: "In quacumque hora peccator ingemuerit, non recordabor iniquitatum eius" (God says: "In the hour in which the sinner sighs deeply I shall no longer remember [all] his transgression"). Cf. *Decretum Gratiani*, De poenitentia, d. 1, c. 32 (the edition of Aemilius Ludovicus Richter/Aemilius Friedberg, vol. 1, Leipzig 1879, p. 1165); Hödl (as n. 26) pp. 81, 87 and 96; Ohst (as n. 24), p. 56 with n. 32. Even in the late Middle Ages this aphorism remained a classical proof for the direct connection between repentance and the forgiveness of sins.

[29] On the use of this passage in early Scholasticism cf. e.g. Hödl (as n. 26), p. 226 and idem: "Busse (liturgisch-theologisch), D. Westkirche, II, Scholastische Busstheologie", in: *Lexikon des Mittelalters*, vol. 2 (Munich/Zürich, 1983), cols. 1137–1141: 1139.

of the sinner's repentance including the atoning penitential acts but simply the profession of repentance and confession. The atoning action imposed by the priest then relates simply to a certain residue of temporal punishments for sin. Anyone who does not discharge this quantum within his lifetime must wipe it out hereafter under harsher conditions in Purgatory before he reaches Paradise.[30] But the decisive condition for a sinner to inherit eternal salvation is not any sort of penitential act or merit, but the state of his heart at the moment of death: whether it is in a state of loving God and consequently repents its sins – is, as it were, in the emotional orbit of God – or whether it remains caught up in its own orbit because the love of self is dominant.

II. *The Late-Medieval Transformation in the Understanding of Love, Penance and Contrition*

In principle this decisive centrality of the love of God did not change during the whole of the later Middle Ages. People in the late Middle Ages were told in an easily-remembered way that God the Father would judge their souls at the moment of death, each individual personally, according to the principle: "I will show mercy to all those who depart this life with true repentance."[31] That was and remains the point decisive for salvation in the Roman Catholic understanding from the 12th century.

What changed in the High and Late Scholasticism of the 13th to 15th centuries and in the pastoral theology of piety in the late Middle Ages will become clear if we now take a great leap from the 12th century and look at the last four decades before the Reformation, at the period between 1480 and 1520. The following aspects seem

---

[30] On the early and high Scholastic theory of Purgatory as it developed from the second half of the 12th century cf. Jacques Le Goff: *La naissance du-purgatoire*, 1981.

[31] Thus the text of a banner on a picture of the divine judgment of the individual painted by Hans Holbein the Elder in 1508; cf. Berndt Hamm: "Von der spätmittelalterlichen *reformatio* zur Reformation: der Prozess normativer Zentrierung von Religion und Gesellschaft in Deutschland", in: *Archiv für Reformationsgeschichte* 84 (1993), pp. 7–82:36f. The same text could also be seen on a gravestone in the choir of the church in the Franciscan monastery in Nuremberg: v. Ulrich Schmidt: *Das ehemalige Franziskanerkloster in Nürnberg*, Nuremberg 1913, p. 18.

to me to be particularly important if we are to locate and portray adequately the necessity of loving repentance for salvation in comparison with the theology of the 12th century.

1.) The love of God, the *caritas*, is no longer identified with the coming of the Holy Spirit into the human soul as in Peter Lombard (†1160), the most influential teacher of early Scholasticism.[32] This kind of direct proximity to God is no longer simply a matter of the soul being stirred by the power of the Holy Spirit but is now – as a gift of the Holy Spirit – an attribute created in the soul itself, its fundamental habitual virtue which gives all other virtues their loving orientation towards God.[33] In this case the love of God is absorbed more fully into the human soul; it can even be dissociated from the merciful working of the Holy Spirit as was held by William of Ockham and his followers. Ockhamists like Gabriel Biel (†1495) could say that a person may perform acts of pure divine love and true penitence using his own innate powers.[34] The majority of theologians around 1500 challenged this potentiality and always saw in man's love of God the influence of God's justifying grace which was poured into the human soul and transformed it. But they, too, usually stressed that the sinner had to prepare himself by exerting his own innate spiritual powers to receive this grace which brings true love of God and penitence.

2.) When at the close of the Middle Ages the portrayal of the suffering Christ, the wretched Man of Sorrows, became a central

---

[32] Petrus Lombardus: *Sententiae*, Lib. I, dist. 17, cap. 1 (Quod spiritus sanctus est caritas, qua diligimus deum et proximum), Edition of the P. Collegii S. Bonaventurae: *Magistri Petri Lombardi Sententiae in IV libris distinctae*, Tom I, Pars II; Liber I et II, 3rd edition (Grottaferrata, Rome, 1971) [= Spicilegium Bonaventurianum 4], pp. 141,25–143,20; this kind of Augustinian doctrine of grace was unable to assert itself in the early Scholasticism of the 12th century but is an indication that it was only in the first half of the 13th century that the idea of the habitual character of justifying grace and love was developed: cf. Artur Michael Landgraf: *Dogmengeschichte der Frühscholastik*, vol. I/1 (Regensburg, 1952), pp. 220–237.

[33] Cf. Landgraf, ibid. pp. 141–219; Johann Auer: *Die Entwicklung der Gnadenlehre in der Hochscholastik mit besonderer Berücksichtigung des Kardinals Matteo d'Acquasparta*, Part One: *Das Wesen der Gnade* (Freiburg i. Br., 1942); Charles Baumgartner; Paul Tihen: "Grâce", in: *Dictionnaire de Spiritualité ascétique et mystique*, vol. 6, pp. 701–750.

[34] Cf. Leif Grane: *'Contra Gabrielem'. Luthers Auseinandersetzung mit Gabriel Biel in der 'Disputatio Contra Scholasticam Theologiam' 1517* (Gyldendal, 1962) [= Acta Theologica Danica 4], pp. 223–261; Heiko Augustinus Oberman: *Spätscholastik und Reformation*, vol. 1: *Der Herbst der mittelalterlichen Theologie* (Zürich, 1965) [*The Harvest of Medieval Theology*, 1963], pp. 139–146.

theme in theology and piety,[35] human love of God became more intensely, almost exclusively, related to the earthly figure of the Christ of the Passion. The love which responds to his suffering love awakens pangs of contrition in the depths of the soul; and this true contrition together with all the sinner's acts of satisfaction should be nothing other than suffering with the suffering Christ, emulation of the Way of the Cross and conformity with him in his Passion.[36]

3.) This indissoluble conjunction of love of God, pangs of contrition and inner fulfilment of Christ's sufferings signals a fundamental change compared to the position of the love of God in the mysticism of the 12th to 14th centuries. For mystic theologians like Bernard of Clairvaux the love for Jesus, the suffering Son of God who had become human, is only the first stage in a mystical ascent which – transcending all that is earthly and profane – unites the soul directly with the otherworldly spirit of the eternal Word.[37] Love mounts above the purifying, cleansing, penitential level of spiritual sighing. At the end of the Middle Ages, if I see it properly, such mysticism of spiritual 'alpinists' had been left behind. That there were stages in the love of God, a gradation in its intensity, was still accepted,[38] but now all the grace of love is related to the inner rela-

---

[35] Cf. Hamm (as n. 31), pp. 24–41.

[36] Cf. Martin Elze: "Das Verständnis der Passion Jesu im ausgehenden Mittelalter und bei Luther", in: Heinz Liebing/Klaus Scholder (eds.): *Geist und Geschichte der Reformation, Festschrift for Hanns Rückert*, Berlin 1966 (= Arbeiten zur Kirchengeschichte 38), pp. 127–151; Petra Seegets: *Passionstheologie und Passionsfrömmigkeit im ausgehenden Mittelalter. Der Nürnberger Franziskaner Stephan Fridolin (gest. 1498) zwischen Kloster und Stadt* (Tübingen, 1998) [= Spätmittelalter und Reformation. Neue Reihe 10].

[37] Cf. Ruh (as n. 13), pp. 234–275, e.g. p. 242: "For Bernard the recalling of Christ's sufferings is always only a starting-point, has scarcely any intrinsic value." On the stages of love according to Bernard, cf. ibid. pp. 229–234 and p. 258 (the ascent of the bride-soul from kissing the feet, the hands and then the union with the heavenly Bridegroom in the kiss on the mouth [cf. above, n. 15]). Kissing the feet corresponds to the humble attitude of contrition: "First we fall before the feet of him who created us and weep for all (the evil) that we have done". (*Sermones super Cantica Canticorum*, sermo 3.5). Cf. also e.g. the graduated path of the "impetuous" love of God in the tract *De quattuor gradibus violentae caritatis* by the mystical theologian Richard of St. Victor (†1173) in Ruh, ibid. pp. 387–395, on the first step, p. 389f.: "The first step – that of wounding love – reveals most clearly the Ovidian model. It pierces the heart, love's fiery arrow penetrates the spirit to the marrow. This then 'burns with desire, glows with ardour, it blazes, it pants, it groans from the bottom of its heart and long-drawn sighs burst from it'."

[38] On the 'gradualism' characteristic of medieval theology, piety and devotion – envisioned in terms of ascending and descending steps and stages further intensified in comparison with the Early Old Church and its neoplatonic impulses – cf. Günther

tionship of the painful, contrite heart to the suffering Christ and to a lifelong existence of identification with the tortured Son of Man. Such a reduction and concentration on the mystical love of God to the '*via purgativa*' of making the Passion one's own through replication was particularly characteristic of the teaching on piety before and after 1500. The intention of the works of art completed in these decades is to inspire fervor and give an instructive illustration of this way to Salvation through the Passion.

4.) For all the weight which falls, in the late Middle Ages as before, on the decisive criterion of loving contrition, compared with the 12th century the emphasis swings again more heavily to the external dimension of penitence, to the sacrament of penance with confession and absolution by the priest and the works of satisfaction by the sinner. There are various reasons for this. The increasing importance of the aspect of sufficient satisfaction and the accompanying total eradication of all temporal punishments for sin was doubtless principally a reaction to the doctrine of Purgatory which developed from the end of the 12th century.[39] During the late Middle Ages the horror of the punishments in Purgatory was pictured in an excessive, detailed, terrifying manner,[40] and in consequence the faithful made increased efforts to save themselves from Purgatory and enter into Paradise immediately after their death, either by making satisfaction themselves, (above all by fasting, prayer, giving alms and making endowments), or by the purchase of indulgences. The more Purgatory – not as a salutary episode of purification but as a fearful place of punishment – took hold of the imagination of priests and laity, the greater was the importance attributed to the penitential act. In general, in late-medieval piety the opinion is widespread that the acquisition of salvation is dependent on works done for the love of God and one's neighbor, i.e. on the effect of good works which pay the penalty and earn merit. A mercantile mentality revolves less around the heavenly treasure of the soul which loves God than around the 'treasury of good works'.

Müller: "Gradualismus", in: *Deutsche Vierteljahrsschrift für Literaturwissenschaft und Geistesgeschichte* 2 (1924), pp. 681–720; see also my contribution in: Berndt Hamm/Bernd Moeller/Dorothea Wendebourg: *Reformationstheorien – ein kirchenhistorischer Disput über Einheit und Vielfalt der Reformation* (Göttingen, 1995), pp. 69–71.

[39] Cf. above, n. 30.

[40] Cf. the articles and illustrations in: Peter Jezler (ed.): *Himmel, Hölle, Fegefeuer. Das Jenseits im Mittelalter. Exhibition catalogue* (Zürich, 1994).

5.) From the 13th century the priestly power of the keys in the form of absolution was also coming to be massively more important right across the scale of scholastic doctrinal thinking.[41] Particularly in the school of Duns Scotus (†1308) great weight was placed upon a theory of the power of absolution which, in short, runs as follows: Most people, because of their emotional weaknesses, are not in a position to achieve a true, loving repentance – i.e. *contritio* – without the help of the sacrament of penance. When they come to the priest and confess their sins they have only an imperfect pain of remorse, the so-called *attritio*. But through the sacramental absolution – i.e. through his words *"Ego te absolvo a peccatis tuis"* (I absolve you from your sins) – the imperfect is changed to a perfect, true contrition. By virtue of the words of absolution there enters into the heart of the sinner the justifying grace through which *attritio* becomes *contritio*, and consequently the sinner is given pardon for his sins, the *remissio peccatorum* – i.e. is freed from guilt and eternal damnation.[42] Hence it lies in the priest's power of authority and in the effectiveness of the sacrament of penance to compensate for man's weak inner repentance by means of an external stimulus, and to elevate the sinner in an instant, as if by the magic of the ecclesiastical ritual, to the plane of the true saving contrition of love. From the 13th century

---

[41] Cf. Herbert Vorgrimler: *Buße und Krankensalbung* (Freiburg i.Br./Basle/Vienna, 1978) [= Handbuch der Dogmengeschichte, vol. 4, Section 3], pp. 131–138; Vorgrimler, considering the heightened evaluation of priestly absolution, speaks of a "change of direction in the Scholastic theology of penitence" in the 13th century (e.g. in Bonaventura, Thomas Aquinas and Duns Scotus). What is new is, for example, that the efficacy of the grace of the *contritio* is attributed to the performance of the sacrament.

[42] On the medieval Scotist teaching on repentance cf. particularly the works of Valens Heynck, e.g. his essay "Zur Lehre von der unvollkommenen Reue in der Skotistenschule des ausgehenden 15. Jahrhunderts", in: *Franziskanische Studien* 24 (1937), pp. 18–58. Cf. also Ohst (as n. 24), pp. 117–138; he shows how this theory of the sinner's imperfect striving for repentance being transformed and ennobled by the sacramental absolution evidently begins with William of Auvergne (†1249). Ohst sees the fact that repentance became a problem in the 13th century as being directly connected with a sophisticated legal set of standards which were increasingly obscure for laypeople: "How can a person ever find spontaneous, genuine repentance for a deed which objectively, measured by the prevailing standards, is sinful but which he himself does not recognize as such because he does not understand the standards?" (p. 118). Whether there really is, as Ohst assumes in his richly facetted study, a direct connection between this problem of an understanding of sin which was becoming more complicated legally and the sacramental reinterpretation of absolution along with the corresponding theory of *attritio/contritio* needs to be explored further in the sources.

there developed a massive sacramentalism which was able to gain all the more weight the less one trusted man's inner spirituality.[43] The obvious but also ambiguous interest of many theologians and priests in seeing the prestige of the effective authority of ecclesiastical office intensified joined forces with the awareness of the sins, anxieties and the need for assurance of the faithful. Consequently external penance – the Sacrament of Penance, the acts of penance and Indulgences – again became more important, while concurrent tendencies to internalize penitence continued unbroken from the 12th century to the end of the Middle Ages.

6.) A typical question raised by theologians at the end of the Middle Ages was: What is the understanding, feeling, willing, acting person as a religious subject capable of accomplishing if he strains to the limit all his innate spiritual powers – such as are left to him after the Fall?[44] Of what kind of love and remorse is a person capable without the attractive power of the Holy Spirit and the potency of God's grace flowing into his heart? The formulation of the question surely reveals how much one had learned to see a person's natural earthly living space as his own independent sphere of activity, and to focus on his worldly subjective existence. In the assessment of the religious capacities of the natural, sinful person, however, the opinions of the theologians around 1500 diverge totally.

7.) Let us take a look at the range of these opinions! We have already mentioned the Ockhamist conception. This holds that in his moral freedom man has a natural capacity to love God above all else and consequently to achieve true contrition.[45] This, then, is a moral optimism which cannot really explain why the person also needs an inner working of divine grace.[46] The most extreme counterposition to this Ockhamist understanding of penance was held above

---

[43] This over-exaggeration of the effect of the sacraments and indulgences in contrast to man's minimal ability to repent attains its most extreme form in the Augustinian monk, Johannes von Paltz (†1511) who was a member of the Erfurt community at the very time when Luther joined it (in July 1505). Cf. Berndt Hamm: *Frömmigkeitstheologie am Anfang des 16. Jahrhunderts. Studien zu Johannes von Paltz und seinem Umkreis* (Tübingen, 1982) [= Beiträge zur historischen Theologie 65], pp. 266–291.

[44] This is the question so typical for late-medieval theology of the *"facere quod in se est"* (What can the sinner before God achieve when he does all that he can?); cf. Heiko A. Oberman: *"Facientibus quod in se est deus non denegat gratiam.* Robert Holcot, O.P. and the beginnings of Luther's theology", in: *The Harvard Theological Review* 55 (1962), pp. 317–342.

[45] Cf. above, p. 137 with n. 34.

[46] Consequently the Ockhamist school bases the need to be filled with grace not

all by the theologians of the Augustinian Order – i.e. the order into whose Erfurt community the young Luther entered in 1505. From the theologians and spiritual instructors of his order, Luther could learn that the sinful person with his own innate powers is only capable of achieving egoistic flickers of emotion,[47] that he cannot achieve an emotion of love of God and true contrition through the loving imitation of Christ's Passion, but simply a sinful pang caused by selfish fear of punishment. He is like a criminal who is led to the gallows and repents his crimes not because he feels remorse or inner abhorrence but simply from fear of the gallows. Hence every sinner who does not have God's justifying and reforming grace is only capable of a shabby 'gallows remorse' ("*Galgenrew*"). It is only the merciful love of God entering his soul which brings him back into God's orbit. Only its spiritual power of grace transforms him into a truly loving and repentant person who follows in the footsteps of Christ.

III. *Johannes von Staupitz: The Significance of his Understanding of True Contrition for Luther*

Immediately before the Reformation it was above all the Augustinian monk, Johannes von Staupitz, who stressed that the sinner's repentance from beginning to end depended entirely upon grace.[48] Staupitz (†1524) was not only Luther's Superior in the Order and his teacher, but also his pastor, friend, and surrogate father.[49] In later years

---

on the sinful deficiency of human nature but on God's voluntary bond with humankind: In his complete freedom God has decided to accept as worthy of merit and satisfactory only such acts of love for God and one's neighbor as have been created by the divine quality of grace and love instilled in them. No qualitative or ethical change is brought about in the essence of man's ability to love through this infusion. Cf. Berndt Hamm: *Promissio, pactum, ordinatio. Freiheit und Selbstbindung Gottes in der scholastischen Gnadenlehre* (Tübingen, 1977) [= Beiträge zur historischen Theologie 54], pp. 361–365.

[47] Cf. Adolar Zumkeller: *Erbsünde, Gnade, Rechtfertigung und Verdienst nach der Lehre der Erfurter Augustinertheologen des Spätmittelalters* (Würzburg, 1984) [= Cassiciacum 35]; cf. idem: "Das Ungenügen der menschlichen Werke bei den deutschen Predigern des Spätmittelalters", in: *Zeitschrift für katholische Theologie* 81 (1959), pp. 265–305.

[48] Cf. Lothar Graf zu Dohna/Richard Wetzel: "Die Reue Christi. Zum theologischen Ort der Buße bei Johann von Staupitz", in: *Studien und Mitteilungen zur Geschichte des Benediktiner-Ordens und seiner Zweige* 94 (1983), pp. 457–482.

[49] For orientation (with literature details) on Staupitz and the topic 'Staupitz-Luther' cf. Wolfgang Günter: "Johann von Staupitz (ca. 1468–1524)", in: Erwin

Luther frequently emphasized in letters to Staupitz and in other rem-
iniscences what pioneering insights he owed to the elder monk, who
however did not join in his own break with the papal Church.[50] Let
us take a closer look at the theological proximity of the two and
Luther's step beyond Staupitz, for it is here we shall see the decisive transition from the soteriological centrality of the love of God
in the Middle Ages to the centrality of justification by faith alone
in the Reformation. This is a piece of theological microhistory which
changed the course of world history.

When Luther published the detailed commentary on his terse 95
Theses on Indulgences in the early summer of 1518, he prefaced
the edition with an accompanying letter to Staupitz in which he
describes how, years before, the esteemed *Pater* had helped him to
a new understanding of penance.[51] Through his instruction the bitter word 'penance' (*poenitentia*) became sweet. For earlier – no doubt
influenced by Ockhamist teachings[52] – Luther had always understood

---

Iserloh (ed.): *Katholische Theologen der Reformationszeit* 5 (Münster, 1988) [= Katholisches
Leben und Kirchenformen im Zeitalter der Glaubenspaltung 48], pp. 11–31; Lothar
Graf zu Dohna: "Staupitz und Luther. Kontinuität und Umbruch in den Anfängen
der Reformation", in: *Pastoraltheologie* 74 (1985), pp. 452–465; Richard Wetzel:
"Staupitz und Luther", in: Volker Press/Dieter Stievermann (eds.): *Martin Luther.
Probleme seiner Zeit* (Stuttgart, 1986) [= Spätmittelalter und Frühe Neuzeit 16], pp.
75–87; a revised version of Wetzel's essay in: *Ebernburg-Hefte* 25 (1991), pp. 369(41)–
395(47).

[50] Cf. e.g Luther's last letter to Staupitz, dated 17th September 1523, *WA Br*
3,155f., 6–8 Nr. 659 = Otto Scheel (ed.): *Dokumente zu Luthers Entwicklung*, 2nd edition (Tübingen, 1929), p. 30 Nr. 74: Staupitz is the one *"per quem primum cepit evangelii lux de tenebris splendescere in cordibus nostris"* (cf. 2 Cor. 4.6); Luther's letter to
Count Albrecht of Mansfeld, dated 23rd February 1542, *WA Br* 9.627, 23–25 Nr.
3716 = Scheel p. 167 Nr. 461: "Jnn disen gedancken oder anfechtungen [. . .] ich
etwa [= einst] auch drinnen gestecket. Vndt wo mihr D. Staupitz, oder viel mehr
Gott durch Doctor Staupitz, nicht heraus geholffen hette, so were ich darin ersoffen
vndt langst in der helle." (I was once bogged down in such thoughts and doubts.
And if Dr. Staupitz – or rather God through Dr. Staupitz – had not helped me,
I would have drowned in them and long been in hell.)

[51] Letter from Luther to Staupitz dated 30th May 1518, *WA Br* 1,525–527 =
Scheel (as n. 50) pp. 9–11 Nr. 18; Wetzel (as n. 49, version in the Ebernburg-
Hefte), pp. 374–385.

[52] Since it is well-known that Luther's theological development was strongly
influenced by the Ockhamist, Gabriel Biel, the following reminiscence (from his
Enarratio Psalmi LI, 1538) clearly relates to the Contritionism of the Biel school (cf.
above, n. 34): "Hac doctrina [scil. de contritionibus et attritionibus] sane ita sum
ego in scholis corruptus, ut vix magno labore, Dei gratia, me ad solum 'Auditum
gaudii' (Ps. 51.10) potuerim convertere. Nam si expectandum eo usque est, donec
sufficienter conteraris, nunquam pervenies ad auditum gaudii. Id quod in monas-
terio magno cum dolore saepissime expertus sum, sequebar enim hanc doctrinam

penance as something enforced and wrested out laboriously, as a
strain and an obligation with the goal of the true contrition of love,
confession and works of satisfaction. Staupitz, however, opened his
eyes to what true penance really is: (1) that the love of God and his
righteousness is not its consummation but its starting-point, a love
which is not strained but is gratefully given thanks to the encounter
with the suffering of the "sweetest Redeemer"; (2) that we cannot
understand penance in the biblical sense as the acts the person performs: what is meant is a fundamental change in his attitude and
emotions, a "*transmutatio mentis et affectus*"; (3) that this existential change
of direction is not a human achievement but is caused by the grace
of God; put precisely: it is not changing oneself, but being changed.

Much of what Luther describes here as a joyful discovery of true,
biblical penance bequeathed to him by Staupitz might bring to mind
certain characteristics of the reorientation of the understanding of
penance in the 12th century: how at that time the emphasis was
shifted from the external level of making satisfaction to the inner
penitential emotion of remorse, how this remorse was understood as
growing out of the impetus of God's love and man's answering love
and was anchored in the event of the Incarnation and Passion of
Christ. The change which took place in the 12th century was connected with the renaissance of interest in Augustine just as we must
understand the theological insights of a Staupitz and Luther from
the Augustine-renaissance of their era.[53] They too, in their day, had
to contend with types of 'archaic' piety obsessed with deeds and
tariffs. Just as after 1100, the 'true' biblical sense of *poenitentia* needed
to be rediscovered. But in the late Middle Ages this was not the
same as in the days of Abelard and Bernard. If we compare Staupitz'
sermons and tracts from the years before the Reformation the vast
difference from the beginning of the 12th century is obvious.

The theologians of the High Middle Ages were in no doubt that
the love awakened in the heart of the sinner through God's Spirit
endued his life with the powers of spiritual transformation and perfec-

---

de contritionibus" (in contrast to the Scotist *doctrina de attritionibus*); *WA* 40/II,411,36–
412,17 = Scheel (as n. 50), p. 95,11–16 Nr. 241.
  [53] Cf. Heiko A. Oberman: *Werden und Wertung der Reformation. Vom Wegestreit zum
Glaubenskampf* (Tübingen, 1977), pp. 82–140 (The Augustinian renaissance in the
late Middle Ages); on the Augustinian renaissance of the 12th century cf. above,
n. 7.

tion and that consequently there was also a direct causal connection between loving repentance, the forgiveness of sins and justification. Staupitz on the other hand, as an attentive pastor, has particularly intensely absorbed the spiritual disillusionment at the end of the Middle Ages and worked this into his radical Augustinian theology of grace. He contrasts man's total wretchedness and spiritual poverty with God's abundant mercy in Jesus Christ.[54] Certainly he too thinks that the soul of the human sinner is led to a true, loving contrition through the gift of transforming grace. Indeed, every person who is drawn into the force-field of Christ's Passion experiences the spiritual rebirth which makes him capable of true love of God and genuine pangs of remorse. But this human remorse, as Staupitz stresses in the same breath, is always so miserably insignificant that there is no way it can ever come up to the standard of achieving forgiveness of sins by its own emotional quality.[55] There can only be any causal connection between the sinner's loving contrition and the forgiveness of sin because Christ's infinitely priceless pain of remorse in the Garden of Gethsemane and the mental suffering of his Passion (which far exceeded his physical suffering on the Cross) compensates for all the inadequacy of our human contrition. Human love of God is elevated only through Christ's Passion. Only so can it be a justifying and saving love.[56] As Staupitz sees it, the contemporary illusion that

---

[54] Cf. Staupitz' tract printed at the beginning of 1517 (arising from his Advent sermons in Nuremberg in 1516): *Libellus de exsecutione aeternae praedestinationis*, ed. by Lothar Graf zu Dohna/Richard Wetzel (Berlin/New York, 1979) (= *Johann von Staupitz: Sämtliche Schriften*, vol. 2) [= Spätmittelalter und Reformation/Texte und Untersuchungen 14] §64 (p. 150): "Ego admiror coniunctionem summae misericordiae cum summa miseria."

[55] Cf. Staupitz: *Salzburger Predigten* 1520, Codex St. Peter b V 8, Pr. 6. fol. 96v–97r; quoted in Dohna/Wetzel (as n. 48), p. 466: "O mein got, wie ain klaine reu ist es umb mich [= bei mir], das ich ain missfallen umb mein sündt hab und traur darüber." ("Oh my God, what a tiny regret that is in me, that I have displeasure and sorrow for my sin.")

[56] Cf. the continuation of the Staupitz text in n. 55: Christ answers the sinner – who surely feels a true contrition from his love to God but is aware of the lifelong worthlessness and inadequacy of his own pangs of remorse – by pointing to his own remorse in the Garden of Gethsemane. The sinner can make this perfect, eternally precious vicarious remorse his own if he only relates his own suffering to this suffering of Christ: "Nain, nain, fleuch nuer zu meinem herzenlaid und zeuchs in dich, so ist die sündt schon volkömen pereut" ("No, no, fly only to my heart's suffering and draw it to yourself and so your sin is fully repented of.") Quotation from Dohna/Wetzel ibid. Cf. also the theologically even more dynamic text of a sermon on repentance which Staupitz preached in Nuremberg in Lent 1517 and which was recorded by the Nuremberg council clerk, Lazarus Spengler: ed. by

such an egocentric grief over one's sins as apprehensive gallows-con-
trition might be transformed into a true contrition of love through
the power of the Sacrament of Penance is completely erroneous.[57]
A cast of mind which is worthy to be called 'repentance' can only
have as its central starting-point a heartfelt love of God; but it is
only the power of Christ's vicarious suffering which makes this true
human contrition – as Staupitz says – a "sufficient" contrition, i.e.
a contrition which is enough, "sufficient" to receive the divine forgiveness for all sins.[58] Put in a metaphor: Only because we human
beings with our paltry feeling of love can climb on to the shoulders
of Christ's great love and great suffering can our contrition – which
in itself is so inadequate – become a contrition which wipes out our
sins. Lilliputian human contrition can reach heaven only on the
shoulders of the giant Christ.[59]

Knaake (as n. 18), pp. 15–19: especially p. 16 (that man must "ground" his contrition on that of Christ – i.e. find in this the ground for the forgiveness of sins).
On the relationship between human contrition and that of Christ in Staupitz – like
that of the analogous relationship of human merit and that of Christ – cf. generally Dohna/Wetzel ibid. passim and Hamm (as n. 43), pp. 238–243.

[57] Staupitz: Nuremberg sermon on repentance (as n. 56), ed. Knaake, p. 16:
Gallows' repentance, the characteristic of which is that it only relates to "human
gain and loss" is "totally useless and sterile".

[58] Ibid. p. 16: Through the "schmerzen, rew und traurigkeit unsers seligmachers"
(suffering, remorse and sadness of our Saviour) man's true loving contrition is
"allererst angezundet und lebendig gemacht und dan zu abtilgung unnser sonden
mer dann genugsam" (first kindled and brought to life and then becomes more
than enough to wipe out our sins). Here as is clear from the context and his other
writings Staupitz has in mind a twofold effect of Christ's suffering: On the one
hand, as an inner working of grace, it enflames the answering contrition of the sinner; on the other, through its immeasurable merit it complements externally all the
imperfection of this human contrition so that it becomes "more than enough" to
achieve forgiveness of sin. Consequently the valency of contrition to wipe out sin
is an external valency bestowed by God for Christ's sake. Cf. Hamm (as n. 43),
pp. 240–243 and n. 59 following.

[59] The 'sufficiency' of repentance is thereby the assumption of Christ's contrition, of which Staupitz says (ibid. p. 16): "Dieser schmerz und berewung Christi,
wo wir unser rew darein ergrunden, ist zu abwaschung aller unser missethat
genungsam und so vellig, wo es moglich were, das tausent welt weren, das sie durch
diese engstliche plutschwaissung Christi [Lk. 22.44] irer sonden entledigt wurden."
(This pain and remorse of Christ upon which we base our repentance is sufficient
to wash away all our transgressions, and is so plenteous that if there were a thousand worlds their sins would be discharged through Christ's fearful sweating of
blood.) The comparison with the giant's shoulders is not taken from the sources.

IV. *Luther's New Understanding of Contrition:*
Faith is Love, but Love does not Justify

It is precisely here that we find the decisive point where Luther goes beyond the late-medieval confines of a Johannes von Staupitz. Typical of the late Middle Ages is the question of sufficient penance: Of what kind and how much repentance, confession, satisfactory deeds or purchase of indulgences is necessary and "sufficient" to wipe out guilt and eternal and temporal punishments for sin? What kind of help does the sinner need to kindle at least a spark of that true love of God, that painful love of true contrition without which no one in the end reaches salvation? And how does this true contrition become a saving contrition? When at the end of May 1518 Luther wrote his letter to Staupitz on true penitence it was no longer a question for him of adequate "sufficient" penance and contrition.[60] He, too, once began with this question,[61] but the radicality of his own experience of sin and his encounter with the sovereignty of God's free mercy led him to realize that it can never be the quality of one's inner love of God and feelings of remorse which allow a person to be blessed with the forgiveness of sins and save him from damnation. Repentance – whatever form it takes and upon whatever kind of shoulders it rests (thereby including the loving contrition which leans upon Christ's remorse) – can never be a sufficient, saving repentance in relation to the forgiveness of sins and heavenly salvation. Consequently the peace of the troubled can not be grounded in it.[62]

---

[60] Cf. Luther's polemic against the question of "*satis contritum esse*" – of "sufficient" contrition – in his commentary on the 38th thesis on Indulgences (written quite some time before the letter to Staupitz). In the justification of the sinner it is not a question of the "*fervor contritionis*" but of the "*fides absolutionis*". Whatever the state of your contrition ("*quicquid sit de contritione tua*"), however inadequate it is, the only important thing is the faith in Christ's word of forgiveness (given by the priest) *WA* 1,594,37–595,5.21–34 = Otto Clemen (ed.): *Luthers Werke in Auswahl*, vol. 1, 6th Edition (Berlin, 1966), pp. 105,5–16 and 105,37–106,14.

[61] Cf. Luther's retrospective glance in 1538, already cited in n. 52, which begins with the question which once tormented him: "*Utrum fuerit contritio sufficiens*": *WA* 40/II, 411,10f. = Scheel (as n. 50), p. 94,27.

[62] Cf. Luther's theses (which were probably developed in the early summer of 1518) '*Pro veritate inquirenda et timoratis conscientiis consolandis conclusiones*', *WA* 1,629 – 633, e.g. thesis 18 (p. 631,23f.): "Super contritionem edificantes remissionem super arenam, id est super opus hominis, fidem dei edificant" and Theses 8 and 9 (p. 631,3–6): "Remissio culpe non innititur contritioni peccatoris, nec officio aut potestati sacerdotis, innititur potius fidei, que est in verbum Christi dicentis: 'Quodcunque

It is true that, because Luther takes mankind's lifelong sinful deca-
dence so seriously, he cannot imagine a Christian life without the
pain of true penance; and by this he means that the person reaches
the end of his own possibilities, safeguards and certainties, that he
becomes humbly aware that before God he is a beggar with empty
hands[63] and that he sincerely regrets his sins. The letter to Staupitz
shows how important such a heartfelt repentance is for Luther as
he was also concerned in the famous 95 Theses with just such true
repentance and true contrition.[64] But what is decisive in comparison
with the Middle Ages is that in his view this pain of true repentance which arises from love of God does not in itself justify and
save – i.e. is not a "sufficient" repentance.[65] It is simply man's admission that he cannot contribute anything towards his salvation, not
even the smallest spark of a loving, contrite emotion. For Luther
this is not simply a subjective, humbly pious attitude of a sighing
ego but formulates an objective, doctrinal reality: The human being,
no matter how great his love of God and pain for his sins, cannot
really contribute anything towards his redemption either through his
pious emotions or his moral activities. "*Hoc est verum!*"[66]

---

solveris etc.'" On this cf. the interpretation by Oswald Bayer: *Promissio. Geschichte
der reformatorischen Wende in Luthers Theologie* (Göttingen, 1971) [= Forschungen zur
Kirchen- und Dogmengeschichte 24], pp. 164–202, especially pp. 182–202.

[63] Cf. the famous words of the one-time mendicant Luther in his last note and
Heiko A. Oberman's commentary: "Wir sein pettler. *Hoc est verum*. Bund und Gnade
in der Theologie des Mittelalters und der Reformation", *Zeitschrift für Kirchengeschichte*
78 (1967), pp. 232–252.

[64] Cf. from the '*Disputatio pro declaratione virtutis indulgentiarum*' (31st October 1517)
e.g. Thesis 4: "Manet itaque pena, donec manet odium sui (id est penitentia vera
intus), scilicet usque ad introitum regni celorum" and Thesis 40: "Contritionis veritas
penas querit et amat, veniarum autem largitas relaxat et odisse facit, saltem occasione":
WA 1,233,16f. and 235,16f. = Clemen, vol. 1 (as n. 60), pp. 3,26–28 and 5,37f.
In interpreting the 95 Theses we must take into consideration the fact that they
are not concerned with justification (and consequently not with faith) but with indulgences (and consequently with penance and remorse). This means that Luther is
not concerned in them to explain in a comforting way how the sinner enters into
Christ's grace and righteousness but wishes to make it clear, in a sharp and provoca-
tive way, how the sinner – on the basis of the grace bestowed upon him and in
the emulation of Christ – leaves himself open to the gravity of the penitential life
with its destruction of human possibilities and certainties and consequently denies
himself the escape of a deceptive assurance of grace and salvation.

[65] Cf. the quotation from the Theses '*De veritate*' above, n. 62 and below, n. 69.

[66] Cf. above, n. 63. Already in Luther's first lecture series on the Psalms the
statements about the subjective-existential prayerful attitude before God (*humilitas*)
and the didactic objectified truth coincide in one and the same *modus loquendi*; cf.
Chapter 5, below: "Why did 'Faith' become for Luther the Central Concept of the
Christian life?"

During the years 1513–1518 Luther, gradually drawing away from medieval spirituality, had brought the love of God and loving contrition theologically to the point where he relocated faith into the central position held by love in the Middle Ages.[67] Consequently after 1516 faith and contrition drift farther and farther apart in his writings.[68] Faith remains connected with contrition – there is no faith in Christ without the pain of repentance[69] – but faith itself now loses its characteristic note of pain and takes on for Luther the characteristic of the undoubting, joyful confidence which clings to the word of promise in the Gospel, to that biblical promise which assures the sinner personally: Your sins are forgiven. Hence Luther replaces the medieval association of loving repentance and the forgiveness of sins with the connection of faith and the word of forgiveness. But what does this mean? Is not faith as Luther sees it a kind of unmitigated love of God even if it is no longer a painful, loving contrition but a joyful, confident love of God? As he constantly reiterates, faith is a sincere confidence in God's saving loving-kindness, in his unconditional mercy for the sake of Jesus Christ. Can this faith then be understood as anything other than a warming of the soul through the power of the Holy Spirit and consequently as a confident love which *is* totally love in that it expects and receives everything from God?

Although this was indeed the case[70] Luther displays the greatest

---

[67] Already in this form in the 'Dictata super Psalterum' 1513–1515; cf. below p. 167f.

[68] This development can first be seen in the second half of Luther's lecture course on the Epistle to the Romans; cf. Matthias Kroeger: *Rechtfertigung und Gesetz. Studien zur Entwicklung der Rechtfertigungslehre beim jungen Luther* (Göttingen, 1968) [= Forschungen zur Kirchen- und Dogmengeschichte 20], pp. 152–163; this development reaches its conclusion in the Theses *'De veritate . . .'* (as n. 62). This in no way signifies that, as Oswald Bayer claimed, we should see this set of theses as Luther's first reforming texts.

[69] Cf. the Theses *'Pro veritate . . . conclusiones'*, Thesis 40: "Finge casum (per impossibile) sit absolvendus non contritus, credens tamen sese absolvi, hic est vere absolutus" (*WA* 1,632,28f.). Hence Luther cannot envisage a justifying faith without a simultaneous loving repentance inextricably bound to this faith (*"impossibile"*!); yet what he means to say in the thesis is that it is not the repentance but the faith that receives the justifying forgiveness of sins. No faith without contrition, but no *contritio justificans*!

[70] On the metaphor of 'being warmed' cf. Luther's sermon from 9th June 1532 on God's love to humanity: "Denn es nicht moeglich ist, were solch fewr seiner liebe fuelet, das er nicht auch solt ein wenig davon erwermet und entzundet werden." (For it is impossible for one who feels the fire of his love not to be a little warmed and inflamed by it) *WA* 36,429,28–30 (though without mention of the concept of faith). Cf. occasional phrases used by Luther which characterize the essence of faith and its "joy" as love of God, e.g. in the tract *Von der Freiheit eines Christenmenschen,*

restraint, indeed a kind of inhibition about defining faith as love of God.[71] He talks effusively of God's self-offering, saving love[72] and of the exalted love of Christ, the Bridegroom, for his bride, believing humanity[73] just as he characterizes the living, active essence of faith as love of one's neighbor.[74] Love flows from God to the believer and from the believer to his neighbor.[75] But for the confident reciprocal relationship of humankind to God Luther typically no longer employs as a basic term the traditionally favored concept of *love* but of all things the concept of *faith*, which in Scholastic theology stood for the emotionally weakest and least pious dimension of Christian exis-

§21: "die seel durch den glauben reyn ist, vnd gott liebet" (the soul is pure through faith and loves God), §27: "also fleusset auß dem glauben die lieb vnd lust zu gott" (hence out of faith flows love and joy in God), §20: "Vnd stett alle seyn [des Glaubens] lußt darynn, das er widderumb mocht gott auch vmbsonst dienen ynn freyer lieb" (since faith itself is grateful love of God, its joy consists in serving God too without reward in free love); *Martin Luther Studienausgabe*, ed. by Hans-Ulrich Delius, vol. 2 (East Berlin, 1982), pp. 287,24f.; 299,14f.; 287,9f. On the character of faith as love of God cf. also Luther's sermon-postille: *WA* 10/I/1,73,8f.; 102,11; 260,15f.; 10/I/2,187,25. Cf. also below, n. 73 (Elert) and Peter Manns "*Fides absoluta – Fides incarnata*. Zur Rechtfertigungslehre Luthers im Großen Galater-Kommentar", in: Erwin Iserloh/Konrad Repgen (eds.): *Reformata Reformanda, Festgabe für Hubert Jedin*, vol. 1 (Münster, 1965), pp. 265–312: 288–312; Reinhard Schwarz, "Die Umformung des religiösen Prinzips der Gottesliebe in der frühen Reformation. Ein Beitrag zum Verständnis von Luthers Schrift 'Von der Freiheit eines Christenmenschen'" in: Stephen E. Buckwalter, Bernd Moeller (eds.): *Die frühe Reformation in Deutschland als Umbruch* (Gütersloh 1998) [= SVRG 199], pp. 128–148, especially the comment on the strongly affective component of faith, p. 145.

[71] Cf. e.g. Luther's exegesis of the first Commandment in the Greater Catechism: *Die Bekenntnisschriften der evangelisch-lutherischen Kirche*, 5th Edition, Göttingen 1963, pp. 560–572. The faith which carries out the first Commandment is here described by Luther as trust and sincere confidence but is not called love – in contrast to the famous exegesis of the first Commandment in the Lesser Catechism: "We should fear, love and trust God above everything" (ibid. p. 507,42f.) but where Luther does not mention faith.

[72] The divine being as "feur offen und brunst solcher liebe, die himel und erden fuellet": ("the fiery oven and heat of such love as fills heaven and earth"): *WA* 36,424,18f. (Sermon from 9th June 1532): cf. also 429,1–5,13–24.

[73] Cf. Werner Elert: *Morphologie des Luthertums*, vol. 1, Munich 1931, pp. 147–154. Elert shows how, in Luther's understanding, the "moment of reciprocity" is contained in this "relationship of love", i.e. "that God's love engenders our love for him" (with reference to *WA* 10/III,157,9ff.); hence for Luther faith is "the relationship of a mutual love between the 'I' and 'Thou' in the most personal sense" (p. 151).

[74] Cf. Rudolf Mau: "Liebe als gelebte Freiheit der Christen. Luthers Auslegung von G 5,13–24 im Kommentar von 1519", in: *Lutherjahrbuch* 59 (1992), pp. 11–37.

[75] Cf. Luther: *Von der Freiheit eines Christenmenschen*, '29: *Studienausgabe* (as n. 70), p. 305,1–11.

tence.[76] In choosing this concept as central in the justification of the ungodly, Luther wants to say that the human person is not justified and saved through personal spiritual emotions, through pious feelings like love of God and loving contrition, but solely through the passive reception from without. For him faith is the manner of pure receiving, of being vouchsafed the righteousness of Jesus Christ;[77] it is granted to the believers when they put their trust in the Gospel – i.e. have no confidence in themselves but put all their trust in God's saving acts.

By contrast, the concept of the love of God was highly problematical in Luther's eyes. In the theological tradition it was easily connected with the idea of a spiritual quality which increases a person's affective and operative capacity. But Luther patently wanted to keep such a view of religious quality and activity out of the sinner's relationship to God and salvation. This also corresponded to his own fundamental, primary experience that as a sinful human being he was incapable of feeling true love of God[78] and would be lost if he were somehow to base his access to salvation on his own ability to love – even if this was an ability to love bestowed upon him through God's mercy and his Spirit. Here the concept of faith should banish any association with distinction, virtue, uprightness or good works and indicate 'only' a *relationship* consisting in being the recipient of a gift. Faith then means to be liberated from all the conditions of salvation involved with feeling and acting. Certainly faith is a kind of loving feeling, indeed the most radical form of love because it depends on God alone; but it justifies and saves not by its emotion nor by its affective ardor and fervor but only because it is received. Faith is love of God, but it is always a broken love because of the fundamental sin of lovelessness, radical love cast in doubt by radical sin. Hence faith justifies and saves not through its loving but through its reception; not the loving but the sinful person is acquitted. This

---

[76] Piety (*pietas, devotio*) here in the sense of a manner and structuring of one's life in relationship to God. On the medieval concept of faith cf. Chapter 5.

[77] "Ingressus in Christum est fides, quae nos colligit in divitias iustitiae dei." *Operationes in Psalmos: WA* 5,408,4f.

[78] Luther traces the experience of the "*semper peccator*" (first lectures on the Psalms) and the "*simul iustus et peccator*" (lectures on the Epistle to the Romans) back to that attitude of faith with which he can perceive himself as a hopelessly recreant sinner who is incapable of love and at the same time see himself in the light of Christ's righteousness.

is what Luther is trying to say when he names not love but faith as the saving relationship between man and God.[79]

V. *Summary*

Let me summarize the main conclusion of this chapter. For the theology of the 12th century it was a pioneering discovery to overcome the fixation on outwardly visible religious acts by turning to the inner emotion of love of God. Almost 400 years later, however, Luther not only opposed a religiosity of good works. For him it was liberating to surmount both the fixation on pious action and the fixation on the inwardness of true love of God by listening to the exculpating word of the Gospel and consequently by receiving the saving righteousness which comes from outside us – *extra nos*.[80] This was his discovery of faith. In doing this Luther took up a position beyond that of late-medieval tendencies to trivialize and internalize penance.

---

[79] Zwingli, in contrast to Luther, has no qualms about identifying faith and love within the existential movement of trust in God. Cf. Berndt Hamm: *Zwinglis Reformation der Freiheit* (Neukirchen-Vluyn, 1988), pp. 76–78.

[80] Cf. Karl-Heinz zur Mühlen: *'Nos extra nos'. Luthers Theologie zwischen Mystik und Scholastik* (Tübingen, 1972) [= Beiträge zur historischen Theologie 46]; Wilfried Joest: *Ontologie der Person bei Luther* (Göttingen, 1967).

WHY DID 'FAITH' BECOME FOR LUTHER THE CENTRAL CONCEPT OF THE CHRISTIAN LIFE?

I. *The Question from the Medieval Perspective*

It is a well known fact that the cardinal position held by the concept of faith provides a link between the different currents of the Reformation.[1] In pamphlets and tracts from all sides, we continually come across the programmatic slogan: "Man is justified by faith alone and not by works!" – faith being understood as direct access to the Word of God and consequently as confidence that one will attain salvation.[2] The question how this typical Reformation position of *'sola fide'* came into being takes us back to the roots of the Reformation and faces us with the fact that the first stages of the Reformation were essentially a result of theology and piety, embedded in the teachings of medieval theology and in the empirical context of an Observant monastery. This means that the question leads us back to the first beginnings of a new theology developed circa 1509/10 in Erfurt and Wittenberg by the young Augustinian monk, Martin Luther, and documented in his own hand between 1509 to 1516: in the marginal notes to Lombard in 1509/10[3] and especially in the notes for his first lectures on the Psalms (1513–1515)[4] and the Epistle to the Romans (1515/16).[5]

I should like to ask from a medieval perspective how such an

---

[1] I owe many suggestions for this article to the students who took part in my Erlangen seminar on "Luther's Discovery of Faith" in the summer semester of 1996, and to my assistant Dr. Petra Seegets.

[2] Cf. most recently Thomas Hohenberger: *Lutherische Rechtfertigungslehre in den reformatorischen Flugschriften der Jahre 1521–22* (Tübingen, 1996) (with bibliography).

[3] *WA* 9, pp. 28–94; cf. for the same period Luther's marginal notes on Augustine: ibid. pp. 2–27.

[4] The first edition of the *Tractata super Psalterium: WA* 3 and 4 (1885 and 1886); new edition: *WA* 55/I (1993) = complete edition of Luther's glosses on the Psalms and *WA* 55/II/1, 1. Lieferung (1963) = edition of Luther's scholia on Psalms 1–15.

[5] *WA* 56 (1938).

astonishing shift of the centre of gravity to faith could take place
when for the Middle Ages, at least from the 12th century onwards,
love and not faith had been held to be the Christian form of life
decisive for salvation. I emphasize 'from a medieval perspective' not
simply because I am thinking of the radical change – as is customary in research on Luther – but particularly because, going beyond
the current state of research, I wish to call attention to his continuity with certain aspects of the medieval understanding of faith. I
would begin by formulating my thesis as follows: If Luther had not
positively taken up the late medieval scholastic theology and the theology of piety, the new centrality of '*sola fide*' in his theology would
be incomprehensible. There were particular aspects of the medieval
concept of faith which were important for Luther when in his lectures on the Psalms in 1513, for the first time he made the key
terms *fides*, *fidelis* and *credere* the decisive concepts for Christian existence and church life.[6] But at the same time (within this continuity)
Luther gave faith a new defining content that allowed it to super-
sede the medieval centrality of *caritas* and its works.

II. *The Medieval Understanding of Faith:*
The Levels of Faith, Humility and Hope

How was this process of displacement, so fundamental for the
Reformation, accomplished? To describe this I must first, at least in
brief outline, say a little about the common factors in the high and
late medieval concept of faith. I shall naturally start from such authors
as were particularly familiar to the Augustinian monk as a student.
The understanding of faith mediated to him by, for example, Gabriel
Biel[7] and Johannes von Staupitz[8] has the following characteristic
features:

---

[6] On the centrality of the concept of faith in Luther's *Dictata super Psalterium* cf.
the seminal study of Reinhard Schwarz: *Fides, spes und caritas beim jungen Luther, unter
besonderer Berücksichtigung der mittelalterlichen Tradition* (Berlin, 1962), p. 212 (in relation
to *caritas*) und p. 227 (in relation to *spes*). On occasion, though not yet as a formula, the young Luther also already uses the verbal combination *sola fides*, e.g. *WA*
4, 380, 19f. On the significant comparison with the exegetical tradition of medieval
interpretation of the Psalms cf. below n. 36.
[7] Gabriel Biel: *Canonis misse expositio I–IV*, ed. by Heiko Augustinus Oberman,
William J. Courtenay (Wiesbaden, 1963–1967); *Collectorium circa quattuor libros Sententiarum*,
ed. by Wilfrid Werbeck, Udo Hofmann, 5 vols. (Tübingen, 1973–1984, with indexes
by W. Werbeck, Tübingen, 1992). Biel not only shows himself in his Commentary

1.) Already in the Middle Ages, faith – together with baptism – is the fundamental principle of Christian existence, the basic attitude which differentiates the Christian from non-Christians. It is the fundamental principle, but also – we must immediately add – the least important element of Christian existence, as yet completely insufficient for the attainment of salvation.

2.) Faith always stands in a constitutive relationship to the revealed truth of God. In this sense it is 'accepting as true' through hearing what the person himself cannot say or observe intuitively but is transmitted to him by the authority of Holy Scripture and the Church.

3.) From this arises the fundamental orientation of faith to the word: It is meant to hear and obey the authoritative word of the divine truth.[9]

---

on the Mass (first printed 1489) and Commentary on the Sentences (first printed 1501) to be a decided adherent of the Occamist line of teaching, but also represents in his quotations a certain breadth and "harvest" of the medieval school tradition – and in this respect he serves me as a source for the common traits of the understanding of faith in the various streams of the high and late Middle Ages. Thus for instance Thomas Aquinas is the most frequently cited theological authority in Biel's Commentary on the Sentences; cf. the index, pp. 140–144. On Biel's concept of faith cf. Heiko Augustinus Oberman: *Spätscholastik und Reformation, vol. 1: Der Herbst der mittelalterlichen Theologie*, pp. 68–87 (ch. 3).

[8] Johann von Staupitz, *Tübinger Predigten*, ed. by Richard Wetzel (Berlin – New York, 1987) = J.v.S., *Sämtliche Schriften*, ed. by Lothar Graf zu Dohna, Richard Wetzel: *Lateinische Schriften I*, p. 552f. and 564f. (subject index: see 'credere' and 'fides'). Luther of course did not know these sermons on Job, extant only in Staupitz' autograph, which probably date from between 1495 and 1500. Yet they show what kind of theology of piety was represented by the man who cultivated such intensive contact with the young monk Luther as the superior of his order, as his teacher and confessor. Certainly Staupitz appears in this cycle of sermons as a profiled pupil of Augustine, but at the same time he represents a broad spectrum of theologically reflected spirituality and in the situating of faith, for example, he closely follows formulations of Jean Gerson, so that he too, like Biel in his own way, can be read as representative of a certain theological consensus in the field of high and late medieval understanding of faith.

[9] It appears to me that medieval theology was never able to make clear what the so-called infusion and formation of faith by grace (on "fides infusa" and "formata") actually meant for the character of faith itself – as a virtue of the Christian in its own right distinguished from hope (*spes*) and love (*caritas*) – beyond the elementary stage of faith acquired by hearing. This formation of faith was always qualitatively determined by the formative caritas but not described as a feature of the virtue of faith itself. Consequently "fides ex auditu" (Ro. 10.17) in its elementary meaning was decisive for the description of the specific nature of the "virtus fidei", while the intensified forms of infused and formed faith as fides remained remarkably pale and acquired their whole coloring from love.

4.) In its relationship to the binding doctrine of the truth of God, faith is always a recognition, knowledge and consent on the part of the intelligence, the *intellectus.* Hence faith is essentially cognitive.[10]

5.) Faith is a firm adherence to the truth (as Biel formulates it in accord with tradition)[11] and consequently possesses in its recognition an infallible certainty, *certitudo* and *securitas*, of the contents of faith.

6.) Faith is always receptive: a receiving and acceptance of the truth as taught and proclaimed, not creative, active or working – in contrast to the medieval *caritas*, which is always characterized as operative in its realm.

7.) Hence faith is first and foremost conceived as a relationship *ad extra* describing the receptive relationship of the person to the church's truth, while love is the dominant qualitative concept for the innermost heart. Faith is the way by which the person comes to an assured knowledge of God; love is the way by which God comes to dwell in his heart.

8.) This means at the same time: Of all the concepts of medieval theology which describe a spiritual change and adjustment in the inner person, 'faith' is the least qualitatively characterized. Only

---

[10] It can be said without qualification: Faith has its place in that human capacity to know and understand (the *intellectus*) which is directed towards spiritual truths. Certainly the will is also always involved in faith – in ways variously defined according to the different schools – insofar as the believer willingly assents to what he recognizes, i.e. accepts it as true. Yet these willed acts of *assensus* are directly coupled with the rational character of the *intellectus*; there is no shifting of faith to the level of the powers of emotion (affects) in the "heart". The reference to *voluntas* underscores the free nature of faith, whose subject remains solely the *intellectus* and its *ratio*. Faith is thus the freely willed movement from apprehension of the content of faith through its cognition and recognition to rational comprehension of what is believed, – Cf. *Lehrverurteilungen – kirchentrennend?, vol. I: Rechtfertigung, Sakramente und Amt im Zeitalter der Reformation und heute*, ed. by Karl Lehmann, Wolfhart Pannenberg (Freiburg i.Br./Göttingen, 1986), p. 56: "Die Trienter Konzilsväter denken mit der mittelalterlichen Tradition bei dem *Wort* 'Glaube' (in der semantischen Spannung von 'fides' und 'credere'!) zunächst an die Zustimmung des Verstandes zum geoffenbarten Wort Gottes einerseits und an den 'objektiven' Glauben andererseits, wie er in Bekenntnis und Lehrverkündigung der Kirche niedergelegt ist."

[11] Cf. Gabriel Biel: *Collectorium circa quattuor libros Sententiarum III*, ed. Wilfrid Werbeck, Udo Hofmann (Tübingen, 1979), dist. 23, q. 2, art. 1, not. 1 (p. 407, l. 3–5): "Fides est notitia adhaesiva certa et firma veritatis ad religionem pertinentis per revelationem accepta." Cf. also there p. 408,18f. ("intellectus adhaesio"), 410,3 ("firmitas adhaesionis"), 411,9 ("apprehensio credibilis, id est veritatis credendae") und 424,23f. (the "fides acquisita" as "intellectualis virtus seu habitus derelictus ac causatus ab actibus intellectus apprehensivis vel adhaesivis, inclinans intellectum ad obiecti cognitionem aut ad veri adhaesionem").

in a limited sense is faith a moral virtue[12] since it is primarily receptive and not active. While a life lived in *caritas* brings sinners into an intimate relationship to God's loving-kindness, frees them from their egoism and qualitatively changes the orientation of their life, faith is not constituted by the existential relationship to God's loving-kindness but by the cognitive relationship to divine truth, not becoming good but becoming free of error. Consequently to have faith does not *eo ipso* mean to be good and perform good deeds. Faith *in itself* – as amorphous, naked faith – is perfectly compatible with lovelessness and reprobation. Even Judas Iscariot had faith.

9.) Hence faith is the lowest stage in the life of the Christian climbing step by step to Paradise. *Fides* certainly plays a part in the ascent; hence there are diverse types and degrees of faith, the way from a faith acquired to one infused or from an unformed to a formed faith. But the principle which brings about perfection does not lie in faith itself but in the form of the justifying grace and love flowing into the sinner. It is the formative principle of love mediated by grace which raises faith to that level of spiritual quality and morality which enables the attainment of salvation. Hence for medieval theology and piety what is most important in the life of a Christian is not *fides* but *caritas* and the meritorious and satisfactory good works it motivates in the justified person.[13]

So far we have discussed the location of faith compared to the pre-eminent concept of love. To understand Luther's new approach, however, we must go beyond the nine points just mentioned. In the medieval understanding faith is not simply constituted by the differentiation and co-operation between faith and love, but also by the tension between faith and hope. Here I am thinking particularly of the 15th century theology of piety which – as one can see in the

---

[12] Cf. Biel: op. cit., art. 3, dub. 4 (pp. 424,1–425,38); on this Schwarz: *Fides, spes und caritas* (as n. 6), p. 44f.

[13] A characteristic example is the following formulation of Johann von Staupitz on the human faith in salvation – closely bound up with hope and love – worked by the Spirit: "Vitam autem gloriae non vidimus, sed speramus et cognovimus per fidem, movemur autem ad eam per caritatem; ipsa namque caritas pondus est quo coelum attingimus. Caritas autem non consentit malo, ideo simul cum peccato mortali non stat." *Tübinger Predigten* (as n. 8), Sermo 24, line 191–195 (p. 368).

example of Johannes von Staupitz[14] – was shaped above all by Jean Gerson.[15] In his pastoral theology hope (*spes*) takes on a new weight. In contrast to faith, hope takes its place beside love since in the general medieval understanding *spes*, like *caritas*, is not rooted in the epistemic capacity but in volition and emotional life, not in the cognitive but in the affective area of the higher spiritual soul.[16] While faith is the acceptance of a way of teaching and thinking and consequently enlists the *intellectus* and *ratio* to understand the divine truth, hope like love is a way of life which orientates the heart's emotions to God's loving-kindness and the attainment of heavenly bliss. Here, however, there emerges a distinction which is extremely important for theology and piety at the end of the Middle Ages, up to and including religious art.[17] We can discern a kind of dichotomy here which I should like to characterize as follows:

Faith and hope are assigned to different levels of expression, which means at the same time: to different degrees of certainty and assurance. Christian faith moves in its cognition and confession towards an objectifying and generalizing level of validity – i.e. to the level of truth and certainty of the teaching church which transcends that of the individual. When believers take their stand on this level they

---

[14] On Staupitz' reception of Gerson cf. op. cit. p. 517f. (s.v. Gerson in the register of authorities and sources) and in particular the definition of the relation of fides to spes and caritas in Sermo 24, line 287–315 (pp. 371–373): mostly literally from Gerson.

[15] Certainly every theology has somehow to do with piety, but in the late middle ages only that type of theology which I call *theology of piety* was totally orientated towards piety in the sense of the pious (authentic) shaping of life – and indeed so exclusively that all theological themes and modes of reflection not directly relevant for piety fall out of the program of the theology of piety or are reshaped to fit it. Cf. Berndt Hamm: "Von der spätmittelalterlichen reformatio zur Reformation: der Prozeß normativer Zentrierung von Religion und Gesellschaft in Deutschland", in: *Archiv für Reformationsgeschichte* 84 (1993), pp. 7–82: 18–41, especially p. 19f. n. 26 (the relation of the theology of piety to scholastic and 'monastic' theology of the 15th century).

[16] Cf. e.g. Gerson: *De consolatione theologiae*, ed. Palémon Glorieux: *Jean Gerson: Oeuvres complètes*, vol. 9 (Paris, 1973), p. 196 above. Cf. too Thomas Aquinas, *Summa theologiae* II/II, q. 18, art. 1 (voluntas as subiectum of spes) and q. 24, art. 1 (voluntas as subiectum of caritas) in comparison with q. 4, art. 2 (intellectus as subiectum of fides). On the doctrine of hope (and its certainty) in Thomas and other scholastic theologians cf. the work of Basse cited below in n. 23.

[17] Think particularly of texts, particularly of the captions on devotional pictures of the century before the reformation. Such textual images, for example doctrinal formulations or short prayers, can be precisely assigned to the various levels of expression which I distinguish below.

know that their relationship to God is established by definite, universally valid rules made known in the divine revelation of salvation according to the rule: Only such as are free from mortal sin and die in a state of justified grace – i.e. love God with their whole heart and feel the pangs of true repentance for their sins – attain salvation. The knowledge of this rule is part of the sure certainty of faith. But even the person who thus firmly believes cannot know the answer to the question which is crucial for him personally, namely whether he himself is in a state of grace and love and consequently a candidate for salvation. On the general level of the knowledge of truth and its certainty as bestowed through faith there can be no personal, individual assurance of grace and salvation; at best there can only be a conjecture that one is in a state of grace.[18]

The situation is quite different at the level of expression of hope, which – we must immediately add – is always also the level of humility (*humilitas*). *Spes* and *humilitas* are for Gerson, as for the other teachers of the spiritual life before and after him, two sides of the same affective Christian stance.[19] In contrast to faith, however, humility and hope are expressed on a subjective, existential level – not on that of doctrine but of prayer. It is the personal, prayerful attitude in which a person in humble fear confesses his sins before the righteous, judging God and trustingly places all his hope on the merciful, saving God. Here faith's fixed knowledge of truth evaporates along with its specific uncertainty. For in the attitude of humility the awareness of the normal necessity for salvation of the inner quality of love in one's own heart and of the consequent satisfactions and merits is at once wiped out. Then sinners before God can see only their own emptiness, accuse themselves and despair – as Gerson demands – of their own possibilities of attaining salvation by their own merits.[20] In this humility the person makes himself even more

---

[18] On this 'coniecturaliter' cf. e.g. Thomas Aquinas: *Summa theologiae* I/II, q. 112, art. 5, "corpus".

[19] Cf. e.g. Gerson: *De consolatione theologiae*, ed. Glorieux (as in n. 16), vol. 9, p. 195 below; cf. also Staupitz: *Tübinger Predigten* (as in n. 8), Sermo 11, line 21–27 (p. 186).

[20] Cf. e.g. Gerson: *De vita spirituali animae*, ed. Glorieux (as in n. 16), vol. 3, Paris 1962, p. 126: "Denique perspicuum est, quanta necessitate desperare debeamus de viribus nostris ... nec confidere in homine, sed projicere totam spem nostram in Deum, ne confundamur, sed liberemur et nutriamur et glorificemur." Idem, *De praeparatione ad missam*, ed. Glorieux, vol. 9 (as in n. 16), p. 50: "Deum time, de te desperans, in se fidens, et mandata eius observa, quod in te est non omittens; hoc est omnis homo." With this pregnant summation Gerson's text closes.

insignificant than he actually is; he confesses guilt where there is no guilt, as is commonly said.[21] This means: In the self-condemnation of humility he obscures the truth, the reality of his actual standing before God. Yet just such humility is *de facto* of the highest spiritual quality and meritorious.[22] Analogous to this, hope, the sister of humility, leaps over the uncertainty characteristic of faith. In an attitude of pure trust, hope detaches itself from the uncertainty of its own quality, clings alone to God's gracious promises and thus wins a personal assurance of salvation which is not possible on the level of the knowledge of truth available to the *intellectus*.[23]

Consequently in medieval theology and piety there is a very instructive differentiation between the knowledge of truth and the uncertainty of faith on the one hand and blind humility and assurance of hope on the other. One can see here the cleft between a theoretical, objectifying, strongly rational form of teaching and the existential form of life of a personal situation before God, the polarity between an intellectualized religion of the lecture-hall[24] and an affective

---

[21] Corresponding to a much quoted sentiment of Gregory the Great: "Bonarum mentium est ibi culpam agnoscere, ubi culpa non est." Cf. Epist. XI, 64 (Migne *PL* 77, 1195 B). It is typical that this dictum is received and applied by Gerson (in the version of the text quoted) in the sense that the sinner should exaggerate his sense of guilt ("exaggerans quantum potest") as his own prosecutor, witness and judge; *De consolatione theologiae*, ed. Glorieux (as in n. 16), vol. 9, p. 232f. Cf. Sven Grosse: *Heilsungewißheit und Scrupulositas im späten Mittelalter. Studien zu Johannes Gerson und Gattungen der Frömmigkeitstheologie seiner Zeit* (Tübingen, 1994), pp. 54 and 122.

[22] Cf. Grosse, ibid., pp. 113–118 (merit and grace).

[23] Cf. e.g. Gerson: *De consolatione theologiae*, ed. Glorieux (as in n. 16), vol. 9, p. 195f.; on this Grosse: ibid., pp. 106–111 (certainty of hope) and also on this whole thematic Michael Basse: *Certitudo Spei. Thomas von Aquins Begründung der Hoffnungsgewißheit und ihre Rezeption bis zum Konzil von Trient als ein Beitrag zur Verhältnisbestimmung von Eschatologie und Rechtfertigungslehre* (Göttingen, 1993) (without taking account of Gerson and medieval theology of piety and with only minimal attention to late scholasticism – in a word, one of the systematic-theological Thomas-Luther-studies of the old style). On personal certainty of hope according to Staupitz cf. the texts cited below in n. 27.

[24] The concept "lecture-hall" is one-sidedly pointed to refer as *pars pro toto* to the entire field of the church's academic and catechetical mediation of knowledge in teaching and instruction. Equally selective is the following description "religion of monastic prayer", with which I refer to the whole expressive dimension of the stance of prayer before God. The reading in the lecture-hall and the prayer in the choir or in the monastic cell represent in particularly typical fashion the difference between the objectified form of doctrinal teaching and the existential living-out of faith in humility and hope. On the corresponding existential type of expression in Gerson's theology of consolation, which aims to accentuate humility and the certainty of hope, cf. Sven Grosse: "Existentielle Theologie in der vorreformatorischen Epoche

religion of monastic prayer. In the form of an internalized, mystically-tuned piety of prayer the latter soon outgrew the specifically monastic sphere and in the late Middle Ages became a form of spirituality not only for members of all the various monastic orders but also for pious secular clergy and lay people. In the history of the institutions we can trace the separation of the levels of speech and certainty back to the 12th and 13th centuries, when the teaching of the cathedral schools and nascent universities made space for the new spirit of the rational and philosophical that pervaded theology and thus came into conflict with the molding of life through the practice of prayer in spiritual communities.[25] The emergence of this academic Scholasticism left its mark on the late medieval concept of faith. It solidified the didactic, cognitive understanding of ecclesiastical truth transmitting a universally valid *certitudo*. In humility and hope, on the other hand, there is concentrated the model of the closest affective communion with God which raises the sinner from insignificance to the comforting certainty of salvation. It was in the same 12th century that the theologians of western Europe discovered both a new intellectuality of the grounds for faith and a new emotional interiority of love including its penitential emotions of humility and hope.[26] Because of this the historical course was set in theology and piety

---

am Beispiel Johannes Gersons. Historische Überlegungen zum ökumenischen Disput", in: *Kerygma und Dogma* 41 (1995), pp. 80–111.

[25] It is characteristic when Petrus Comestor (†1179) concludes: "Sunt qui orationi magis operam dantes lectioni minus insistunt, et hi sunt claustrales. Sunt alii qui lectioni invigilant, rarius orantes, et hi sunt scholares." Sermo 9 (Migne *PL* 198, 1747A). Quoted by Arnold Angenendt: *Geschichte der Religiösität im Mittelalter* (Darmstadt, 1997), pp. 44–68; here p. 50; cf. there the section on the high Middle Ages, which briefly and appropriately characterizes the shift in the history of science in the 12th and 13th centuries (with bibliography).

[26] Cf. Peter Dinzelbacher: "Über die Entdeckung der Liebe im Hochmittelalter", in: *Saeculum* 32 (1981), pp. 185–208. Theologically important in the framework of this reorientation "inwards" is above all the shifting of the center of gravity from the external penitential works of satisfaction to the inner penitential sense of contrition (of humble pain at one's sins) and of hope (which takes flight to God's forgiveness). This new view of penance, which comes to the fore above all in the school of Anselm of Laon (†1117) and with Abelard (†1142), understands the genuine contrition and attrition of the heart as an awakening of love to God. From the 12th century on the 'vera contritio' arising from the motive of love to God comes to constitute the decisive condition at the moment of death for admission to purgatory and/or paradise. Cf. the article 'Buße', in: *Lexikon des Mittelalters*, vol. 2 (1983), col. 1123–1141: 1137–1139 (Ludwig Hödl); also Hödl: *Die Geschichte der scholastischen Literatur und der Theologie der Schlüsselgewalt*, 1. Teil (Münster, 1960), passim.

for a new type of polarity between knowledge and emotion in western Christianity.

The antithetical positioning of faith and humility/hope shows clearly once again why in the Middle Ages faith could not be the central concept of Christian life since the humility and hope of a spiritual life was not yet contained in the truth reference of faith alone. According to medieval understanding only love could unlock the inner relationship of the heart both to truth and to God's loving-kindness and thus make possible the humble confidence to hope.

Certainly as soon as faith was understood as "faith formed by love" and thus seen in a closer connection with humility and hope, the concept of faith could express the saving relationship of the sanctified person to God without any diminution at all. Hence time and again before the Reformation we come upon sermons which employ a concept of faith filled out in this way to give expression to the intensive relationship of trust in God's mercy and Christ's saving righteousness.[27] In this way the tension between *intellectus* and

---

[27] Cf. for example the way in which the Franciscan Stephan Fridolin in his sermons on Compline towards the end of the 15th century relates "by faith alone" to the righteousness in the passion of Jesus Christ, quoted by Hamm: "Von der spätmittelalterlichen reformatio" (as in n. 15), p. 39 with n. 98 and Petra Seegets: *Passionstheologie und Passionsfrömmigkeit im ausgehenden Mittelalter. Der Nürnberger Franziskaner Stephan Fridolin (gest. 1498) zwischen Kloster und Stadt*, esp. p. 272. Staupitz too in his Tübingen sermons on Job (as above, n. 8) frequently employs the concept of faith in the full soteriological sense of 'fides caritate formata', without specially mentioning the (naturally assumed) 'infused' quality of love – an abbreviated form of speech which elsewhere too seems to be quite common in texts of the theology of piety; cf. e.g. ibid., Sermo 22, line 108–111 (p. 341): "Tertium fundamentum in bonitate collocatur. Et secundum hoc sic imbuendi pueri sunt, quod deus optimus dedit nobis sua bonitate fidem rectam, in qua sperantes salvi erimus. Cuius fidei fundamentum positum in Christo." A comparison with other passages shows how carefully Staupitz distinguishes in the traditional style between fides, spes und caritas, in particular between general certainty and personal uncertainty of faith on the one hand and the personal certainty of salvation given in hope on the other as well as particularly in regard to the decisive key position of love, which alone can save and build the form of life for faith and love; cf. ibid. Sermo 4, line 194–203 (p. 83), Sermo 24, line 203–212, 300–315 (p. 368f. 372f.), Sermo 27, line 219f. (p. 403) and Sermo 28, line 113–118 (p. 408f.) as well as Staupitz' tract published at the beginning of 1517: *Libellus De exsecutione aeternae praedestinationis*, ed. *by Lothar Graf zu Dohna, Richard Wetzel* (Berlin – New York, 1979) = *J.v.S.: Sämtliche Schriften*, ed. by idem: *Lateinische Schriften* II, §51 (p. 138), §171 (p. 236), §228 (p. 278), §237 (p. 284) and §§238–240 (pp. 286–288). In the Staupitz literature, so far as I can see, the relation between fides, spes and caritas is not presented with the clarity that might be wished.

affectus could be bridged – particularly in the mode of the theology of piety with its focus on the life-context of the *vita spiritualis* – but the divergence between the two levels of expression of Christian existence could not be cancelled out.

Amid the doubts and problems typical of the spiritual life in the late Middle Ages we can discern the difficulty, indeed the impossibility – particularly for the scrupulously religious – of keeping this divergence under control emotionally and pastorally.[28] How can people attain the unambiguous, humble, confident assurance of hope when they are aware that, according to the Church's binding knowledge of faith, no one can be saved without the sanctifying quality of justifying love and its meritorious possibilities, and when at the same time a certain knowledge of their own state of grace and love is denied them? How can one find the consolation of hope solely in the sufferings of Christ (*pro nobis*) when one must at the same time ascertain whether Christ is living through the power of love in one's own heart (*in nobis*)? Staupitz calls the first without the second a "tzu unbescheidenes vortrawen in gottes barmhertzigkeit" (too immodest trust in God's mercy) because the '*pro nobis*' only leads to salvation through the '*in nobis*'.[29] With this he indicates the whole dilemma of late medieval pastoral theology in the field of tension between fervid examination of one's conscience and comforted trust in God's mercy.

III. *What Luther Means by Faith:*
The Question from the Perspective of the Judgement of God

If we now turn again to the early Luther, what we initially find remarkable (though not altogether astonishing) is how positively he takes over the medieval concept of faith outlined in the nine points above, in his marginal notes on Lombard's Sentences (1509/10) and then in his first two lecture-courses on the Psalms and the Epistle

---

[28] Cf. Wilfrid Werbeck: "Voraussetzungen und Wesen der scrupulositas im Spätmittelalter", in: *Zeitschrift für Theologie und Kirche* 68 (1971), pp. 327–350; Grosse: *Heilsungewißheit und Scrupulositas* (as in n. 21).

[29] Johann von Staupitz: "Von der Nachfolgung des willigen Sterbens Christi" (1515), cap. 7, in: *Johann von Staupitzens sämmtliche Werke*, ed. by Joachim Karl Friedrich Knaake, vol. 1: *Deutsche Schriften* (Potsdam, 1867), p. 66; cf. on this Heiko Augustinus Oberman: *Werden und Wertung der Reformation. Vom Wegestreit zum Glaubenskampf* (Tübingen, 1977), pp. 106–108.

to the Romans (from 1513). It was particularly important for Luther that, following theological tradition, faith was defined not as an operative *virtus*, a moral activity, but as a receptive occurrence, a comprehending and consenting acceptance of the truth of God which is made known in his authoritative revealed Word.[30] This relationship of Truth and Word remains constitutive for Luther's understanding of faith,[31] just as he emphatically retains a firm hold of the cognitive, informative basis of the concept of faith: Faith is fundamentally a hearing and understanding of verbal truth, a perceiving *cognoscere* and *intelligere*.[32] Here it was very important for Luther that this believ-

---

[30] Cf. Luther's marginal notes on the Sentences of Petrus Lombardus: *WA* 9,91,4–6: "Videt quisque intellectualiter fidem suam certissima scientia, hoc est non actu secundo, sed actu primo, id est intellectus habet earn praesentem sibi certissime, sed non per opera etc." Cf. also ibid. 92,13–36, especially the closer definition of 'fides ex auditu' (Röm. 10.17) as "sensus seu intellectus, id est qui recipit sensum illorum (seil, verborum sonantium, d.h. des verbum Christi), ille habet fidem; assensus enim ad istum sensum est fides, licet non videat, quomodo sensus ille verus sit" (line 23–27) – "fides, id est assensus, fit ex auditu, id est apprehensione [darüber: perceptione] significationis seu sensus verborum" (line 28–30). A shift away from the tradition announces itself at the point where Luther pointedly summarises the content of faith in the concept of the "verbum Christi"; cf. Schwarz: *Fides, spes und caritas* (as in n. 6), pp. 51–54.

[31] For Luther the concepts veritas, intellectus and fides belong together, whereby he stresses with the tradition that the truth-relation of believing apprehension of truth is not a *seeing* of the truth (cf. above n. 30: "non videat"), rather a "firmiter credere" in what the Holy Spirit has revealed (*WA* 9,92,13–17). Cf. ibid. 38,12–15: "Veritas est intellectio activa/passiva rei, sicut se habet. Bonitas est amatio activa/passiva amabilis sive rei." The orientation of faith to veritas and intellectio is directly connected with the fact that faith is related to preaching and the level of doctrine, leading to the sequence fides, spes und actio: "Spes enim servat, quae fides praedicat et docet" – "sine qua [seil, fide] nemo potest sperare et per consequens bene agere" (ibid. 91,12.33). These thoroughly traditional differentiations between veritas and bonitas or fides and spes respectively reflect Luther's theological thinking at the time of the marginal comments on Peter Lombard. At the same time these marginalia are evidence for what was so important to him in the medieval understanding of faith that he reproduced it in his own formulations and in later years did not give it up but integrated it in his significantly altering understanding of faith.

[32] This line of cognitive/intellectual understanding of faith is continued by Luther beyond his comments on the Sentences in the lectures on the Psalms (cf. n. 47 below: "solum intellectu et fide", and *WA* 3,507,35: "solo intellectu et fide") – whereby admittedly it must be observed (as we shall see) that it is by no means rationally and intellectually confined. It is rather that the cognoscere and intelligere of faith spreads out into the entire emotional life of the human "heart". How strongly the cognitive recognition of truth remained the basis of Luther's concept of faith – in the connection between apprehension, knowledge, recognition and confession – can be seen more than clearly, for example, in his exegesis of the Vulgate-Ps. 95.6 (the words "confessio et pulchritudo"), where in Gerson's style he links

ing acceptance of the truth according to the medieval understanding should not be morally qualified – i.e. it is possible even without
the quality and activity of love – so that even a person caught up
in lovelessness and mortal sin can have faith. That faith in itself, in
contrast to love, is not a description of a pious quality but is a concept of relationship directed outwards, characterized by its receptive,
apprehending attitude to the absolutely certain, assuring Word of
the truth of revelation[33] – this is as it were the medieval dowry to
the concept of faith in Luther's early theology. Seen from the perspective of late medieval theology and piety, there was no other concept which could appear to him so suited to express what was crucial
in the relationship between God and humankind than this ready-
minted understanding of faith. But how could faith suddenly attain
its new soteriological centrality in Luther's first lectures on the Psalms
when for centuries, during a great era of rediscovered and further
developed Augustinian religiosity, it had occupied a place subordinate to the decisive importance of love?

This radical change was only possible because faith, love and the
other concepts of the spiritual life fell into the maelstrom, so to speak,

---

faith as the light of the soul to *intelligentia* and its *intellectus*, *ratio* and *speculativa virtus*, while assigning spiritual *amor* as the beautifying color of the soul to *voluntas* and
its *affectus*, *practica virtus* and *vis appetitiva*; WA 4,109,12–31. Cf. Bernhard Lohse: *Ratio
und fides. Eine Untersuchung über die ratio in der Theologie Luthers* (Göttingen, 1958), pp.
38–41 (Faith as recognition and understanding of *intellectus* and *ratio*); Albert
Brandenburg: *Gericht und Evangelium. Zur Worttheologie in Luthers Erster Psalmenvorlesung*
(Paderborn, 1960), pp. 73–76; Schwarz: *Fides, spes und caritas* (as in n. 6), pp. 134–153
(The *intellectus fidei*). The specific recognition and understanding of faith is not a
natural human capacity but a gift of the biblical revelation of Christ and therefore
stands sharply opposed to all natural cognitive human ability. The latter proves
itself to be blind to divine truth, i.e. to the recognition of Christ (cf. WA 4,356,23f.:
"Sic enim fides non intellectum illuminat, immo excecat"). In his Dictata super
Psalterium Luther differs from medieval theologians like Gerson und Biel by interpreting the *intellectus fidei* precisely not in philosophical style as a faculty of the soul
of the *homo intelligens*, but exclusively in terms of the truth of Christ which opens
the way to its own recognition (cf. WA 3,176,3f.: "'Intellectus' in scripturis sanctis
potius ab obiecto quam potentia nomen habet, contrario quam in philosophia"); cf.
Gerhard Ebeling: *Lutherstudien*, vol. I (Tübingen, 1971), p. 39f. This exclusive con-
ditioning of the *intellectus fidei* by grace admittedly does not prevent Luther too from
relating the theological *cognoscere/intelligere* and the theological *velle* to the anthropological base of the *intellectus* with its *ratio* and *voluntas* respectively (cf. above) – yet
only to the extent that he was concerned with the existential movement of the
human soul and its real cognition and will, not because he had a psychological
interest in its various areas.

[33] Cf. above n. 30: "apprehensione", "perceptione"; also n. 11 (*fides* as *apprehensio*
in Biel).

of an experience of truth and untruth completely new in its radicality, and in consequence altered their positions fundamentally. With
the motto 'experience of untruth' I have in mind that crisis of doubt
endured by the young theologian and monk which he then worked
out theologically in the lectures on the Psalms.[34] Luther experienced
in a shattering way the deep cleft between divine and human reality; he had personally reached the end of his human possibilities
before God – in every respect: both as an epistemological subject
and as an ethical agent. In his eyes all human speculation, speech
and judgment about God is untrue, just as he denies human nature
any capacity for a truly genuine love of God and one's neighbor.
He sees humanity caught up for life (*semper!*) in the radical sins of
blindness and egoism.[35]

But this means – and here we come to the nerve of a fundamentally new theological approach – that while he is delivering his
Dictata super Psalterium he is already no longer thinking in the categories of a qualitative, habitual, operative constitution of human
nature – and if he does so, then only in such a way that human
quality can only be un-quality in the face of God's judgment and
mercy. The salvation or damnation of a person is not decided by
his quality because this state of his being and action can always only

    [34] The most important literature on Luther's 'Dictata super Psalterium' is col-
lected in Karl Heinz zur Mühlen: Art. 'Luther II', in: *Theologische Realenzyklopädie*,
vol. 21 (1991), p. 562 (on 1.2); Reinhard Schwarz: *Luther*, 1st edn. (Göttingen, 1986),
p. 24f.; Bernhard Lohse: *Luthers Theologie in ihrer historischen Entwicklung und ihrem
systematischen Zusammenhang* (Göttingen, 1995), p. 61. Cf. also Jared Wicks: *Man Yearning
for Grace. Luther's Early Spiritual Teaching* (Wiesbaden, 1969), pp. 41–94.
    [35] On the lutheran 'semper' see – apart from n. 37 below (quoting from the let-
ter to Johannes Braun) – e.g. *WA* 3,289,5–7: "Quare verum est nos esse in peccatis coram illo semper, ut scilicet ipse in pacto suo et testamento, quod nobiscum
pepigit, iustificator sit." The concepts 'pactum' and 'testamentum' point to Luther's
view – explored in more detail below – that the justifying reorientation of sinful
human existence does not consist in a natural, qualitative change, but in a new
definition from without through the address of the divine word of covenant; vgl.
Berndt Hamm: *Promissio, pactum, ordinatio. Freiheit und Selbstbindung Gottes in der scholastischen Gnadenlehre* (Tübingen, 1977), pp. 377–389. On the problematic of sin and
truth as developed in the following, see especially *WA* 3,287,20–293,21; 4,266,1–4
and 266,22–273,23 (with the intensive combination of *veritas* and *fides* to the point
of their identification in 266,25–27 = *WA* 55/I,756: "q.d.: Vidi, quod qui credere
nolunt et resistunt verbo propter ipsum me humiliantes, sunt mendaces; et solum
qui credunt sunt veraces, quia fides est veritas. Sed hec fides, in qua omne bonum
tenetur, donum dei est."). See on this Berndt Hamm: "Martin Luthers Entdeckung
der evangelischen Freiheit", in: *Zeitschrift für Theologie und Kirche* 80 (1983), pp. 50–68:
especially 54–56.

be sinful from a theological point of view. Therefore love under-stood in qualitative and operative terms can no longer be for Luther the central concept of a Christian life journeying toward salvation. Now what is decisive is no longer the question of quality but rather the perspective of the relationship of judgment between God and the person: how God judges me and how I judge myself before God. Hence Luther shifts the problem of truth from the level of quality to that of relationship and judgment and so finds, as we shall see, an initial escape from the tormenting question of how healing truth can come into a deeply untruthful, warped human existence. Conse-quently he makes the question of salvation a question of faith since, entirely in the sense of traditional terminology, he uses the relational concept of faith for the relationship of a person to the divine truth. And now that everything is concentrated in the question of rela-tionship the concept of faith attains its new dominance.[36]

IV. *Luther's First Commentary on the Psalms: Faith as Humility and Hope*

How this happens first becomes clear if we look more closely at this relational connection between faith and truth in Luther's lectures on the Psalms. Amidst the radical crisis of the *humanum* Luther finds truth only where the person stops speaking and God begins to speak. He thus reduces – first tendencies in this direction can be recog-nized as early as 1509 – the sinner's truthful encounter with God exclusively to the believing relationship with the *biblical* Word of

---

[36] Cf. above n. 6. The centrality of faith is repeatedly thematised by Luther, as for example in the *Scholion* to Vulgata-Ps. 83,6f. (*WA* 3,648,23–651,22), where he characterizes the fides Christi as fountain and source of the whole Christian life and the foundation of the church, e.g. in the formulation: "Siquidem fides, que ex gratia dei donatur impiis, qua et iustificamur, est substantia, fundamentum, fons, origo, principium, primogenitum omnium spiritualium gratiarum, donorum, virtu-tum, meritorum, operum." 649,17–20. – The new dominance of the concept of faith in Luther's theology can be impressively underlined if one compares his exe-gesis of the Psalms at the many places where he speaks of *fides, fidelis* or *credere* although the Psalm text itself does not provide these terms with the previous tra-dition of exegesis of the Psalms. One will then observe that in the majority of these cases Luther's employment of the concept of faith runs counter to the tradition. Cf. the commentary apparatus to Luther's glosses interpreting Psalms 1–30: *WA* 55/I,1–288; further Gerhard Ebeling: *Lutherstudien*, vol. I (Tübingen, 1971), pp. 143–145.167–175.181.

God, or, more precisely, to the Word of Christ.[37] With this critical – also extremely church-critical – reduction there is also connected a considerable broadening of the understanding of truth and faith. For Luther does not relate the truth of God's Word simply to the human cognitive sphere, to *intellectus* and *ratio*. As a Word of direct address it moves the whole of human existence; its truth also grips the affective emotional life of the soul.[38]

This happens, as Luther records again and again, in a twofold way: God's address, the biblical Word of Christ, encounters the sinner as a word of judgment and as a word of promise, as *iudicium* and as *promissio*.[39] The person responds to the divine address of both

---

[37] Cf. the way in which Luther centers his understanding of faith on the Bible and the word as early as his marginal notes on the Sentences of Peter Lombard: *WA* 9,45,2–7 ("veritas scripturae et fidei"); 46,16–20; 62,19–24 ("quicquid supra fidem – scil. to the biblical Word of God – additur, certissimum est figmentum esse humanum"); 65,11–22; 66,9f.; 84,6–8 ("credere oportet et verbis scripturae fidem profiteri et linguam illis aptare et non econtra"). Essentially this already implies the believing relation to the "verbum Christi": *WA* 9,92,24.30–33. Cf. also Luther's letter to Johannes Braun on 17th March 1509 with the sentence: "Sed deus est deus; homo saepe, imo semper fallitur in suo iudicio." *WA Br* 1,17,44f., No. 5. On this whole area see Heiko Augustinus Oberman: *Luther – Mensch zwischen Gott und Teufel* (Berlin, 1981), p. 170f.

[38] Cf. e.g. *WA* 3,649,1–5: The word of Christ and faith in it are fixed in the heart: "in corde, id est in affectu sunt". *WA* 4,313,29 ("'Vivifica', scilicet veritate fidei") combined with 314,7 ("'Revela', scilicet a cecitate primi peccati in intellectu, sicut vivifica' in affectu"). On Luther's understanding of the affects in his Dictata super Psalterium cf. Günther Metzger: *Gelebter Glaube. Die Formierung reformatorischen Denkens in Luthers erster Psalmenvorlesung, dargestellt am Begriff des Affekts* (Göttingen, 1964); Schwarz: *Fides, spes und caritas* (as in n. 6), pp. 172–191; further n. 48, below.

[39] *Iudicium* and *promissio*, judgment and promise, are contrasting ways in which God encounters us in the biblical word. Since however, as Luther continually emphasizes in the Dictata super Psalterium, the salvific presence of God is always hidden for those on earth under the opposing form of the cross of Christ, the saving word of the gospel and its promise of future glory always meet the sinner as the message of the cross and therefore at the same time as the humbling judgment upon all the glory of the world and humankind, just as obversely the assurance of salvation is also hidden within the word of judgment for those who allow themselves to be humbled. *Iudicium* und *promissio* are thus to be clearly distinguished in their character yet at the same time intimately bound together in the spiritual understanding of the word of Christ – in the same way in which as we shall see *humilitas* and *spes* are bound together in the fides Christi. Thus in the *Scholion* to Vulgata-Ps. 118.43 Luther can let the afflicted request in prayer: "... ne sinas verbum fidei taceri a me propter adversariorum resistentiam, sed eo magis adiuva me illud loqui et predicare, quia in iudiciis tuis etc., id est in ipsis verbis promissionis tue, futurorum spem habui. Vel secundo et melius: quando sum in iudiciis tuis, id est passionibus et crucibus tuis, tune non tantum spero, sed et super spero, id est abundantius spero quam alias, cum sum extra ... Nam iudicia sunt ipse passiones Christi, que in nobis abundant, et calix domini, quem bibi oportet." *WA* 4,330,21–32. On the

kinds in faith. The judgmental word exposes and condemns him in his profound malignity. Faith then means that the person admits the truth of this divine judgment, recognizes his desperate condition before God and confesses his sin in prayer to God. Taking over the divine judgment he accuses, judges and condemns himself.[40] Luther groups together recognition, acceptance, confession and self-condemnation under the concept of humility (*humilitas*). Hence faith is now conceptually coincident with humility.[41] This is possible because Luther places humility in a direct relationship to truth.[42] In humility a person does not make himself less significant than he really is, but turns upon himself the truth of the judgmental Word of God and realizes that, as creature and sinner, he is really nothing before God.[43] Thereby, however, the general level of the church's teaching

two sides of Luther's understanding of the cross (judgment and peace) cf. *WA* 3,652,24–27: "Quia Sacra Scriptura secundum spiritalem intelligentiam est nidus; ibi enim Christus latet requirendus et inveniendus. Et eadem est Altare; quia est crux, in qua affigitur caro cum concupiscentiis suis, sicut Christus in sua cruce. Carne enim crucifixa sequitur requies et pax anime." Cf. on this Brandenburg: *Gericht und Evangelium* (as in n. 32), especially pp. 33–42 and 86–88.

[40] Cf. Luthers Scholia on Vulgata-Ps. 50: *WA* 3,287,20–293,21.

[41] Cf. e.g. Luther's *Scholion* on Vulgata-Ps. 70.2 ('In iustitia tua libéra me'): God judges "primo tropologice. Quia condemnat opera carnis et mundi. Ostendit enim, quod omnia, que sunt in nobis et in mundo, coram Deo sunt abominabilia et damnabilia. Et ita qui ei per fidem adheret, necessario sibi vilis et nihil, abominabilis et damnabilis efficitur. Que est vera humilitas." *WA* 3,462,27–30; cf. also n. 53 below. The understanding of faith as *humilitas* continues unbroken into Luther's lectures on Romans (e.g. with such formulations as "humilis fidei gemitus" or "humilitas fidei": *WA* 56,276,34 and 282,12); cf. Matthias Kroeger: *Rechtfertigung und Gesetz. Studien zur Entwicklung der Rechtfertigungslehre beim jungen Luther* (Göttingen, 1968), pp. 41–85. It seems to me important, however, that while Luther integrates *humilitas* completely in *fides*, yet faith is not reduced without remainder to the dimension of *humilitas*, as becomes clear in the following discussion of the *spes*-dimension of faith.

[42] On the fundamental moment of truth in *fides* as *humilitas*, Kroeger (ibid., p. 45) rightly remarks that Luther's main concern in his lectures on the Psalms and Romans is "Gott selber nur überhaupt als Wirklichkeit zu gewinnen, und sei es in Zorn und Unheil, d.h. im Bekenntnis der Sünde und in der Rechtfertigung Gottes allein": "Dieses Wiedergewinnen von Gottes Wirklichkeit, das nur im Bekennen der Wahrheit und im Glauben geschieht, ist der erschütternde und leidenschaftliche Sinn dieser frühen Theologie. Darum ist fides iustificans durchweg als confessio und humilitas verstanden."

[43] Cf. e.g. Luther's *Scholion* on Vulgata-Ps. 115.11 ('Ego dixi in excessu meo: omnis homo mendax'): "Ergo in excessu isto, id est conturbatione, dixi et expertus sum, quod homo solus non staret, sed fieret mendax, nisi desursum adiutus verax permaneret in confessione fidei. Vel quia dixit: 'humiliatus sum nimis', in ea afflictione didicit, quod omnis homo sit mendax et nihil, quia non stat in tentatione, sed cadit a veritate et consentit falso, nisi dominus iuverit." *WA* 4,267,29–33; cf. ibid. 272,32–38. Cf. also the central thought extended by Luther from the mendicant sphere to the

and truth coincides for Luther with the personal existential level of the individual sinner's prayer.

Something similar happens when a person who has reached the end of his possibilities of achieving salvation is given fresh heart and comforted by the divine word of promise. The truth of the *promissio* lies in the truthfulness of God – i.e. in the faithfulness with which he keeps the promises he has made: that he forgives the sinner his guilt for Christ's sake and through pure mercy brings him to eternal life.[44] This strongly guaranteed word of promise awakes in the person the bright, joyful side of his faith. Thus faith becomes identical with confident hope, with *spes* and *fiducia*.[45] As in earlier tradition, humility and hope are closely bound together, but now within faith.[46] Now not only the deep doubt which makes one unsure of

---

universally Christian that the faithful (the "pauperes Christi") *are* poor and *confess* themselves as poor: *WA* 3,87,12–88,14 – *WA* 55/I,80,7–84,5.

[44] Cf. e.g. Luthers *Scholion* on Vulgata-Ps. 118.111 ('Hereditate acquisivi testimonia tua in eternum; quia exultatio cordis mei sunt'), "Felix autem hec hereditas, quia eterna; dicit enim: 'hereditate acquisivi in eternum'. Promissa enim dei cor letificant eorum, qui credunt et sperant in ipsa. Igitur interim exultamus in fide et spe futurorum, que nobis promisit deus; ideo autem exultamus, quia certi sumus, quod non mentitur, sed faciet quod promisit et aufert a nobis omne malum corporis et anime, conferet autem omne bonum et hoc sine fine. Quis enim non exultet, si certus est, quod induetur corpus eius gloria et immortalitate, claritate et virtute etc.? Certus autem est, si credit; tantum est, ut expecto, quia sine dubio fiet, quod expectat." *WA* 4,360,5–13. On the connection between *prommissio* and *veritas* cf. also e.g. ibid. 287,1–9 = *WA* 55/I,776 ("Haec me consolata est spes, quia certa est, deus enim verax est in promissis, in humilitate mea") and *WA* 4,17,4–18,4. On Luther's understanding of promise in the early lectures cf. James Samuel Preus: *From Shadow to Promise. Old Testament Interpretation from Augustine to the Young Luther* (Cambridge/Mass., 1969); Oswald Bayer: *Promissio. Geschichte der reformatorischen Wende in Luthers Theologie* (Göttingen, 1971); Hamm: *Promissio, pactum, ordinatio* (as in n. 35), pp. 377–389.

[45] Cf. e.g. *WA* 3,640,11–641,10 = *WA* 55/I,584 ("Beati fideles omnes, qui habitant per fixam spem . . . in domo tua"); *WA* 4,332,26–33 (the connection of *fides, spes, certificari, consolari* and *gaudium* with the "verbum evangelii tui"); ibid. 264,14–16.31–35 = *WA* 55/I,754 (the "certe credere" establishes the "certa spes"); *WA* 4,314,10 ("fac me confidere et certificari"); ibid. 380,33–382,24 (on the joy of the believer/hoper in God's word of promise) as well as n. 44 above. What applies to *humilitas* (cf. above n. 41), also applies to *spes*: Luther integrates them in the fulfilment of faith without reducing faith to hope; the hope which trusts and is assured of salvation is one of the significant dimensions of faith. To put it another way: faith is the basis of hope (as Luther emphasizes particularly with reference to Hebr. 11.1). Cf. Schwarz: *Fides, spes und caritas* (as in n. 6), p. 112f. 163–169.227–240. On Christ as ground of the trust and assurance of hope cf. e.g. *WA* 3,56,31–42.

[46] Cf. e.g. *WA* 3,566,36–39 (combination *of fides* with "de se et mundo desperare" and "nudus in domino sperare") and *WA* 4,207,7–12 = *WA* 55/I,718 ("humiliati . . . desperantes de se et in deum sperantes").

oneself but also the assurance of hope of personal salvation find their place in the relationship of faith to truth.[47] To the medieval theologians such an assurance of faith remained, understandably, alien. As we saw, they pushed the certainty and surety of faith on to a general level of truth; faith had to remain in uncertainty about the virtuous inner quality of the individual person. Because Luther by contrast freed the question of salvation from this question of a person's qualitative and moral constitution he was able to turn the certainty of hope into the certainty of faith. Hence here, too, the general dimension of the truth of faith coincides with the existential prayerful attitude of the sinner before God.

V. *Results and Consequences*

I come to the following results and conclusions:

1.) In Luther as in the theological tradition faith is related to the verbalized truth of revelation, but this is now understood exclusively as the biblical Word of God. In this sense Word and faith form a unity constitutive for faith so that the new pathos of the divine address brings that of true faith with it.

---

[47] Cf. the evidence of the texts quoted above in notes 44 and 45. In regard to Luther's view of the firm assurance of faith and hope in his first two lecture series it must admittedly be kept in mind that the character of assurance of salvation is also conditioned by the opposed forms of the divine revelation "sub contrario" (cf. n. 39 above). That explains the peculiarly fractured nature of his understanding of faith's assurance of salvation, which has misled some scholars into thinking that in his lectures on the Psalms and Romans Luther does not yet know the personal assurance of faith. He sets great value on this firm *certitudo*, but combines it immediately with the complete despair of the sinner over all he possesses and can dispose of. Just as the saving message of the Gospel is experienced as judgment on all 'flesh' and its self-glorying, so too the believers' assurance in hope, holding fast to God's promise, is closely tied to that existential unsettling and temptation which the humbling word of God works by confronting them with the reality of their desolate state and with the *ire* of the *deus iudex*. The situation of the believing sinner is thus characterized by an oscillation between assurance and uncertainty, between *spes* and *timor*. To this corresponds the formula, taken over from Augustine and repeatedly used in the Psalm lectures, that the believer has grace and salvation 'only' in hope, not yet however in present reality: "tota vita fidelium est tantummodo in spe et nondum in re" (*WA* 4,259,2f. = *WA* 55/I,752); "omnis nostra letitia est in spe futurorum et non in re presentium" (*WA* 4,380,35f.); "opera enim dei sunt intelligibilia, id est solum intellectu et fide perceptibilia in spe, non in re" (*WA* 3,367,34–36); cf. on this Lohse: *Luthers Theologie* (as in n. 34), p. 74.

2.) In that Luther relates the biblical truth as the judging and saving Word of God to the whole of human cognitive and affective existence, the concept of faith also attains an integrative breadth and fullness.[48]

3.) Faith is – and this, we might add, is typical of the Middle Ages too – in a fundamental way a cognitive perception of revelation, a firm grasp of and adherence to the truth, but consequently – very atypical of the Middle Ages – conceptually identical with *humilitas* and *spes*, with despairing self-accusation and certainty of personal salvation.

4.) To be more precise, one must not only say that the concept of faith incorporates humility and hope but conversely that *humilitas* and *spes* align themselves with the concept of *fides*. They are no longer understood as qualities of love which mold from within but are now purely relational concepts which express that the heart is passively stirred by the address of divine truth and loving-kindness.[49]

5.) The same thing happens with the concept of love as Luther uses it in his lectures on the Psalms. Love, too, is assimilated to faith, its perception and judgment, insofar as he understands *caritas*, *dilectio* or *amor* as an external relationship of the sinner to God's loving-kindness and mercy, as a warming of the heart through the power of the Holy Spirit. In this sense love is faith, synonymous with humility and hope.[50] The active, operative side of love – its works – however, is different. Luther sets this apart as a consequence of faith from mankind's justifying relationship to salvation[51]

---

[48] On the relation between *intellectus* and *affectus* in Luther's understanding of faith cf. e.g. *WA* 4,107,31–34; on this Karl-Heinz zur Mühlen: Art. 'Affekt II', in: *Theologische Realenzyklopädie*, vol. 1 (1977), p. 607, and Art. 'Luther II', in; ibid. vol. 21 (1991), p. 546; cf. also n. 38 above.

[49] Cf. Schwarz: *Fides, spes und caritas* (as in n. 6), pp. 169–172 (on *humilitas*, in critical response to Ernst Bizer) and 231–233 (on *spes*, especially on Luther's formulation of the "nuda spes", which ought to cling to the "nuda verba" of God).

[50] On the unity of faith, hope and love cf. e.g. *WA* 4,380,35–37: "Ideo enim gaudemus, quia promissionibus divinis credimus, et que promittit, speramus atque diligimus." Ibid. 8,10f.: Deus "unitur spiritualiter spiritui nostro per fidem et caritatem". On the understanding of faith as love in the power of the Holy Spirit cf. Schwarz: ibid. p. 112f.187.191.253f.

[51] The believer, loving God and hoping in God, performs the works of love, as Luther puts it, "on the backside" ("posteriora dorsi", Vulgata-Ps. 67,14) of his life: *WA* 3,396,14–397,2. The fact that for Luther good works no longer constitute the contact between humankind and salvation does not prevent him at the same time

while he completely abandons the qualitative understanding of *caritas* maintained in the tradition.[52]

6.) The whole of the human relationship to salvation now consists in faith. It is faith which justifies.[53] For Luther this means, as many research essays on the lectures on the Psalms have shown, that faith places sinners in a fundamental relationship to Christ, i.e. in a cognitive and affective relationship to the righteousness of Christ which is brought home to them existentially in the Word of judgment and salvation.[54] In this way faith – combined with the biblical Word – becomes *the* christocentric relational concept for participation in Christ.[55]

7.) This being so faith takes over the central soteriological position and final eschatological validity which love held in the Middle Ages – that leading position which hitherto had been bound to the molding operative quality of love. Now it stands thus: Love no longer molds faith but faith itself has become the way of life which is the compass of love.[56]

8.) Hence the new central position of faith is directly connected with the fact that Luther rejects the medieval differentiation, indeed separation, between the objectifying way of teaching directed towards the cognitive capacity and the subjective way of life of an affective spiritual existence. In the concept of faith he combines the common level of the Church's truth and teaching with the subjective, existential level of the expression of prayer.

---

from still describing works as 'merita', e.g. *WA* 3,396,39 and 4,389,39; cf. on this Hamm: *Promissio, pactum, ordinatio* (as in n. 35), p. 382, n. 177.

[52] Cf. Schwarz: *Fides, spes und caritas* (as in n. 6), pp. 210–213.

[53] Cf. for example the evidence of the texts quoted above in n. 36 and below in n. 55; on the specific *humilitas* character of the *fides iustificans* of those who are 'born' out of the Word of God cf. *WA* 3,345,26–30.

[54] Justification as an event of communication between the *iustitia* Christi and the *fides* Christi through the medium of *iudicium* and *evangelium/promissio* consists in the humbling of the believer together with the humiliated Christ and in being set upright again with the exalted Christ; cf. e.g. *WA* 3,431,40–432,25 and 458,1–7. Cf. on this Schwarz: *Fides, spes und caritas* (as in n. 6), pp. 188–190.

[55] Cf. *WA* 3,369,4; 3,458,8–11; 3,466,26f. ("Iustitia dei ... tropologice est *fides* Christi"); *WA* 4,19,37–39 ("Christus non dicitur iustitia ... in persona sua nisi effective; sed *fides* Christi, qua iustificamur, pacificamur, per quam in nobis regnât"). Cf. Erich Vogelsang: *Die Anfänge von Luthers Christologie nach der ersten Psalmenvorlesung, insbesondere in ihren exegetischen und systematischen Zusammenhängen mit Augustin und der Scholastik dargestellt* (Berlin – Leipzig, 1929), as well as n.s. 57 and 58 below.

[56] Admittedly Luther's relational understanding of faith leaves no room for a concept of form in the sense of the Aristotelian *forma*.

I should like to remark in conclusion that it is striking that Luther developed this new understanding of faith for the first time in a lecture on the Psalter – that he, the Professor of Holy Scripture and Observant Augustinian monk, chose as text for his teaching the prayer-text of the canonical hours. He understood the Psalms to a very large extent as both christological and existential, as words of Christ and about Christ,[57] which in tropological interpretation should be related to the perceptive, comprehending, believing way of life.[58] One could indeed say: It is Luther's concentration on the connection between the christological and tropological sense of the Psalms – directed at the personal dedication of Christ – which first permits us to understand in what sense he allows the truth of God's Word to communicate with the whole cognitive and affective existence of the believing person.[59] The Psalter, interpreted and made topical in this way, allowed him more easily than any other biblical text to express the kind of theology he was concerned about at that time in 1513: It was a kind of integrative biblical theology which allowed the *modus loquendi* of the university lecture-hall to coincide with the prayerful attitude of the cloister, a theology which combined *lectio* and *oratio*, *intellectus* and *affectus*, thinking and feeling, truth and experience.[60]

---

[57] Cf. especially Luther's "Praefatio Ihesu Christi" to the first Psalm lectures, which presents the hermeneutical foundations of his christocentric understanding of the Psalms: *WA* 3,12,11–13,32 = *WA* 55/I,6–11; on this Gerhard Ebeling: *Lutherstudien*, vol. I (Tübingen, 1971), pp. 109–131. Cf. also Luther's view that all the works of creation and the old covenant are signs pointing to Christ as their fulfillment: "ideo Christus finis omnium et centrum, in quem omnia respiciunt et monstrant"; *WA* 3,368,18–24.

[58] Luther described the method of his tropological exegesis of the Psalms like this: "Immo pro tropologia hec regula est. [Canon:] Quod ubicunque Christus in Psalmis conqueritur et orat in afflictione corporali ad literam, sub eisdem verbis queritur et orat omnis fidelis anima in Christo genita et erudita et in peccatum se tentatam vel lapsam agnoscens. Quia Christus usque hodie conspuitur, occiditur, flagellatur, crucifigitur in nobis ipsis. Item insidiatur ei usque modo sine intermissione caro sum sensibus, mundus cum voluptatibus suis et diabolus cum suggestionibus suis et tentationibus, sicut Christo ludei secundum carnem." *WA* 3,167,20–28; cf. 458,8–11; on this Ebeling: *Lutherstudien* (as in n. 57), pp. 1–68. Cf. above n. 55.

[59] On this christological sense of God's *iudicium and promissio* cf. n. 39 above.

[60] Cf. with this Luther's early letter of 17th March 1509 to Johannes Braun; the sentence quoted above in n. 37 is preceded by the following characterization of a genuine theology which he wishes to emulate: ". . . ea inquam theologia, quae nucleum nucis et medullam tritici et medulliam ossium scrutatur." (line 43f.) So on the basis of its integrative character Luther's theology moves both on the "existential" and also on the "objectifying" or "sapiential" level of expression; against Otto Hermann Pesch: *Theologie der Rechtfertigung bei Martin Luther und Thomas von Aquin*

This integrative theological program is deepened in Luther's new understanding of faith which integrates not only knowledge and feeling but also the darkness of grief and the brightness of joy.[61]

Luther did not stop at this concept of faith. In the years following he developed it so much further that modern research cannot agree upon whether the understanding of faith in the lectures on the Psalms and the Epistle to the Romans[62] can be counted as belonging to the Reformation.[63] I content myself with the observation that a significant caesura, perhaps even the most important change over against the medieval understanding of faith, can already be discerned in Luther's first series of lectures on the Psalms. For here the concept

---

(Mainz, 1967), pp. 937–941, who interprets the difference between Luther and Thomas Aquinas essentially as the "Unterschied zwischen existentieller und sapientialer Theologie".

[61] Cf. Heiko A. Oberman: "Simul gemitus et raptus: Luther und die Mystik", in: idem, *Die Reformation: von Wittenberg nach Genf* (Göttingen, 1986), pp. 45–89 (first published 1967). Remarkable as it is that mystical terminology finds its way into Luther's understanding of faith – above all after 1515 – it is equally apparent on the other side that he does not come to his specific concept of faith from medieval mysticism, but finds access to particular mystical traditions and concepts on the basis of his new concept of faith (the first lectures on the Psalms). This can be observed with the mystical concepts of 'raptus' and 'exstasis', which he precisely does not understand in the traditional mystical sense of being transported above the sphere of mere belief (cf. Oberman ibid. pp. 74–79), but as the illuminated recognition of faith – thus in the gloss on Vulgata-Ps. 115.11: "Exstasis illa . . . est raptus mentis in claram cognitionem fidei, et ista est proprie exstatis." *WA* 4,265,32f. = *WA* 55/I,756. Cf. on this Wolfgang Böhme (ed.): *Von Eckhart bis Luther. Über mystischen Glauben* (Karlsruhe, 1981) [= Herrenalber Texte 31], especially the contributions of Heiko A. Oberman, Reinhard Schwarz and Karl-Heinz zur Mühlen (this on Luther's understanding of ecstasy p. 46f.).

[62] This further development already begins in the second half of the lectures on Romans; cf. Kroeger: *Rechtfertigung und Gesetz* (as in n. 41), pp. 152–163. Cf. also Jared Wicks: *Luther's Reform. Studies on Conversion and the Church* (Mainz, 1992), pp. 15–42.

[63] It is striking that those scholars who dispute the Reformation character of this understanding of faith generally do not argue immanent-historically from a comparison with late medieval texts, but take their bearings from a predetermination within systematic theology and from a systematic theological interpretation of Luther. The historiographical value of such an obviously dogmatic interpretation of history is correspondingly limited. Cf. e.g. the early attempt at such interpretation by Lennart Pinomaa: *Der existentielle Charakter der Theologie Luthers. Das Hervorbrechen der Theologie der Anfechtung und ihre Bedeutung für das Lutherverständnis* (Helsinki, 1940); Pinomaa sees the "hervorbrechende Neue" in Luther (p. 143) first in the texts between spring 1515 and spring 1518, without drawing in any medieval texts at all for comparison. The same problematic manifests itself in Ernst Bizer (*Fides ex auditu*, 1st edition Neukirchen, 1958) and those influenced by him to advocate a late dating of the Reformation breakthrough.

of faith already takes over that central position for the mediation of salvation in the Christian life which in the Middle Ages was held by love. At the same time, however, the continuity with the medieval concept of faith emerges clearly. From his theological training Luther found the concept of faith which was exactly right to express what was important for him in 1513–1515 as well as later: a new, fundamental relationship of the inner man to the divine truth which consists not in working but in receiving.

In conclusion let me give a short reply to an obvious question: Why the appeal to the Middle Ages at all? Is not the biblical text itself with its linguistic usage enough to explain why in Luther's first lectures on the Psalms faith became the central concept of the Christian life? Various grounds speak against so simple an explanation, particularly the fact that in the Vulgate text of the Psalms the concept of faith only occurs infrequently[64] and Luther's understanding of faith in these lectures is not altogether biblical and particularly not simply Pauline.[65] The biblical text, therefore, does not itself explain the way it is interpreted.[66] It is the variables that are decisive:

---

[64] The Vulgate formulation of Ps. 115.10: "Credidi, propter quod locutus sum" is at any rate significant; cf. the important *scholion: WA* 4,266,23–268,28. Generally it is striking that at the numerous places where Luther's exegesis of the Psalms uses the terms *fides, fidelis* or *credere*, the Psalm text itself hardly ever supplies them. One can indeed speak of a specific Paulinism in Luther even at the time of the lectures on the Psalms, yet he quotes relevant passages from Paul relatively seldom when thematising the concept of faith in the Dictata. It would therefore be an extreme short-circuit to try to explain the new centrality of faith in the first lectures on the Psalms simply by reference to his intensified reference to the biblical text. It is remarkable, for example, that in seven of ten cases where the Vulgate Psalm text speaks of 'intellectus', Luther's glosses and/or scholia introduce the concept of faith – without explicit reference to Paul – as for example the *scholion* on Ps. 118.73 (*WA* 4,342,4f.): "'Da mihi intellectum', id est spiritualem intelligentiam veritatis et fidei in litera latentis". The combination *of intellectus, veritas* and *fides* indicates the horizon of Luther's theological training.

[65] The weight placed in Luther's early concept of faith on humble self-recognition, self-judgment, self-damnation and confession of sin is alien to the Pauline understanding, as is the style and fashion in which Luther contrasts faith and love.

[66] For such late medieval theologians as engaged zealously in the study and interpretation of Paul – like Johannes von Staupitz – it would have been quite natural around 1513, when Luther began his work on the Psalms, to understand the *Pauline fides* in the sense of the *fides caritate formata* of standard teaching, just as Augustine's biblical exegesis was received in this sense. Neither the concentration of Luther's work on the biblical text nor the influence of an intensified Paulinism can alone offer an adequate explanation for his new way of bringing the concept of faith into play.

which interpreter reads which biblical text through which spectacles; which horizon of interpretation is associated with which horizon of the text. Hence the key to the new position of the concept of faith in Luther is to be found in how the personal horizon of his theological training and his existential struggle were connected with the challenge of the text.

VI. *Postscript*

In view of the overall topic of the symposium "Die frühe Reformation als Umbruch" (Verein für Reformationsgeschichte, 1996) and the question which is constantly discussed as to whether the Reformation should be understood as a radical break from the world of the late Middle Ages or as a process of continuation, I think my essay can show, through the paradigm of the theological *initia reformationis*, that the Reformation is both. It is a radical change, in that it rapidly broke from and re-evaluated tradition; it is a continuation in that it took up and developed crucial themes from within that tradition. The historical perspective through which one views the 15th and 16th centuries, the sources one selects and the motives with which one examines them all play a role in determining whether the abiding impression is of sudden shifts or of persistence and gradual change. This holds true for all epochal breaks within a generation, as for example with the German-European threshold years of the 20th century – 1918, 1945 and 1989. A generation that lives through a time of rapid change will grow up applying rational and emotional categories to the 'good' or 'bad' times. Yet the continuing and changing old is always combined with the abruptly unfolding new.

This is exactly what we can see in Luther. With every fiber of his being, for example, he had absorbed the teachings of late scholasticism and the formation of piety common around 1500; consequently, with all his new theological discoveries he remained within the stream of continuity of the so-called late Middle Ages. In saying this we must note that this late medieval period of the 15th and early 16th centuries can also be seen as the dawn of the early Modern Age, in which are contained many developments characteristic of the 16th and 17th centuries. My research concept of the 'normative centralization' of religion and society is also intended to relate to this two-sidedness of an era.[67] In that process of centralization, the new centrality of faith first defined by Luther in 1513–1515 plays a leading role. What I have described in this article is the process of clarification that led Luther to place faith in the radiant center of the Christian life. The history of Luther's public impact and his concept of faith after 1518/19 then lie on another level.[68] We must admit that both – the clarification of the interpreter of the Bible in cloister and lecture-hall and the success of the author of pamphlets – are inextricably bound together.[69]

---

[67] Cf. Berndt Hamm: "Reformation als normative Zentrierung von Religion und Gesellschaft", in: *Jahrbuch für Biblische Theologie* 7 (1992), pp. 241–279; idem: *"Von der spätmittelalterlichen reformatio zur Reformation"* (as in n. 15).

[68] Cf. Bernd Moeller: "Das Berühmtwerden Luthers", in: *Zeitschrift für historische Forschung* 15 (1988), pp. 65–92.

[69] Cf. Berndt Hamm: "Die Reformation als Medienereignis", in: *Jahrbuch für Biblische Theologie* 11 (1996), pp. 137–166.

CHAPTER SIX

WHAT WAS THE REFORMATION DOCTRINE OF JUSTIFICATION?*

The question I hope to answer in this chapter contains a problematical dimension of breadth – and not just on account of the *genius loci* of Erlangen. I am not asking: "What is the *Lutheran* doctrine of justification?" but "What is the *Reformation* doctrine of justification?" That is to say, what links the Wittenberg Reformation of Luther and Melanchthon, the Reformation of Zwingli in Zurich and Calvin's Geneva-based Reformation in their opposition to medieval Catholic doctrine and the reforming Catholicism of the sixteenth century? The limits I have set to my subject will be obvious, in that I do not intend to discuss Reformation theology in general but only the Reformation doctrine of justification; however, that is a merely apparent limitation, since to those four historically influential leading figures of the Reformation the central point, indeed the whole meaning, of their theology lay in the doctrine of justification.[1]

Is there merely *one* Reformation doctrine of justification, however, in contrast to the wide variety of medieval Roman Catholic doctrinal systems? Let us briefly survey this wider range of issues. Reformation historians in recent decades have encouraged an awareness of the diversity of currents in the Reformation to such an extent that it is becoming increasingly difficult to retain a grasp on those features that are common to the Reformation as a whole, and to define their content precisely. This is particularly true of the doctrine of justification. The various Reformation positions are seen as drifting so far apart

---

* This essay is an extended version of my inaugural lecture at the University of Erlangen on 26 June 1985.

[1] Cf. E. Wolf: "Die Rechtfertigungslehre als Mitte und Grenze reformatorischer Theologie", in: idem, *Peregrinatio II* (Munich, 1965), pp. 11–21, particularly the comment: "The doctrine of justification, consequently, is not to be understood as the natural property of the Evangelical church, always available, but as ground that must always be reconquered. It should not be regarded as a 'dogma' in terms of theological history, or a theologumenon to be revised more or less intensively at a certain opportune or appropriate time; it means an ever-indispensable consciousness that theological self-examination is central to the life of the church" (p. 11).

on this point that either they appear to have no common ground any more,[2] or what they do have in common is formulated in such vague and amorphous terms, such as the principle of grace, that it no longer seems possible to trace any clear dividing line between it and the Catholic concept of grace.[3] It is at this point, and with a certain sense of resignation, that historians come up against enthusiastic ecumenicists who in any case believe that the doctrine of justification does not divide the churches,[4] and this opinion can then be linked to a historical line of argument claiming that the reformers, in particular Luther, were not really attacking a truly 'catholic' doctrine of justification. Instead, their attacks are claimed to have been provoked by the degenerate, Ockham-infected doctrine of the late Middle Ages and then forced into certain prejudices which turn out to have no real basis when compared with a 'fully catholic' theology of grace such as Thomism with some Augustinian influence.[5] And thus the contours become blurred. If we also note how far the question of what is really evangelical has been drawn into the search of today's Evangelical churches for the self-confidence of a confessional identity, then we can understand how difficult it is for the

[2] Cf., for instance, U. Gäbler: *Huldrych Zwingli. Eine Einführung in sein Leben und sein Werk* (Munich, 1983), p. 47: "In view of the diversity of theological positions among sixteenth-century Protestants, it is impossible to trace a historically distinct outline of the term 'evangelical'. Although it generally used to be identified with the theology of the reformer of Wittenberg – and in confessional Lutheran studies it still is – the precise content of the term is less and less frequently discussed in written studies. It may still be in use, but one must indicate that it has come to be detached from the traditional church and its doctrine."

[3] Cf., for instance, H. Scheible: "Reform, Reformation, Revolution. Grundsätze zur Beurteilung der Flugschriften", in: *Archiv für Reformationsgeschichte*, 65 (1974), pp. 108–34, 117.

[4] On the Catholic side the names of H. Küng, S. Pfurtner, O. H. Pesch and V. Pfnür spring to mind. On the Lutheran side, P. Brunner in particular tends this way in his essay "Reform – Reformation, Einst – Heute", in: idem, *Bemühungen um die einigende Wahrheit. Aufsätze* (Göttingen, 1977), pp. 9–33, esp. pp. 28–31. It is significant that in this article Brunner expressly quotes Melanchthon's doctrine that degrees of heavenly reward would be assessed by the merit of a man's works (*Apologie* §366, quoted from the German translation by Justus Jonas §368f.; *Die Bekenntnisschriften der evangelisch-lutherischen Kirche* [Göttingen, 1930], 229, 21–27 and 229, 59–230, 7), for exactly this kind of doctrine lies outside the bounds of any Reformation doctrine of justification. Cf. also the work of Brunner's pupil H. G. Pöhlmann: *Rechtfertigung. Die gegenwärtige kontroverstheologische Problematik der Rechtfertigungslehre zwischen der evangelisch-lutherischen und der römisch-katholischen Kirche* (Tübingen, 1971).

[5] Cf., for instance, E. Iserloh: *Luther und Reformation. Beiträge zu einem ökumenischen Lutherverständnis* (Aschaffenberg, 1974) [= Der Christ in der Welt, XI/4], esp. p. 24f.; cf. also earlier works by J. Lortz, L. Bouyer and W. H. van de Pol.

ecclesiastical historian to separate this historical issue from the embrace
of dogmatism, for the less clear our historical definition of the evangelical is, the more forceful and unchecked the dogmatic premises
applied to the study of this complex subject become. A glance at
the discussion of Luther's turning towards ideas of Reformation and
what it really entailed will amply demonstrate my point.[6] Against
the impressive background of all the currents of the Reformation[7]
and the tensions and contrasts between many genuine reform initiatives,
it seems to me all the more important to ask again what was so
particular to the Reformation in its central doctrine of justification,
and to answer the historical question by applying historical criteria.
I shall do so in the following stages: having established the criteria
(I), I shall then discuss the general medieval Catholic doctrine of
justification (II), and then, in contrast, what was both common to
the individual reformers' understanding of justification and what features of it were particular to the Reformation (III). Finally, I shall
show where this significantly evangelical factor can first be clearly
perceived in historical terms (IV), where it can become reinforced
and intensified in certain doctrinal developments, and where, on the
other hand, its distinct features are lost or even abandoned (V).

I. *Criteria for Defining the Reformation Doctrine of Justification*

By comparison with many other *reformationes*, the specific feature of
the sixteenth-century Reformation was that it was a movement of
radical change from the ecclesiastical and theological system of the
Middle Ages in its return to study of the scriptures. Historically,
therefore, it is only logical to say that whatever broke the mold of
the medieval theological system in returning to the word of God in
the Bible, and whatever can no longer be explained as an extreme
position within the range of medieval theological variation, is of the

---

[6] Cf. the studies by O. H. Pesch: "Zur Frage nach Luthers reformatorischer
Wende", in: *Catholica* 20 (1966), pp. 216–43, 264–80; in B. Lohse (ed.): *Der Durchbruch
der reformatorischen Erkenntnis bei Luther* (Darmstadt, 1968) [= Wege der Forschung,
123), pp. 445–505; idem, "Neuere Beiträge zur Frage nach Luthers 'reformatorischer
Wende'", in: *Catholica* 37 (1983), pp. 259–87; 38 (1984), pp. 66–133.
[7] Cf. H. A. Oberman: "Headwaters of the Reformation. 'Initia Lutheri – Initia
Reformationis'", in: idem (ed.), *Luther and the Dawn of the Modern Era*. Papers for the
Fourth International Congress for Luther Research (Leiden, 1974), pp. 40–88.

Reformation. However, there is certainly wide scope for discretion in determining what it was about the Reformation doctrine of justification that actually did break the mold of the system. Consequently two further and more precise criteria may be added in our search for the features essential to an understanding of the Reformation doctrine of justification.

1. Historically, there is little point in understanding the essential features of the Reformation in such a narrow sense – perhaps on the basis of certain interpretations of remarks made by Luther[8] – that our criterion would prove Zwingli or even Calvin to be the proponents of non-Reformation theology. Or to put it in more positive terms: the nature of Reformation theology must always be defined by comparison. The objective common ground between the reformers when they move away from medieval systems must find a place in our definition of its features. Consequently, the question of what is characteristic of the Reformation is also the question of what is common ground shared by all the reformers, and is not just specifically Lutheran.[9]

2. Another criterion to be taken into account in defining the mold-breaking element of the Reformation doctrine of justification is to

---

[8] For instance, E. Bizer and his followers who support a late date for Luther's turning to ideas of Reformation, particularly O. Bayer: "Die reformatorische Wende in Luthers Theologie", in: *Zeitschrift für Theologie und Kirche* 66 (1969), pp. 115–50; idem, *Promissio. Geschichte der reformatorischen Wende in Luthers Theologie* (Göttingen, 1971) [= Forschungen zur Kirchen- und Dogmengeschichte, 24].

[9] We can thus ascertain what the evangelical doctrine of justification actually was by comparing Luther, Melanchthon, Zwingli and Calvin. I believe that the differences between these four most important of the reformers in their views of the doctrine of justification are wide and representative enough to keep our definition of its strictly evangelical character from becoming too narrow. At the same time, the crucial common ground between them in their opposition to the doctrinal systems of the Roman Catholic church appears quite clearly, as it certainly would not if Osiander and the anti-authoritarian reformers, represented by some very diverse figures, were to be included in a study of the Reformation doctrine of justification. That 'left wing' did indeed subscribe entirely to what we call the Reformation and to Reformation theology, but not every evangelical position in the sixteenth century necessarily contains a genuine Reformation doctrine of justification, that is, one clearly distinct from the Catholic understanding of grace and morality. Where a doctrine of justification no longer contains the fundamental features of opposition to Catholicism, to be studied below from comparison between Luther, Melanchthon, Zwingli and Calvin, its evangelical character is in doubt – not for dogmatic but for purely historical reasons, since application of the historical description 'evangelical' is appropriate only where there has been an obvious break with the ecclesiastical and doctrinal system of the Middle Ages.

determine what the theological exponents of Catholicism in the six-teenth century thought of the doctrine. What features of the doc-trine were perceived as 'mold-breaking' and what features (in their eyes) could be integrated? By those exponents I mean representa-tives of all scholastic orientations, not only Ockhamism and Scotism but also a Thomism and Augustinianism that were extremely sensi-tive to questions of the theology of grace. It is by comparison with men who grappled with the Reformation doctrine of *solus Christus* and *sola gratia* as openly as Johannes von Staupitz,[10] Johannes Gropper,[11] Gasparo Contarini[12] and Girolamo Seripando[13] that a clear outline of what was evangelical will emerge and must be checked.[14] In this context, the religious negotiations between Protestants and Roman Catholic controversialist theologians aiming for unity on the one hand,[15] and the debates and doctrinal statements of the Council of Trent[16] tending towards distinction and separation on the other, will

---

[10] Cf. H. A. Oberman: *Werden und Wertung der Reformation. Vom Wegestreit zum Glaubenskampf* (Tübingen, 1977), pp. 97–118; B. Hamm: *Frömmigkeitstheologie am Anfang des 16. Jahrhunderts* (Tübingen, 1982) [= Beiträge zur historischen Theologie, 65], pp. 234–43 (bibliography).

[11] Cf. R. Braunisch: *Die Theologie der Rechtfertigung im „Enchiridion" des Johannes Gropper. Sein Kritischer Dialog mit Philipp Melanchthon* (Münster, 1974) [= Reformations-geschichtliche Studien und Texte, 109].

[12] Cf. H. Rückert: *Die theologische Entwicklung Gasparo Contarinis* (Bonn, 1926) [= Arbeiten zur Kirchengeschichte, 6].

[13] Idem: *Die Rechtfertigungslehre auf dem Tridentinischen Konzil* (Bonn, 1925) [= Arbeiten zur Kirchengeschichte, 3], pp. 230–8; A. Forster: *Gesetz und Evangelium bei Seripando* (Paderborn, 1963).

[14] Of course we must always consider how far such theologians were already influenced by the Reformation doctrine of justification. There can thus be common ground between reforming Catholic theologians and the leaders of the Reformation, and even though it is common ground it may contain features that are specifically and genuinely of the Reformation.

[15] Cf. B. Lohse in HDGThG II, ed. C. Andresen, 1980, pp. 102–8 (bibl.).

[16] Cf. W. Dantine, ibid., pp. 453–64 (bibl., esp. the works by Rückert, Oberman and Joest). In comparing the decrees and canons of Trent with the doctrine of the reformers, one must always remember that the Council of Trent narrowed ortho-doxy down considerably by comparison with the doctrinal diversity and broad spec-trum of Catholic theology in the Middle Ages. What the Council rejected and condemned as non-Catholic was far from being non-Catholic as that term would have been understood in the Middle Ages and the first half of the sixteenth cen-tury. Anyone contrasting 'Catholic theology' with 'Reformation theology' should thus be aware of what medieval Catholic theology permitted. In particular, the 'Augustinian' school of the Order of Augustinian Hermits must not be overlooked, nor above all should the combination of radical Augustinianism and nominalism in the theology of grace propounded by Gregory of Rimini and his pupils. In speak-ing of nominalism a great many Catholic and Evangelical scholars still automatically

be of great significance for our study of the issue. If we set out from
the criterion defined above, that Reformation features are mold-
breaking and cannot be described as just *one* possible position within
the medieval theological system, then one thing should be clear:
access to a definition of the Reformation doctrine of justification can
be acquired only by studying the characteristics of medieval Catholic
doctrines of grace and salvation, and what they have in common. I
shall now turn to that question.

II. *Medieval Catholic Doctrine*[17]

Let us imagine a late medieval man with a strong consciousness of
his sinfulness, living in fear of the divine judge and the punishments

---

think of Ockhamism, although with its specific doctrine of grace Ockhamism – in
its own turn by no means always unambiguous – is only one aspect of nominalism. On the symbiosis of Augustinianism and nominalism cf. recently M. Schulze:
"'Via Gregorii' in Forschung und Quellen", in: H. A. Oberman (ed.), *Gregor von
Rimini. Werk und Wirkung bis zur Reformation* (Berlin, 1981), pp. 1–126; A. Zumkeller:
*Erbsünde, Gnade, Rechtfertigung und Verdienst nach der Lehre der Erfurter Augustinertheologen
des Spätmittelalters* (Wurzburg, 1984) [= Cass. 35], esp. pp. 2–9.

[17] It is not only sensible but necessary for us to take our bearings in the following account from those medieval doctrines of salvation that, comparatively speaking, come closest to the Reformation doctrine. I am thinking of a doctrine of grace
strongly influenced by Augustine's anti-Pelagianism, for instance in the late works
of Thomas Aquinas (*Summa theologiae*), in the Augustinian Hermit Aegidius Romanus,
and in Gregory of Rimini. These theologians laid particular emphasis on the distance between natural morality and the justifying operation of grace. The differences
separating this Augustinian theology of grace from the theology of the reformers
also apply (indeed, they apply in particular) to the Scotist and Ockhamist doctrine
of grace. To that extent we can detect a common basic feature of medieval theology.
On *one* point, however, we must make a reservation. The Scotists and Ockhamists
agree with the nominalist tendencies of the Augustinian Gregory of Rimini in stressing the fact that the infused 'habit of grace' of *caritas* and the works proceeding
from it do not lead with absolute inevitability to the divine *acceptatio ad vitam aeternam*. In his sovereign power (*de potentia dei absoluta*) God could still withhold eternal
bliss from the man to whom grace has been given. The causal and conditional connection between human morality – that is, its fulfillment of divine law and the
attainment of salvation – is thus not directly derived from the nature of man in
possession of justifying grace. Only God's freely given promise lies at the root of
this causal relationship and thus the connection between merit and reward. In the
context of this order of salvation, ordained by God thus and not otherwise, and
therefore immutable (*de potentia dei ordinata*), the quality of the habit of grace and
the morality of good works can indeed develop fully: a characteristic feature of the
Catholic understanding of salvation. The scope of the *potentia dei absoluta* thus makes
no difference to the immanent stringency of the concept of salvation in the model
of justification described below. The nominalists too see salvation *de facto* as depend-

of hell and purgatory. Let us further imagine that this man acts as he is expected to do by the scholastic theologians. He will be constantly repenting of his sins, confessing to the priest and receiving the sacrament of absolution. He will hope devoutly that God has forgiven him his sins for Christ's sake and is inclined to show him grace. But he knows at the same time that this is not enough to get him into Paradise. He sees the way of probation lying ahead of him, the way of obedience to the law, the way of good works that must be done out of unselfish love for God and for his neighbor. Through such works he will on the one hand make amends (*satisfactio*) for the temporal punishment of sin he bears, and on the other he will acquire merit (*merita*).[18] He will earn continuation in the divine grace, an increase of grace, entrance into eternal life, and finally an increase in the sanctification of eternal life. All this is the object of his works, made possible by active love. Of course, supposing for instance that this man has heard Johannes von Staupitz preach in Nuremberg,[19] he knows that he can never do such good works of his own sinful nature, but only through the supernatural quality of grace infused in him by God and transforming him. Furthermore, he will have a sense of the inadequacy of his works of love:[20] he will feel that even they can never fully atone for his temporal sin and earn a heavenly reward, but the power of the Passion of Christ must always compensate for his inadequacy,[21] and thus that in the end, when his

---

ing on the essential quality and actual morality of man. However, wide differences then arise between those theologians who, like William of Ockham, will even allow natural man the possibility of selfless love of God, and those like Gregory of Rimini who consider a morally good action possible only on condition of the granting of grace and the actual support of God (the *auxilium speciale dei*). Even Gregory of Rimini, however, insists on the morality of human acts as a condition of fitness for salvation. On the tradition of the freely given promise of God in the Middle Ages, cf. B. Hamm: *Promissio, Pactum, Ordinatio. Freiheit und Selbstbindung Gottes in der scholastischen Gnadenlehre* (Tübingen, 1977) [= Beiträge zur historischen Theologie, 54].

[18] The actual content of the concept of merit and the basis on which its possibility is founded are very variable in scholastic theology; cf. Hamm: ibid., pp. 437–62.

[19] Nuremberg sermons of 1517 (Lazarus Spengler's copy). *Johann von Staupitzens sämmtliche Werke I: Deutsche Schriften*, ed. J. K. F. Knaake (Potsdam, 1867), pp. 15–42.

[20] Cf. A. Zumkeller: "Das Ungenügen der menschlichen Werke bei den deutschen Predigern des Spätmittelalters", in: *Zeitschrift für katholische Theologie* 81 (1959), pp. 265–305.

[21] Staupitz applies the idea of inadequacy with particular force to the affect of repentance; cf. L. Graf zu Dohna and R. Wetzel: "Die Reue Christi. Zum theologischen Ort der Busse bei Johann von Staupitz", in: *SMGB* 94 (1983), pp. 457–82; Hamm: *Frömmigkeitstheologie* (as n. 10), pp. 240–2. The christological idea of

works are accepted by God and he is granted eternal life, God is rewarding only his own gifts to mankind,[22] and always through the interceding power of Christ.[23] Even all this, however, will not lead our medieval man to feel a confident certainty of grace and salvation. He will still feel sure (if he sees himself in the light of scholastic doctrines) that he can attain salvation only through works of love, and he will still be convinced that these works must derive from the nature of the human being himself, that is, from a quality of selfless divine love constantly present in him and expelling the affect and the act of hostility to God, that is to say, original sin and mortal sin. However, he will also feel sure that he can never know with complete certainty if he really possesses that love and is thus in a state of grace that will justify him.[24] In pious self-analysis, his conscience will remain anxiously intent on his own condition, however often he is told and assured that everything happens through grace and for the sake of Christ, for the reality of Christ must become the reality in him of a new state of being and acting. At the end of his life, after all, the same Christ who died for him and works in him through grace will call him to reckoning, a stern judge, and will then decide whether he has kept the law of love.

Now let us try to perceive the scholastic understanding of justification as set out in this model of late medieval experience. Here, and indeed here above all, where the primacy and the transforming power of grace are emphasized in line with Augustine's anti-Pelagianism, justi-

---

compensation as held in the late Middle Ages, mainly by the Augustinian Hermits, is taken up in pre-Tridentine reforming theology, particularly by supporters of the doctrine of double *iustitia* (Gropper, Pigge, Contarini, Seripando); cf. Braunisch: *Die Theologie der Rechtfertigung* (as n. 11), pp. 419–37.

[22] According to Augustine's influential formulation, for instance in *De gratia et lib. arb.* 6,15 (Migne, *PL* 44, 891): "Si ergo dei dona sunt bona merita tua, non deus coronat merita tua tamquam merita tua, sed tamquam dona sua"; *Tract. in Ioan.* 3, 10 (*CChr SL* 36, 25, 25f.): 'Coronat autem in nobis deus dona misericordiae suae.'

[23] The Scholastic concept saw merit and satisfaction on mankind's part as possible only in so far as man's finite actions and sufferings are founded in the infinite value of the merit and satisfaction of Jesus Christ. Johannes von Paltz, referring to Johannes Duns Scotus, consequently says of *satisfactio*: "Verum est, quod deo per nos satisfacere non possumus, sed tamen in virtute passionis Christi possumus satisfacere; quia ilia passio in tantum acceptatur a deo trino, ut virtute eius acceptetur satisfactio ilia, quae secundum se accepta non posset esse satisfactio." Johannes von Paltz: *Supplementum Coelifodinae*, 1504, ed. B. Hamm (Berlin, 1983) [= Spätmittelalter und Reformation, 3], p. 290, 11–14.

[24] On the uncertainty of grace and election, cf. Hamm: *Frömmigkeitstheologie* (as n. 10), pp. 222–6 (distinguishing between subjective and objective levels of certainty).

fication is identified with the idea of being made righteous. The nature of justification, its *forma*, is the new quality of grace shown in love, a quality that is acquired by man, and here indeed the giving and working of God[25] has become so much his own that they are the well-spring of his own free movement and a self-realization resulting from his actions, with the aim of achieving eternal life. The person of the man assumes the aspect of an active subject[26] before God, and only in this way can he win eternal life. The working of God as the autonomous first cause opens up to man the possibility of cooperation (*cooperatio*) in his own salvation through the outpouring of grace and perhaps in addition through the actual aid of God's grace.[27]

Here we come to the understanding of the nature of existence characteristic of the medieval doctrine of salvation,[28] an ontology of righteousness determining man's righteous conduct and relation to salvation from the viewpoint of his moral quality, and ideologically relating that morality in action to man's final acceptance into sanctification. A crucial point is the dominant idea here of causality or contingency: the justification of the sinner, his pardon and acceptance as a child of God, are expressed when he is made righteous and his soul transformed through the quality of grace. Only if sin is really set aside is it conceivable that a man's sins can be forgiven

---

[25] The freedom of the *liberum arbitrium*, to medieval followers of Augustine, means simply the participation of the man to whom grace has been shown; the operation of God is transformed into the spontaneous operation of man, and man as an entity guided by God also operates of himself, as an active subject (as distinct from acting under compulsion, *coactio*). Cf. Thomas Aquinas: *S.th.* I–III q. 113 art. 3.

[26] Johannes von Staupitz formulates this idea in accordance with the theological tradition whereby the good works of the justified, although they are the works of God, are *formaliter* present in man: *Libellus de exsecutione aeternae praedestinationis*, 1517, §40, ed. L. Graf zu Dohna and R. Wetzel (Berlin, 1979) [= Spätmittelalter und Reformation, 14], p. 124. The *formaliter* here, according to the editor's comment, means 'subjective', that is, it describes the *esse* of the works as in a subjective relation to the substance of the human person.

[27] The necessity of the actual aid of God's grace for every morally good act is emphasized by Gregory of Rimini and his pupils; cf. C. P. Burger: "Der Augustinschüler gegen die modernen Pelagianer: Das *auxilium speciale dei* in der Gnadenlehre Gregors von Rimini", in: Oberman (ed.): *Gregor von Rimini* (as n. 16), pp. 195–240.

[28] Theologians influenced by nominalism also understand the nature of being in a similar way, although they are more interested than the representatives of the *via antiqua* in unusual rather than in habitual actions. They too are concerned about the moral nature of man in the doctrine of justification, whether in regard to the 'habit' of love or to the separate acts of love of the justified, and they too see morality as a human factor that is a condition of acceptance into salvation.

and not held against him. Here, in the transformation wrought by
the infused habit of grace, lies the real factor making acceptance of
the sinner possible[29] – its "sole formal cause" (*unica formalis causa*), as
the Council of Trent puts it.[30] However, this means that the process
whereby the sinner is made righteous, a process expressed in moral
virtues and good works, is the reason, the necessary prerequisite and
condition for the final absolution of man at the Last Judgment. For
where the grounds of the reality of justification are seen as residing
in the nature and actions of man, the justification of the sinner in
this life is always provisional and incomplete, and will come to a
final conclusion only in the judgment that will absolve man and find
him righteous *because of* his righteous nature and actions. In scholastic thought, then, the two great significant aspects of the Christian
life are separate: first the acceptance of man into grace (the *acceptatio ad gratiam*) occurring when he is made righteous in the process of
justification, then his acceptance into salvation at the end of his life
(the *acceptatio ad vitam aeternam*).[31] Final absolution is *on the grounds* of
righteous actions and obedience to the law, although also, and always,
for the sake of Christ. Here a causal and contingent relationship
prevails, and it is also articulated in the concepts of satisfaction and
merit.[32] The fact that the works of love are described as satisfactory
and meritorious shows that they are the necessary prerequisite or at
least the *causa sine qua non* for making man's sanctification possible.
The Council of Trent consequently condemns the doctrine that the
Gospel constitutes a "naked and absolute" (i.e. unconditional) "promise

---

[29] Cf., for instance, the answer given by Thomas Aquinas to the question "Utrum
ad remissionem culpae, quae est iustificatio impii, requiratur gratiae infusio", and
in particular his concern with the argument that the forgiveness of sin consists in
the *reputatio divina*, and thus requires no *infusio gratiae: S. Th.* I–III q. 113 art. 2 arg.
2 and ad 2. Cf. also ibid., art. 8 ad 1: from God's point of view (*ex parte dei
iustificantis*) the infusion of grace precedes the forgiveness of sins, not temporally but
in an objectively logical sense (*ordine naturae*), for the infused habit of grace is *causa
remissionis culpae*.

[30] *Decretum de iustificatione*, c. 7 (D/S No. 1529). Cf. ibid. can. 11 (No. 1561): "Si
quis dixerit homines iustificari vel sola imputatione iustitiae Christi vel sola peccatorum remissione, exclusa gratia et caritate, quae in cordibus eorum per spiritum
sanctum diffundatur atque illis inhaereat, aut etiam gratiam, qua iustificamur, esse
tantum favorem dei: anathema sit."

[31] Cf., for instance, Johannes von Paltz: *Supplementum Coelifodinae*, p. 227 (as n. 23),
5–7: "Respondetur, quod est duplex acceptatio: una quantum ad praesentem iustitiam, altera quantum ad finalem remunerationem."

[32] On the medieval connection between the concept of merit and ideas of causality cf. Hamm: *Promissio* (as n. 17), p. 443f. and 485–9.

of eternal life", that is to say, sanctification given "without condition of the fulfillment of the commandments" (*sine condicione observantis mandatorum*).[33]

III. *The Reformation Doctrine of Justification*

1. *The Unconditionally Given Acceptance of Mankind*

This doctrine, condemned by the Council of Trent as un-Catholic and stating that the sinner is given an outright promise of unconditional salvation, was at the center of the Reformation doctrine of justification as we encounter it in Luther, Melanchthon, Zwingli and Calvin.[34] In the *Confessio Augustana Variata*, Melanchthon says that the promise of forgiveness of sins and of eternal life is certain, since it does not depend on the condition of our worthiness (*ex condicione nostrae dignitatis*) but is given for Christ's sake. Melanchthon sees the whole consolation of the terrified conscience in this unconditionality, the fact that forgiveness is linked neither to preceding nor to subsequent works.[35] Calvin puts it similarly when he sees the characteristic feature of the promises of the law in its structure of conditionality, the *condicio*: only on condition that the commandment of the law to love is kept does its promise of life come into effect.[36] It

---

[33] *Decretum de iustiflcatione*, can. 20 (D/S No. 1570): "Si quis hominem iustificatum et quantumlibet perfectum dixerit non teneri ad observantiam mandatorum dei et ecclesiae, sed tantum ad credendum, quasi vero evangelium sit nuda et absoluta promissio vitae aeternae sine condicione observationis mandatorum: anathema sit."

[34] Cf. Luther: *Resolutiones*, thesis 38 (*WA*, 596, pp. 7–9): "Cave ergo, ne quando in tuam contritionem ullo modo confidas, sed in nudissimum verbum optimi et fidelissimi tui salvatoris Jesu Christi; cor tuum fallet te, ille te non fallet vel habitus vel desideratus."

[35] "Quamquam igitur evangelium requirit poenitentiam, tamen, ut remissio peccatorum certa sit, docet earn gratis donari, hoc est non pendere ex condicione dignitatis nostrae nee dari propter ulla praecedentia opera aut dignitatem sequentium . . . ideo Paulus dicit: 'gratis salvati estis' [Eph. 2.5]. Item: 'ideo ex fide gratis, ut sit firma promissio' [Rom. 4.16], hoc est: ita erit certa remissio, cum sciemus earn non pendere ex condicione nostrae dignitatis, sed donari propter Christum. Haec est firma et necessaria consolatio piis et perterrefactis mentibus." CAvar (1540), art. 4 (*Melanchthons Werke in Auswahl*, ed. R. Stupperich, VI (Gütersloh, 1955), pp. 15,11–16,24–30).

[36] Cf., for instance, *Inst.* (1559), III, 17, 6 (OS IV, 258, 27–32): "Legales promissiones appello, non quae ubique sparsae sunt in libris Mosaicis (quando in illis quoque evangelicae multae occurrunt), sed quae proprie ad legis ministerium pertinent.

is not so with the gospel: its promises of justice do not depend on the *condicio operum*, but are unconditional, resting solely on the mercy of God and the righteousness of Christ interceding for us.[37] This unconditional promise, the unconditional acceptance of the sinner into righteousness and sanctification, is what Calvin calls justification (*iustificatio*).[38]

It is not a matter of terminology. The term *iustificatio* plays a very subsidiary part in the writings of Zwingli compared with those of the other three reformers, and Luther by no means confines it to the precise sense of God's absolution received in faith, as do the late Melanchthon and Calvin; he also relates divine justification to the living process of justification in human existence.[39] As for the term *condicio*, one might search both Luther and Zwingli in vain for an explicit account of the unconditionality of grace and salvation. The Reformation was concerned not with the term but with the essence of unconditionality: the unconditionality of the process whereby the godless sinner is justified before God and accepted by God into salvation. How can I become just before God and be saved, in view of the total commitment of will and of achievement that God's law demands of me? How can I, as one who breaks that law, be accepted into the family and inheritance of God? This is the essence of the idea of justification at the heart of every fully developed theological system in the Reformation.[40] The connection between justification and unconditionality, as the reformers saw it, requires an explana-

---

Eiusmodi promissiones, quocunque nomine vocare libeat, sub condicione 'Si feceris quod tibi praecipitur' paratam esse remunerationem denuntiant." Cf. ibid. III, 11, 17 (IV, 200, 34–201, 7); III, 17, 2 (IV, 254, 30f.); III, 13, 3 (IV, 218, 8).

[37] Ibid. III, 11, 17 (IV, 200, 33–201, 15), and finally: "Certe et lex ipsa suas habet promissiones. Quare in promissionibus evangelicis distinctum aliquid ac diversum esse oportet, nisi velimus fateri ineptam esse collationem. Quale autem istud erit, nisi quod gratuitae sunt ac sola dei misericordia suffultae, cum legis promissiones ab operum condicione pendeant." Cf. ibid. III, 2, 29 (IV, 39, 6–11) for the distinction between *promissio gratuita* and *promissio condicionalis*.

[38] Cf., for instance, ibid. III, 11, 2 (IV, 183, 4–10): "Contra iustificabitur ille fide, qui operum iustitia exclusus Christi iustitiam per fidem apprehendit, qua vestitus in dei conspectu non ut peccator, sed tamquam iustus apparet. Ita nos iustificationem simpliciter interpretamur acceptionem, qua nos deus in gratiam receptos pro iustis habet. Eamque in peccatorum remissione ac iustitiae Christi imputatione positam esse dicimus."

[39] Cf. P. Althaus: Die *Theologie Martin Luthers* (Gütersloh, 1980), p. 197.

[40] This question, characteristic of the Reformation as a whole, is still central where the answer blurs the dividing line between Reformation and medieval Catholic doctrines, for instance in Andreas Osiander the elder.

tion that will correctly locate its essential difference from medieval theology.

To be precise, we are concerned with the nature of the relationship between divine acceptance of the sinner and the sinner's actual change of life. The close connection between justification and absolution is not a matter of controversy. All the great reformers emphatically taught that justification, the absolution and acceptance of godless man, is fundamentally connected with man's sanctification and renewal in love and the works of love. The difference from Catholicism does not lie here, as if there could be a new divine beginning without renewal in man, and the act of judgment were an abstract and involuntary act of God concerned with himself, not a creative calling of man to life. After Luther, Calvin in particular shows how deeply the connection of justification and sanctification can be founded in the Reformation; to Calvin, the indissoluble link arises from the community of the faithful in Christ.[41] For "Christ justifies no one whom he does not at the same time (*simul*) sanctify", Calvin writes in the *Institutio*.[42] Those who would separate the two would tear Christ apart. "Would you therefore achieve justice in Christ?" Calvin continues. "Then you must first possess Christ. However, you cannot possess Christ at all without at the same time participating in his sanctification [. . .] the Lord gives us both at once [justification and sanctification], never the one without the other."[43] The reason is in the inseparable community of Christ with the Holy Spirit, so that our community with Christ is always at the same time community with his renewing spirit.[44] In a treatise of 1547 against the decrees of the Council of Trent Calvin explicitly says that the question is not whether

---

[41] Cf. W. Kolfhaus: *Christusgemeinschaft bei Johannes Calvin* (Neukirchen, 1939) [= Beiträge zur Geschichte und Lehre der Reformierten Kirche, 3].

[42] "Nullum ergo Christus iustificat, quern non simul sanctificet. Sunt enim perpetuo et individuo nexu coniuncta haec beneficia, ut quos sapientia sua illuminat, eos redimat, quos redimit, iustificet, quos iustificat, sanctificet." Inst. (1559), III, 16, 1 (OS IV, 249, 8–11).

[43] "Vis ergo iustitiam in Christo adipisei? Christum ante possideas oportet; possidere autem non potes, quin fias sanctificationis eius particeps; quia in frusta discerpi non potest. Cum ergo haec beneficia [i.e. *iustitia* and *sanctificatio*] nonnisi se ipsum erogando fruenda nobis dominus concedat, utrunque simul largitur: alterum nunquam sine altero." Ibid. III, 16, 1 (IV, 249, 14–19). On the idea that to separate justification from sanctification would be to tear Christ apart, cf. also n. 46.

[44] Cf. the account and texts in T. Stadtland: *Rechtfertigung und Heiligung bei Calvin* (Neukirchen, 1972) [= Beiträge zur Geschichte und Lehre der Reformierten Kirche, 32], p. 129f.

Christ also sanctifies those whom he justifies. The entire argument, rather, turns around the cause of justification: "Sed tota nostra disceptatio est de causa iustificationis."[45] The question is where the acceptance of man, the totality of his justification and his salvation before God, have their foundation.

We have seen how in medieval Catholic theology neither the acceptance of the sinner into the process of justification nor his acceptance for eternal salvation is seen as causeless, that is, without foundation in sanctification and the renewal of human morality. Absolution and acceptance by God never occur without such cause. God's forgiveness of sins and justification of man is made possible by the granting of grace to man and by his subsequent good works and freedom from acts of mortal sin; these aspects of his nature then also become the condition of his sanctification after death. These ideas of the possible and necessary grounds of righteousness and sanctification are what the reformers dispute. It is here that the Reformation doctrine of justification breaks the mold. There can be no valid cause for man to be justified before God; not even God himself stands in such a causal relation to man and his actions. The acceptance of God, his bestowal of grace on his creature, is not subject to reasons or conditions, although justification always has consequences in the shape of sanctification in the renewing power of love and the works of love.

---

[45] A distinction may be drawn between justification and sanctification, but they cannot be divided: "[. . .] perpetuo coniunctae sint ac cohaereant duae istae res: sanctificatio et iustificatio. Sed perperam inde infertur unam ac eandem esse. Exempli gratia: Solis lumen, etsi nunquam separatur a calore, non tamen calor existimandus est; nemoque tarn rudis invenitur, qui non unum ab altero distinguat. Fatemur ergo, simul atque iustificatur quispiam, necessario innovationem quoque sequi. Neque vero de eo ambigitur, an sanctificet Christus nee ne, quoscunque iustificat. Hoc enim esset lacerare evangelium adeoque Christum ipsum discerpere, si quis iustitiam, quam fide consequimur, separare velit a poenitentia. Sed tota nostra disceptatio est de causa iustificationis. Hanc Tridentini patres duplicem esse fingunt: ac si partim remissione peccatorum, partim spirituali regneratione iusti essemus; vel, ut aliis verbis exprimam quod sentiunt: ac si partim imputatione, partim qualitate iustitia nostra constaret. Ego autem unicam et simplicem esse assero, quae tota continetur gratuita dei acceptione. Earn praeterea extra nos constituo, quia in solo Christo iusti sumus." *Acta Synodi Tridentini cum antidoto* (CR 35, 448).

2. *Radical Sin*

The way taken by the reformers in reaching this view of unconditionally is through insight into man's pitiable nature and sinful frailty before God. To the scholastic understanding, the life of man is always marked in one way or another by sin. However, sin dividing man from God, original and mortal sin that of its nature excludes the love of God, is a human fault that can be remedied. The infusion of the habit of grace compensates for this lack in man by making him a creature that loves God,[46] and thus goes to meet God through obedience to the law. The reformers, however, particularly Luther, thought and taught that the original sin of rebellion against God was not a human fault that could be cancelled out, but was the perverse and basic tendency of the whole person until death. Throughout his life, the Christian remains an unrealized being, incapable of love for God and his neighbor, trapped in a self-centered way of life, lacking even the roots of humanity.

3. *Grace Preceding Perfect Righteousness*

This understanding of radical sin has its precise counterpart in the understanding of grace. Just as sin is not an aspect of man, but is the whole man, justifying grace is not an appendage of man, a quality inherent in him, something that man as subject possesses. Grace, in direct contrast to the scholastic doctrine, is nothing but God himself in his mercy, the grace of God, God giving himself in community with the sinner. Grace is not something made in man, but his new standing in the sight of God. Since man is guilty before God, and owes total righteousness and selfless love throughout his life, the reality and possibility of God's grace can have no foundation based in man. Furthermore, even if man could obey God's law and owe nothing to God's favor, as a created being he would not be worthy or deserving of the boundless grace and splendor of God;[47] to quote

---

[46] Here we may disregard the scholastic doctrines that allow the possibility of acts of divine love even in the natural state, before the reception of *caritas* – in line with our basic proposition (see n. 17 above) to take medieval theology seriously where it most strongly emphasizes the gulf between nature and grace.

[47] Cf. Zwingli: "Eine kurze christliche Einleitung", in: *Huldreich Zwinglis sämtliche Werke* (abbreviation Z) II, 63, 7, 3–6 and 24–26: "And even if we were always devout and without frailty, and served God all our days according to his will, yet man's life is unworthy of long, immeasurable eternity."

Luther: "God has laid it down that man is to be saved not by the law but by Christ."[48] To the godless, then, grace becomes real in the form of groundless acceptance into the family of God, the beginning of a new relationship. A conceptual approach in terms of the relationship replaces the traditional qualitative and moral attitude. Sin remains real in ourselves, but outside ourselves (*extra nos*), in the relationship, that is to say, we are justified in the way in which we are seen by God (*coram deo*).

A little further interpretation of what Luther and the other reformers understood by this relationship of grace should be added. The propitiatory righteousness of Jesus Christ acting vicariously for us is of fundamental importance. It alone is the cause of justification; it alone provides satisfaction and wins merit. The new relationship in which grace justifies us means that God sees man in the light of Christ's righteousness, and allows it to stand for the righteousness of sinners. That in turn means that through Christ man acquires a total righteousness that he could never qualitatively possess as a frail sinner and a created being with such a being's limitations.

Luther, and Melanchthon and Calvin with him, expresses this understanding of justification in terms of the relation by speaking of the imputation to us of righteousness (*reputatio, imputatio*), and by describing the righteousness of Christ imputed to the sinner as a righteousness that is external and alien to mankind (*iustitia aliena, externa*). It is indeed truly given to us, but it never exists in us, only in the manner of its acceptance and of divine absolution. 'Righteousness' is the acknowledgement of the sinner before the judgment seat of God in the face of accusations against him from all sides, including his own heart. This extremely forensic terminology articulates the change from the scholastic understanding of the nature of man in particularly concentrated form;[49] however, the example of Zwingli

---

[48] "Est autem quaestio non, utrum lex vel opera rationis iustificent, sed an lex facta in spiritu iustificet. Respondemus autem, quod non, et quod homo, qui per omnia legem virtute spiritus sancti impleret, tamen debeat implorare misericordiam dei, qui constituit non per legem, sed per Christum salvare." *WA* TR 1, 32, 9–13, no. 85.

[49] Cf. O. H. Pesch: *Theologie der Rechtfertigung bei Martin Luther und Thomas von Aquin* (Mainz, 1967, repr. 1985 Walberberg, Ger. Albertus-Magnus-Academie) [= Walberger Studien, 7, T 4], p. 182: "Secondly, the requisite distinction from scholastic doctrine can best be perceived through forensic understanding. We may indeed wonder, with some justice, whether Elert is right in suggesting that scholasticism bases its certainty of justification not on faith but on 'empirical facts'. However, it is true

clearly shows how the basic attitude of the Reformation to the doctrine of justification can still be the same where this specific kind of terminology is not to the fore. Once again, the crucial point is not the forensic terminology but the nature of what it implies. Zwingli never equates the righteousness we derive from Christ with the righteousness of renewal expressed by good works and wrought in us by the Holy Spirit. He too sees the righteousness of Christ as the pre-given totality of our acceptance for salvation in the forgiveness of our sins, while the renewal itself is the partial element in an existence shattered by sin. Our righteousness and innocence, preserving us before the judgment of God, as Zwingli constantly emphasizes, are nothing but the righteousness of the son of God interceding for us.[50] "Everyone who is in Christ," he says, "is saved in the perfection of the law and by it. To be 'in Christ' means to have faith in him and to continue firm in our belief."[51]

Although Zwingli seamlessly links righteousness received in faith with the sanctification of life under the dominant perspective of the workings of the divine spirit, and although he therefore identifies belief and love in his concept of faith,[52] his own theology displays the characteristic profile of the Reformation doctrine of justification: indissoluble as the link between justification and sanctification appears to the reformers,[53] they all, even Zwingli, clearly point out that, in

---

that on the issue of justification, the scholastics enquire not about empirically verifiable processes but about *internal* processes, about *man*, while Luther, on the other hand, is concerned with the new attitude of *God* to man. In fact a forensic understanding thus does express the most important difference between the Reformation and scholasticism."

[50] Cf., for instance, Zwingli: *Auslegen und Grunde der Schlussreden* (Zürich: Froschower, 1523); Art. 5 (Z II, 40, 26–28); B. Hamm: *Zwinglis Reformation der Freiheit* (Neukirchen-Vluyn, 1988). As yet there is no complete study, free of polemics and apologetics, of Zwingli's understanding of righteousness and justification. The monograph of H. Schmid: *Zwinglis Lehre von der göttlichen und menschlichen Gerechtigkeit* (Zurich, 1959) [= Studien zur Dogmengeschichte und systematischen Theologie, 12] does not give a precise account of the specifically evangelical features of Zwingli's doctrine of justification.

[51] In *Epist. ad Rom.*, on Rom. 10.4 (M. Schuler and J. Schulthess: *Huldrici Zwinglii Opera VI/2*, Zurich 1838, 112): "Omnis, qui est in Christo, est in perfectione legis et per hoc salvus. In Christo esse est ei fidere et firma fide haerere."

[52] Cf., for instance, *Commentarius de vera et falsa religione*, 'De merito' (Z III, 848, 29, and 849, 33).

[53] This is particularly true, to an even greater degree, of those reformers who saw justification and sanctification less *a partis hominis* than from the perspective of the works of God. Since in Zwingli the main viewpoint is always the omnipotence

contrast to scholastic theology, justification is not the same thing as
to be made righteous. Justification as the totality of obedience to the
law and of righteousness, given to the sinner in advance through
Christ and protecting him, that perfect righteousness in the sight of
God, can never be congruent with partial renewal through the spirit
of love. This tenet also means that the sinner's acceptance into the
grace and salvation justifying him can never derive the basis of its
existence from the change to a Christian way of life. Justification
through the righteousness of Christ which is outside us, and the
process whereby we become just within ourselves in a sanctified life,
are always separate, like cause and effect, like the immeasurable fullness of God and the emptiness of created beings, the purity of the
innocent and the guilt of outcast, ever-sinful man. To this extent
there is agreement between the reformers, if not terminologically
then on a common "evangelical conviction of the unconditional predominance of 'alien righteousness (*iustitia aliena*)'" (Dantine).[54] And
Elert is right to locate the crucial difference from scholasticism in
this 'alien righteousness'.[55]

4. *Simul Iustus et Peccator*

In the thinking of the Reformation, the approach to this distinction
and to the irreversibility of cause and effect is directly connected
with the approach to the idea of what is *simul*, existing "at the same
time". *Simul*, in the Reformation[56] means simultaneity, the inseparable
and yet distinct existence side by side of four carefully distinguished

---

of the spirit of God, justification and sanctification, faith and love, the fruits of love
and its social consequences, seen from that angle, all cohere to form a spiritual
unity, with faith in God alone at its center, wrought by the spirit. This theocen-
tric perspective of unity, however, must not be misunderstood. As soon as the question of the cause of salvation is raised, and attention is directed to the created
being, Zwingli distinguishes clearly between the righteousness of the son of God
passively received in devout faith, and the activity of the loving human being; the
latter can never be a cause of salvation but always shows the workings of the abundance of righteousness and salvation that has been received.

[54] Dantine, in *HDGThG* II (as n. 16), p. 459.

[55] W. Elert: *Morphologie des Luthertums I* (Munich, 1931, repr. 1965), pp. 68–70.
However, Elert confines his definition of this opposition to Luther.

[56] On the "evangelical" character of the idea inherent in the Lutheran formula
simul iustus et peccator, cf. W. Link, *Das Ringen Luthers um die Freiheit der Theologie von
der Philosophie* (Munich, 1940, repr. 1979) [= Forschungen zur Geschichte und Lehre
des Protestantismus, IX/3], p. 77f.

aspects of the Christian's life;[57] and in fact the emphasis on simultaneity derives only from this distinction. Simultaneous realities are (1) sin lasting all our lives, and received by the Christian in the form of penance; (2) the righteousness in the sight of God won for us by Christ (*extra nos*), and received in the form of faith; (3) the righteousness of renewal in sanctification that wrestles with sin, active in the form of love; and (4) liberation from our sinful natures and complete renewal after death, already present in the form of hope. This fourfold reality is expressed in Luther's famous phrase *simul iustus et peccator*, "a just man and at the same time a sinner".[58] Yet again, however, the Reformation doctrine of justification does not depend upon such formulaic expressions. So far as I am aware Zwingli, who was a great deal more independent of Luther than Melanchthon and Calvin, did not employ this formula, but the simultaneity of the fourfold reality of sin and righteousness is at the very heart of the content of his theology.[59] He too makes it clear that because man always stands before God as a created being and a sinner, the totality of his simultaneous righteousness must always be outside himself, in Christ, must antedate all the good works of his new life, and must always be considered the sole grounds for the reality and possibility of salvation.

5. *The Eschatological Final Validity of Justification*

Having located the new element in the Reformation understanding of sin and grace, we must now go a step further. Since in Reformation thinking justification is the *unconditional* acceptance of the sinner, for Christ's sake and not because of any previous, present or future quality in his life and morals, and is always founded outside us in God

---

[57] The classic text in which these four realities of sin and justice are first ranged side by side in Reformation theology is in Luther's course of lectures on the Epistle to the Romans, Rom 4.7f. (*WA* 56, 269, 21–273, 2).

[58] Cf the pioneering work of R. Hermann: *Luthers These 'Gerecht und Sünder zugleich'* (Göttingen, 1930, repr. 1960). The Lutheran *simul* is not Pauline but does signify a further creative development of St. Paul's interpretation, and thus represents a genuine assimilation of Pauline thinking at a period much concerned with the refinement of the scholastic theology of sin and grace; cf. W. Joest: "Paulus und das Luthersche Simul Iustus et Peccator", in: *Kerygma und Dogma I* (1955), pp. 269–320.

[59] Cf. G. W. Locher: *Huldrych Zwingli in neuer Sicht. Zehn Beiträge zur Theologie der Zürcher Reformation* (Zürich, 1969), p. 30 (quoting texts).

himself – since that is the case, justification acquires an eschatological meaning in the Reformation that is foreign to it in Catholic theology.[60] In scholastic thinking, as we have seen, man's acceptance
into grace and righteousness in justification, and his acceptance into
sanctification at the Last Judgment, are two separate things, divided
by the way of life inherent in obedience to the law and the principles of satisfaction and merit. Man's morality is the prerequisite of
his final acceptance. Reformation unconditionality brought the two
aspects together: the sinner has already been accepted for salvation
through his justification and in advance of his new life and good
works, despite the enduring power of sin. This is the eschatological
final validity of justification. Through the acceptance of the sinner,
his entering into the righteousness of Christ, something final has
taken place; it cannot be superseded even by the Last Judgment, but
will then be brought out of concealment into the revelation of bliss.
Why does his acceptance for sanctification become so conclusively a
present event in the justification of godless man? Because in giving
grace to man God is giving not a thing but himself, in his whole
and undivided love, and God himself cannot be superseded.[61]

At the same time, this conclusive finality in Reformation theology
derives from Christ. The justice of Jesus Christ interceding for human
guilt thus makes the here and now of justification the *eschaton*, the
final event in the divine plan, since Jesus Christ "is the same yes-
terday, and today, and forever" (Heb. 13.8) and consequently his
protective righteousness is eternal too.[62] The godless are therefore
safe in his righteousness for all eternity.[63] In the last resort the dogma
of Christ's divinity is at the heart of this line of argument: through
his divine nature, and through his human suffering and death in
man's stead, he is part of the divine eternity. This is the sole reason why the "existence in Christ" of the justified already denotes
existence in everlasting bliss.

Luther and the other reformers with him express this final acceptance of mankind in Christ by saying that in the act of justification

---

[60] Cf. U. Aschendorf: *Eschatologie bei Luther* (Göttingen, 1967), pp. 36–48.
[61] Cf. H. Rückert: *Vorträge und Aufsätze zur historischen Theologie* (Tübingen, 1972),
p. 306f.
[62] Cf. A. Sperl: *Melanchthon zwischen Humanismus und Reformation* (Munich, 1959)
[= Forschungen zur Geschichte und Lehre des Protestantismus, X/15], pp. 48–61
(on Luther).
[63] Cf. Calvin: *Inst.* (1599) III, 24, 6 (OS IV, 416, 38–417, 14).

the sinner becomes "righteous *and* saved", *iustus et salvus*,[64] that is, not righteous now and saved at some future date, but already the recipient of righteousness and salvation in faith. Luther, for instance, comments in his Small Catechism on the sacrament of communion: "We are shown it in this saying: given for you and shed in forgiveness of sins, that is to say, in the sacrament such words offer forgiveness of sins, life and salvation. For where there is forgiveness of sins [to Luther, this was what justification entailed] there is also life and salvation."[65] Calvin puts it thus: "Through faith in Christ we achieve not only the ability to win righteousness and become sanctified, but they are both [*iustitia* and *salus*] given to us [through faith]."[66] The faithful, as he says, are those who "have achieved sanctification" already through their community with Christ.[67]

In this context we repeatedly encounter the Pauline image of the "heir of God" (Rom. 8.17; Gal. 4.7). By adoption or birth through his justification, the sinner becomes the child and heir of God and his glory: "He has not earned his position as heir to that fortune through his work, nor does he work and act so that he may become heir to it, but when he was born he was already heir to those patrimonial estates on the grounds of birth, not as a result of his own merit. Even if he persists steadfastly in his work he asks no reward, for he knows that all is his already." The justified man, then, as God's heir, is already in possession of salvation; he is an heir before he performs any works, and is not paid for them later; he is a child and not a servant.[68]

---

[64] Cf. for instance Luther's famous preface to the first volume of the complete edition of his Latin writings, Wittenberg, 5 March 1545 (*WA* 54, 183, 27–9): "[. . .] deinde primitias cognitionis et fidei Christi hauseram, scilicet non operibus, sed fide Christi nos iustos et salvos fieri." In retrospect, Luther writes that he came to this conclusion after the most careful public and private reading of holy Scripture and after teaching it for a period of seven years ("sacras litteras diligentissime privatim et publice legeram et docueram per septem annos"). Since we know that Luther gave his first public course of biblical lectures after attaining the degree of *Baccalaureus biblicus* on 9 March 1509, we can date his conclusion to 1515 (assuming he used the manner of counting customary at the time, including both the first and last years involved) and thus, at the latest, to his lectures on the Epistle to the Romans.

[65] *Die Bekenntnisschriften der evangelish-lutherischen Kirche* (Göttingen, 1930), p. 520, 24–30.

[66] "Non enim aut comparandae iustitiae aut salutis tantum acquirendae facultatem fide Christi! obtingere significant sed utrumque nobis donari." *Inst.* (1559) III, 15, 6 (OS IV, 245, 17–19).

[67] Ibid. (IV, 245, 12–16).

[68] Quotation from Zwingli: *Expositio fidei*, in: Schuler and Schulthess: *Huldrici Zwinglii*

6. *The Certainty of Salvation*

Salvation means the unconditional and thus final acceptance of the
godless, an acceptance that cannot be reversed. The epoch-making
break with medieval theology in this tenet becomes even clearer
when we see that the unconditional nature of salvation propounded
by the reformers makes it possible for the sinner to equate certainty
of salvation with certainty of *belief*. The historical point at which the
opposition between the Reformation and Catholicism first emerged
on this question was Luther's interrogation by Cardinal Cajetan in
Augsburg in October 1518.[69] When the Thomist Cajetan read Luther's
resolutions on indulgences he recognized this point, with admirable
acuity, as the greatest threat to the papal church: subjective certainty
of salvation on the part of the believer could replace obedience to
the church. In line with tradition, Cajetan would allow only the idea
of objective certainty of belief, which to him meant the sacrament
of penance: the Christian, obedient to the faith of the church, must
be convinced that generally speaking the priest's absolution freed
men from the guilt of sin, and that those who receive the sacrament
in a fit state of mind, truly repenting of their sins, will acquire grace
that justifies them. According to Cajetan, on the other hand, a subjective certainty of faith is not permitted to the Christian; that is,
he can never have undoubted certainty on the question of whether
he himself is in a state of grace, for no one can know if he truly
repents of his sins and has received the sacrament worthily. Cajetan
accuses Luther of mingling the objective and subjective aspects of
the certainty of faith, and the new Reformation approach to the
question of the certainty of belief does indeed reside in this combination of the objective and subjective. Luther and the other reformers after him make a connection between the objective validity of
the actions of Christ, of the New Testament and its promise, and
the advent of his promise in the shape of subjective certainty of faith
in the man who receives it. This connection is possible only in the

---

Opera IV (Zurich, 1841), p. 63; Cf., for instance, Luther: *Rhapsodia seu concepta in
librum De loco iustificationis* (*WA* 30/11, 670, 21–32).
[69] Cf. G. Hennig: *Cajetan und Luther. Ein historischer Beitrag zur Begegnung von Thomismus
und Reformation* (Stuttgart, 1966) [= Arbeiten zur Theologie, 7]; Hamm: *Frömmigkeitstheologie*, (as n. 10), pp. 22, 5f.

light of unconditionally. Only because the question of whether the person receiving grace is worthy or unworthy becomes irrelevant, only because the sinner's gaze no longer remains fixed on himself with his imperfect repentance and his inability to love, only because this subjective uncertainty is no longer necessary and the sinner's attention is diverted away from his own potential for works and towards Jesus Christ as the sole grounds of salvation, does the subjective certainty of salvation become possible: man is unconditionally accepted by God for salvation although he is a sinner, indeed *as* a sinner. Unconditional certainty, to the reformers, is thus the outcome of unconditional grace.[70]

In their view, moreover, this certainty of being safe in Christ is the source of all that they call the peace, calm, joy and consolation of a Christian life. The whole typical late medieval yearning for security and the certainty of grace and salvation[71] finds an outlet and a solution here.

7. *Freedom and the Absence of Freedom*

The central concept of Christian freedom must also be mentioned at this point. Every Reformation doctrine of justification is essentially a doctrine of freedom. Above all it means freedom from the law, even in Zwingli and Calvin, and not just freedom from human statutes but even from the divine law of love that still holds good. Christ frees the sinner's conscience from the accusation and condemnatory curse of disobedience to the law, and from the pressure of his obligation to obey that law as a condition of salvation, so that now – backed by the total obedience to the law shown by Jesus Christ – he can obey the law "freely and cheerfully".[72] Again, everything depends on the idea of salvation unconditionally given, free of insistence on the law.

This Christian freedom, according to the Reformation understanding of it, is protected by a radical doctrine of our lack of freedom. For

---

[70] In neither Melanchthon and Zwingli nor in Calvin, however, are unconditional grace and certainty bound to the effective power of external consent, as we encounter it in Luther after 1518, particularly in his dispute with Cajetan.

[71] Cf. Hamm: *Frömmigkeitstheologie*, pp. 216ff. (chapter 5: "Im Umkreis der Suche nach Gnaden- und Heilsgarantien").

[72] A favorite phrase of Zwingli's: e.g. in Z II, 649, 32.

only where the sinner's freedom to decide is taken from him by
God, where God's gift of grace and man's own remaining in that
grace do not in the last resort depend upon man's free will, do the
reformers see the doctrine of *solus Christus* and unconditional grace
maintained. In this, like the anti-Pelagian Augustine and his medieval
followers, they take up the fight against the moralism of all periods
which rests on the basic axiom that man has moral autonomy in
his freedom to decide. This insistence on the sinner's lack of freedom is not specifically of the Reformation and did not of itself break
the mold of the scholastic systems. However, for all the major reformers, including the young Melanchthon of the *Loci communes*,[73] a strict
doctrine of predestination forms the foundation of their Reformation
doctrine of justification. And the understanding of justification that
is specifically evangelical, the unconditional gift of salvation, is essentially and indeed indissolubly bound up with the doctrine of election and the absence of freedom.

The new element in Reformation ideas of predestination, as opposed
to those of the scholastics, is perceptible where it becomes clear that
not a speculative but a highly soteriological and christological interest in the believer's certainty of salvation is controlling the line of
doctrinal argument. Where the idea of conditionality has collapsed,
the believer knows his salvation is assured by God's immutable decision alone: no power, not even his own sin, can part him from God's
unconditional will for his salvation.[74]

8. *By Faith Alone*

Is it not possible, however, that with faith playing so important a
part in salvation, with the typically evangelical principle of *sola fide*,
a subtle element of conditionality creeps into the doctrine of justification

---

[73] For Melanchthon's radical doctrine of determination see the *Loci communes* of
1521, the section "De hominis viribus et de libero arbitrio", in: *Melanchthons Werke
in Auswahl*, ed. R. Stupperich, II/1 (Gütersloh, 1952), pp. 8–17.
[74] Cf. Luther: *De servo arbitrio* (*WA* 18, 783, 28–33): "At nunc, cum deus salutem
meam extra meum arbitrium tollens in suum receperit et non meo opere aut cursu,
sed sua gratia et misericordia promiserit me servare, securus et certus sum, quod
ille fidelis sit et mihi non mentietur, turn potens et magnus, ut nulli daemones, nul-
lae adversitates eum frangere aut me illi rapere poterunt." We may also compare
the manner in which Calvin, in the *Inst.* (1559), presents the doctrine of predestination as a doctrine of consolation, e.g. III, 15, 8 (OS IV, 247, 22–248, 7).

by the back door? We here encounter an area of problems concerning faith and the word within which the various Reformation positions are relatively far apart. Even behind this diversity of views, of course, common evangelical ground in contrast to medieval Catholic doctrine as a whole is clearly perceptible, and so we should now look at the Reformation principle of "by faith alone". The Reformation concept of faith, unlike the cognitive aspect of scholasticism usually identified with the affective concept of faith, derives its nature from rejecting reliance on good works and from its close connection with the word of the Gospel. In this context the Reformation principle of *sola fide*, which may look like the last bastion of conditionality, on the contrary becomes a principle of unconditionality. But I must explain this proposition further.

What exactly does it mean to say that man is justified by faith *alone*, not by the works of the law? To the reformers, it meant that the sole grounds and cause of justification reside in God's mercy in Jesus Christ, not any morality inherent in man and manifesting itself in works.[75] Faith, in their eyes, is not located on man's active plane as a spiritual quality, a virtue or a work. Instead, it is a purely receptive mode – and not just because faith is a gift of the Holy Spirit (to the scholastics, after all, grace was also a divine gift), but because of its very nature it means that the sinner's attention is directed away from himself,[76] away from any condition on which his own salvation depends,[77] and shelters in the righteousness of Christ. This is the confidence of the believer: he is sure that in faith he is taken outside himself, away from the necessity of proving himself to God in works, and instead is taken into the righteousness of Christ. Luther put it thus: "Entering into Christ is the faith that gathers us together

---

[75] Cf. Melanchthon: *Loci theologici* (*CR* 21, 750): "Quare cum dicitur 'fide iustificamur', non aliud dicitur, quam quod propter filium dei accipiamus remissionem peccatomm et reputemur iusti. Et quia oportet apprehendi hoc beneficium, dicitur 'fide', id est fiducia misericordiae promissae propter Christum. Intelligatur ergo propositio correlative: 'fide sumus iusti', id est per misericordiam propter filium dei sumus iusti seu accepti." On the (exclusively) christological central point of justification by faith in Luther, cf. esp. H. J. Iwand: *Rechtfertigungslehre und Christusglaube* (Leipzig, 1930, repr. 1966).

[76] Cf. Calvin: *Inst.* (1559) III, 19, 2 (OS IV, 283, 16f.): "averse a nobis aspectu unum Christum intueri".

[77] Cf. Calvin: *Comm. on Hab.* 2.4 (CR 71, 529): "Ergo [homo] nihil affert proprium, quia fides quasi precario mutuatur, quod non est penes hominem."

in the wealth of divine righteousness."[78] Zwingli states that faith is "peace and security in the merit of Christ".[79]

The eschatological final validity of justification that I have mentioned corresponds exactly to the supremacy of this faith, divorced from all virtues and morality. In scholasticism the primacy of faith represents only a beginning; it has only a "temporal root" as a necessary interim stage in the process of justification.[80] Not faith, but the quality of grace through love determines the specific order of being of the justified; the quality of that grace "forms" faith. That is to say, only such a quality authenticates faith and its validity in justification, and only active love makes possible the dynamic and teleology of good works in the form of satisfaction and merits rendering mankind acceptable into salvation. The Council of Trent therefore tried to "hold the necessity and the impossibility of 'faith' in equilibrium".[81] Reformation theology insists that all is given to faith and faith alone. It is a justifying, saving faith: *fides iustificans et salvifica*. For faith is the means whereby man is led from his moral subjective existence into the final validity of the righteousness of Christ, in which he is preserved for salvation – outside himself, where God looks graciously on him. Faith therefore derives its justifying form not from internal love but through the external righteousness of Christ, to which it is bound in trust. The medieval *fides caritate formata* is replaced by the Reformation *fides Christo formata*, the "faith that lives in Christ".[82] In such fulfillment, faith is of course internal

---

[78] "Ingressus in Christum est fides, quae nos colligit in divitias iustitiae dei." *Operationes in Psalmos* (*WA* 5, 408, 4f.).

[79] *Auslegen und Gründe der Schlussreden*, 1523, Art. 20 (Z II, 182, 4–9): "Faith is nothing other than a secure certainty whereby man relies on the merit of Christ, and it is not a work [. . .] but it is peace and security in the merit of Christ, which security and faith comes not from man but from God." Cf. Calvin: *Comm. on Rom.* 3.21 (CR 49, 58): "Ideo fide iustificamur, quia in solam dei misericordiam et gratuitas eius promissiones nos recumbere necesse est." *Inst.* (1559) III, 11, 18 (OS IV, 202, 8f.): "fides sine operum adminiculo tota in dei misericordiam recumbit".

[80] W. Joest: "Die tridentinische Rechtfertigungslehre", in: *Kerygma und Dogma* 9 (1963), pp. 41–69, here 65.

[81] Dantine, in *HDGThG* II (as in n. 16), p. 464.

[82] Cf. H. A. Oberman: "'Iustitia Christi' und 'Iustitia dei'. Luther und die scholastischen Lehren von der Rechtfertigung", in: Lohse (ed.), *Durchbruch*, (as in n. 6), pp. 413–44, here 436 and n. 45; T. Mannermaa: "Das Verhältnis von Glaube und Liebe in der Theologie Luthers", in: M. Ruokanen (ed.), *Luther in Finnland*, SLAG, A22 (Helsinki, 1984), pp. 99–110, 102f; B. Hägglund: "Was ist mit Luthers 'Rechtfertigungs'-lehre gemeint?", in: *Zugänge zu Luther* (Publication of the Luther-Akademie Ratzeburg 6, 1984), pp. 110–20, here 117.

too and before the exposition of any system of ethics it denotes rebirth and the transformational vitality of the inner man.[83] This creative advent of the righteousness of Christ into the very center of man's existence, into his conscience, heart and mind, is part of justification.

The reformers see the fact that faith is also extremely active, operating through love and its works, in a different context. That activity is not a matter of doing good works in order to acquire justification and salvation; it derives from salvation that has already been received. When St Paul (Gal. 5.6) says that faith "worketh through love", Luther explains that he is speaking, "not of becoming just, but of the life of the just. *Fieri et agere* is one thing, *esse et facere* another, as boys learn *verbum passivum* and *verbum activum* at school."[84] The sphere in which faith is active in love does not, as in scholasticism, constitute its justifying nature; faith is justified only passively[85] in that the sinner is accepted into salvation in advance of any good works he may perform. Every Reformation doctrine of justification in fact (though not necessarily in terminology) distinguishes in this way between the passive and active nature of faith, between its *soteriology* and its *ethics*.[86]

9. *The Bond Between Faith and the Biblical Word*

As I pointed out above, passive faith meant taking of man out of himself. As a believer, he stood outside himself and in Christ. To the reformers this meant that faith was located in the biblical word of God, the gospel of Jesus Christ, and only there – outside man himself – did it have a firm foothold. This point brings us to the

---

[83] Cf. the quotations from Luther in Hägglund: ibid., pp. 114–17.

[84] *WA* Br 9, 407, 40–2 (No. 3614, 10 or 11 May 1541); cf. K.-H. zur Mühlen: "Die Einigung über den Rechtfertigungsartikel auf dem Regensburger Religionsgespräch von 1541 – eine verpasste Chance?", in: *Zeitschrift für Theologie und Kirche* 76 (1979), pp. 331–59, here 352f. Cf. also Calvin's interpretation of Gal. 5.6 in *Inst.* (1559) III, 11, 20 (OS IV, 204, 18–22): "Fatemur quidem cum Paulo non aliam fidem iustificare quam illam caritate efficacem; sed ab ila caritatis efficacia iustificandi vim non sumit. Imo non alia ratione iustificat, nisi quia in communicationem iustitiae Christi nos inducit."

[85] Cf. Calvin: ibid. Ill, 13, 5 (IV, 220, 24–26): "Nam quoad iustificationem res est mere passiva fides, nihil afferens nostrum ad conciliandam dei gratiam, sed a Christo recipiens, quod nobis deest."

[86] Cf. Hägglund, "Luthers 'Rechtfertigungs'-lehre" (as in n. 82), p. 118.

Reformation principle of scripture and the word. At the heart of the activities of all the reformers we find the bond between man and God's word: his conscience was bound to that word alone and was thus free from all the words of men. The faith of man was bound to the word of holy scripture addressed to him and to the preaching that continued this biblical message. Zwingli, unlike Luther, did not think this meant that in the workings of his spirit *God* had also bound himself to his *verbum externum*.[87] However, Zwingli too stresses that *man* and his faith are bound to the biblical word.[88] Man must not base his trust on what he himself says, for he is a sinful creature, called to answer for himself yet not responsible for himself; in his faith he should cling only to the revelations of God's liberating word. This view of faith shows the direct connection between the scriptural principle of the Reformation and the principle of grace that brings justification: man's false reliance on his own word reflects a distortion in himself, a belief in what he himself has achieved in works as well as words. Conversely, the reformers saw belief in God's word alone and reliance on holy scripture as faith solely in the grace of God, who forgives sins, gives absolution and accepts us into salvation.

Through grace and the scriptures, that is, the promise of the Gospel, man is led out of himself, out of his self-accusation and self-justification and any kind of 'pious' ministering to himself. We have seen how 'grace' in the thinking of the Reformation is determined not through the internal dimension of human qualities, but in relation to the external dimension of the righteousness of Christ, in which God unconditionally gives himself in grace. Grace is a reality that always flows in afresh from outside, not from any inner experience of reality; it justifies man and brings absolution from the accusations of sin. This attitude precisely reflects the importance of the word in the Reformation and the bond between faith and the biblical word. For the word is a relational process: the sinner is taken out of himself, away from anything he himself could say, and is liberated from the realities of virtue and morality. Through the word that brings absolution, forgiveness and a promise, the totality and

---

[87] Cf. Locher: *Huldrych Zwingli* (as in n. 59), p. 222f.
[88] Cf. on the following B. Hamm: "Freiheit zur Freude – der Weg des Schweizer Reformators Huldrych Zwingli", in: *Evangelisch-reformatorisches Kirchenblatt für Bayern* 3 (1984), pp. 5–11, here 8.

final validity of his acceptance become present to the sinner and precede any partial achievement of righteousness.

10. *Breaking the Mold: the Contrast with Medieval Theology*

Let us return to our initial question: what was specifically evangelical in the Reformation doctrine of justification? Historically, as I have pointed out, the evangelical element lies in the mold-breaking contrasts between the theology of the various reformers and the medieval Catholic systems. We have explored the frontiers of the medieval understanding of grace, which are also the frontiers of sixteenth-century Catholic controversialist theology, while on the other hand we have defined what is common ground in the evangelical antitheses to Catholicism, or at least what was common ground to the four reformers who most influenced the structure of Protestantism in the sixteenth century in their theological doctrine of justification. A considerable body of mold-breaking contrasts has emerged in the process. They are found in the understanding of sin and grace, and the way in which sin and righteousness can be regarded as simultaneous in Reformation thinking; they are found in the eschatological determination of justification, in the doctrine of the certainty of salvation and the understanding of freedom from the law; finally, they are found in the role of faith and the bond between the scriptural principle and the principle of grace. If we ask what binds these various aspects of Reformation thinking together, we shall see that the unconditional nature of salvation is the overriding theme: an abundance of righteousness and salvation is given to the godless man in his justification. His total, unconditional acceptance by God for Christ's sake precedes any partial renewal of the still sinful man himself: such rudiments of the regenerating sanctification of man can never become a condition in which his value before God is founded, but are merely the consequence and creative advent of the abundance and totality of grace bestowed upon him. The reformers express this immutable consequential relationship in describing 'good works' – by which they mean all the reality of man renewed – as the fruits and signs of faith and of justification received in faith.[89] This is the doctrine that the church fathers condemned at the Council of Trent:

---

[89] Cf. Luther: *Rhapsodia* (*WA* 30/11, 663, 5f.): "Et opera fidei signa sunt et fructus iustitiae. Sic opera incredulitatis signa et fructus iniustitiae sunt."

"If a man says . . . that good works are only the fruits and signs of justification already achieved, not the cause of an increase in justification, then let him be anathema!"[90]

11. *The Evangelical Understanding of the Person*

Behind this epoch-making change in the understanding of justification and salvation, as Wilfried Joest has shown, lies a new view of the person.[91] To a great extent Joest's account of it in Luther can also be applied to Melanchthon, Zwingli and Calvin. The Reformation no longer defines the human person before God in the manner of medieval philosophy and theology, that is, as the substance of the natural or spiritual man, distinguished by reasonable and voluntary possession of himself, a subject with qualities deriving from his essence and a morality made manifest in works. To the reformers the presence of the human personality before God entails a break with the subjectivity of the sinner: he is taken out of himself, and outside himself he is in Christ. The person accepted by God is thus not man in the mode of ethical realization, but man solely *coram deo*, as he is seen by God,[92] in what has become the basis of his salvation through Christ.[93]

---

[90] "Si quis dixerit iustitiam acceptam non conservari atque etiam non augeri coram deo per bona opera, sed opera ipsa fructus solummodo et signa esse iustificationis adeptae, non etiam ipsius augendae causam: anathema sit." Concilium Tridentinum, *Decretum de iustificatione*, can. 24 (D/S No. 1574).

[91] W. Joest: *Ontologie der Person bei Luther*: ibid., "Martin Luther", in: *Gestalten der Kirchengeschichte*, ed. M. Greschat, V (Stuttgart, 1981), pp. 129–85, here 156–9 (on man as person).

[92] Cf. G. Ebeling: *Luther. Einführung in sein Denken* (Tübingen, 1964), pp. 219–38 (the person in Christ and in the world), esp. pp. 220–30 (the fundamental meaning of the *coram* relation in Luther).

[93] Seen in this way, 'self-realization' does not enter into Reformation Christianity: the realization of man, yes, but not self-realization. For the person accepted by God is never man in the mode of ethical realization. He has *been* realized, in that an abundance of righteousness and salvation and thus total and unconditional acceptance have become his through Christ; man is therefore free from the compulsion to realize himself and be concerned for himself, and can give himself up to loving care for his neighbors (which is where the realization of his new nature begins, in the reality of sanctification). On the other hand, man is truly realized only in death and resurrection, when he passes into eternal freedom.

IV. *Luther's Lectures on the Epistle to the Romans as Evidence of the Reformation Doctrine of Justification*

This understanding of the person as wholly man who is yet wholly absolved by God and accepted into salvation has manifested itself to us under various aspects of unconditionality. If we ask where this break with the medieval Catholic doctrine of justification first becomes historically perceptible in the Reformation, we must look at the early stages of Luther's evangelical theology. Having begun by determining historical criteria for the use of the term 'evangelical' and thus the content of the Reformation element in the doctrine of justification, let us conclude by looking at the interesting question of the content and timing of Luther's turn towards evangelical thinking. The features of the general understanding of justification in the Reformation, as set out in my comparative analysis above, bring us to Luther's lectures on the Epistle to the Romans of 1515/16. If we move forward historically from the scholastic systems to study the Reformation as a whole, without setting out from too narrowly defined a postulate in the systematic and theological essence of what is truly evangelical, then we shall find that the break with the medieval system came in this work *at the latest*. The structural antithesis of Reformation theology is not yet fully worked out in the lectures on Romans. It was not until 1518 that Luther developed the relationship between faith and the word in the process of justification into the assessment of the external word as the pledge which, in his view, makes the certainty of salvation possible. However, we should not think that the mold-breaking element was not present in Luther's theology until the Reformation doctrine of justification was mature and complete, with all its features in place. Although the lectures on the Epistle to the Romans occupy a central place in the development of Luther's Reformation theology, they already clearly illustrate the break with the Middle Ages.

The way in which various different aspects come together in this work makes it particularly impressive. I will mention only some of the most important:

– a radical approach to the understanding of sin, typical of the Reformation;[94]

---

[94] Cf., for instance, *WA* 56, 271,1–272, 2.

- also characteristic of the Reformation is the definition of grace as proceeding exclusively from the favor of God shown in absolution; Luther intensifies his understanding of grace in the new concept of *iustitia dei*, a righteousness conveyed by God, who draws the nature of the sinner into his own righteous nature by justifying him;[95]

- the evangelical understanding of the righteousness of the sinner, in that the righteousness of Jesus Christ is credited to him (*iustus ex reputatione*),[96] and in this connection the forensic emphasis on the *extra nos*;[97]

- hence the Reformation development of the doctrine *simul iustus et peccator*,[98] and the first emergence of the theme of christological exchange and interchange, which is particularly forceful in Luther's Reformation doctrine of justification: 'This (Christ) has made his righteousness mine and has made my sin his.';[99]

- freedom from the law, seen in the Reformation as freedom from a conditional understanding of the law (obedience to the law as a condition of acceptance into salvation);[100]

- the Reformation identification of the justification of the godless with his acceptance into salvation, eschatological final validity, and the total righteousness credited to him in advance of any partial renewal of his life;

- the basic view, evident in all these aspects, that salvation is unconditional and has no grounds *a parte hominis*: forgiveness of sins, righteousness and sanctification are bestowed only for Christ's sake and never because of any partial involvement of human virtues and morals, satisfaction or merit;

---

[95] Cf. *WA* 56, 172, 3–5.

[96] Cf., for instance, *WA* 56, 272, 18.

[97] Cf., for example, *WA* 56, 268, 26–269, 19; cf. also K.-H. zur Mühlen: *'Nos extra nos.' Luthers Theologie zwischen Mystik und Scholastik* (Tübingen, 1972) [= Beiträge zur historischen Theologie, 46], on the Epistle to the Romans, pp. 93–176.

[98] Cf. notes 57 and 58 above.

[99] "Hic suam iustitiam meam fecit et meum peccatum suum fecit." *WA* 56, 204, 18f. On this text and its context cf. H. J. Iwand: "Glaubensgerechtigkeit", in: *Gesammelte Aufsätze* II, ed. G. Sauter (Munich, 1980) [= TB 64], 1980, pp. 118–20; B. Hamm: "Martin Luthers Entdeckung der evangelischen Freiheit", in: *Zeitschrift für Theologie und Kirche* 80 (1983), pp. 50–68, here 59f.

[100] Cf., for instance, *WA* 56, 274, 11–275, 16.

– and finally the basically new understanding in the Reformation of the person: the righteousness of the person *coram deo* is by its nature outside itself, in Christ and in the eyes of God.[101]

None of this can still be accommodated in the scope for variation found in medieval theologies, even if we take their most extreme stances on the theological doctrine of grace. Against the background of the reformers' common ground in the doctrine of justification, even thinkers like Gregory of Rimini and Johannes von Staupitz appear the exponents of a very Catholic theology, and in fact comparison with them shows how far away Luther had moved from this Augustinian scholasticism and the devotional theology of the late Middle Ages as early as his course of lectures on the Epistle to the Romans.[102] Comparison with Catholic controversialist theologians of the sixteenth century such as Gropper, Contarini and Seripando leads to the same conclusion. Even at the time of his lectures on Romans, Luther was aware of the fundamental antithesis of his ideas to scholasticism, as is clear from his general polemic against the *theologi scholastic!* ('Oh *stulti*, Oh pig-theologians!')[103] and their amalgamation of theology with Aristotelian philosophy.[104] The direct confrontation with Catholic thinking is new by comparison with Luther's earlier lectures on the Psalms, in which he can still cite the doctrine of the sinner's duty *facere quod in se est* and add an approving *recte dicunt doctores*.[105] Another new feature is the fact that in putting forward his opposition to scholasticism in his lectures on Romans, Luther also depicts his own theological past as one of wrestling while he was held captive in error.[106]

In this confrontation between scholasticism and the elucidation of his own position, Luther sees the crucial contrast as the conflict between two entirely different ways of thinking and speaking. It is,

---

[101] Cf., for instance, *WA* 56, 158, 10–159, 14.
[102] Cf. D. C. Steinmetz: *Luther and Staupitz. An Essay in the Intellectual Origins of the Protestant Reformation* (Durham, NC, 1980) [= Duke Monographs in Medieval and Renaissance Studies, 4], (this work pays special attention to Luther's lectures on the Epistle to the Romans). There is no similar comparative study on Gregory of Rimini and Luther; for Gregory's doctrine of grace, see most recently Burger: "Der Augustinschüler gegen die modernen Pelagianer" (as in n. 27), cf. also n. 17.
[103] *WA* 56, 273, 4; 274, 14.
[104] Cf., for instance, *WA* 56, 273, 3–2, 74, 2.
[105] *WA* 4, 262, 4–7.
[106] Cf. *WA* 56, 274, 2–11 (in connection with his understanding of *remissio peccatorum*).

as he likes to put it, the contrast between the *modus loquendi theologicus*
or *modus loquendi Apostoli (Pauli)*, that is, the biblical approach to theology, and the *modus loquendi philosophicus* or *metaphysicus seu moralis*, an
approach to theology that is guided by philosophy, and is non-bib-
lical, metaphysical and moral.[107] The metaphysical and moral approach,
as Luther understands it, is characteristic of the entire scholastic and
medieval understanding of theology. He sees the interest of scholastic theology as being bent on human morality, man's moral quality
before God, and his natural quality in accordance with his creation,
its diminution through sin and its restoration and improvement
through the metaphysical quality of grace. Luther sees the Pauline
approach to theology, on the other hand, as leaving aside the entire
field of virtue and morality, physics and metaphysics, and man's ability to act for better or worse. He is not concerned with man's human
ability but with his new creation by God, and a new relationship
between merciful God and sinful man in which man is outside himself in Christ. Consequently Luther can formulate the whole mold-
breaking antithesis to the Catholic doctrine of the Middle Ages, the
contrast between the two approaches, cogently as follows: Paul says
that man is removed but sin remains. The moral approach, however, says that sin is removed and man remains.[108]

This and other formulations of antitheses in the lectures on Romans
mark the epoch-making turning point between scholasticism and the
Reformation. The question of how far Luther's *Dictata super Psalterium*
(1513–15) already subscribe to the Reformation doctrine of justification
may be left open; the clarity and the sharp distinctions drawn in the
lectures on Romans are absent from that work. Here Luther's early
theology of humility still seems bound to the conditional structure
of the medieval theology of grace and judgment,[109] although the
break with scholasticism is already perceptible, particularly in the

---

[107] Cf. L. Grane: *Modus loquendi theologicus. Luthers Kampf um die Erneuerung der Theologie
(1515–1518)* (Leiden, 1975) [= Acta Theologica Danica, 12], esp. pp. 94–96 (on
WA 56, 334, 2f.).

[108] "Modus loquendi Apostoli et modus metaphysicus seu moralis sunt contrarii.
Quia Apostolus loquitur, ut significet, sonet hominem potius auferri peccato rema-
nente velut relicto et hominem expurgari a peccato potius quam econtra. Humanus
autem sensus econtra peccatum auferri homine manente et hominem potius purgari loquitur. Sed Apostoli sensus optime proprius et perfecte divinus est." *WA* 56,
334, 14–19.

[109] Cf. Hamm: "Martin Luthers Entdeckung" (as in n. 99), p. 56.

field of hermeneutics,[110] in Luther's understanding of sin[111] and in his relational view of personal righteousness *coram deo*.[112] The first lectures on the Psalms are obviously a transitional work between two periods neither clearly of the Reformation nor – if we are looking for the roots of Luther's Reformation theology – unambiguously not of the Reformation.

V. *Further Prospects: the Intensification and the Boundaries of the Reformation Doctrine of Justification*

Our object has been to trace the characteristic evangelical element in the doctrine of justification, and a study of the common ground between the reformers was a determining factor. In relation at least to further prospects, however, I must not omit to say that this characteristic element, the essence of Reformation thinking, can at certain points undergo reinforcement and intensification in many reformers, while in others it is diluted so far as to be unrecognizable.

I would speak of the reinforcement or intensification of the Reformation doctrine of justification when, in marked contrast to medieval or contemporary Catholic theology, the subject of unconditionality emerges even more strongly than was already obvious in our study of the common ground between Luther, Melanchthon, Zwingli and Calvin. I will cite a few examples: by comparison with the consensus of the reformers, there is certainly some intensification in Luther's new understanding of the righteousness of God, for here he works out God's unconditional communication with sinful man to the point where God in his righteousness abandons his own self to participate with man.[113] He thus fundamentally does away with the traditional understanding of satisfaction, whereby Christ provides satisfaction before God's avenging righteousness;[114] this comes out particularly clearly in the theme of the fortunate interchange, the direct exchange

---

[110] Cf. G. Ebeling: "Die Anfänge von Luthers Hermeneutik", in: ibid., *Lutherstudien I* (Tübingen, 1971), pp. 1–68.

[111] All his life man is a sinner in the sight of God: for instance, *WA* 3, 289, 6f.

[112] Cf., for instance, *WA* 3, 287, 20–293, 21.

[113] Cf. *WA* 56, 172, 3–5; cf. also Iwand: "Glaubensgerechtigkeit" (as n. 99), pp. 107–11: "God's own righteousness includes us in it rather than excluding us."

[114] The understanding of *iustitia dei* in the other reformers (apart from Andreas

between the righteousness of God and the sin of man. Another intensification of Reformation thinking is Luther's new understanding of the word, breaking with the western and Augustinian tradition of the hermeneutics of signification.[115] The fact that God's word not only conveys meaning and points the way, but is an active word creating faith and effectively conveying forgiveness and salvation, liberates faith even more from considerations of virtue and qualities, and makes man fully at home outside himself and in the word. In his understanding of faith Zwingli also finds a way – admittedly a different way – of stressing the unconditionality of salvation. Strictly speaking, he says, human faith is not the cause of salvation and does not bring our salvation about; it is done solely through God's free election.[116] Faith is merely the consequence and the sign of election; election is not a consequence of faith.[117] God, then, can save even unbelievers.[118] Here assurances against the misunderstanding of faith as a condition and cause of salvation are built into the theology of justification. We find similar assurances expressed by Calvin, although in a considerably diluted manner,[119] when he emphasizes the fact that faith does not justify through itself or through any intrinsic power (*virtus intrinseca*). In the real sense, God himself alone justifies us, and Christ justifies us because he was given us for the sake of righteousness; faith itself is only a receptive, empty vessel.[120]

Intensifications of Reformation thought all attempt to make conceptual distinctions illustrating the fact that the regenerative sanctification

---

Osiander and Johannes Brenz), on the other hand, moves exclusively in the traditional context of righteousness that judges and recompenses

[115] Cf. Bayer: *Promissio* (as n. 8), p. 161f. (Part II).

[116] Cf. *Freundliche Verglimpfung über die Predigt Luthers wider die Schwärmer* (Z V, 781, 21–7).

[117] Cf. *Fidei ratio* (Z VI, 2, 799, 15–18); *De providentia dei* (Z VI, 3, 169–192: *De fide*, esp. 181, 11f.; 183, 11–184, 3).

[118] Zwingli is thinking of dead infants (including unbaptized infants) and certain elect heathens of antiquity. On infants, cf. the text from *Fidei ratio* quoted in n. 117; on the heathens the text, also quoted in n. 118, from *De providentia dei* (182, 15–183, 6); cf. also R. Pfister: *Die Seligkeit erwählter Heiden bei Zwingli. Eine Untersuchung zu seiner Theologie* (Zurich, 1952).

[119] Calvin can still call faith the *causa formalis vel instrumental* of salvation; *Inst.* (1559) III, 14, 17 (OS IV, 235, 27f.). To Zwingli, on the other hand, faith is merely in the nature of a sign and has no causal function; cf. Locher: *Huldrych Zwingli* (as n. 59), p. 219.

[120] *Inst.* III, 11, 7 (IV, 188, 24–189, 9); cf. Ill, 18, 8 (IV, 279, 1–3. 7–10); in 18, 10 (IV, 281, 9–13).

of man does not stand in any fundamental or causal relation to the acceptance of the sinner into grace and salvation. For instance, distinctions are drawn between faith and love (Luther, Melanchthon, Calvin), justification with sanctification and renewal (Melanchthon and Calvin) or regeneration and renewal (developed in particular by Matthias Flacius Illyricus).[121] In this area, orthodoxy concentrated on the famous maxim *Qui bene distinguit, bene docet.* Such differences are logical abstractions intended to clarify the issue of cause and effect through precise conceptual distinctions, and to illustrate the fact that justification is unconditional and separate from any alteration of the sinner's life on his own part. A logical and causal distinction, however, is of its nature not identical with the distinction between a temporal 'before' and 'after'.[122] To take the example of Calvin, he does not see the distinctions mentioned above as impairing the unity of the connection between faith and love or between justification and renewal;[123] faith is always love at the same time, and justification is always renewal as well.

The boundaries of the Reformation doctrine of justification, the place where it begins to lose its clear contours, is also the nerve-center where the causality and unconditionality of justification and sanctification are located. The boundary is crossed when the quality and morality of natural or spiritual man are again seen to some extent as the real or potential reason for the sinner's justification and the outcome when he faces judgment. Setting out from this point, one may question, in particular, Osiander's effectively judicial understanding of justification,[124] and the later Melanchthon's doc-

---

[121] On Flacius, cf. B. Hägglund: "Rechtfertigung – Wiedergeburt – Erneuerung in der nachreformatorischen Theologie", in: *Kerygma und Dogma* 5 (1959), pp. 318–37, here 326f. Regeneration, to Flacius, is the imputed relational process of man's adoption as a child of God. While Flacius is not content with forensic categories but equates the crediting of Christ's merit to man (forensic justification) with *regeneratio* (as distinct from *renovatio*), he makes it clear that justification is not merely an external verdict but indicates a profound change of the inner man (in faith) preceding any gradual renewal of the heart.

[122] Cf. the very instructive quotation from Hesshusen's *Examen theologicum*, 1587, in Hägglund: "Rechtfertigung", p. 336.

[123] Cf. notes 41–45 above.

[124] It was from this that the whole difficulty of agreement on the article on justification arose at the Regensburg dialogues on religion of 1541. For instance, when the formula agreed says that those who have done greater or more works attain a higher degree of sanctification on account of the increase of their faith and their love (*propter augmentum fidei et caritatis*), we have the classic formulation of a non

trine of freedom. In principle we must accept that some reformers and writers of evangelical theology promoted the scriptural Reformation principle of the word in opposition to the Roman Catholic church and its authorities, but without developing any doctrine of justification that was really of the Reformation and that broke away from dogmatic Catholic systems.[125] Historically, then, it is inappropriate to limit our ideas of the essence of the Reformation to the doctrine of justification and the criticisms of the church that arose directly from it. That does not, of course, alter the fact that the stimulating *center* of the Reformation was its theology, and the structural centre of that theology was the doctrine of justification as I have tried to outline it here.

Reformation doctrine in line with Catholic thinking. The agreed formula, however, also contains Reformation elements of Melanchthonian theology. Text in: Acta reformationis catholicae [. . .] 6 (Regensburg, 1974), pp. 52,3–54,37.

[125] This corresponds to the observations on the Reformation pamphlets in Scheible: "Reform, Reformation, Revolution (as n. 3)."

CHAPTER SEVEN

REFORMATION "FROM BELOW" AND REFORMATION "FROM ABOVE". ON THE PROBLEM OF THE HISTORICAL CLASSIFICATIONS OF THE REFORMATION

The subject that was originally suggested for this essay was "People's, City and Princes' Reformations – Rivals or Phases?" Yet the longer I was engaged upon this theme, the clearer it became that I could not accept the notions of rivalries or phases which dominate current historiography. Consequently I rephrased the topic and shall question the delimitations that are currently made between People's Reformation, City Reformation and Princes' Reformation – between Reformation "from below" and Reformation "from above". I voice my uneasiness about this and other well-known and long accepted classifications of the historiography of the Reformation, not because I desire to discard conceptualizations that certainly made sense and will continue to do so, but I intend to show their limitations and dubious nature, to free them from a tendency to become fossilized, to include them in an extended network of connections and in this way open them up. In so doing I take up the results of recent research which have already stirred up the familiar classifications.[1]

I. *Widespread Conceptions of Types and Phases of the Reformation*

I should like to note in a few words how forcefully even in today's Reformation research sharply delimited typologies are combined with

---

[1] Here I am grateful – to mention only one segment of the more recent research projects important for my own endeavors – for the stimuli I received in the former Tübingen *Sonderforschungsbereichs* 8 "Spätmittelalter und Reformation". Under the umbrella title of "Continuity and Change" the SFB 8 united in a unique way specialists in the Early Modern era from various disciplines and thus widened the perspectives of all those participating. With regard to the current subject I thank the following members of the SFB 8 for particularly valuable stimuli: Heiko A. Oberman, Volker Press, Hans-Christoph Rublack, Eberhard Isenmann, Olaf Mörke and Dieter Stievermann.

the notion of competitive rivalry and succession in phases, of lines
of demarcation and breaks. It is still common practice to compare
the Reformation of the "common man" – also known as "reforming movement(s)" – with the Reformation of the authorities – i.e.
the Reformation brought about by the councils in the cities and by
the princes in their territories – and consequently to construct a
model of phases. Initially the Reformation was a widespread, spontaneous, many-voiced popular movement which included members
from all walks of life and mobilized in particular those excluded from
power and wealth, among them the manual laborers in the cities
and the peasants in the countryside. This popular movement, which
had been greatly enhanced through sermons, tracts, translation of
the Bible and hymns in German was quashed by a one-sided
Reformation implemented and administered by the authorities. With
the consent of the most important Reformers, the model of a Church
ruled from above took the place of the original reformation model
of a Church ruled from below. The defeat of the peasants in 1525
was a major factor in bringing about this change. Looked at in this
way the end of the Peasants' War forms the break between a natural, creative Reformation born by the whole community and a
Reformation essentially channeled and directed by the authorities,
developing into a Church ruled by those in power. This Reformation
of the princes and magistrates, organized and institutionalized from
above, which was given its legitimizing fundamental basis by the
conclusion of the Imperial Diet of Speyer in 1526, is accompanied
by conditions such as domestication,[2] discipline, direction, supervi-

---

[2] Cf. Thomas A. Brady, Jr: "Göttliche Republiken: die Domestizierung der Religion
in der deutschen Stadtreformation", in: Peter Blickle, Andreas Lindt, Alfred Schindler
(eds.): *Zwingli und Europa* (Zürich, 1985), pp. 109–136; idem: "In Search of the Godly
City: The Domestication of Religion in the German Urban Reformation", in:
R. Po-Chia Hsia (ed.): *The German People and the Reformation* (Ithaca/New York, 1989),
pp. 14–31.

[3] Robert Scribner's description of the situation after 1525 is a typical example:
"The various acts of legislation establishing the formal framework of church reform
throughout Germany and Switzerland also attest the effective control of the church
by the secular power. Almost everywhere this was achieved by means of Ecclesiastical
Statutes, issued by secular authorities to regulate religion, in much the same way
as other 'policing' legislation regulated many other areas of life. The institution of
ecclesiastical reform was the conclusion of a long struggle between church and state
over who should control ecclesiastical life, and the state clearly emerged as the victor." Robert W. Scribner: *The German Reformation*, 2nd edition (London, 1987),
p. 37. Cf. n. 73; cf. also n. 7 below (Ozment).

sion and control[3] – in contrast to the spontaneity and liberality, simplicity and authenticity of the time before 1525/26.

If this is the view taken of the critical period – i.e. as a 'Constantinian conversion' so to speak within the Reformation – then it is almost always accompanied by the idea of a "turning-point", of a serious change in the attitude of the Reformers themselves.[4] Because of his clash with Karlstadt and his congregation at Orlamunde (1524)[5] and even more because of the peasants' demands in 1525, Luther revised his earlier view of the spiritual responsibility of the congregation ("that a Christian assembly or congregation has the right and power to judge all doctrine and to call, appoint and remove teachers from office") and placed the "improvement" of the Church in the hands of the secular authorities.[6] In a similar way Zwingli, too, relinquished the freedom of a Christian congregation to form itself from below and joined forces with the dictated policy of the municipal authorities. For Luther, Zwingli, Bucer, Melanchthon and other influential Reformers, original ideals of a spiritually justified lay Christianity give way to a new theological and practical stress on the divinely legitimated secular office to care for the ordering of the Church and the ecclesiastical office of the minister of the Church, educated at university and legally appointed – i.e. with the support of the civic authorities.

Corresponding to this picture of the rejection of the basic ecclesiological tendencies of the Reformation stands the image of a reforming authenticity and continuity living on among the Baptists. In this view the small Baptist congregations carried on the original tendencies of a congregational and lay Christianity, of sacred and spiritual independence, of voluntarism and immediacy to God unmediated by theological erudition and secular power. Within the Reformation of the major Reformers that was controlled by the secular authorities,

---

[4] Cf. John H. Yoder: "The Turning Point of the Zwinglian Reformation", in: *Mennonite Quarterly Review* 32 (1958), pp. 128–140; Robert Walton takes a contradictory view in "Was there a Turning Point in the Zwinglian Reformation?", in: *Mennonite Quarterly Review* 42 (1968), pp. 45–56.

[5] Cf. e.g. Scribner (as in n. 3), p. 50.

[6] Cf. e.g. Peter Blickle: *Die Reformation im Reich* (Stuttgart, 1982), p. 141: The "secularization" of the Reformation "was easier to bring about because after 1525 the Reformers, with Luther at the forefront, distanced themselves from their earlier conception of community which was based on the conviction that the Gospel would create its own place and create the proper Christian community life through its own persuasiveness."

however, moral constraint and law took the place of protestant voluntarism, and a new hierarchy took the place of the equality of the
baptized.[7]

The conception of rival types of Reformation (from below – from
above) and of contrary phases also dominates the distinction commonly made between the "City Reformation" and that of the princes.[8]
The sharply contrasting comparison of the "two basic types of reformation Church establishment"[9] has endured into the most recent
research. The co-operative urban Reformation of the *bonum commune*

---

[7] Cf. e.g. Steven E. Ozment: *The Reformation in the Cities. The Appeal of Protestantism
to Sixteenth-Century Germany and Switzerland* (New Haven/London, 1975), pp. 151–166:
the erstwhile "freedom fighters" as "new papists". Cf. also the catastrophic depiction of the development of the Reformation and its practice of indoctrination in
Gerald Strauss: *Luther's House of Learning. Indoctrination of the Young in the German
Reformation* (Baltimore/London, 1978), especially pp. 300–308.

[8] The concept of the "Princes' Reformation" so dear to Marxist research as a
designation of the Reformation controlled by the territorial rulers has in the meantime established itself in western writings on the history of the Reformation. Cf.
e.g. Rainer Wohlfeil: *Einführung in die Geschichte der deutschen Reformation* (Munich, 1982),
p. 66 (on the Marxist approach of Gerhard Brendler, Siegfried Hoyer and Wolfgang
Küttler); Arthur Geoffrey Dickens: *The German Nation and Martin Luther* (London,
1974), p. 182 and p. 196; Heiko A. Oberman: *Werden und Wertung der Reformation.
Vom Wegestreit zum Glaubenskampf*, 1st edition (Tübingen, 1977), p. 352f. (in critical
confrontation with the widespread negative evaluation of the Princes' Reformation);
cf. also idem: "Stadtreformation und Fürstenreformation", in: Lewis W. Spitz (ed.):
Humanismus und Reformation als kulturelle Kräfte in der deutschen Geschichte: ein Tagungsbericht
(Berlin/New York, 1981) [= Veröffentlichungen der Historischen Kommission zu
Berlin 51], pp. 80–103 and 181–187; idem: *Die Reformation. Von Wittenberg nach Genf*
(Göttingen, 1986), pp. 21–24; Harm Klueting: *Das Konfessionelle Zeitalter 1525–1648*
(Stuttgart, 1989), p. 108. – I would call attention to two conceptual differentiations:
The Princes' Reformation (Reformation by territorial rulers, territorial/state Reformation and the like) is a part of the authoritarian Reformation but is not synonymous
with it since the concept of the authoritarian Reformation includes the reformations brought about by municipal councils and members of the lower aristocracy.
The Reformation referred to as the "Princes Reformation" is because of its goal
not necessarily synonymous with a developed control of the Church by temporal
rulers – i.e. a reformation totally administered by territorial rulers and integrated
into the state-run bureaucracy; on the character of the territorial rule of the Church
cf. the concise outline by Bernd Moeller: *Deutschland im Zeitalter der Reformation* (Göttingen, 1977) [= Deutsche Geschichte 4], p. 119f. with literature on p. 197. Luther,
for example, – in the framework of his view of the "crisis" and of territorial rulers
as "emergency bishops" – wished for an authoritarian and princely reformation in
a particular sense but not for that government of the Church by the territorial
rulers that developed in the territories. In principle "reformation" denotes a process;
by contrast (established, princely) government of the Church denotes a state (certainly capable of development, variable and rich in variation) that existed *de facto*
at the end of the Reformation due to the actions of the civic authorities but was
not really intended by those who welcomed it.

[9] Oberman: "Stadtreformation und Fürstenreformation" (as n. 8), p. 90.

with its socio-political dynamic and conception of a "construction of the Church from below" is compared with the magisterial Reformation of the princes and "the princely agenda of an organization of the Church from above".[10]

It is true that the fixation on the antithesis of urban Reformation and princely Reformation was moderated somewhat in the last decade by Peter Blickle's new concept of "Communal Reformation" which closely related the important branch of the "Peasants' Reformation" and a rural understanding of reformation with the municipal process of Reformation in the cities.[11] But this concept, too, – like the old concepts of People's Reformation and City Reformation – is defined as sharply dissociated from the authoritarian Reformation, which is to a large degree equated with the Princes' Reformation.[12] For characteristic of Communal Reformation is the movement "from below", which takes up the co-operative "community" consciousness of the traditional communalism of the town and rural communities – "without any involvement or against the resistance of the rulers or civic authorities".[13] The Communal Reformation counts as the Reformation

---

[10] Ibid., p. 184f. (in the concluding words of the discussion): on the example of the contrasting ideas of reform held by the municipal Reformer, Ambrosius Blarer, and Duke Ulrich of Württemberg; cf. p. 90. The extent to which the comparison of urban and princely Reformations can lead to a two-phase model can be seen above all in Dickens (as n. 8), p. 196; he talks of two Reformations following one upon the other (i.e. not of many different reformation movements and many individual reformations but of two diverse, indeed opposing, characteristically contrasting reformations): "Thus a second Reformation, stabilizing yet sterilizing, followed upon the popular and enthusiastic Reformation of the cities."

[11] Blickle introduced the concept of "Communal Reformation" (*Gemeindereformation*) into the discussion in 1982: "Die Reformation im Reich" (as n. 6), pp. 86, 95–97. Cf. idem: "Der Kommunalismus als Gestaltungsprinzip zwischen Mittelalter und Moderne", in: *Gesellschaft und Gesellschaften. Festschrift für Ulrich Imhof* (Bern, 1982), pp. 95–113; idem: *Gemeindereformation. Die Menschen des 16. Jahrhunderts auf dem Weg zum Heil* (Munich, 1985).

[12] Cf. Blickle, *Gemeindereformation*, p. 205ff. (Princes' Reformation v. Communal Reformation); cf. also Klueting (as n. 8), p. 108: "As a result we must now understand under 'Communal Reformation' that reforming movement of the citizens *and* country folk in town *and* country roused by the reforming teachings of Luther and Zwingli. The Communal Reformation defined in this way consequently stands over against the authoritarian Princes' Reformation which in most cases chronologically followed the Communal Reformation and superseded it." Admittedly Klueting adds that here we are dealing with ideal types of classification since "as a historical fact the transition from Communal Reformation to Princes' Reformation could be fluid".

[13] Klueting: ibid., p. 107. Cf. Blickle: *Unruhen in der ständischen Gesellschaft 1300–1800* (Munich, 1988), [= Enzyklopädie deutscher Geschichte 1], pp. 67–71: City Reformation as a Reformation "from below".

movement(s) of the common man – i.e. of the urban and rural population who possess no authoritarian power and who do not belong
to the nobility. The relatively rigid model of phases is also retained
here as is shown by Blickle's formulation in his book on "Communal
Reformation" from 1985: "For stormy years, proliferation, reforming movements and revolt against the priests end around 1525, and
therewith begins the princely, authoritarian, state-run Reformation
– in short, the 'Princes' Reformation'".[14]

The Marxist conception of the Reformation as an "early bourgeois revolution" shows in a forceful way the stark difference between
an anti-feudal, revolutionary people's Reformation and a reactionary
princes' Reformation associated with Luther's development. Here,
too, (as in the thesis of the Communal Reformation) the year 1525
of the Peasants' War is interpreted particularly as a year of change with
serious consequences for the Reformation.

This criticism of the highly overburdened ideological concept of
the early bourgeois revolution in no way signifies a relativizing of
the traditional classifications and categorizations of competing types
and distinguishable phases of the Reformation. On the contrary: the
serious objections and reservations expressed against this – in many
respects justifiable – model of community Reformation foster a new
view which leads away from the rigidity of the old classifications and
disjunctions.[15] This direction should be pursued farther.

---

[14] Blickle: *Gemeindereformation* (as n. 11), p. 14. The strong emphasis on the break
of 1525 ("the dialectic change from the Communal Reformation to the Princes'
Reformation") is also found in pp. 205–215 (the above quotation is from p. 207)
– with reference to works by Ernst W. Zeeden, Bernd Moeller, Heinrich Lutz, Marc
Lienhard, Hans-Jürgen Goertz, Heiko A. Oberman, Winfried Becker and Rainer
Wohlfeil (p. 205f.); cf. also idem: "Die soziale Dialektik der reformatorischen
Bewegung", in: *Zwingli und Europa* (as n. 2), pp. 71–89: 71–73. Here in addition to
Moeller, Oberman and Wohlfeil he refers to Franziska Conrad, Heinrich R. Schmidt
and Hans-Joachim Köhler, the last-named with the statistical proof "that the production of tracts, after increasing rapidly from 1517, fell again sharply in 1525",
with the exaggerated statement: "Most recent research shows that the year 1525 is
to be interpreted in principle rather as a break than as a structural change in the
process of reformation." The social dialectic that Blickle has in mind is the antithesis between the two phases or epochs of the Reformation separated by the caesura
of 1525, i.e. between the "horizontally"-structured Communal Reformation of the
Common Man and the Princes' Reformation/City Reformation characterized by
"vertical references", at the same time the antithesis between the "Reformation of
the ordinary people" and the "Reformation of the Reformers" (ibid., p. 89).

[15] A critical discussion of Blickle's conception of the Communal Reformation
which points in the direction of what I shall say in the following can be found
above all in Heinz Schilling and Olaf Mörke: cf. Schilling: "Die deutsche Gemein-

It is my aim at this point to collate aspects of historical evidence that indicate the permeability and interrelation between the People's Reformation from below and the authoritarian Reformation of the magistrates and princes from above. Connections between the municipal and the territorial Reformations, between a co-operative and a lordly conception of reformation will also become obvious – without being expressly expounded. While emphasizing such permeability, connections, continuity and areas of association I should like to relativize the formations of types and models of phases with their delimitations and clarify the very restricted reach of their explanatory capacity.

First let us look at some factors "from above" which even before 1525 influenced the successful course of the Reformation, and were very closely connected with the Reformation movements of the common man in the cities and in the countryside – indeed, supported and promoted them. Then in a second step I shall ask, inversely, which aspects of the reforming movement "from below" live on after the late 1520s within an authoritarian Church government. There appear synchronous connections and diachronic continuities, social and chronological permeabilities (also from a geographical aspect – in the comparison of Southern Germany and Switzerland with Northern Germany and the Netherlands – one must achieve a new permeability in the observation of simultaneous phenomena which cannot, however, be pursued further in what follows).[16]

---

dereformation. Ein oberdeutsch-zwinglianisches Ereignis vor der 'reformatorischen Wende' des Jahres 1525?", in: *Zeitschrift für historische Forschung* 14 (1987), pp. 325–332; idem: *Aufbruch und Krise: Deutschland 1517–1648* (Berlin, 1988) [Siedler Deutsche Geschichte/Das Reich und die Deutschen], p. 184f.; Mörke: Review of "Zugänge zur bäuerlichen Reformation", ed. Peter Blickle, in: *Zeitschrift für historische Forschung* 16 (1989), pp. 488–491; idem: "Die städtische Gemeinde im mittleren Deutschland (1300–1800)". Comments on Blickle's concept of communalism, in: Blickle (ed.): *Landgemeinde und Stadtgemeinde in Mitteleuropa* (Munich, 1991) [= *Historische Zeitschrift*, Beiheft 13], pp. 289–308.

[16] Schilling in particular drew attention to this in referring "to the general problem that German research into the Early Modern era, followed by American research – particularly insofar as it dealt with the Reformation and the 16th century – reveals a curious, objectively unjustified dichotomy between Southern and Northern Germany": Schilling: "Die deutsche Gemeindereformation" (as n. 15), p. 328.

II. *Factors "from above" in the Broad Reformation Movement before 1525*

1. *The "prae" of the Educated Upper Strata of Society*

It is well known that from the very beginning (and not only after the
Peasants' War and the Imperial Diet of Speyer in 1526) the Reformation was facilitated and supported by princes, municipal magistrates
and nobility but also by attitudes of neutral (even if secretly well-
disposed) non-intervention.[17] To this extent it had from the outset
an authoritarian dimension. Even if one disregards this aspect of
political control we must consider a further important aspect that
likewise leads to the upper strata of society. The Reformation was
not initially a broad popular movement that then experienced a con-
traction through the rapid political intervention of the powers in authority; rather, from the very first – after the radical change in Luther's
own theology – it was supported by a social elite which was at the
same time an educated elite. Initially, in 1518–1521, it was an intellectual and religious movement among humanists, intellectuals impressed
by humanism, and those educated people (among them priests and
monks) who may not have been entirely dedicated to humanist ideals
but still were part of the humanist lines of communication.

People from this humanist or quasi-humanist milieu important for
the dissemination and institutional establishment of reforming ideas
were, as is well-known, especially numerous amongst *predicants* (generally, holders of endowed urban preaching posts), preachers in a
religious Order (particularly that of the Augustinian monks), legal
scholars (professors and above all erudite court councilors), clerks
employed by city councils, and schoolmasters. If we designated these
litterati – among whom we can also include members of other learned
professions such as doctors or printers – as an "intellectual middle
class"[18] we should in fact be hitting the mark, since most of these

---

[17] Cf. Eike Wolgast: "Formen landesfürstlicher Reformation in Deutschland.
Kursachsen – Württemberg/Brandenburg – Kurpfalz", in: Leif Grane, Kai Hørby
(eds.): *Die dänische Reformation vor ihrem internationalen Hintergrund/ The Danish Reformation
against its International Background* (Göttingen, 1990) [= Forschungen zur Kirchen- und
Dogmengeschichte 46], pp. 57–90: 61; as examples of how "the ruler" could "promote the process of penetration of his territory from below by remaining neutral"
Wolgast names Frederick the Wise of Electoral Saxony, Henry V of Mecklenburg,
Ludwig V and Frederick II of the Palatinate as well as the Jülich Dukes John III
and William V or the Margraves Philipp and Ernest of Baden.
[18] Cf. Wolfram Wettges: *Reformation und Propaganda. Studien zur Kommunikation des*

people – apart from a few exceptions (like the patrician Willibald Pirckheimer in Nuremberg) – did not belong to the ruling circles who exercised the decisive political power. On the other hand such educated people did belong to the social elite in a broader sense, to that "honorable estate" which, e.g. in a city, was established between the ruling class of the patriciate and the upper middle class of the wealthier master craftsmen and lesser merchants.

With respect to Nuremberg I could show that all the humanists and their followers, both laymen and clerics, were at least on the social level of the "honorable estate" which was represented in the Great Council, and many were even members of the patriciate.[19] It was out of this sector of the educated "aristocracy", which looked down on the "common man",[20] that the Reformation in Nuremberg was set on its way after 1518. It is characteristic of the course of the Lutheran movement in these early years that the "Sodalitas Staupitziana" in Nuremberg, that circle which was the breeding-ground of reforming ideas in Nuremberg, was exclusively a circle of patricians and "honorable" people infused with humanist ideals. Among them were – alongside great merchants – a legal counselor to the Council (Christoph Scheurl the Younger), a council clerk (Lazarus Spengler), an artist (Albrecht Dürer), a provost (of St. Laurence: Georg Beheim) and a preacher from a religious Order (the Augustinian monk, Wenzeslaus Linck, previously Professor in

---

Aufruhrs in süddeutschen Reichsstädten (Stuttgart, 1978) [= Geschichte und Gesellschaft 17], pp. 69–96; Wolfgang Zorn: "Die soziale Stellung der Humanisten in Nürnberg und Augsburg", in: Otto Herding, Robert Stupperich (eds.): *Die Humanisten in ihrer politischen und sozialen Umwelt* (Boppard, 1976) [= Deutsche Forschungsgemeinschaft, Kommission für Humanismusforschung, Mitteilung III], pp. 35–49.

[19] Berndt Hamm: "Humanistische Ethik und reichstädtische Ehrbarkeit in Nürnberg", in: *Mitteilungen des Vereins für Geschichte der Stadt Nürnberg* 76 (1989), pp. 65–147: 67–115, with the conclusion on p. 115: "Anyone who was active or interested in the spirit of Humanism was almost always on the social level of the 'honorable' and belonged to their sphere of social communication. This means: Humanism in Nuremberg was socially, economically and spiritually bound to the respected upper strata of society and in a particular respect especially to the patrician ruling classes even if its ideas time and again extended beyond what was specific to a particular social stratum into the universal human, Christian and middle-class." The "honorable estate" in Nuremberg, composed of respected citizens both patrician and non-patrician, made up about five per cent of the population; ibid., p. 80 and p. 84. It is important to remember that here and in what follows we are not talking about the *background* of the cultured people (who occasionally were from families of humble origin) but about their actual social *status*.

[20] Cf. ibid., p. 95.

[21] Cf. ibid., pp. 133–143 (cf. also particularly n. 302b: on the later decision in

Wittenberg).[21] The Nuremberg reformer Andreas Osiander also came
from the Augustinian monastery which was the institutional focal-
point of the Staupitz circle of friends.[22]

What is also characteristic is that people from this circle of the
first admirers of Luther and the first "multiplicators" of Reformation
theology were the very ones who later, after the spring of 1525,
numbered among those who called for a speedy authoritarian
Reformation of the Council, brought this about in word, writing and
deed, and both realized and stabilized it (even if differences arose
on particular questions such as the implementation of ecclesiastical
discipline). Lazarus Spengler, Christoph Scheurl, Wenzeslaus Linck,
Andreas Osiander and the councilors Hieronymus Ebner, Kaspar
Nützel, Martin Tucher and Sigmund Fürer were such bearers of
continuity.[23] They took part in the beginning of the Reformation in
Nuremberg; they initiated and drove forward its expansion into the
movement of the common man by means of sermons and tracts, or
through council policy or influence on council policy provided the
necessary shelter for the Communal Reformation; and finally, they
supported a continuing Reformation by the Council.

Certainly we must take into account the fact that Nuremberg in
many respects represents a special case, with its powerful patriciate
and governing Council, its unusually high level of humanistic education and outstanding representatives of a late medieval spirituality
predisposed to reform. Admittedly what is special and unusual – as

---

favor of the Reformation by the majority of the "Staupitzians" – at the time of the
Nuremberg Religious Dialogue in March 1525).

[22] Before Osiander became preacher at St. Laurence he was a teacher of Hebrew
in the Nuremberg Augustinian monastery from 1520 to 1522: cf. Gottfried Seebaß:
Das reformatorische Werk des Andreas Osiander (Nuremberg, 1967) [= Einzelarbeiten aus
der Kirchengeschichte Bayerns 44], p. 73. On Osiander's social position, over and
above my study of Nuremberg humanism already quoted (as n. 19, on Osiander:
p. 87), we should note that Osiander's father, Andreas Schmid, was seven times
mayor of Gunzenhausen, the Reformer's home-town, between 1506 and 1521; cf.
Gunter Zimmermann: "Der Familienname des Nürnberger Reformators", in: *Zeitschrift
für bayerische Kirchengeschichte* 52 (1983), pp. 45–51: 48.

[23] Cf. the synopsis of the course of the Nuremberg Reformation by Gottfried
Seebaß: "Stadt und Kirche in Nürnberg im Zeitalter der Reformation", in: Bernd
Moeller (ed.): *Stadt und Kirche im 16. Jahrhundert* (Gütersloh, 1978) [= Schriften des
Vereins für Reformationsgeschichte 190], pp. 66–86; particularly on the Nuremberg
Religious Dialogue of 1525 cf. idem: "Der Nürnberger Rat und das Religionsgespräch
von 1525", in: *Jahrbuch für fränkische Landesforschung* 34/35 (1974/75), pp. 467–499;
unreliable: Gunter Zimmerman: "Das Nürnberger Religionsgespräch von 1525", in:
Mitteilungen des Vereins für Geschichte der Stadt Nürnberg 71 (1984), pp. 129–148.

in the case of Nuremberg – is often simply an intensification or sharpening of the exemplary and typical. And so we can discern – with all due caution – something basic and characteristic for the course of the Reformation in this example. A comparison with the course of the Reformation in other cities and territories should confirm this. The third main phase of the Reformation – i.e. the authoritarian Reformation of the princes and magistrates (after the first "calm" phase of educated communication[24] and the second more turbulent phase of popular agitation), only partly signifies something new but is frequently in essential aspects a chance for success for those reforming forces of the educated and social elite which had already set their mark on the beginning of the process of reform. To this extent the years 1525/26 appear from this political and social aspect not as a break but, at least in southern Germany, as a continuous extension of long-existing priorities and initiatives.[25]

We cannot, however, simply transfer this view to the north. It appears that in many north German cities the link between humanism and the beginnings of the Reformation was not as close as in the southern and central regions.[26] But this must be the subject of closer examination.

2. The Reformation of the Middle

From what has been said, yet another detail has emerged which is of great importance for understanding the so-called "Communal Reformation", the reformation of the authorities [Obrigkeiten], and

---

[24] Cf. Heiko A. Oberman: Werden und Wertung der Reformation. Vom Wegestreit zum Glaubenskampf, 1st edition (Tübingen, 1977), p. 347: "We should not underrate the function of the monastery, particularly the closed Augustinian monastery, as a center of intellectual exchange during the first 'calm phase' of Luther's work before the Edict of Worms."

[25] Looking at the continuity of the importance of imposed authority and exertion of influence during the Reformation Scribner also can say: "On this view of the process of Reformation, there is no decisive break in the phases of development, with 1525 as a watershed. The same trend is present in the early 1520s as in the later 1520s and 1530s. What changes is, first, the possibility of erastian action, which is greatly strengthened after 1525; second, the willingness to take such action; third, the extent to which the state takes the church into its tutelage." Robert W. Scribner: "Paradigms of Urban Reformation: Gemeindereformation or Erastian Reformation?", in: Grane, Hørby: Die dänische Reformation (as n. 17), pp. 111–128: 127.

[26] Cf. Bernhard Lohse: "Humanismus und Reformation in norddeutschen Städten in der 20er und frühen 30er Jahren des 16. Jahrhunderts", in: Grane, Hørby: Die dänische Reformation (as n. 17), pp. 11–27.

particularly for the understanding of the connection between the two. It would appear that the opposition of authoritarian rule and the Common Man (i.e. ruled subjects, socially: the middle and lower classes) is all too simplified and leads to an overly sharp, distorting impression of contrast.[27] What is not taken into consideration is that dimension of the Reformation that lies between the two, at the pivotal point between authorities and subjects, and is important for the interactions and connections between the authoritarian perspective and that of the common man. The literary and humanistically educated people, the *litterati* and *eruditi*, among whom are to be found the first supporters and disseminators of a reforming organization of the Church – scholarly preachers, students of law, leading chancellery officials *et al.* – were mediators between the rule of their princes and magistrates and the Common Man.[28] On the one hand they mediated reforming impulses to their authorities (particularly in the form of evaluations, advice and letters) while on the other hand they brought home the message of the Reformation to the Common Man via inflammatory polemics and propaganda, didactic description and devotional instruction. Their extensive literary competence enabled them to use variable styles of argumentation on various linguistic levels with diverse emphases in content. In the city it is pre-

---

[27] The concept "Common Man" as used here and in what follows is determined by the situation at Nuremberg and consequently denotes those groups of the population excluded from the ruling class and not belonging to the "honorable" stratum. It is, however, necessary to point out that the term "Common Man" could be interpreted very differently according to local context and instrumental application. It can extend upwards or contract downwards; it can also include partial participation in control (as, for example, through the medium of co-operative committees in the city). The variability of the term can be seen for example – in a critical discussion of Blickle's definition of the "Common Man" – in Heinz Schilling: "Aufstandsbewegungen in der Stadtbürgerlichen Gesellschaft des Alten Reiches. Die Vorgeschichte des Münsteraner Täuferreichs, 1525–1534", in: Hans-Ulrich Wehler (ed.): *Der Deutsche Bauernkrieg 1524–1526* (Göttingen, 1975), pp. 193–238: 237f. Schilling's comments provide an important supplement to what I say in the following. He calls attention from the other side to precisely that urban permeability between "above" and "below" which is so remarkable for the course of the Reformation (cf. especially below, p. 242). To this extent I am quite open to a use of the phrase "Common Man" which differs from my own.

[28] This intermediary position becomes clear in the example of the Nuremberg council clerk, Lazarus Spengler: cf. Berndt Hamm: "Stadt und Kirche unter dem Wort Gottes: das reformatorische Einheitsmodell des Nürnberger Ratsschreibers Lazarus Spengler (1469–1534)", in: Ludger Grenzmann, Karl Stackmann (eds.): *Literatur und Laienbildung im Spätmittelalter und in der Reformationszeit. Symposion Wolfenbüttel 1981* (Stuttgart, 1984) [= Germanistische Symposien Berichtsbände 5], pp. 710–731: 711f.

cisely these mediators, open to "above" and "below", who theologically legitimate and exalt the power of the authorities but also appeal
to the co-operative ideals of the community[29] and can also – based
on the command of love – give them higher spiritual intensification.[30]
Already in the 1520s they make themselves, on the one hand, spokesmen for an increasing secular authoritarian responsibility over the
Church; on the other, they emphasize the priesthood of all believers, and the right of simple lay-people to gain knowledge of God's
Word and to judge the doctrines of the Church.

These mediators (e.g in Nuremberg, the preacher Andreas Osiander
and the council clerk Lazarus Spengler;[31] in Constance, the preachers
Johannes Zwick and Ambrosius Blarer,[32] and council clerk Jörg Vögeli)[33]
give their authorities important stimuli towards a re-formation of the
church pushed through by the authorities, while at the same time
they stimulate the Reformation movement of the common folk in
sermons and tracts. This shows the extent to which the Reformation
cannot simply be described in the categories "from above" and "from
below", in mutually exclusive terms of competition or co-operation
between authority and the common man. In the last years it has
become increasingly more obvious how much the Reformation is
also a "midway" phenomenon between "above" and "below" and
to what a great extent – particularly in the early years – it was stimulated by people who cannot simply be assigned to the party having power or to the subject-group of the common man. It becomes
clear that this political and social middle role, which is bound to
the function of theological conversion and negotiation, particularly
in the key role played by the erudite court counselors[34] and the

---

[29] Cf. Hans-Christoph Rublack: "Grundwerte in der Reichstadt im Spätmittelalter
und in der frühen Neuzeit", in: Horst Brunner (ed.): *Literatur in der Stadt* (Göppingen,
1982) [= Göppinger Arbeiten zur Germanistik 343], pp. 9–36.

[30] Cf. Hamm (as n. 28), p. 716f.; idem: "Laientheologie zwischen Luther und
Zwingli: Das reformatorische Anliegen des Konstanzer Stadtschreibers Jörg Vögeli
aufgrund seiner Schriften von 1523/24", in: Josef Nolte, Hella Tompert, Christof
Windhorst (eds.): *Kontinuität und Umbruch. Theologie und Frömmigkeit in Flugschriften und
Kleinliteratur an der Wende vom 15. zum 16. Jahrhundert* (Stuttgart, 1978) [= Spätmittelalter
und Frühe Neuzeit 2], pp. 222–295: 282–286 and 292f.

[31] Cf. Seebaß: *Stadt und Kirche* (as n. 23), pp. 76 and 80f.; Hamm: "Stadt und
Kirche" (as n. 28).

[32] Cf. Rublack (as n. 29), p. 25.

[33] Cf. Hamm: "Laientheologie" (as n. 30).

[34] On the key role played by scholarly counselors and officials in the princely
seats, in the rural councils and in the chancelleries of the provincial and free cities

municipal council clerks, was important for the success of the
Reformation movement.[35]

If one starts from the perspective of this middle group which (particularly in the cities) thought both on an authoritarian/ruling level
as well as on a community/co-operative level, one will have strong
reservations about describing the years before 1525/26 (or later in
the north) as "Communal Reformation", which equates the socially
widely diversified Reformation movement with a Reformation of the
Common (in the sense of the underprivileged) Man. Within the
framework of a comprehensive understanding of "Christian community" these "mediators" experienced and aspired to reformation
as an event that combined 1) the preaching of government-appointed
servants of the Church, 2) elements of a lively lay Christianity 'from
below' and 3) authoritarian structuring (in the sense of a lay Christianity
'from above'). Such an integrative understanding of "Communal
Reformation" may well be seen as characteristic of the intermediary position of the "intellectuals", corresponding to the intentions of

---

cf. particularly the works of Volker Press, above all: "Stadt und territoriale Konfes-
sionsbildung", in: Franz Petri (ed.): *Kirche und gesellschaftlicher Wandel in deutschen und
niederländischen Städten der werdenden Neuzeit* (Cologne/Vienna, 1980) [= Städteforschung,
Series A, vol. 10], pp. 251–296. In regard to the further development of the
Reformation and confessionalization in the 16th century Press describes (p. 295)
these scholarly employees as "a bourgeois stratum of civil servants" . . . "who took
the place of the celibate clergy and moved alongside the nobility": "The group
taking shape became simultaneously the main support of the new reforming creeds."
Press speaks of the "coincidence of a Reformation and a development of a bourgeois
stratum of civil servants which identified with it" and which was in practice closely
connected "with the likewise newly developing position of protestant parish clergy".
In the early years of the Reformation, even before 1525, the decisive role played
by this supportive function on the part of scholarly counselors and civil servants –
which can be seen in a closer association (frequently mediated by Humanism) with
the forerunner-role played by the predicants – is described by Dieter Stievermann:
"Sozial- und verfassungsgeschichtliche Voraussetzungen Martin Luthers und der
Reformation – der landesherrliche Rat in Kursachsen, Kurmainz und Marsfeld",
in: Volker Press, Dieter Stievermann (eds.): *Martin Luther. Probleme seiner Zeit* (Stuttgart,
1986) [= Spätmittelalter und Frühe Neuzeit 16], pp. 137–176.
[35] Luther was aware of his debt to the clerks (recording secretaries) of the city
councils. In a "Tischrede" in 1542 he remarked: "Es liget mechtig viel an einem
gutten stadtschreyber in einer stadt, wenn etwas sol ausgerichtet werden. Ich halte,
wenn Lazarus Spengeler zu Nurmbergk gethan hette, das euangelion were so bald
nicht auffgangen. Die stadtschreiber thun, wie es die propheten vorzeitten thetten
bey der konigen." ("It is very important that a city should have a good council
clerk when something is to be achieved. I believe that if Lazarus Spengler had not
been in office in Nuremberg the Gospel would not have emerged so soon. The
council clerks perform the function that the prophets in olden times performed for
the kings.") *WA TR* 5, 132,30–133,2, Nr. 5426.

the supra-regional reformers such as Luther, Melanchthon, Zwingli, Bucer, Brenz, Osiander, Blarer *et al.*

3. *The Authoritarian Orientation of the Reformers before 1525*

In connection with what has just been said I shall now briefly comment on the attitude of the reformers, particularly with regard to the widespread thesis of their "turning-point" – i.e. their renunciation of the Reformation of the common man and their turn toward the authoritarian Reformation with its rule of the Church by secular authorities. This "turning-point" belongs to the area of legend even if there were important alterations and developments in individual Reformers. The idea of a break or a total change of direction in the ecclesiology and understanding of the Reformation by the reformers is false: On the contrary, the aspect of continuity must be emphasized. This will become clear as we briefly consider the examples of Zwingli, Bucer and Luther.

It is true that *Zwingli* underwent a momentous change in his attitude to the problem of coercion. At the latest in 1526 he reaches the opinion that the "free" preaching of God's Word must be defended and secured by means of force, capital punishment, and military might.[36] But from the very beginning – recognizable already in measures taken in 1522 and quite obviously after the First Zürich Disputation (29th January 1523) – Zwingli laid the competence of decision for the reform and restructuring of the Church in the hands of the municipal authorities. Zwingli saw in the authority of the Christian council the legitimate representative of the christian community, accompanied by the preacher's office of guardian and led by the Word of God, which was responsible for questions of church order.

---

[36] Even before 1526 Zwingli was never a pacifist in the general sense but always approved of an armed battle for the freedom of the Confederation. His approval of a forceful engagement for the freedom to preach the Reformation in the Confederation was not a break in his reforming thought and action but corresponded to his basic understanding of the political dimension of God's Word and its right to be made public. In a climate of intensifying violence, in the face of aggressive power politics hostile to the Reformation on the part of the opposing party who still believed in the old order, his call for the use of military force was completely natural from this understanding – particularly since the consideration of the Imperial "authority", which played such an important role in Lutheran territories, did not apply for the Swiss Zwingli. Cf. Berndt Hamm: *Zwinglis Reformation der Freiheit* (Neukirchen – Vluyn, 1988), p. 8f. with n. 25 and pp. 10–20.

Zwingli could not envisage Reformation in any other form than this kind of authoritarian Reformation.[37]

A similar view was held by *Bucer* (whose ecclesiology has recently been very thoroughly examined),[38] another of many other Reformers who, like Zwingli, could only think of Reformation under the aegis of a competent authority. For Bucer, too, it is characteristic that, right from the start, commencing with his first Strasbourg publication in August 1523,[39] he makes the municipal authorities of the free Imperial City responsible for reform, restructuring, and the enforcement in the whole city of the Two Tables of the biblical Law.[40] For the duty of the authorities relates both to the temporal welfare and the eternal salvation "einer gantzen gemeyn" (of the whole community).[41] The authorities should "am leib straffen" (physically punish)[42] any who oppose the "uffgang göttlichs worts" (emergence of God's Word).[43] Like Zwingli and the other Reformers, Bucer does distinguish between the specific "internal" office of the preacher and the "external" work of the secular authorities,[44] but he locates the service of the Christian authorities within the one Kingdom of Christ

---

[37] Cf. ibid., p. 9 and pp. 113–120, especially p. 114: "The freedom of the Church community in the face of the state consequently does not concern Zwingli. He always critically challenges the authorities to fulfill their Christian duty to protect the Gospel and subordinate all sections of society and politics to the highest standard of God's Word."

[38] Gottfried Hammann: *Martin Bucer 1491–1551: Zwischen Volkskirche und Bekenntnisgemeinschaft* (Wiesbaden/Stuttgart, 1989) [= Veröffentlichungen des Instituts für Europäische Geschichte Mainz, Abt. Religionsgeschichte, vol. 139]. Cf. also – to mention only one important older publication on this topic – Martin Brecht: *Die frühe Theologie des Johannes Brenz* (Tübingen, 1966) [= Beiträge zur historischen Theologie 36], pp. 271–292 and 313–318; especially important is the conclusion on p. 292: "[. . .] it is at the same time definite that Brenz was in no way forced to change his theological stance because of the Peasants' War"; "Brenz' alleged change caused by the Peasants' War never happened."

[39] "Das ym selbs niemant, sondern anderen leben soll, und wie der mensch dahyn kummen moeg", edited in: *Martin Bucers Deutsche Schriften, vol. 1: Frühschriften 1520–1524*, ed. by Robert Stupperich (Gütersloh, 1960), pp. 29–67 (revised by Johannes Müller).

[40] Cf. Hammann (as n. 38), pp. 252–261.

[41] "Das ym selbs [. . .]" (as n. 39), pp. 55,1–59,26 ("einer gantzen gemeyn": p. 55,6.16).

[42] Ibid., pp. 57,20–24: "[. . .] vor allem schaffen, das dem volck das goettlich wort fürtragen wurd und am leib straffen, die das felschten oder in einich weg hynderten, wie dann solchs auß goettlichem gesatz christlicher magistrat und oberkeit schuldig ist und habens auch alweg die gottseligen Künig und Fürsten als Moses, Josue, David, Ezechias [Hezekiah] und andere bewisen."

[43] Ibid., p. 55,25.

[44] Ibid., p. 55,2–4.22f.; cf. Hammann (as n. 38), p. 259f.

and understands it in the light of the working of the Holy Spirit desiring to gain acceptance in the external area of ecclesiastical and political order as well. There is only "one single Kingdom – the Kingdom of Christ! – which aspires to expand by both 'spiritual' and 'external' means. No longer do we find two different divine ways of acting as in Luther but rather two special spheres in the service of one and the same Kingdom which is embodied in the Church."[45]

Bucer is not original in this, but reflects a standard way of thinking arising from the late medieval idea of the *Corpus Christianorum*, which can be recognized in most of the city Reformers of southern Germany and Switzerland (it is particularly evident, for example, in Zwingli[46] and Osiander)[47] and perhaps also in the Reformers of the north German area (and presumably not only in city Reformers).[48] With a strong pneumatological emphasis, which takes as its starting point the unifying effect of the Holy Spirit in the body of Christ, these Reformers consider as one the political and ecclesial community;

----

[45] Hammann, ibid., p. 260.

[46] Cf. Hamm (as n. 36), pp. 113–120; Hans Rudolf Lavater: "Regnum Christi etiam externum – Huldrych Zwinglis Brief vom 4. Mai 1528 an Ambrosius Blarer in Konstanz", in: *Zwingliana* 15 (1981), pp. 338–381.

[47] Cf. Berndt Hamm: "Wort Gottes und Menschensatzung. Notizen zur Osiander-Gesamtausgabe und zu Osianders Theologie", in: *Zeitschrift für bayerische Kirchengeschichte* 51 (1982), pp. 54–72: 62; on Osiander's unitive thinking as a development of a particular doctrine of God (emphasizing the unity of God) and ontology cf. Martin Stupperich: *Osiander in Preussen 1549–1552* (Berlin/New York, 1973) [= Arbeiten zur Kirchengeschichte 44], pp. 200–203; cf. also Hamm: "Stadt und Kirche" (as n. 28), p. 719f. (This article is mainly concerned with the unitive thinking of the council clerk, Lazarus Spengler, who admittedly did not put as much stress on pneumatology as did Zwingli, Bucer and Osiander.)

[48] Oberman derives the urban Reformers' thinking and striving for unity – which fitted in with the temporal-spiritual "public benefit" ("under the succinct aspect of the *bonum commune*") – from the medieval scholastic teaching of the *via antiqua*, for: "The leading Upper German urban Reformers almost without exception stem from the *via antiqua*." Oberman (as n. 24), pp. 362–378 (quotations from p. 361 and p. 377). We must carefully test how far all that has been considered typically urban (i.e. especially pertaining to the Free Cities) in Reformation theology was not also represented on the territorial level and how far the historical derivation from the *via antiqua* can be proved in individual cases (in most cases it will be neither provable nor disprovable). Nevertheless Moeller has in the meantime revised his earlier thesis of the specifically co-operative character of the theology of the Upper German and Swiss City Reformation in view of more recent works on the history of the Reformation in north German cities (especially those of Heinz Schilling and Olaf Mörke); Bernd Moeller: *Reichsstadt und Reformation. Bearbeitete Neuausgabe* (Berlin [GDR], 1987), p. 92f. Further revision will no doubt have to overcome many previously accepted theological lines of separation between City Reformation and territorial Rulers' Reformation.

authority and the political-spiritual community; internal and external;
Law (divine justice) and Gospel; spiritual discipline and authoritarian, civic discipline; the offices of preacher and civil servant; earthly
well-being and eternal salvation; God's indwelling in humanity and
a spiritual penetration of the social body. This is their fundamental
theological and socio-ethical approach, which enables us to understand why their conception of reformation and Church government
from the outset included an authoritarian dimension and – without
a Constantinian conversion or betrayal of original reforming principles – steered quite consistently towards Church government by secular authority. In their eyes the authorities are spiritually legitimized
for this task through the priesthood of all believers, but especially –
and this aspect plays a far greater part – through the institutional
holiness of the governing offices they hold, acting for the whole congregation (Rom. 13.1–14; 1 Pet. 2.13f.).[49]

Luther's approach to ecclesiology and especially his concrete ideas
as to how the Reformation ("improvement of the Christian community") should be carried out only partially vary from the unifying ideas described above in the differentiation of the Two Kingdoms
of God, designed to interlink *ecclesia* and *politia*. The differentiation
was directed specifically against a "papist" Church that exercises
authority with secular instruments of power and against an ungodly
secular authority that attempts to suppress the progress of God's
Word instead of fostering its dissemination.[50] At the same time, however, it is clear that from the beginning (i.e. at the latest from 1520),
Luther definitely had in mind a change in the Church brought about
from above: by authoritarian princes, noble lords and municipal
authorities. He is not thinking of a Church ruled *by* the authorities

---

[49] At a time which is marked by an intensifying trend towards oligarchy and by
the juxtaposition of developed congregational structures and rising early absolutis-
tic tendencies, a line of thinking which is oriented on the authorities and one which
is co-operative do not necessarily constitute a contrast within this ecclesiological and
political synopsis of the theologians. Cf. the very instructive textual examples in
Rublack (as n. 29), p. 24f. This combination of authoritarian thinking (under the
rubric "by the grace of God") and co-operative consciousness of worth can also be
seen in the views of the council clerks (e.g. Lazarus Spengler). Cf. also the example of Nuremberg city counselor Christoph Scheurl, in: Rublack: ibid., p. 27f.

[50] Cf. the conditions required for the emergence of this differentiation and the
polemic involved in his fundamental pamphlet on the issue, "Von weltlicher Oberkeit,
wie weit man ihr Gehorsam schuldig sei" (published in March 1523); see also an
Introduction and Edition of the text by Sieghard Mühlmann, in: *Martin Luther
Studienausgabe*, vol. 3, ed. Hans-Ulrich Delius (Berlin [GDR], 1983), pp. 27–71.

but – in view of the failure of the ecclesiastical authorities who are actually responsible – of a secular authoritarian Reformation. He did not adopt this position only after the turmoil at Wittenberg (1521/22),[51] or after his confrontation with Karlstadt and his congregation at Orlamünde (1524/25).[52] Rather, it is already clearly recognizable in his treatise "To the Christian Nobility of the German Nation Concerning the Reform of the Christian Estate" (June 1520). Here he argues that the priesthood of all believers legitimates the holders of secular authority as "fellow Christians" and "fellow priests" to function in the spiritual "Body of Christ",[53] and that the official position of those in authority elevates them and makes them particularly suitable – more than all other Christians – for this task of improving the substance of the Church.[54] In this connection it becomes clear that Luther's conception of reformation furnishes not only the idea of Two Kingdoms or Two Regiments, but also a binding christological idea of One Body which unites secular authority and Christian community: "Christus hat nit zwey noch zweyerley art corper, einen weltlich, den ander geistlich. Ein heubt ist und einen corper hat er." (Christ does not have two bodies or two kinds of body, the one earthly and the other spiritual. He is the one Head and has one Body).[55]

---

[51] On the emphasis on the authorities' responsibility in this connection – rooted in Luther's basic attitude to anything tainted with the odium of "rabble-rousing" or which might even come close to it – cf. Ulrich Bubenheimer: "Luthers Stellung zum Aufruhr in Wittenberg 1520–1522 und die früh-reformatorischen Wurzeln des landesherrlichen Kirchenregiments", in: *Zeitschrift der Savigny-Stiftung für Rechtsgeschichte*, Kan. Abt. 71 (1985), pp. 147–214.

[52] Cf. Gert Haendler: *Amt und Gemeinde bei Luther im Kontext der Kirchengeschichte* (Stuttgart, 1979) [= Arbeiten zur Theologie 63], pp. 43–49 (Luther's criticism of the congregation at Orlamünde in 1524/25); Martin Brecht: *Martin Luther*, vol. 2 (Stuttgart, 1986), pp. 158–172.

[53] "An den christlichen Adel deutscher Nation von des christlichen Standes Besserung", *WA* 6, 408,8–11 and 413, 27–33; on the Body of Christ cf. n. 55.

[54] See ibid., 408, 11–410, 2 and 413, 27–414, 3.

[55] Ibid., 408, 33–35 with the preceding sentence (lines 31–33): "Unnd das ist sanct Paul Ro. xij. und i. Corint. xij. unnd Petrus i. Pet ij. wie droben gesagt, das wir alle ein corper sein des heubts Jesu Christi, ein yglicher des andern glidmaß." (St. Paul in Rom. 12 and 1 Cor. 12 and St. Peter in 1 Pet. 2 said that we are all one Body of the Head, Jesus Christ, each a member of the other.) Cf. 410, 3–6: "Also meyn ich, disse erste papyr maur lig darnyder, seyntemal weltlich hirschafft ist ein mitglid worden des Christlichen Corpers, unnd wie wol sie ein leyplich werck hat, doch geystlichs stands ist, darumb yhr werck sol frey unvorhindert gehen in alle glidmaß des gantzen corpers [. . .]" (So I believe that this first paper wall has fallen, since the worldly power has become a member of the Body of Christ, and though her work is physical, yet her status is spiritual, thus her work should run

The secular authorities with their special office, which legitimates
and commits them to reform the Church in the present state of
emergency, belong, as Luther stresses, within this one Body of Christ,
which is the Christian community.[56]

At the same time, while Luther keeps a firm hold on his view of
Reformation by the authorities, in a familiar writing of 1523 he can
still maintain the principle "that a Christian assembly or congregation has the right and power to judge all doctrine and to call, appoint
and remove teachers from office."[57] For Luther the Reformation perspective from "above" (with respect to the special office of the authorities or the special office of the preacher called to the congregation)
always corresponds to an ecclesiological perspective from "below"
(with respect to the "authority"[58] or "power", the legitimation and
warrant of the whole congregation). This is not a contradiction as
he sees it, for the following reasons:

1. When Luther talks of *Gemeine* he is normally thinking of the
Christian community within which he includes the secular authorities.[59] This concept of community is *not* determined by the political
polarity between authority and community (in the sense of subjects)
but presupposes – e.g. in the calling or deposing of pastors – an
agreement between secular authority and the "rest" of the church
community, indeed even includes a predominance of the authorities
in the right to make decisions. In any case Luther energetically
opposed demands from congregations wishing to push through the
Reformation and appoint or depose pastors without regard for the
secular authorities: "Darumb hab acht auff die ubirkeyt! So lange
die nit tzu greyfft und befilhet, szo haldt du stille mit hand, mund

free and unhindered through all the limbs of the whole body.) This view of the
one Body of Christ which is based on the conception of the priesthood of all believers and hence also of the spiritual dimension of all secular vocations (cf. 409, 5–10)
is not cancelled but supplemented shortly afterwards by the first development of
Luther's idea of the Two Kingdoms/Regiments.

[56] Cf. particularly in the letter to the nobility, *WA* 6, 408, 8–11: On the basis
of the priesthood of all believers and baptized one should count the office of the
authorities as an office which is part of and useful to the Christian community
("zelen als ein ampt, das da gehore und nutzlich sey der christlichen gemeyne").

[57] *WA* 11, 408–416.

[58] Cf. "An den christl. Adel", *WA* 6, 407, 30f.: "die alle gleiche gewalt haben"
(who all have the same power); cf. *ibid.*, 408, 15.

[59] Cf. Luther's formulation in n. 56: that the office of the secular authorities "is
part of [...] the Christian community", i.e. has its place *within* the community and
consequently has to serve the community.

unnd hertz und nym dich nichts an. Kanstu aber die uberkeyt bewegen, das sie angreyffe und befelhe, szo magistu es thun; will sie nicht,
szo soltu auch nit wollen." (Therefore pay attention to the authorities. If they do not act or give the command you must remain quiet
with hand, mouth and heart and take no action. But if you can per-
suade the authorities to act and give the command, then you also
may act; but if they are unwilling to do so, you should also be
unwilling) (December 1521).[60]

2. With Luther one must always take into consideration (and this
is closely connected with what has just been said) that within the
rights of the community – i.e. the Christian community – he always
differentiates:

a) between the general legitimacy that applies to all believing
Christians in the same way (as a warrant to make judgments between
true and false doctrine based on their understanding of the Bible
and in the power of the Holy Spirit; to teach; to appoint and depose
teachers; to proclaim God's Word to the neighbor; to rebuke and
to grant forgiveness), and the *ius executionis* – i.e. among other things
the right to take measures regarding ecclesiastical order, which, in
the situation after 1520, Luther grants first and foremost to the secular authorities within the community;[61]

b) between the general Christian warrant to teach[62] and the
particular commission of teachers and preachers. Everyone may be
able to preach but only a few with special gifts are called to be
preachers;[63]

c) with regard to preachers themselves, between the simple preachers

---

[60] "Eine treue Vermahnung M. Luthers zu allen Christen, sich zu hüten vor
Aufruhr und Empörung", *WA* 8, 680, 27–31; cf. Introduction in: *Martin Luther
Studienausgabe*, vol. 3, ed. Hans-Ulrich Delius (Berlin [GDR], 1983), pp. 12–14
(literature).

[61] Cf. Bubenheimer (as n. 51), p. 206 on Luther's *Invocavit* sermons in 1522:
"Nevertheless the differentiation between word and deed is a red thread that runs
through the sermons. It is also phrased canonically by the contrast of the *ius verbi*,
which is the right of the preachers, and the *(ius) executionis* which spiritually is the
prerogative of God and physically of the secular authority."

[62] Cf. e.g. "Daß eine christl. Versammlung [. . .]", *WA* 11, 411, 31–412, 13 (since
– according to Jn 6.45 – all Christians are taught by God, all Christians are entitled to teach – i.e. to proclaim the Word of God).

[63] Ibid., 411, 22–30 ("die ienigen, so man geschickt datzu findet und die gott
mit verstand erleucht und mit gaben datzu getziert hatt" [those who are found to
be skilled in this and whom God has inspired with intellect and graced with gifts
thereto]).

of the faith who – having no knowledge of the original biblical languages, nevertheless "Christum verstehen, leren und heyliglich leben und andern predigen" (understand Christ, teach, live a holy life and preach to others) but cannot really interpret the Bible, and the preachers trained in the biblical languages who can in their own autonomous interpretation reconstruct the sense of the biblical text and thus protect against error;[64]

d) between normal times and a state of emergency, i.e. between a hypothetical state of normalcy (as should be the case in the Christian congregation) in which upright bishops appoint evangelical preachers with the consent of the congregation;[65] a hypothetical state of emergency (in which every Christian – without being appointed by any external agency – has a duty to teach and preach publicly)[66] and the emergency actually "existing" (in which the bishops are failing in their duties and the congregations, including their secular rulers, are appointing preachers).[67]

Hence not everyone who believes and is inspired by the Holy Spirit is consequently appointed preacher of the Church, and not every preacher has the ability to interpret Holy Scripture, just as the Christian entitlement to judge doctrine *in concreto* does not adequately give one the right to appoint and depose teachers. Existing legal and administrative conditions provide the framework. Luther reaches these distinctions already in the early 1520s.

From what has become clear in the examples of Zwingli, Bucer and Luther we can draw two further conclusions:

---

[64] "An die Ratsherrn aller Städte deutschen Lands, daß sie christliche Schulen aufrichten und halten sollen" (early in 1524), *WA* 15, 40, 14–26 and 42, 1–14.

[65] Cf. "Daß eine christl. Versammlung [. . .]", *WA* 11, 413,28–414,29 (with reference to the situation of the early congregations i.e. to the practice of the "bishops" Titus, Timothy, Paul and Barnabas).

[66] Cf. ibid., 412,14–413,10: Luther is thinking, again with reference to the early congregational practice, of two possible emergencies: 1. if a Christian is living among non-Christians (412,16–29); 2. if a Christian is living in a Christian environment but the appointed teachers are in error (412,30–413,10). In both these emergencies the Christian comes to the fore as teacher of God's Word – not because he is appointed by men but by virtue of his "inner" calling and anointing by God (412,17f.).

[67] Cf. ibid., 413,10–22 and 414,30–416,10 ("wie es denn alltzeyt und sonderlich itzt ist"; "nu aber zu unsern zeytten die nott da ist [. . .]"); in the same connection the reference to the authoritarian warrant to appoint within the Christian community: 414,5–7 and 415,19–25.

1. The problematic nature of a concept of "Communal Reformation" becomes more obvious insofar as it analogously transfers without qualification the socio-political antithesis between communalism and authoritarian rule to the reforming perspective of the Christian community. On the other hand it has become clear that the Reformers named here (and indeed almost all of the Reformers) already in this early phase before the Peasants' War had a strongly authoritarian conception of communal Reformation. The reformation concept of the "community" (*Gemeine*) is, as we see from the example of Luther, not simply construed as analogous to the socio-political concept of community with its antithesis of community and authority (e.g. in the usual comparison of "council" and "commons") but includes authority and political community, integrating the *membrum* of authority within the *corpus* of the community.[68] This conception (as indeed a large part of the Reformation Movement in the early 1520s) is *not* determined by the political tension between authority and subjects as such, but by the characteristic anticlerical contrast between a protestant movement on the one side, and on the other a hierarchy clinging to the old ways together with those authorities who opposed the Reformation or reacted to it by evading the issue.

2. What has also become clear is that the dynamic of the history of the Reformation did not run one-sidedly from a Reformation determined by the "community" (from below) to one determined by the secular authorities (after 1525). Already at the start there is close

---

[68] Cf. e.g. the letter of the Orlamünde community to Luther, 16th August, 1524: *WA* 15, 343. In the title it states: "Deß Rahts und der gemeyn brieff an Doctor Martinum Lutther" (A letter from the Council and Congregation to Dr. Martin Luther). In the letter itself, when the subject is the church congregation, this differentiation quite naturally disappears as we read: "Hirauß goetliche einigkeyt unnd christliche gemeine zu dem sonnderlichen lob Gottis auffgericht und erbawet werde" (Hence divine unity and Christian community were raised up and uplifted to the special praise of God) (343,33f.). Consequently there is good reason for reservations about Blickle's monolithic understanding of community (as assumed in his thesis of "Communal Reformation") and about his emphatic statement that the social and reforming theological conceptions of community were mirror-images; Blickle: *Gemeindereformation* (as n. 11), p. 203f. Only as long as a co-operative understanding of unity remains effective in the political self-understanding of the inhabitants of a city – as a contrary element to autonomous authority or in combination with authoritarian thinking (cf. n. 49) – can one draw parallels between a strongly co-operatively inspired and inspiring understanding of Christian community in the Reformation and political communalism. In this respect Blickle's approach is very illuminating; cf. my assenting acceptance of Blickle in my book on Zwingli (as n. 36), p. 123.

co-operation between the decisive forces of the Reformation and the
ruling elite. Significantly that trend of the Reformation movement
which emphatically (and in conflict with the secular authorities) emphasized the community element from below – as a Reformation of
the Common Man, as a fully empowered spiritual Christianity of
the simple laity – arose in opposition to authoritarian characteristics
of the Reformation which were already present or were beginning
to appear. Protestant dissidence did not begin only after 1525; it was
already taking shape in the early 1520s against the co-operation of
Reformers with municipal authorities or princes. This was the case
with Karlstadt, who after 1522 stood up against the loyal alliance
of the theological faculty at Wittenberg with the Elector of Saxony,
and it was the case in Zürich, where in 1523 the group around
Conrad Grebel and Felix Manz made their mark against Zwingli's
agreement with the town council. Thomas Müntzer himself originally
assumed authoritarian participation in the task of reforming, then
after 1524 – disappointed with the reaction of the rulers – he adopted
the anti-authoritarian Reformation way. Long before 1525, therefore,
we can clearly discern an authoritarian tendency in the Reformation,
which intensified greatly after 1526.

Several factors "from above" have now been mentioned which
played an important part in the Reformation already before the
Peasants' War. We must now examine how central impulses of the
broad popular reform movement were taken up *within* the secular
authorities' government of the Church, and lived on after 1525/26.
Consequently I am inverting the question to take up the connect-
ing threads from the other side, as it were: To what extent is the
communal movement "from below" still present in later years?

III. *Factors of the Early Reformation Movement within the Later Government of the Church by Secular Authorities*

1. After-effects of the Reformation of the "Common Man" in the Authorities' Governance of the Church

Primary concerns of the broad Reformation movement before 1525
(and in the north much later) were taken over by the authoritarian
Reformation of the municipal councils and princes and converted
into reforming measures and guidelines. Olaf Mörke rightly ques-

tioned whether, on socio-historical grounds, it is right to understand reformation "from below" and reformation "from above" simply as opposing forces; it would be more correct "to judge the urban Reformation as an occurrence within an integrated social structure in which the reformations 'from below' or 'from above' represent simply two sides of the same cause".[69] A "change of political rule in the direction of increased authoritarian domination" should consequently be "examined as to whether the authoritarian components developed into co-operative components as a countermovement or as a positive consequence".[70]

What Mörke cautiously suggests – an authoritarian Reformation which takes up, to positive effect, impulses of the co-operative communal Reformation – is scaled up to a massive assertion by Gunter Zimmermann, who bases his thesis particularly on Nuremberg. The deeply decisive changes after the Nuremberg Religious Disputation on 3rd March 1525, when the council deprived the old clergy of power, remodeled the nature of the Church in the protestant spirit and integrated it into the lay society and government, perhaps making potentially rebellious citizens and peasants aware "that the secular authorities were courageously putting into effect one of their own most urgent concerns – a Church community independent of Rome in which the clergy were allowed no special privileges. In view of this obvious political demonstration citizens and peasants could be so content with the city council in matters relating to Church and religion that to a large extent they could abstain from further rallies, demands and protests. In the case of Nuremberg the introduction of secular governance of the local church prevented the spread of agitation on the part of the common man. On the other hand this shows that this form of Church constitution corresponded

---

[69] Olaf Mörke: *Rat und Bürger in der Reformation. Soziale Gruppen und kirchlicher Wandel in den welfischen Hansestädten Lüneburg, Braunschweig und Göttingen* (Hildesheim, 1983) [= Veröffentlichungen des Instituts für Historische Landesforschung der Universität Göttingen 19], p. 9f.

[70] Ibid., p. 10. It is to be "investigated whether a strengthening of the authorities, of the council as an independent norm-establishing body and not as one which is merely appointed to apply norms, may not also be the result of a communally occasioned widening of its social basis among the citizenry. In other words, whether the council, influenced by the Reformation and perhaps also altered in its personal composition, does not take over the task of independently establishing norms ('authority') precisely as a consequence of the changes brought about by the citizens as a community?"

to the needs of the great majority of the population who were anxious for reform. Consequently it is more meaningful to understand Church rule by those in power locally not as a contraposition to the Peasants' War but as its consistent continuation on the political level."[71]

Even if it was hardly possible that Zimmermann should succeed with such a rough-hewn one-sided argument (which totally ignores the fact that the demands of the peasants and citizenry in 1525/26 contained fundamental social objectives that were *not* taken up by the authorities), the observation deserves to be respected that there was a strong element of continuity and exchange between the reform goals of the common man and the measures carried out in the authorities' Reformation. The co-operative communal Reformation left a positive mark on the authoritarian Reformation. Research on the city reformation has been able to show clearly with a wealth of examples the great extent to which the pressure for reform applied by the common man influenced the course of Church policy taken up by the councils – even in those cities where no citizen's committees were established, no changes made in the council's government, and no loss of magisterial control over the people's Reformation.

In any case a one-sided Reformation "from above" did not correspond to the social structure in the cities, where interdependent relationships demanded a certain degree of co-operative agreement if policies were not to provoke revolt. And it certainly did not correspond to the special climate of the Reformation, where the fronts for or against the late medieval ecclesiastical system ran diagonally through all the social strata – and usually through the council itself. If the councils in their authoritarian Reformation took up the desires and demands of the socially diverse communal Reformation we must not assume automatically that this was an opportunistic reaction caused by fear of the common man, or a tactically necessary accommodation to populist demands: in each case, in varying ways and degrees, such actions were also taken by the authorities because of their own convictions of faith.[72]

---

[71] Gunter Zimmermann: "Die Einführung des landesherrlichen Kirchenregiments", in: *Archiv für Reformationsgeschichte* 76 (1985), pp. 146–168: 167.

[72] Cf. Wolgast (as n. 17), p. 62f. where – with regard to territorial rulers – he cautiously weighs the diverse motives and interests of the authorities. Here one must certainly differentiate very carefully between the Reformation of the 1520s and 1530s and the later Reformation – i.e. between a much more spiritually inspired attitude of the authorities in the early period (when to profess acceptance of

To this extent all interpretations oversimplify if they attempt to understand the reforming measures in the cities and territories one-sidedly, under the rubric of the control and regulation of doctrine, worship, spiritual welfare, education and piety.[73] Understandably, in carrying out the Reformation the authorities were quite happy to take advantage of increased possibilities of exerting influence over the Church. Conversely, however, councilors, nobles and princes themselves were also subject to religious influences, swayed by religious beliefs, confessions and doctrines, particular sermons, theological writings, and sundry ecclesiastical personalities. Consequently the slope of influence did not run one-sidedly from the secular authorities to the Church; it also ran inversely from Church to secular authorities – in different ways and with varying intensity according to each individual case.

In this way, reciprocal connections developed between "above" and "below" and between "worldly" and "spiritual". On the basis of their common faith and common anticlerical attitude to a Church ruled by Pope, bishop, priest and monk and because of a common lay feeling against the rigid ideas of doctrine and moral discipline held by the reforming preachers, there evolved a communication and permeability from above to below and *vice versa*. From this vertical permeability there arose horizontal continuities in the history of the Reformation.

The fact that the reforming activities of the common man – e.g. in the drafting of reform pamphlets – lessened rapidly after 1525[74] is

---

Reformation teaching meant that one exposed oneself in a dangerous way to the laws of the Empire) and a more juridical tendency of the later secular authoritarian rule of the Church. Martin Heckel in the discussion at Tübingen pointed out the necessity of making this differentiation. My observations are restricted to the earlier period of the Reformation.

[73] Cf. again Scribner (as n. 25), who defines the authoritarian dimension of the Reformation – that which he understands as "Erastian Reformation" – as "state control of the church exercised by lay authorities, including control over doctrine and religious cult" (p. 121); cf. p. 128: "control", "regulation", "determination", "coercive sanctions". With regard to the authoritarian Reformation Scribner describes only this one-way movement from above to below. Cf. also above, n. 3.

[74] Cf. Hans-Joachim Köhler: "Erste Schritte zu einem Meinungsprofil der frühen Reformationszeit", in: Volker Press/Dieter Stievermann (eds.): *Martin Luther. Probleme seiner Zeit* (Stuttgart, 1986) [= Spätmittelalter und Frühe Neuzeit 16], pp. 244–281. Köhler, however, at the same time (p. 251f.) emphasizes a certain continuity in the production of pamphlets above and beyond the break of 1525/26: "In the years 1525 and 1526 the production curve drops considerably; but even in the years

therefore not necessarily to be seen as a symptom of resignation or as a sign that the spontaneity from below was crushed and "silenced" by measures from above. In the eyes of the populace it was in any case the duty of the authorities to ensure the reform of the Church. Such expectations were naturally directed at the temporal rulers in view of the patent failure of the proper ecclesiastical authorities. This is quite understandable, given the late medieval trend toward secular authoritarian power within the Church. And the common man really could find at least a partially satisfactory clarification to questions over the propriety of such activity in the way that councils and princes took up populist demands and carried out the Reformation. The large number of pamphlets is characteristic of an open, unresolved, unstable situation that provoked much debate. When the secular authorities relinquished their hesitant, dissimulating reserve, took up a stance and resolutely eliminated the old ecclesiastical system, a public war of words waged in pamphlets was no longer what the hour required. Massive efforts by a city council to re-Catholicize might possibly have immediately provoked a polarization and sparked renewed activity by the common man. At any rate warnings about the mood of the common man such as we meet e.g. in memoranda and suggestions prompted by the Diet of Speyer in 1529 point in this very direction.[75] And the fact that the Augsburg Interim in 1548 brought a renewed outbreak of disagreement and stimulated another pamphlet war[76] also shows how careful we must be in interpreting

1527–1530 it still remains at a level which is twice as high as that of 1518/19 and more than twenty times as high as that before 1518. This result means nothing other than that even after the beginning of the reduction of pamphlet production at the end of the Peasants' War there still remained a quantity of publications which were perfectly adequate to guarantee public accessibility to printed information and appeals calculated to have an effect on the masses. At any rate even in this period every person who could read could each year have a copy of a newly-published pamphlet." "The general public readership called into being by pamphlets (and leaflets) remained even after the canalization of the reforming movement – albeit on a clearly lower level."

[75] Cf. e.g. the warning voice of the Nuremberg preacher, Osiander: "Gutachten für Nürnbergs Verhalten auf dem Speyerer Reichstag von 1529, 22nd März 1529", edited by Gerhard Müller in: *Andreas Osiander d. Ä. Gesamtausgabe*, vol. 3, ed. by G. Müller/Gottfried Seebaß (Gütersloh, 1979), pp. 341–359, Nr. 112: pp. 355,5–356,6.

[76] Köhler (as n. 74), p. 252, cites as an example of "streams of pamphlet journalism" those which are continually produced by "times of spiritual or political unrest": The attempted reform in Cologne, the Schmalcaldic War and the Interim, the Siege of Magdeburg, the Thirty Years War, the Napoleonic Wars, the furor

the relative calm in the southern German cities after 1525/26 simply as an indication of the paralyzing effect of secular authoritarian "management" of the Reformation.

2. *Theological Continuity*

A further aspect, related in particular to the history of theology, is closely connected to that line of continuity evident when the authoritarian Reformation takes up desires of the broader communal Reformation. Overstating slightly, I should like to formulate it thus as a thesis: It is in the authoritarian Reformation carried out by the city councils and princes and codified in their church governance that the theological "Reformation" substance[77] of the early reform movement first becomes really effective. Most of what the original Reformers intended by theologically true doctrine and proclamation, by confession and worship according to the Bible, only attains written form in the late 1520s and 30s, in mature theological works and in doctrinal confessions, in catechisms and Church ordinances, in the practical (if partial) realization of liturgical reform, the integration of the "clergy" into secular society, and in many other transformations in the nature of the Church.

Certainly one cannot say that the years before the Peasants' War were the time of a "wild growth" which ran to seed unrestrained.[78]

---

over Paul's Church in Frankfurt. On the Interim cf. Horst Rabe: *Reich und Glaubensspaltung. Deutschland 1500–1600* (Munich, 1989) [= Neue Deutsche Geschichte 4], p. 278f.: "To this was added a broader resistance among the population for which there are many proofs. A stream of pamphlets such as had not been seen since the reforming movement of the early 1520s was both the expression and means of such resistance; hundreds of satirical and confessional songs against the Interim did the rounds."

[77] On the concept of "reformation" cf. Berndt Hamm: "Was ist reformatorische Rechtfertigungslehre?", in: *Zeitschrift für Theologie und Kirche* 83 (1986), pp. 1–38: 3f. English translation in chapter 6, above (here p. 181f.). I should like, however, to broaden the definition of "reformation" given there: reformation is – in respect of medieval theology, Church and society – that which breaks open the system in the manner in which it goes back to the Bible and which can no longer be explained as an odd position within the breadth of variations in medieval theologies and models of reform.

[78] The concept of "wild growth" (*Wildwuchs*) in a pejorative sense was introduced into research on the history of the Reformation by the Leipzig church historian, Franz Lau – with his eye on the positive contrast of the pruned horticulture of Luther's *pura doctrina*: Franz Lau, Ernst Bizer: *Reformationsgeschichte Deutschlands bis 1555*, 2nd. Edition (Göttingen, 1969) [= Die Kirche in ihrer Geschichte, vol. 3, Lief. K]: Franz Lau: "Reformationsgeschichte bis 1532" (MS completed in 1962),

Bernd Moeller rightly pointed out how strongly before 1525 Luther's theology was adopted and adapted at the grass roots level, and how deeply the central points of his doctrine of justification were understood by many preachers and pamphlet writers.[79] This is also true in the Swiss and Upper German region where, before the dispute over the Lord's Supper, the influences of Luther and Zwingli overlapped, mutually strengthening rather than impeding each other.[80] But on the other hand the impact and reception of Luther was an extremely complex phenomenon.[81] This means among other things: conceptions of reform and socio-ecclesiastical ideals were associated with the reforming impulses of Luther, Zwingli and other Reformers, which were already at work in the late Middle Ages, and which cropped up again in their characteristic form in the early years of the Reformation (1522–1526/27). These either blended with the

---

p. K 32f. and 43. The whole of §2 (p. K 17–43) has the title: "Decay and Wild Growth in the Reformation".

[79] Bernd Moeller: "Was wurde in der Frühzeit der Reformation in den deutschen Städten gepredigt?", in: *Archiv für Reformationsgeschichte* 75 (1984), pp. 176–193; 192f.; idem: "Die Rezeption Luthers in der frühen Reformation", in: *Lutherjahrbuch* 57 (1990), pp. 57–71: 58f. and 69.

[80] Recent examinations of the relationship between the theology of Luther and that of Zwingli show that on central theological points, particularly in the understanding of justification, Zwingli stands far closer to Luther than was previously assumed. Hence it is not surprising that Lutheran and Zwinglian ideas combine harmoniously in the reformation theology of the south German cities. Luther was the dominant authority in the south German free cities just as Zwingli could also make an impact in the territorial reformations. Cf. Martin Brecht: "Zwingli als Schüler Luthers. Zu seiner theologischen Entwicklung 1518–1522", in: *Zeitschrift für Kirchengeschichte* 96 (1985), pp. 301–319; Hamm: *Zwinglis Reformation* (as n. 36), particularly pp. 51–62. At the same time, however, one must acknowledge the great independence of manner by which Zwingli adopted Luther's thought, and the fundamental differences in the theological starting-points of the two reformers (e.g. in Pneumatology and Christology, cf. Hamm: ibid., p. 128f. with reference to Gottfried W. Locher).

[81] This could be developed in a direction critical both of Moeller's thesis of a "Lutheran constriction" during the early period of the Reformation before 1525 (see Moeller's articles cited in n. 79) as well as against Lau's metaphor of "wild growth" (see n. 78). On the multiformity and coherence of the early Reformation as is apparent in the pamphlets within the frame of a dominant reception of Luther cf. Berndt Hamm: "Geistbegabte gegen Geistlose: Typen des pneumatologischen Antiklerikalismus – zur Vielfalt der Luther-Rezeption in der frühen Reformationsbewegung (vor 1525)", in: Peter Dykema/Heiko A. Oberman (eds.): *Anticlericalism in Late Medieval and Early Modern Europe* (Leiden/New York, 1993) [= Studies in Medieval and Reformation Thought 51], pp. 431–437 (= Nr. 11: "'rank growth' nor 'Lutheran constriction'".) Miriam U. Chrisman notes social aspects of a variety of lay pamphlets in the early Reformation: Chrisman: *Conflicting Visions of Reform. German Lay Propaganda Pamphlets* (Atlantic Highlands/New Jersey, 1996).

reformation body of thought, or first found new articulation in the language of the Reformation: humanist ideals of reform, education and morality; slogans about the ineptness of the scholars and the genuineness of the simple, unspoiled, biblical lay piety;[82] mystical, spiritualistic notions of proximity to God and liberation from natural relationships; apocalyptic expectations of the ultimate purging of the godless from the congregation of the faithful; social utopian dreams of a society free of class distinctions and political servitude; idealistic longing for pure communities largely cleansed of sin, practicing sanctity, like islands of purity in a sea of social filth.

In their designs for integrity of life and spirituality, these conceptions of reform – not specific to the Reformation – reveal to a large extent tendencies running counter to particular implications of the Reformation doctrine of justification (including its understanding of sin, Church, and the bondage of the will)[83] and to particular Reformation hermeneutics (relating to the proper relationship to the external biblical Word). It is not "wild growth", because these models of reform were natural outgrowths of medieval trends and aspirations. They do not presuppose any hypertrophic growth; rather, they combined quite clearly with Reformation ideas of an intensified struggle against the hierarchy. But this also means that for the years before and after 1525 the largely *unresolved* situation is characteristic: incomplete conceptions, modifications and consequences of reform, dissociations and dissolutions, a merging and co-operation of potentially contrary factors. New Reformation impulses that threatened to smash the old system were combined – often in one and the same person – with late medieval reform ideals of individual and social cleansing and restoration.[84] Only during the period of the territorial and urban

---

[82] Cf. Heiko A. Oberman: "'*Die Gelehrten die Verkehrten*': Popular Response to Learned Culture in the Renaissance and Reformation", in: Steven E. Ozment (ed.): *Religion and Culture in Renaissance and Reformation* (Kirksville/Missouri, 1989) [= Sixteenth Century Essays and Studies 10], pp. 43–62: on the late medieval background of such slogans in the Dutch *Devotio Moderna*.

[83] This also holds true if we do not too narrowly restrict a conception of "reformation" to the doctrine of justification, nor define it from a uniquely Lutheran understanding but, as is explained in n. 77, take as our starting point the criterion of *what breaks the system* (i.e. the medieval theological system).

[84] Hence in Andreas Bodenstein von Karlstadt and Thomas Müntzer there are proposals for purification derived from late medieval mystic theology that are closely connected with the Reformation theology of penitence and sanctification and with the Reformation renunciation of the Roman Catholic understanding of tradition and office. On the continuity between late medieval mysticism and ideas of how

Reformation is there any polemical or defensive clarification on a
wider level. What was earlier available in terms of Reformation doctrinal substance – e.g. in the sermons and pamphlets mentioned by
Moeller – admittedly in many different tones (but not exclusively
and not without competition)[85] now took shape against individual,
ecclesiological and social ideals of sanctification and transformation
which contradicted the Reformation notion of man and God with
its message of the justification of the sinner as *semper peccator*.[86]

This at any rate is the judgment of the most influential Reformers
from Luther through Zwingli, Melanchthon, Bucer, Brenz and Bugenhagen to Calvin and Bullinger. In their opinion it was only the years
after the Peasants' War that brought the fruits of the reformation of
doctrine, confession and Church. To be sure this assessment of the
Reformation is not the only valid one, but it must be taken seriously.
And it lets us see that we must look upon the years and decades
after the People's Reformation not as a time of dialectical change
and the surrender of original ideals, but as a clarifying continuation
of the initial impulses and – in spite of all the disappointments, in
spite of centralization, constraint, legitimation, formalization, bureaucratization and nationalization – as a gain of volume of the *pura*

---

to live a pious life in the early reformation period cf. Steven E. Ozment: *Mysticism
and Dissent. Religious Ideology and Social Protest in the Sixteenth Century* (New York/London,
1973); cf. also Werner O. Packull: *Mysticism and the Early South German-Austrian Anabaptist
Movement 1525–1531* (Scottdale/Pennsylvania, 1977) [= Studies in Anabaptist and
Mennonite History 19]. In principle we must assume that there were Reformers
and Reformation writers who were active against the Roman Catholic Church and
its authorities on the Reformation principle of Scripture and the Word, but who
did not represent a truly Reformation understanding of justification with its departure from the traditional late medieval Roman Catholic system of doctrine and
piety. If we look at Luther's conflicts with Karlstadt and Müntzer it is obvious that
the clarifications and separations have already started before 1525 – hence in this
aspect, too, there is continuity!

[85] Taking account of the summaries of sermons in Reformation pamphlets which
he has examined Moeller names e.g. the following points of agreement on the theology of justification: "Everywhere, for example, love is described as a fruit, not as
a form of faith; the concept of Christian freedom always has the double sense known
from Luther; everywhere the Law as a way to Salvation is considered as having
been superseded; and the idea that the Law can be fulfilled by Justification is foreign to our texts." Moeller: "Was wurde in der Frühzeit . . .?" (as n. 79), p. 192.

[86] Here one may think of the wide spectrum of antiauthoritarian (spiritualistic,
"consistent", violent and baptist) reformation movements which started in the early
1520s, but also of the later conflicts in the generation after Luther around Osiander's
doctrine of justification, the beginnings of which are already recognizable in the
early period of the Nuremberg Reformer (e.g. in his "Großen Nürnberger Ratschlag"
at the end of 1524 = *Osiander Gesamtausgabe* Nr. 25).

doctrina evangelii and of the *recta administratio sacramentorum*. As a historian one might reject this kind of theological perspective or consider it questionable,[87] but it was an extraordinarily relevant concern during this theological period. It was the way in which the Reformation theologians, authorities and congregations developed their Reformation identity and rejected other ways of life related to late medieval ideals of righteousness and purity.

In this way we can distinguish important lines of continuity which – on the personal, socio-historical and purely theological levels – lead from the beginnings of the Reformation through successive phases of community and social expansion, and of authoritarian reform. In saying this, the significance of the antagonism between forces "from above" and "from below", which even after 1525 was still a factor in the history of the north German Reformation, does not pale. On the contrary! Under aspects that have been necessarily abbreviated here, one cannot stress sharply enough the social tensions that accompanied such Early Modern trends as the formation of oligarchies, the re-imposition of feudalism, the increasing polarization of classes and the estrangement between political authorities and their "subjects" (even in the cities). The strong links between Reformation and socio-political unrest could be a topic unto itself. But it should become clearer that the intensifying social antagonism of the sixteenth century represents only a partial truth while from other angles the so-called people's Reformation and the authorities' Reformation form a continuous flow. The most important reason for this probably lies in the theological dimension of the Reformation,

---

[87] All the same it is interesting that Robert W. Scribner (as n. 25, p. 120 and p. 126f.) wished to use the concept "Reformation" only when it reaches the stage of development in which, under the directive of the authorities ("by an erastian intervention of secular authority"), there is a new formation of the institutional church. In his view the foregoing phase was not yet Reformation but "a reforming or evangelical movement". Without making any judgment Scribner thereby in part took over an assessment held in the Sixteenth Century, while most modern historians tend to see and value the early period of the Reformation as the epitome of Reformation. The highly problematical two-phase schema of "evangelical movement" and "Reformation" (after 1526) can be found already in Wilhelm Diehl: *Evangelische Bewegung und Reformation im Gebiet der heutigen hessen-darmstädtischen Lande* (Darmstadt, 1926); critically opposed to this is Gottfried G. Krodel: "'Evangelische Bewegung' – Luther – Anfänge der lutherischen Landeskirche: Die ersten Jahre der Reformation im Schnittpunkt von Kirchengeschichte und Sozialgeschichte", in: Wolf-Dieter Hauschild, Wilhelm H. Neuser, Christian Peters (eds.): *Luthers Wirkung, Festschrift für Martin Brecht*, pp. 9–45, particularly p. 25, n. 3 (with reference to the criticism by Karl Dienst).

which also impinges upon the generally human element. This was what made it possible for reforming impulses to be effective across the developing social and political fronts.

IV. *The Outlook*

What I have emphasized about the permeability and interconnectedness of the communal Reformation from below and the authoritarian Reformation from above – against erroneous delimitations, the formation of isolating contrasts, and excessively rigid standardization and division into phases – can also be applied to the two types, City Reformation and Princes' (or Territorial) Reformation.

It would be profitable to carry on from the beginning I have made here on the history of the Reformation by qualifying (though not destroying) the construction of types and breaks, and emphasizing (while not making absolute) permeability and interactions by including a third large complex: the co-operation of magisterial Church government and those confessional forces that were *not* guided by the authorities; indeed, that ran contrary to the authorities' action from the late 1520s to the end of the sixteenth century and far beyond. Here I am thinking particularly of the history of the development of church governance, especially within the princely territories, and the attendant conflicts between the representatives of church doctrine, preaching and discipline and secular rulers, about attitudes of resistance and nonconformity on the part of churchmen. The long struggle between State and Church did not come to an end, but entered a new phase.[88]

---

[88] Cf. e.g. the following more recent works which provide examples of a critically resistant attitude on the part of Lutheran ministers, superintendents, court preachers and professors of theology to the secular authorities of the same protestant persuasion in the 16th and 17th centuries: Wolfgang Sommer: "Obrigkeits- und Sozialkritik in lutherischen Regentenpredigten des frühen 17. Jahrhunderts", in: *Daphnis* 10 (1981), pp. 113–140; Peter Friedrich Barton: "Obrigkeitshöriges Luthertum? Eine Anfrage an die Kirchengeschichte", in: *Amt und Gemeinde*, ed. by the Bishop of the Protestant Church, Augsburg Confession, in Austria, 34th Year, Vienna, Feb. 1983, pp. 13–20; Luise Schorn-Schütte: "Prediger an protestantischen Höfen der Frühneuzeit", in: Heinz Schilling/Herman Diederiks (eds.): *Bürgerliche Eliten in der Niederlanden und in Nordwestdeutschland* (Cologne/Vienna, 1985), pp. 275–336; idem: "'Papocaesarismus' der Theologen? Vom Amt des evangelischen Pfarrers in der frühneuzeitlichen Stadtgesellschaft bei Bugenhagen", in: *Archiv für Reformationsgeschichte* 79 (1988), pp. 230–261; Wolfgang Sommer: *Gottesfurcht und Fürstenherrschaft* (Göttingen,

As I see it, the story of this intra-evangelical conflict between Church and secular authority on a wider front begins with the argument about church discipline; in particular, about the possibility of excommunication (exclusion from holy communion and worship) in the south German and Swiss cities at the end of the 1520s and during the '30s and '40s.[89] The dissension over the Augsburg Interim of 1548 constituted a first climax.[90] One might say that the story of such insubordinate attitudes to Protestant rulers is – under changed circumstances – the continuation of the early Reformation resistance to authorities hostile or hypocritical toward the Reformation. Here again we see the element of continuity beyond the break of 1525/26, both in the conflict situations and in the relevant theological points of reference, for the ecclesiastical representatives, the preachers and professors, wished to carry on and show to advantage what from the very beginning was of central importance in the battle against Roman Catholicism. They did not intend to stop half way or allow

---

1988) [= Forschungen zur Kirchen- und Dogmengeschichte 41]; Inge Mager: "'Ich habe dich zum Wächter gesetzt über das Haus Israel'. Zum Amtsverständnis des Braunschweiger Stadtsuperintendenten und Wolfenbüttelschen Kirchenrats Martin Chemnitz", in: *Braunschweigisches Jahrbuch* 69 (1988), pp. 57–69. An overview of the history of criticism directed against the territorial rule of the Church in Lutheranism up to Spener can already be found in Martin Kruse: *Speners Kritik am landesherrlichen Kirchenregiment und ihre Vorgeschichte* (Witten, 1971) [= Arbeiten zur Geschichte des Pietismus 10]. These works correct the widespread cliché of the Lutheran "pathos of obedience" and a "Lutheranism enslaved to the authorities". Admittedly they do not give *eo ipso* only a positive evaluation of the Lutheran attitudes of resistance. Combined with this resistance there could also be elements of a *rabies theologorum*, a tendency toward the sovereignty of the theologians, an excessive awareness of office over against the congregation and fixations of problematical content. Thus Martin Chemnitz in 1578 considered it the duty of his office as pastoral guardian to protest against Duke Julius' pro-Semitic policy in Brunswick-Wolfenbüttel since, as he saw it, "a policy tolerant to the Jews is blasphemy and a betrayal of the Lutheran Confession"; Mager, ibid., pp. 64–66 (quotation from p. 66).

[89] Cf. Walther Köhler: *Zürcher Ehegericht und Genfer Konsistorium*, vol. 1: "Das Zürcher Ehegericht und seine Auswirkung in der deutschen Schweiz zur Zeit Zwinglis"; vol. 2: "Das Ehe- und Sittengericht in den süddeutschen Reichsstädten, dem Herzogtum Württemberg und in Genf" (Leipzig, 1932/42) [= Quellen und Abhandlungen zur schweizerischen Reformationsgeschichte 7/10]. On the dispute about excommunication in Nuremberg in 1531 while the rules for the ordering of the Church were being drawn up cf. Hamm (as n. 28), pp. 718–721; *Andreas Osiander d. Ä. Gesamtausgabe*, vol. 4, ed. by Gerhard Müller/Gottfried Seebaß (Gütersloh, 1981), pp. 344–369, Nr. 167.

[90] On the resistance of the theologians cf. e.g. Wolf-Dieter Hauschild: "Zum Kampf gegen das Augsburger Interim in norddeutschen Hansestädten", in: *Zeitschrift für Kirchengeschichte* 84 (1973), pp. 60–81; Schorn-Schütte: "'Papocaesarismus' der Theologen? . . ." (as n. 88), p. 258f. (with literature).

themselves to be pushed back again into confessionally unclear, equiv-
ocal positions. Connected to this is the tendency on the side of the
Church to oppose the intensified control and discipline exerted by
the secular authorities' governance of the church with counter-control
and counter-discipline exercised under the supervisory and disciplinary
function of the theologians.

In conclusion I should like to stress: I do not want merely to break
down the well-worn lines of differentiation but rather to break down
the customary apportionment of light and shade in the traditional
assessments. The one-sidedness of counter-assessments must also be
amended. It is not true that the City Reformation was particularly
liberal and creative while the Princes' Reformation was wholly judicial,
authoritarian and sterile,[91] nor, *vice versa*, was the urban Reformation
a stronghold of intolerance and bigotry while the liberalizing presence of universities in princely territories made the princes' Reformation
a shelter for the freedom of sciences, preserving them from being
squeezed into the corset of the religious-worldly common good.[92]
The early years of the Reformation before the Peasants' War were
not a time of hypertrophic wild growth which was then pruned back,
under the secular authoritarian rule of the Church, to healthy proportions by the horticultural skills of the theologians and their doctrinal
confessions. Nor is the early phase of the Reformation to be judged
simply as a realization "from below" of genuine communal reform,
the initial ideals of which were lost and betrayed in the years after

---

[91] Cf. above, n. 10: Arthur Geoffrey Dickens on the "second Reformation" of
the princes.

[92] By considering "the" City Reformation together with the *via antiqua* and because
the main perspective of the *bonum commune* is somewhat restricting, Oberman inclined
toward such an inversion of the positive and negative omens. Taking as examples
the city Reformers Blarer and Bucer and their "urban ideology of the *bonum commune*" he tried to show that urban thinking attemptes to tie university education to
the Church to such an extent "that there is no freedom left for secular research".
Hence "the replacement of the 'city Reformation' by the 'princes' Reformation'
introduced anything but sterility": "There was space made for the investigation of
secular empirical knowledge contrary to all superficial feedback to the *bonum commune*, which it desperately needed against the claims to leadership of the self-assured
blossoming theology. . . . Under the short-breathed perspective of the *bonum commune*
any space for science was unthinkable at the moment it was taken over by the
Church." Oberman: *Werden und Wertung der Reformation* (as n. 8), p. 359 and p. 361;
cf. also its context in pp. 329–378. I consider Oberman's contribution to lie in the
fact that he led us out of the dead end of the negative evaluation of the later
princes' Reformation and the positive picture of the early city Reformation. His re-
evaluation needs further critical examination.

the Peasants' War. The anti-authoritarian Reformation, particularly that of the Baptists, was not in the main a degeneration of the Reformation and a surrender of the essence of reformation doctrine, nor was its ecclesiology simply a genuine continuation and conservation of the authentic reforming goals.[93] The reformation movement of the early years was not predominantly antiauthoritarian or anti-feudal, neither was the Reformation of the later period in the thrall of the authorities.[94]

This much is certain: by avoiding a fixation on competing types and phases of the Reformation, we may better glimpse the latitudinal and longitudinal connections – the theological, personal, social, political, institutional continuities and communications conditional upon piety and mentality – which resist reduction to one-sided assessments without thereby sinking everything into relativism.

---

[93] Thus not only the evaluation of the Baptist writing on the history of the Reformation but also of a fair number of social historians; cf. e.g. Scribner (as n. 3), p. 51.

[94] Cf. the literature mentioned in n. 88.

CHAPTER EIGHT

HOW INNOVATIVE WAS THE REFORMATION?[1]

I. *Defining the Question*

My question concerns the character and consequences of the changes
which were brought about by the Reformation of the Church in the
first half of the 16th century. How new was what contemporaries
called the 'new faith', how real the radical change they experienced
subjectively? How great was this change compared to the innovations of the preceding 'Late Middle Ages' or the subsequent 'confessional age' or compared with contemporary changes outside the
church? Was not the 'Reformation transition' to a new age – so
heavily emphasized by confessionally and nationally colored historiography – more a significant thrust within a movement which extended
from the 12th to the 18th centuries – i.e. not a break but the continuation of a movement?

Before I go into these questions in more detail I must make three
preliminary remarks:

1.) 'Innovation' was not the aim of the Protestants in the 16th
century inasmuch as they pointedly did not desire to introduce anything new into the Christian faith. They strove for a *reformatio* in the
sense of a restoration of the original form of the true congregation
of Jesus Christ – and in this respect a renewal of the contemporary
Church: *renovatio*, not *innovatio*! The Church of the Roman papacy
accused them of being too innovative in a fatal way. In fact, the

---

[1] This article is an expanded version of a lecture delivered in September 1999
at the Münster Kolloquium for the 65th birthday of Arnold Angenendt, and in
April 2000 at the conference of the church history section of the Wissenschaftliche
Gesellschaft für Theologie in Brandenburg. I limit myself in the footnotes almost
entirely to source references; for the rest I would refer to a thematically related
article in which I deal with the situating of the Reformation epoch between the
Middle Ages and the Modern Era: "Die Stellung der Reformation im zweiten
christlichen Jahrtausend. Ein Beitrag zum Verständnis von Unwürdigkeit und Würde
des Menschen", in: *Die Würde des Menschen* (Neukirchen – Vluyn, 2000) [= *Jahrbuch
für Biblische Theologie* 15], pp. 181–220. An English translation of this article, with
abbreviated references, appears below as chapter 9.

Protestant appeal to the original biblical norm of Christendom was certainly highly innovative for its time – a strikingly new way of interpreting the old Holy Scripture and asserting it against the authoritative structure of traditional interpretations, rituals and institutions.

2.) This should make clear what I mean when I use the terms 'innovation' and 'innovative'. In the language of modern technology these words imply something distinctly positive in the sense of progress, while in the Middle Ages and in the age of the Reformation novelty was considered the essence of heresy. No such value judgment is intended here; rather, as a historian I wish to use the word "innovation" purely descriptively. I ask: What in the Reformation was 'novel' in the sense of a discovery, an invention, a striking historical change by comparison with the preceding state of affairs? To be more precise: in what follows I am not concerned with the most complete possible phenomenological record of such changes but with the categorical question that can be clarified with the help of various examples: In what way did the Reformation bring about change?

3.) Finally I should like to recall the remarkable non-uniformity of early Protestantism which produced widely differing degrees of change *within* the Reformation. Certain innovations touching the traditional understanding of the Church in its fundamental principles were only propagated by the outsiders of the Reformation, by Baptists and spiritualists – as in the rejection of infant baptism or the use of force by the civil authority in matters of faith. Even the conflict about the Eucharist must be seen in this light. On the question – so central to contemporary devotion centered on Christ's Passion and the Mass – of the real physical presence of Christ's body and blood in the bread and wine, the followers of the Swiss/Upper German movement were, as we know, much more open to innovation than were the Lutherans; and the same can be said of the consistency with which church buildings were cleared of images and the whole service remodeled around the hearing of God's word preached. In what follows, however, I concentrate on aspects of the change which are generally valid for all the main currents of the Reformation.

The questions I posed initially about the scope of Reformation change are old topics of research taking us back to Ernst Troeltsch and Max Weber. But recently, as a result of international research, particularly under the influence of the history of religion, historical anthropology, the history of civilization, mentality and religiosity and gender studies, they have become so explosive that in 1996 Heinz

Schilling could oppose the (still widely maintained) thesis of fundamental change with the sobering counter-thesis: "We have lost the
Reformation!"[2] He means by this that research into the Late Middle
Ages and the era of confessionalization has so convincingly exposed
the long-term qualitative alteration in the centuries and decades
before and after the Reformation that the years of the Reformation
themselves are in danger of being totally swallowed up by this longer
lasting tide of reforming change. This is not what Schilling wants.
He would like to see a model which takes seriously "the spiritual
innovative energy of the reformers" as a "breakthrough" and the
Reformation "as a 'cardinal stage' within a longer 'age of reforms.'"[3]
Schilling's lecture was the introduction to a conference of the *Verein
für Reformationsgeschichte* which was documented in the collection of
papers published in 1998 under the title "Die frühe Reformation in
Deutschland als Umbruch" ("The Early Reformation in Germany
as Radical Change").[4] An examination of the papers and reports
gives us – along with many valuable research results – an insight
into a dilemma: how little this conference succeeded in surmounting the rivalry between the conceptions 'continuous change' and 'revolutionary transition' which have already occupied and wearied us
for decades. I mean surmounting them in the sense of not sticking
fast by these very crude and extremely reductionist categories of
'continuity' *or* 'revolution', or postulating at best a combined model,
'continuity *and* revolution' – something like Schilling has in mind –
but of developing a more subtle historico-hermeneutical apparatus
which would do justice to the variety of historical innovative processes
in the 15th and 16th centuries. Here I am thinking particularly of
those innovative developments which were neither continuous change
nor earth-shaking revolution.

When I say that current research on the Late Middle Ages and

---

[2] Heinz Schilling: "Reformation – Umbruch oder Gipfelpunkt eines Temps des
Réformes?", in: *Die frühe Reformation in Deutschland als Umbruch* (cf. n. 4), pp. 13–24.
In this essay Schilling takes up the theme of an earlier article in which he had
posed the question of the loss of the Reformation: "Die Reformation – ein revo-
lutionärer Umbruch oder Hauptetappe eines langfristigen reformierenden Wandels?",
in: *Konflikt und Reform, Festschrift für Helmut Berding*, ed. Wilfried Speitkamp/Hans-
Peter Ullmann (Göttingen, 1995), pp. 26–40, here 36 and 38f.
[3] Schilling: "Reformation – Umbruch oder Gipfelpunkt" (as n. 2), pp. 27f. and 29.
[4] Stephen E. Buckwalter/Bernd Moeller (eds.): *Die frühe Reformation in Deutschland
als Umbruch*. Wissenschaftliches Symposion des Vereins für Reformationsgeschichte,
1996 (Gütersloh, 1998) [= Schriften des Vereins für Reformationsgeschichte, 199].

the Reformation has become bogged down in all too simplifying categories of interpretation and seeming alternatives, I also have in mind the anthology edited by Bernhard Jussen and Craig Koslofsky and published in 1999 under the title "Kulturelle Reformation. Sinnformationen im Umbruch 1400–1600" ("Cultural Reformation. The Formation of Consciousness in Radical Change 1400–1600").[5] It was the intellectual challenge of this volume and its extremely instructive cultural-historical extension of the understanding of religious changes which provoked me to the subject of this paper – and this because neither the conception of the volume as a whole nor the individual contributions lead out of the dead end of the simple opposition or combination of long-term change and abrupt 'radical transformation'. There is, e.g. a chapter by Susan Karant-Nunn,[6] which represents an out-and-out thesis of radical change in respect of her subject, "Gedanken, Herz und Sinn". Over against the holistic emotional piety of the Late Middle Ages which combined fervent emotionalism with physical and ritual actions, she sets a rigid strategy of purification, promoted by Protestant preachers, which suppressed, indeed despised religious emotions with their corporeality, their rituals and their feminine traits, while at the level of popular piety, particularly in rural areas, traditional patterns of emotional expression often continued uninterrupted. Noticeable in Karant-Nunn's essay is the brusque distinction between 'before' and 'after', between 'religious leaders' and 'ordinary believers'.

If we once set aside the stereotyped simplifications of this view of the Reformation the fundamental problem still remains: how does the revolutionary change with its far-reaching consequences – which Karant-Nunn rightly registers – relate to that longer-term change which e.g. Thomas Lentes in the same volume also detects in central aspects of sentiment, reason and corporeality?[7] All in all it is the

---

[5] Bernhard Jussen/Craig Koslofsky (eds.): *Kulturelle Reformation. Sinnformationen im Umbruch 1400–1600* (Göttingen, 1999) [= Veröffentlichungen des Max-Planck-Instituts für Geschichte, 145].

[6] Susan C. Karant-Nunn: "'Gedanken, Herz und Sinn'. Die Unterdrückung der religiösen Emotionen", in: op. cit., pp. 69–95 (chapter two of the volume).

[7] Thomas Lentes: "'Andacht' und 'Gebärde'. Das religiöse Ausdrucksverhalten", in: op. cit., pp. 29–67 (chapter one of the volume). Lentes shows how the piety of the 14th and 15th centuries was innovative in driving forward long-term processes of internalisation to the point of separation of the inwardness of the soul and the outwardness of the body, whereas in this respect the Reformation is not to be understood as an innovative fresh beginning, but simply as the one-sided continuation of the medieval dynamics.

long-term perspective which predominates in this collection of essays:
that one starts from important historico-cultural changes *before* the
beginning of the Reformation and from there largely relativizes the
events of the Reformation as a revolutionary caesura. Indicative of
this is how, in the editors' introduction, Bernhard Jussen programmatically rejects a characterization of the Reformation as a 'systematic breach' with the medieval Church, theology and piety.[8] Now
my own research, starting out from medieval scholasticism and the
theology of piety, has led me to understand the Reformation of
Luther, Karlstadt, Zwingli and Calvin, as opposed to the many late-
medieval *reformationes*, as a breach in the system or a far-reaching
shift in the matrix of standards and rules in Christendom.[9] On the
other hand, on the basis of this same research it is quite clear to
me that we must also understand the Reformation in the context of
the Late Middle Ages – so to speak as a late medieval event in the
course of a long-term change in the formation of meaning. Consequently I read the whole collection presented in Jussen and Koslofsky's
volume partly with positive approval but partly also with a nagging
wish for fundamental correction. It seemed to me that the time was
now ripe to develop an integrative working model for innovation
which would lead out of the oscillation between continuous change
and rapid transition. I should now like to present a brief preliminary sketch of this panorama.

II. *Four Categories of Reforming Innovation*

First of all I think it proper to distinguish between at least four categories of reforming innovation:

For the *first category* I choose the customary term 'radical change'

---

[8] Bernhard Jussen: "Epochen-Imaginationen: 'Reformation', 'Mittelalter', 'System-
bruch' und einige Relikte des strukturalen Blicks", in: op. cit., pp. 22–27 (section
3 of the introduction to the volume). In this section Jussen discusses two of my
publications: 1.) "Von der spätmittelalterlichen reformatio zur Reformation. Der
Prozeß normativer Zentrierung von Religion und Gesellschaft in Deutschland", in:
Archiv für Reformationsgeschichte 84 (1993), pp. 7–82; 2.) "Einheit und Vielfalt der
Reformation – oder: was die Reformation zur Reformation machte", in: Berndt
Hamm/Bernd Moeller/Dorothea Wendebourg: *Reformationstheorien. Ein kirchenhistorischer
Disput über Einheit und Vielfalt der Reformation* (Göttingen, 1995), pp. 57–127.
[9] Cf. e.g. the publications cited in n. 8 and most recently the article referred to
in n. 1: "Die Stellung der Reformation im zweiten christlichen Jahrtausend."

in the sense of a fundamental change in direction. Something which was previously valid and highly esteemed is discontinued – is indeed condemned – and something new takes its place. Hence the category 'radical change' signifies a radical, decisive transition in the sense of devaluation, demolition, re-evaluation and new beginning. It is characteristic of the Reformation that this process of radical change takes place with amazing speed within a few years, at least on the level of the intellectual spokesmen and propagators – i.e. in sermons, pamphlets, and demonstrative actions. Corresponding measures of institutional change then follow the rapid revaluation of values with greater or lesser consistency.

As an example with eminent religious and historico-cultural implications I would refer to the late classical and medieval understanding of holiness, particularly as explained, following Ludwig Bieler,[10] in the work of Wolfgang Speyer,[11] Peter Brown[12] and Arnold Angenendt:[13] holiness understood not simply as a provision of grace for all true Christians in the scholastic sense of the *gratia infusa*, but above all as an exceptional divine gift bestowed on special people because of their meritorious asceticism. These so-called 'people of God' or 'saints' become thereby bearers of a supernatural *virtus*, a purifying and miracle-working quality of power which draws them into a healing proximity to God – draws the people themselves, but also all those who, seeking protection, confide in them, pray to them, make pilgrimages to their graves and venerate their power-charged relics. It is a well-known fact that in a revolutionary process of desacralization, the Reformation broke with this understanding of holiness as sacredness inherent in a person or object and mediating blessing and salvation. Holiness is reduced to what is simply and commonly Christian and simultaneously given a fundamentally new interpretation. If it is true,

---

[10] Ludwig Bieler: *Theîos anér. Das Bild des "göttlichen Menschen" in Spätantike und Frühchristentum*, 2 vols., (Vienna, 1935/36, repr.: Darmstadt, 1976).

[11] Wolfgang Speyer: "Die Verehrung des Heroen, des göttlichen Menschen und des christlichen Heiligen. Analogien und Kontinuitäten", in: *Heiligenverehrung in Geschichte und Gegenwart*, ed. by Peter Dinzelbacher/Dieter R. Bauer, (Ostfildern, 1990), pp. 48–66.

[12] Peter Brown, "Aufstieg und Funktion des Heiligen in der Spätantike", in: idem: *Die Gesellschaft und das Übernatürliche* (Berlin, 1993), pp. 21–47.

[13] Arnold Angenendt: *Heilige und Reliquien. Die Geschichte ihres Kultes vom frühen Christentum bis zur Gegenwart* (Munich, 1994), pp. 69–88 (ch. 6: Der Gottesmensch); idem: *Geschichte der Religiosität des Mittelalters* (Darmstadt, 1997), pp. 160–166 (ch. 6: Der Gottesmensch).

as Speyer maintains, that the holy person "as the type of the exceptional religious person" is one of the most fundamental elements of
the world of religious imagination,[14] the Reformation represents an
epochal historico-religious transition.

The breach is even more apparent when we consider the direct
connections existing between this change in the understanding of
holiness and the reformers' fundamental criticism of an institutional
and status-related sanctity. Here I am referring to the radical devaluation of the sacral hierarchy from the Pope down to the simple
parish priest, the devastating criticism of papal canon law, the monastic orders, virginity and celibacy, the priestly power of consecration,
the sacrifice of the Mass, confirmation, the last rites, etc. Sacral-institutional holiness becomes the work of the Devil; after 1520 from
being the Vicar of Christ the Pope becomes the Antichrist.

There were also close connections between the medieval understanding of holiness and the idea of the intimate communion of the
faithful: a communion in which the living intercede for the living
and for the unsanctified dead, the sanctified dead for the living,
achieving blessing, winning merit and wiping out punishment. The
Reformation not only puts an end to the concepts of merit, satisfaction,
purgatory and indulgence, but makes a total break with the whole
idea of a communion of fellowship, service and assurance, mediating grace and salvation. Instead it develops other, congregationalist
models of community and communion, restricted to the living. In
all these processes of radical change the new, comprehensive principle
of legitimation and abrogation – *sola scriptura* – plays a central part.

What I have said is enough to indicate briefly what I understand
by 'radical change' in the sense of a rapid, fundamental and permanent
change. It is also clear, however, that there are no such sweeping
innovations which are not already heralded in certain elements of
change in the Late Middle Ages. Craig Koslofsky, for example, has
shown how the Reformation's abolition of the communion of the
living and the dead should be seen in connection with a change in
attitude that led, even before 1500, to the relocation of cemeteries
outside the city walls.[15] Or consider the more or less widespread crit-

---

[14] Speyer: "Verehrung" (as n. 11), pp. 48–50.
[15] Craig Koslofsky: "'Pest' – 'Gift' – 'Ketzerei'. Konkurrierende Konzepte von
Gemeinschaft und die Verlegung der Friedhöfe (Leipzig, 1536)", in: *Kulturelle Reformation*
(as n. 5), pp. 193–208 (chapter six of the volume).

ical comments and opinions voiced against papacy, curia, canon law, clerics, monasteries, the worship of images and relics, pilgrimages, indulgences etc.;[16] even the particularly sacred status of virginity could be relativised.[17] But the fundamental change of direction from the broad cultivation of the Church and its partial relativisation up to total invalidation, desacralization and demonisation only came about through the Reformation. So much for the first category – that of radical change.

I define the *second category* of Reformation as that of 'intensification' or 'acceleration'. This is not a category of transition or change of direction but of a continuous extension: Certain threads of late-medieval innovations and changes that had already achieved considerable significance before the Reformation were carried further by it and at the same time strikingly reinforced and accelerated. Consider, for example, the dynamics by which provincial rulers and city councilors came to control the church, or the burgeoning development of popularizing media such as sermon, tract, pamphlet and congregational singing in the Reformation.[18]

In this connection I think two aspects of a piety which was more cognitive and more closely based on the Bible are particularly worth mentioning: I mean (1) the late medieval path from a sacred, ritualized text which – without being understood – is salutary simply by being spoken, to a text whose meaning should be understood by those who hear and read it in such a way that they feel the appropriate reverence. This is the historico-culturally important long-term prelude to a new connection of external and internal, an internalization of Christianity.[19] Hand in hand with this went a revaluation of religious knowledge, the vernacular mediation of practical theology and the new literacy possessed by lay people, including women, who did not belong to a religious order. This change was carried

---

[16] Cf. e.g. Wilhelm Ernst Winterhager: "Ablaßkritik als Indikator historischen Wandels vor 1517: Ein Beitrag zu Voraussetzungen und Einordnung der Reformation", in: *Archiv für Reformationsgeschichte* 90 (1999), pp. 6–71.

[17] Cf. Bernhard Jussen: "'Jungfrauen' – 'Witwen' – 'Verheiratete'. Das Ende der Konsensformel moralischer Ordnung", in: *Kulturelle Reformation* (as n. 5), pp. 97–127 (chapter three of the volume).

[18] Cf. Berndt Hamm: "Die Reformation als Medienereignis", in: *Glaube und Öffentlichkeit* (Neukirchen-Vluyn, 1996) [= *Jahrbuch für Biblische Theologie*, 11], pp. 137–166.

[19] Cf. *Lentes*: "'Andacht'" (as n. 7), pp. 33–41 (section one: Vom heiligen Text zum Textverstehen).

forward and intensified by the early Reformation, particularly in the close relationship between the external text and its understanding by faith. Now the laity in the Church could and should hear the words of institution of the Lord's Supper loud and clear and in their own language.

Closely connected to this I would point (2) to a late medieval shift in the use and understanding of religious images. In place of the sacred religious symbol whose ability to mediate grace was worshipped as if it had the power of a relic,[20] there comes more strongly to the fore the edifying, commemorative image which encourages feelings of reverence and gives moral instruction – with the tendency to measure the religious value of an image solely by how well it succeeded in shaping a person's innermost being and motivating devout behavior.[21] The Reformation reinforced this dynamic in that it only permitted a religious image – if at all – as a representation of the proclamation of the biblical text: as a medium of an edifying message imparting knowledge of faith and teaching how to act in faith. What is already at hand in the so extensively textual illustrations of the 15th century was brought to perfection by the Reformation: the image becomes the text.

We need only mention a *third category* of innovation very briefly since it is very closely connected with the second. It is the prolonged change or continuing alteration – as seen from the Late Middle Ages – *without* any serious intensification or acceleration. Here, the innovative character of the Reformation is very much weaker: new aspects come on to the scene, significant alterations must be registered – but all within the framework of a long-term, gradual process of change. As an example I refer simply to the manifest intensification of fears of the onslaught and temptations of devilish powers in the Late Middle Ages, particularly following the great plague in the 14th

---

[20] On various views of the salvific materiality and appeal to the senses of images in the late middle ages ("sacramental contemplation", with affirmation or rejection of an *ex opere operato* effectiveness of images) cf. *Bob Scribner*: "Das Visuelle in der Volksfrömmigkeit", in: idem (ed.): *Bilder und Bildersturm im Spätmittelalter und in der frühen Neuzeit* (Wiesbaden, 1990) [= Wolfenbütteler Forschungen, 46], pp. 9–20: here 13–17; for examples of images as 'relics' opening the way to salvation cf. Christoph Geissmar-Brandi/Eleonora Louis (eds.): *Glaube Hoffnung Liebe Tod – Von der Entwicklung religiöser Bildkonzepte*, Exhibition Catalogue, 2nd edn. (Vienna, 1996), pp. 144–147 and 152–155 (Thomas Lentes).

[21] Cf. (also for the following) Lentes: "'Andacht'" (as n. 7), pp. 45–54 (third section: Vom Bildgedächtnis zum Schriftgedächtnis).

century, and the development of a corresponding counter-arsenal. Typical of this is the image which the Augustinian hermit of Erfurt, Johannes von Paltz, imparted to his readers in 1504: Satan, the demons and their human agents, the forerunners of the Antichrist, are storming the citadel of the Church and the Christian faith on all sides with mighty armies to bring about its collapse.[22] It is exactly this idea of the fundamental demonic threat to the true faith which would find further development in the writings of Luther and in the confessional conflicts of the 16th century.[23]

In my view the most important type of innovation is the *fourth category*, which has been given too little attention in research and which I have consequently placed at the end although, if we were to follow a systematic order, it should really follow the first. I am referring to the continuation of a late medieval change in the same direction – as in categories 2 and 3 – but with an additional qualitative leap; i.e. not only intensification or acceleration on the same level but the jump to a new level while yet maintaining the late medieval dynamic. Such leaps without change of direction can be seen above all in the transition from the late medieval theology of piety to the theology of the Reformers.

Thus we find in several theologians between 1450 and 1520 a strong tendency to maximize the gracious bestowal of God's mercy, particularly through Christ's Passion, in such a way that the contribution required from our human side can be reduced to a minimum. The weak sinner can be told something like: If you cannot feel true repentance – i.e. any sincere regret for your sins – then at least feel regret that you cannot feel regret and entrust yourself to the divine mercy, to the eternal merit of Christ's suffering. Hence within the framework of the medieval cultivation of repentance and regret the emotional requirements were scaled down to a minimum of personal remorse.[24] The qualitative leap of the Reformation then lies in the step from that minimum to nothing at all. At the latest by 1518

---

[22] Johannes von Paltz: *Supplementum Coelifodinae*, ed. Berndt Hamm (Berlin – New York, 1983) [= J. v. P., *Werke* 2]. In this handbook for spiritual advisers, Paltz divided the material into five sections representing five armies of Lucifer, each to be combatted with different spiritual artillery.

[23] On the third category of innovation cf. also for example the historical changes in law carefully analyzed by Susan Pohl: "'Ehrlicher Totschlag' – 'Rache' – 'Notwehr'. Zwischen männlichem Ehrencode und dem Primat des Stadtfriedens (Zürich, 1376–1600)", in: *Kulturelle Reformation* (as n. 5), pp. 239–283 (chapter eight of the volume).

[24] On this program of emotional minimalisation (e.g. in the two Erfurt theology

Luther came to the conviction: forgiveness of sins does not depend at all on the repentant pangs of the sinner's heart, but solely on God's mercy and on the faith which allows itself to be given that mercy.[25] When compared with the late medieval shifts to a Christocentric theology of mercy, Luther's new understanding of justification appears an almost logically necessary implication, and yet is a contingent qualitative leap. The innovation consists above all in the fact that Luther takes absolutely no account of the medieval question of sufficient repentance – i.e. of the question: what quality and quantity of repentance, confession, satisfaction or acquisition of indulgences is necessary and sufficient to wipe out the guilt of sin and its eternal and temporal punishment? For Luther this question is superfluous because he makes admission to salvation completely independent of the conditions of an emotional and operational capacity to repent.[26] That is his discovery of Christian freedom.

As significant as are this and other innovations in the area of the Reformers' understanding of justification – *sola gratia*, *sola misericordia*, *solus Christus* and *sola fide* – it is clear here too that a late medieval concentration on the wealth of grace in Christ's Passion, on mercy,

---

professors of the Augustinian order, Johannes von Dorsten, who died in 1481, and Johannes von Paltz, who died in 1511) cf. Berndt Hamm, "Wollen und Nicht-Können in der spätmittelalterlichen Bußseelsorge", in: Berndt Hamm and Thomas Lentes (eds.), *Spätmittelalterliche Frömmigkeit zwischen Ideal und Praxis* (Tübingen, 2001), pp. 111–146 [= Spätmittelalter und Reformation. Neue Reihe, 15]; English translation in chapter 3, above.

[25] Cf. especially Martin Luther's theses (probably drawn up in the early summer of 1518): 'Pro veritate inquirenda et timoratis conscientiis consolandis conclusiones', *WA* 1, (629) 630–633, e.g. thesis 18 (631, 23f.): 'Super contritionem edificantes remissionem super arenam, id est super opus hominis, fidem dei edificant' and theses 8 and 9 (631, 3–6): 'Remissio culpe non innititur contritioni peccatoris, nec officio aut potestati sacerdotis, innititur potius fidei, que est in verbum Christi dicentis: Quodcunque solveris etc. [Matt. 16, 19].' See on this the interpretation by Oswald Bayer, *Promissio: Geschichte der reformatorischen Wende in Luthers Theologie* (Göttingen, 1971) [= Forschungen zur Kirchen- und Dogmengeschichte 24] pp. 164–202, especially 182–202.

[26] It is particularly remarkable how intensively Luther relates the faith of the Christian to love for God and life-long penitence, and yet vigorously separates the justifying power of faith completely from love and penitence and bases it solely on the promise of the gospel 'extra nos'. On the combination of faith and love to God see for instance Luther: "Von den guten Werken" (1520), *Martin Luther Studienausgabe*, ed. Hans-Ulrich Delius, vol. 2 (Berlin [DDR], 1982), p. 44, 8–10 (on the Testament of the Last Supper): 'Wan nu disser glaub recht gehet, so musz das hertz vom dem testament frolich werden und in gottis liebe erwarmen und tzurschmeltzen.' On the interpretation cf. Berndt Hamm, "Von der Gottesliebe des Mittelalters zum Glauben Luthers. Ein Beitrag zur Bußgeschichte", in: *Lutherjahrbuch* 65 (1998), pp. 19–44, here 35–44; English translation in chapter 4, above; here pp. 142–152.

exoneration, consolation and trust, is being taken up and carried forward.[27] This conjunction of continuity and qualitative leap is characteristic of many areas and facets of the Reformation change.

Thus far my synopsis of four categories of Reformation innovations which I have introduced to overcome the log-jamming alternatives of long-term change and abrupt transition. They are no more than theoretical working models. In particular I would emphasize how fluid are the borders between the categories, and how problematic it can be to assign certain phenomena to only one category. We can only see what was innovative in the Reformation in the correct proportions if we do not underrate two different factors: on the one hand the amount of change which took place outside the religio-ecclesiastical sphere *without* any innovative impetus from the Reformation; and on the other how much in the realms of faith and Church was *not* changed by the Reformation.

Two examples can illustrate this – in many respects remarkable – conservatism of the Reformation: (1) where the Reformation was able to exert influence on the religious policy of the authorities it also pleaded for a public Christian prosecution of religious deviants and Jews. It was the leading theologians who maintained the principle that there should be only one public form of belief, the true form of the Gospel, in one territory or one city, and that its monopoly must be maintained, by force if need be. (2) In spite of the doctrine of the priesthood of all believers, those same theologians continued to exclude women from the ecclesiastical office of preaching the Word and dispensing the Sacraments, indeed – in contrast to the medieval church – from any special professional Christian status. The traditional opinion that woman by nature has an imperfect disposition, and by the will of God the Creator is destined to be subordinate to man even in the Christian community, was continued without a break in the Reformation even if it did bring radical change in the view of the ideal lifestyle of a pious woman.[28] Religious change and traditional conservatism lie directly alongside each other.

---

[27] Cf. Berndt Hamm: "Normative Zentrierung im 15. und 16. Jahrhundert. Beobachtungen zur Religiosität, Theologie und Ikonologie", in: *Zeitschrift für historische Forschung* 26 (1999), pp. 163–202, here 191–202; English translation in chapter 1, above, here pp. 32–46.

[28] Cf. Petra Seegets: "Professionelles Christentum und allgemeines Priestertum – Überlegungen zum reformatorischen Frauenbild", in: Heidemarie Wüst/Jutta Jahn (eds.), *Frauen der Reformation* (Wittenberg, 1999) [= Tagungstexte der Evang. Akademie Sachsen, 5], pp. 167–180.

III. *The Double Integrative Model: Long-term Change Integrated in Transition and Transition Integrated in Long-term Change*

The intensity and range of innovative power one attributes to the Reformation in the cultural context of 16th century society as a whole is always dependent on the subjective standpoint and academic perspective of the particular observer. The same is true about the answer to the question whether the Reformation marks the beginning of a new age. A historian engaged in research on the history of nutrition or the history of the natural sciences will give an answer different from that of one who is researching questions of confessionalization. Certainly anyone who takes account of how massively the confessionalization of the 16th and 17th centuries can be traced back to the novel confessional character of the Reformation and the ecclesiastical changes it brought about, up to and including the break with the Church of Rome, and anyone who also sees what confessionalization meant for the culture of Europe in general, will understand the Reformation as an epochal caesura. But in the end the answer to the question always depends on how much weight is given to the elements religion, church, confession, theology and piety in the network of factors in the 16th century.

Even if we agree to give great weight to these factors we can still have very divided views about the character of the Reformation as an innovative caesura. I have put forward the working model of a fourfold innovation, but the question remains open as to the mutual relationship of the four categories. When we compare the Reformation with the Later Middle Ages, do the aspects of continuation and reinforcement generally outweigh those of qualitative leap and radical change – or is the opposite true? I should like to conclude by giving some thought to this narrower definition of my model. I cannot entirely resist the tendency to synthesize the perspectives, although it would certainly be a virtue to keep the different aspects in tension with no further attempt at a combining construction.

First I should like to emphasize how massively the character of an aspect of continuity or change alters if one takes into consideration its late medieval and Reformation context. In the second category – that of continuation as reinforcement – I mentioned the example of religious images: how the displacement from sacred religious symbol to didactic picture is continued in the Reformation.[29] At the

---

[29] Cf. p. 262 above and n. 20 and 21.

same time this extends and drives forward a particular tradition of medieval image-critique. Admittedly in this case reinforcement means that the Reformation picks up only one particular – internalizing and critical – thread of the late medieval relationship to images. While for many 15th century theologians, priests, members of orders and laypeople, religious images retained their cultic significance as mediators of grace, worthy of veneration, this visual and tangible sacrality is literally shattered and eliminated by the followers of the Reformation – not only by the Swiss and Upper Germans but also in principle by the Lutherans. They too expunge the whole broad horizon of veneration relating to the effective sacrality of images and the saving power of their contemplation. But the destruction and diminution also applies to the images which mediate a didactic message: The new yardstick of commensurability with Holy Scripture admits only a thematically purified selection. Finally, the Reformation critique of images also bears upon the place given in late medieval piety to charitable donations as meritorious works of satisfaction.

Thus the innovation appropriated by the Reformation from the late Middle Ages turns into the setting for a radical break with images, i.e. with particular, very dominant characteristics of their iconic piety. One could even say: the continuously extended transformation from sacred image to didactic and proclamatory illustration becomes through the Reformation's one-sided reduction the carrier of the radical change. Because of the way it is concentrated and its function determined, continuity becomes an instrument of fundamental, rapid change.

The Reformation's engagement with religious images can serve as a paradigm for the relationship of the Reformation innovations to the religiosity of the 14th and 15th centuries. The innovation takes place to a large extent simply in that certain threads of the late medieval development are taken up while others are not continued but discarded. Thereby, however, the stimuli which are taken up acquire a different character in a changed framework. Hence to a very large extent innovation occurs as selection.

I mentioned as an example that aspect of the late medieval theology of piety which in its view of the human way to salvation put the emphasis totally on the inviting, provenient and exonerating mercy of God and on the inadequacy of the person in need.[30] But as we all know there was also the other side which could prominently

---

[30] Cf. p. 263f. above.

push to the forefront in sermons and catechetical literature, in the treatment of pastoral questions in confessional books and in the religious practice of the faithful: The appeal to a person's spiritual capacities and ability to achieve merit; the emphasis on the strictly judging, precisely weighing, rewarding and punishing righteousness of God; a devotion within the coordinates of gift and gift in return, *do ut des*, counting and calculating. The theologians of the Reformation take up, in an abbreviated form, only the '*sola gratia* thread' of the Middle Ages, the Early Church Fathers and the New Testament, and with that they simultaneously transform it into a qualitative leap. This leap, however, is directly connected with all that they do not accept in that they delete the whole religious complex of performance and merit. The result is that grace, God's mercy, Christ's passion and human humility acquire a substantially different function in a completely changed context. Thus the qualitative leap in the understanding of justification – i.e. the innovative continuation of a particular medieval tradition – has at the same time the character of an abrupt break with other features of medieval theology and practice of devotion.

A complementary variety and tension-laden polarity are, by and large, typical of the religiosity of the Late Middle Ages. The two faces are frequently combined in the theology and devotion of one and the same person – as e.g. when the Strasbourg Cathedral preacher, Johannes Geiler von Kaysersberg, emphasizes either God's gift of grace or the severe logic of retaliation according to the occasion and target group.[31] Frequently too a thoroughly spiritualized devotion which is directed at the recollection, feeling, thinking and desire of the soul is combined with aspects of a corporeal piety which repeats and multiplies external performances in stereotyped fashion.[32]

---

[31] Cf. Berndt Hamm: "Between Severity and Mercy. Three Models of Pre-Reformation Urban Reform Preaching: Savonarola – Staupitz – Geiler", in: *Continuity and Change: The Harvest of Late Medieval and Reformation History. Festschrift for Heiko A. Oberman*, ed. by Robert J. Bast/Andrew Colin Gow (Leiden, 2000), pp. 321–358: here 344–356 (on Geiler); English translation in chapter 2, above, here pp. 73–86.

[32] Cf. e.g. the exercise of bodily meditation leading to spiritual contemplation of the Passion as exemplified by Heinrich Seuse in his 'Vita' (e.g. chapter 13; Heinrich Seuse, *Deutsche Schriften*, ed. Karl Bihlmeyer (Stuttgart, 1907), pp. 34–37. 'Outward' and 'inward' are often combined in late medieval understanding of the Passion in the following way: in Jesus Christ the path leads from the inner suffering of Gethsemane, with the subordinating of his will to the Father's, to the outward

The affective and cognitive spiritualization then has a bodily and ritual external dimension which leads many historians of piety, particularly on the Protestant side, to juxtapose this 'merely outward' to 'true' inwardness. But it is just as characteristic of the 15th century that the poles are not integrated in *one* person or *one* group but – becoming one-sided – drift apart and stand on opposite sides: e.g. extreme reification of the sacred and mystically rarified spirituality; strict Augustinian thinking on grace and predestination and a crass mentality of religious acquisition of merit; a terrifying sermon on God's severity and a comforting sermon on the divine mercy; intensive encouragement of a biblically informed Christian laity and extreme aversion to translations of the Bible and to laypeople reading the Bible; admiration for Rome and criticism of Rome; missionary promotion of the Papal Jubilee campaigns and their uncompromising rejection. But even in this kind of polarization and contrast the late medieval Church is characterized by a balance of differences or at least – if that is putting it too harmoniously – by a variety of horizontal juxtapositions and vertical layering. The innovatory thrust of the Reformation consists above all in the fact that it breaks with the tensions and contradictions in the pluralism of the medieval Church. It carries forward certain long-term processes of change, including certain sources of long-term tension,[33] but only in

---

suffering of Golgotha (in the bleeding of his wounded side his saving love issues forth visibly and sacramentally). In the contemplation of his followers, by contrast, the path leads from Jesus' physical suffering at Golgotha, i.e. from the sympathetic realisation of Golgotha by imitation, to the inner opening and wounding of the heart through love, repentance and willingness to suffer, so that the followers progress from Golgotha to their personal Gethsemane. Seuse describes this inner experience of Gethsemane, which then immediately expresses itself outwardly in prostration and loud calling upon God, in chapter 20 of his 'Vita' (in Bihlmeyer's edition: 57, 25–58, 2).

[33] Think for example of the late medieval tension between a powerfully spiritual and mystical spirituality and a religiosity which was totally oriented towards the institutional mediation of salvation; or of the tension between the theological culture of learning and the slogans about the foolishness of the learned which run on from the late middle ages into the 16th century and then take on a radicalised form in the Reformation. On this second tension see Carlos Gilly: "Das Sprichwort 'Die Gelehrten die Verkehrten' oder der Verrat der Intellektuellen im Zeitalter der Glaubensspaltung", in: *Forme e destinazione del messaggio religioso. Aspetti della propaganda religiosa nel cinquecento*, ed. by Antonio Rotondò (Florence, 1991), [Studi e testi per la storia religiosa del cinquecento . . .] pp. 229–375; Heiko A. Oberman: "Die Gelehrten die Verkehrten: Popular Response to Learned Culture in the Renaissance and Reformation", in: Stephen E. Ozment (ed.): *Religion and Culture in the Renaissance*

such a way that it abandons a wealth of medieval polarities in favor of a new type of concentration on Bible and Gospel.[34] Every kind of religious continuity is consequently directly surrounded and pervaded by aspects of radical change and qualitative leap.

Out of these Reformation processes of selection, diminution and transformation there arises overall a fundamentally changed religious framework. Many aspects remain the same; but the whole with its mixture of old and new is itself new. That is why it caused the division of western Christianity and could no longer be assimilated into the astonishing plurality of the old Church. Even Johannes von Staupitz – perhaps the most innovative late medieval theologian immediately preceding Luther – who like no other with his radical theology of mercy led up to the Reformation and beyond it,[35] could not find a home in the Reformation. Its break with the religious orders and the hierarchical institution of the papacy remained incomprehensible to him. He remained an outsider in the new religious constellation with its fundamentally changed understanding of holiness and unholiness.

If we look at the total ecclesiastical and religious structure as it was changed by the Reformation we can definitely speak of a 'break in the system' insofar as there was a kind of religious and ecclesiastical system in the Late Middle Ages – i.e. a framework ordering and legitimating plurality, polarity and gradual layerings, containing complementary juxtaposition, superordination and conflict. In the Introduction to the collection of essays, 'Kulturelle Reformation', mentioned above, Bernhard Jussen rightly opposes a harmonizing concept of the system in the sense of a rational, consistent coordination.[36] But he himself speaks of "dominant 'formations of meaning'

---

and Reformation (Kirksville, 1989) [= Sixteenth Century Essays and Studies, 10], pp. 43–62.

[34] It is admittedly characteristic of the Reformation understanding of the central normativity of the biblical Word of God that it is interpreted in various dimensions – by Luther for instance in view of such polar tensions as those between Law and Gospel; the twofold use of the Law; Faith and Love; the Kingdom of Christ and the Kingdom of the World; Christian identity and innerworldly responsibility; *deus absconditus* and *deus revelatus*. The break with the later medieval plurality and polarity thus had the effect of unleashing the very different internal theological differentiations of the Reformation.

[35] Cf. Berndt Hamm: "Staupitz, Johann[es] von (ca. 1468–1524)", in: *Theologische Realenzyklopädie*, vol. 32 (2000), pp. 119–127 (with bibliography).

[36] Cf. above n. 8.

and systems of signs" of a culture.[37] Taking this up we could say: in the Reformation there arose a new formation of meaning for theology, piety and the Church with a new structure of signs, legitimations and norms, and that precisely in the *way* the long-term processes of change from the 14th and 15th centuries were incorporated.

The question remains: what is integrated into what? It appears as if in the end I would interpret the innovation of the Reformation principally as a radical break and leap since I see the elements of continuity inserted into a total constellation that is completely changed. This is indeed the case, but at the same time I insist on the possibility and obligation to make the converse integration: nothing speaks against seeing the epochal radical break of the Reformation integrated into the long-term continuities of the change in the centuries-long persisting processes of internalization, rationalization, individualization, laicization, education, disciplining, normative centralization, 'disenchantment' of the world etc. Indeed, much speaks for it. Why should the 'Age' of the Reformation not be understood along with the Late Middle Ages as a stage in a larger era of cultural, institutional, intellectual and religious history? It is merely a matter of one's point of view! But the change in viewpoint is necessary to free the Reformation from a grim epochal isolation and overloading as the "pivot and turning point of the whole Modern Age",[38] – to say nothing of a glorifying mythology. In recent times international research has furnished us with sufficient convincing examples of a long-term perspective which integrates and relativizes the Reformation in this way. I would mention only the recent American "Handbook of European History" which programmatically deals with the period of time 1400–1600 – Late Middle Ages, Renaissance and Reformation – as a continuum.[39] This approach in no way detracts from the

---

[37] Bernhard Jussen: "Der Blick auf die Sinnformationen", in: *Kulturelle Reformation* (as n. 5), pp. 13–17 (section two of the introduction to the volume, quote on p. 14). The term 'Sinnformation(en)' was adopted by the editors of the volume from Jan Assmann, *Ägypten. Eine Sinngeschichte* (Munich-Vienna, 1996).

[38] Cf. the opinion of *Heide Wunder* in the report of the conference discussion: *Die frühe Reformation in Deutschland als Umbruch* (as n. 4), p. 488.

[39] Thomas A. Brady Jr./Heiko A. Oberman/James D. Tracy (eds.): *Handbook of European History, 1400–1600: Late Middle Ages, Renaissance, and Reformation*, 2 vols. (Leiden, 1994 and 1995).

fascination of the contingent, epochal and tremendously diversified event of the 'Reformation'.

I therefore propose a twofold integrative model of innovation: factors of long-term change are integrated into a total Reformation constellation of abrupt transition, which in its turn is integrated into other processes of long-term change.

CHAPTER NINE

THE PLACE OF THE REFORMATION IN THE SECOND CHRISTIAN MILLENNIUM

I. *The Effects of the Reformation and the Question of its Relevance*[1]

Almost everything about the Reformation is the subject of controversy. Were Martin Luther's famous '95 Theses' really nailed to the doors of the castle church in Wittenberg or is this a fiction invented by a later generation who wanted to see in Luther not merely the Professor who takes up his pen but the Reformer who takes action? Does the Reformation only start after 31st October 1517 in the course of the dispute over indulgences or does it already appear in Luther's early lectures between 1513 and 1516 as a radical theological revolution which then dragged all areas of the Church into the maelstrom of change? There is certainly no dispute about the fact that this change in the middle of the second Christian millennium led to the confessional split in western Christendom – to the shattering of the universal Catholic Church of the West, which had already separated from the Byzantine Church of the East in 1054 at the beginning of the millennium. The Reformation, therefore, doubtless had epoch-making consequences in that it set up confessions, mutually excluding their religious opponents, fostering the confessionalization of Europe and the missionary fields beyond it. 'Confessionalization' labels this process, which unfolded over centuries, particularly the 16th and 17th, involving the drifting apart and parallel development not simply of differing church structures and forms of worship but also of different everyday mores and mentality very largely colored by the respective confession. The majority

---

[1] The footnotes have been kept as brief as possible and chiefly supply the necessary evidence from the sources. Fuller references to the literature are to be found in the extended version of this article entitled: "Die Stellung der Reformation im zweiten christlichen Jahrtausend. Ein Beitrag zum Verständnis von Unwürdigkeit und Würde des Menschen", in: *Die Würde des Menschen* (Neukirchen-Vluyn, 2000) [= *Jahrbuch für biblische Theologie* 15], pp. 181–220. An English translation of this article, with abbreviated references appears below as chapter 9.

of Roman Catholics think and feel, observe and perceive, read and
write, eat and make love, work, keep house and use their political
vote differently from most Protestants. But it should not be overlooked
that the deep divisions within the Evangelical camp also begin in
the third decade of the 16th century – the split between the Lutheran
and Reformed (Zwinglian or Calvinist) confessional types and – even
more radical and aggressive – the separating-out of uncompromising Reformation churches strongly critical of secular authority and
predominantly pacifist.

The consequences of this schism in the Church and the resulting
religious diversification, neither of which were intended by the Reformers but were in fact brought about by their Reformation, can
still be observed in the Holy Year 2000 proclaimed by the Pope.
But now, as a result of modern secularization, these have become
more and more faded, pushed to the periphery of our culture and
considerably toned down by the ecumenical movement of the 20th
century. The 'Common Declaration on the Doctrine of Justification'
which was signed in 1999, and the protest of many German university teachers of theology against the Augsburg Agreement[2] each
in their own way witness to this social marginalization of the confessions. The Declaration largely moves in categories of thought and
theological formulae from the 16th century. The vast majority of
our contemporaries, even the loyal churchgoers among them, cannot see the existential connection between this level of discussion
and their own hopes and fears or ecumenical practice. Is this an
indication that at the end of the second Christian millennium the
historical effects of the Reformation are fading from sight? Have its
old revolutionary energies become exhausted so that today we have
before our eyes only their confessional and cultural relics, the fossilized remains of an extinct volcano?

---

[2] The 'Gemeinsame Erklärung zur Rechtfertigungslehre' and the 'Gemeinsame
offizielle Feststellung' of the Lutheran World Alliance and the Roman Catholic
Church of June 11, 1999 with 'Anhang (Appendix)' are published in: *Texte aus der
VELKD* 87, June 1999, pp. 1–11 and 30–33; the ceremony celebrating the 'Gemeinsame Erklärung zur Rechtfertigungslehre' is documented in: *Texte aus der VELKD*
97, MARCH 2000. The 35 statements of Protestant university teachers "Wider den
Augsburger Rechtfertigungsvertrag" are published in: epd-Dokumentation Nr. 43/99
of 11th October 1999: Streit um Texte zur Rechtfertigungslehre.

II. *The Reformation as a Breach in the System*

As a historian I believe that we can only approach this topical question in a meaningful way if we come to an understanding on the kind of impulses for change which existed at the time of the Reformation – i.e. in what way the Reformation with all its multiformity and diversity was innovative. 'Innovation' was not the goal of the 16th-century Protestants in that they emphatically did not desire to introduce something new into the Christian faith. Indeed, they strove for a *re-formatio* of the original, true community of Jesus Christ, while they accused the Church of the Roman Papacy of having been too innovative in a disastrous way. Yet the Protestant appeal to the original biblical norm of Christendom was in fact highly innovative in its time, an electrifying new way of interpreting the old Scriptures and directing them against traditional interpretations. This other version of the Gospel was so novel and unusual that it is possible to define the Reformation as a fundamental breach in the system – i.e. as a radical break with the medieval system of Church, theology and piety. Here I am not using the word 'system' in the strict philosophical sense of a rational, consistent conformity but in the sense of a structure of rules and authorization, whose pluriformity included tensions, in part even contradictions. In contrast to this kind of late medieval religious system the Reformation, beginning with Luther's first lectures, made a fundamental break in the pattern of legitimization by invalidating the bases of the previous understanding of divine right, ecclesiastical authority and human dignity – indeed of the whole previous definition of the relationship of God and the world.

III. *The Medieval Catholic Synthesis of Divine and Earthly*

Characteristic of medieval piety was the differentiating – sometimes sharply polarizing – contrast between the sacred/spiritual and profane/worldly spheres, between the temporal and the eternal, nature and grace, divine holiness and the sinfulness of a fallen world. But at the same time it is striking how intensely the two poles of God and the world are related to one another, even fused together. Because the divine mediation of grace is seen as descending and man's participation as ascending in various ways and in different degrees, the divine and human spheres become intermingled in graduated steps and there arises a spiritual-worldly structure of different degrees of holiness. God as Creator has endowed mankind with the faculties of knowledge and will which are the initial conditions for moral progress towards the goal of eternal life. Into those who have fallen through sin God infuses the healing and sanctifying grace which enables them to act freely according to their anthropological destiny and moral worth. In the form of the ecclesiastical hierarchy from the Pope down to the simple parish priest and the nun God supplies for the needy an institutionalized holiness, the sacrality of the priesthood, the sacraments and the religious orders, which in highly differentiated and graded ways guarantee the presence of God, the working of his Holy Spirit and the influence of the operations of divine grace.

But that is not all. There is also the holiness of the exceptionally religious – holiness not merely in the sense of the provision of grace given to all true Christians but also understood as an extraordinary gift from God. One becomes equipped to receive this gift by particularly meritorious achievements, specifically by ascetic living and above all by untiring prayer. These so-called 'people of God' or 'saints' become thereby bearers of a divine energy, a supernatural 'virtue' which dwells within them as a purifying, miraculous power making them capable of even greater merits and drawing them into a protective, salvific proximity to God. With their exceptional holiness they are consequently able to assist all those who turn to them for help, pray to them, make pilgrimage to their graves and venerate their powerful relics.

The example of saints' graves and relics shows how, in the course of the medieval fusion of divine and earthly elements, personal and institutional holiness came to include particular places, times, objects and actions and raised them above the profane. The faithful could experience them as sacred spheres, substances and events; the sacral space of the altar with the immured relics of the holy person, the periods of fasting, the saints' feast-days, the consecrated hosts, sacramental forms, images, candles, rosaries, liturgical instruments and vestments, the processions, pilgrimages and ordinances of sanctity. Seen in terms of religious history these are forms of what is in part a very primeval, archaic piety which have survived from late antiquity and the early Middle Ages to the present day and which were very much alive in the period immediately prior to the Reformation. In an era of panic-stricken fears of the hereafter and a frantic search for reliable guarantees of salvation, late medieval piety attempted to bring the remote, strict, judging God into an accessible, attainable proximity, rich in grace and mercy. Hence the insistence on a holiness immanent in earthly things which becomes available and can be experienced, even quantified, counted and measured in people and institutions, places, times, objects and good works. Hence also the intensified concentration of piety upon the Passion as a possibility of seeing God in the sufferings of the world, touching him, receiving him in the form of the consecrated wafer and emulating him till one reached perfection. And hence also the cult of the Virgin Mary as the veneration of the purest earthly vessel of heavenly grace and the most compassionate, most effective earthly advocate before the heavenly tribunal. Mary is the ideal figure of the person who is not God but is yet filled with the divine, the embodiment of the catholic-ecclesiastical synthesis of earthly humility and heavenly majesty.

Renaissance humanism in the 14th–16th centuries, with all its variety, was much closer to the conventional ecclesiastical piety, and especially to the scholastic doctrinal tradition, than older research was prepared to admit, even when, as in the Florentine Academy, copious use was made of sources from pagan antiquity. The synthesis of *humanum* and *divinum* in the fusion of nature and grace runs in different varieties throughout Humanism, and connected with it the idea of humanity possessed of divine dignity because the image of God in it has never been destroyed. The modern view of human dignity as something that cannot be lost or encroached upon has its roots in the doctrine of creation, in the scholastic conception of natural law and in the religious anthropology of a humanism which revered the creation. The Reformation's evaluation of humanity on the other hand was not the godparent of this universal placing of increased value on natural human existence – of which we must say more. If we recognize the graduated integration of the divine and human spheres as characteristic of the Roman Catholic devotion of the Middle Ages, including humanism, we must also mention – at least in passing – the political religiosity it involved, particularly the recognition of crowned and anointed Christian rulers not only as patrons of the Church but also as consecrated sacred figures. Thus the Emperor Charles V still understood and wished to assert his universal dignity in the Holy Roman Empire as the worldly spiritual head of Christendom.

IV. *The Reformation as Desacralization of the World and Humanity*

With his universal temporal and religious claims Charles V encountered opposition on principle from representatives of the free cities – e.g. the prominent council clerk of Nuremberg, Lazarus Spengler – who endorsed Martin Luther's reform of the Church but in all else wished the citizens to remain loyal subjects of the Emperor. On December 12th 1524 a group of evangelical free cities under Spengler's leadership wrote a letter to the Emperor in Spain.[3] In this they presented him with the following distinction corresponding to Luther's doctrine of the two kingdoms: in temporal matters – "soviel unser leib und gut belangt" (as far as our persons and property are concerned) – they wish to obey the Emperor and continue to be loyal to him as is the tradition of the free cities of the Empire; but where it is a matter of the word of God, the "hail unser seelen" (salvation of our souls) and their consciences, the municipal authorities intend to maintain the Reformation conviction, even against the Emperor, and will resist his orders. What can be seen in this letter and in the subsequent religious policy of the evangelical free cities is a kind of desacralization of the Emperor's office, and to this extent a break with a particular idea of sacred-temporal unity. We should not draw any false conclusions from this for even in the Protestant cities and territories political power and earthly prosperity continued to be interpreted as a matter of course in religious categories. Indeed it is a well known fact that by destroying the traditional ecclesiastical hierarchy, the Reformation led to an even more intensive fusion of religion and politics, of civil authority, control of the church and confessionalization. And yet the letter sent by the free cities, with its disentangling of earthly obedience in temporal matters from absolute obedience to God's word and the Gospel where the soul's welfare is concerned, is very typical of that Reformation innovation in which, as I said, we can see the breach in the system with the medieval formation of Church, theology and piety. If this Catholic system is

---

[3] Letter of the Ulm city council to Emperor Charles V, edited in: Gerhard Pfeiffer: *Quellen zur Nürnberger Reformationsgeschichte. Von der Duldung liturgischer Änderungen bis zur Ausübung des Kirchenregiments durch den Rat (Juni 1524 bis Juni 1525)* (Nürnberg, 1968) [= Einzelarbeiten aus der Kirchengeschichte Bayerns 45], pp. 308–310 (Br. 81a); on the interpretation of this letter cf. Berndt Hamm: *Bürgertum und Glaube. Konturen der städtischen Reformation* (Göttingen, 1996), pp. 107–110 (with a partial facsimile of the letter).

marked by a concentrated commingling of the heavenly and earthly spheres, a graduated indwelling of the sacred in the creaturely, then the radical change brought about by the Reformation consists above all and under the most various aspects in a desacralization of the world, in a radical secularization of the earthly and creaturely, particularly of humankind and its works, no matter how holy they may appear.

When speaking of humanity and all human achievements even the term 'profanisation' is too weak to express the boundary drawn by the Reformation between God and the world. The Reformers speak of humanity's fundamental sinfulness, of its egoistic selfishness in the pursuit of happiness, which ever and again leads it into an unholy competition with God. In this regard the Reformation brings about a total debasement of humanity. The person who desires to virtuously fulfill his obligations before God, and so to reach the goal of eternal life, has lost the image of God in which he was created and consequently has lost his worth as God's beloved creature. In the view of the Reformation the only kind of human religious worth there can still be after the Fall is that which the merciful God bestows on the ungodly by justifying them despite their sinful unworthiness, i.e. by adopting them by grace and – quite undeservedly – giving them the right to the heavenly inheritance. This means that, from a religious standpoint, the Reformation knows no such thing as natural human rights in the modern sense. When the concept of 'human right(s)' appears in Reformation texts it means exactly the opposite: a collection of statutes, sayings, fabrications and customs by means of which humankind exercise their high-handed willfulness[4] and, particularly in the ecclesiastical sphere, give it the appearance of divine right and sanctified tradition. What the Reformers have in mind here is first and foremost the Papacy with its tradition of canon law. At this point, with respect to the sacral institutional church, to the papacy and priesthood with their hierarchical powers, we can see particularly clearly the extent to which the Reformation as a desacralizing

---

[4] Cf. for example an anonymous Nuremberg opinion on freedom of cult from the spring of 1530, which criticises the injustice and the fatal arbitrariness of a magistracy acting "so on Gottes forcht und wort auß lauter tirannei, auss aigim gutduncken oder menschenrechten"; *Andreas Osiander d. Ä. Gesamtausgabe, vol. 3: Schriften und Briefe 1528 bis April 1530*, ed. by Gerhard Müller und Gottfried Seebaß (Gütersloh, 1979), p. 653, 14–16.

event brings down authority and destroys legitimacy. As I have already said, according to Roman Catholic understanding the hierarchy of the Roman Church is the institutional consolidation of the working of the Holy Spirit and the mediation of grace in the sinful world. Consequently immediately prior to the Reformation one of Luther's brother monks could say: "God is more merciful and generous through the priests than through himself."[5] From the Reformation standpoint this is the way of the Antichrist who puts himself in God's place and encourages others to declare the human to be divine.

V. *The New Understanding of Holiness*

The Reformation, however, does not signify simply a complete desacralization of what was earlier considered the embodiment of holiness and consequently a breach with authority and legitimation. At the same time it signifies a change of authority in that it proclaims the sole and universal validity of another religious manner of legitimation. This 'true' authority, freed from the shackles of a human hierarchy, ought to become the basis of all Christian liberty and obligation and thereby establish a new, evangelical understanding of holiness and sanctification based on the Gospel – new and yet old, since the original text of the old Holy Scriptures would be brought to bear, now opposed in its striking freshness to the accreted sacral contexts of centuries. How far is the holiness of Holy Scripture an anti-holiness compared to the previous synthesis of divine and earthly? In the understanding of the Reformation the Bible is a holy text as the revealing word of God, to the extent to which God speaks to people in it and to the extent to which it testifies to his revelation in Jesus Christ. Certainly this is a revelation in human form and in human words, but in such a way that through this very word of God the infinite gulf between God and every worldly being is made manifest. This takes place in such a way that it also makes clear

---

[5] "Dominus deus est magis misericors et liberalior per sacerdotes quam per se ipsum, loquendo non quantum ad naturam suam, sed quantum ad effectum et exhibitionem, quia plura beneficia exhibet mediantibus sacerdotibus quam sine ipsis: Quia sine ministerio sacerdotum paucissimos salvaret [. . .]". Johannes von Paltz: *Coelifodina (1502)*, ed. by Christoph Burger und Friedhelm Stasch (Berlin – New York, 1983) [= J. v. P., *Werke* 1], p. 264, 6–10.

that this dividing chasm cannot be bridged by hierarchical mediations of God's grace manifested in earthly, creaturely holiness and by a corresponding ascent of the person to God. Salvation cannot be achieved by various combinations of God and the world or by any sort of contribution of human causality. God grants salvation without qualification, through unconditional forgiveness. Consequently the Reformation's message of salvation is in a radical sense a proclamation of the effectiveness of God alone in his unilateral movement of giving to the sinful, pitiful world. This movement, which is identical to the movement of Christ into the world, begins with God's free election that determines people for salvation. It continues under the sign of God's faithfulness in the exculpating and encouraging promise: "Your sins are forgiven." Finally, it manifests its creative power in a faith that, freed from the necessity of religious self-realization, passes on to others the love it has itself received.

What is here described as an emancipation that enables one to accept God's gift and pass it on to others, to have unwavering faith, to love and show compassion, is what the Reformers call human 'sanctification' and 'holiness'. What they mean by that is not a sacredness in the sense of the medieval understanding of holiness – i.e. not a holiness which is a property of particular people, things, places and actions as an inherent quality of gracious, salvific power. The person whom God makes holy does not "have" anything holy in himself. Grace does not enter into a person, but the person enters into grace, into a sanctifying relationship in which God alone as the Holy Spirit remains the giver of salvation. Hence in the understanding of the Reformation it is unthinkable that particular human saints with "their" holiness could independently of the divine Giver become mediators of grace between other people and God. But since grace, salvation and holiness remain so closely and persistently bound to God's own presence and sole effectiveness and do not become inherent in exceptional earthly bearers or spheres, the whole world in its sheer worldliness and disenchanted secularity becomes the field of activity for sanctification. Where God takes people into his service as saints he does not lead them into fenced-off, sanctified reserves but into the everyday areas of work, politics, family and neighborhood, enabling them to become active witnesses of his self-giving love here in the midst of the unholy world. This corresponds to their own personal status as being at one and the same time justified and sinners. It is an incredibly unholy holiness of which the Reformation

speaks, a revolutionary unleashing of sanctification. The new understanding of faith, priesthood, divine service and good works tears
down the traditional barriers between sacred and profane, priesthood
and laity, religiosity and worldliness although (or rather, precisely
because) the Reformation puts such strong emphasis on the eternal,
absolute distance between God and the world. When one sees the
world, at such a distance from God, as sinful and drawn towards
death there is no longer room for the traditional conception of distinctions and gradations within a world more or less moving towards
God, a creation saintly and sinful in varying degrees. All that is left
is the trust in God's providential movement into this world in Jesus
Christ, establishing a unique, unsurpassable, redeeming divine proximity to the doomed world. In this way every believing Christian is
given immediate access to God – a newly proclaimed immediacy in
which lay the roots of the history of freedom in Protestantism.

VI. *The Reformation as a Break in the Religio-historical Logic of*
Gift and Return

From the point of view of religious history this Reformation process
of secularizing, of the unleashing of holiness centered in faith in an
unconditionally self-bestowing God, constitutes a major caesura, a
historico-religious interruption. It already has its beginnings in the
Old Testament, attains a new radicality in the New Testament and
is further intensified in a different context by the Reformation. It is
the radical break with an extremely diversified religious logic, on the
one hand very ancient, on the other ever and again very modern,
which has a high degree of inherent plausibility because it clearly
corresponds to particular basic human needs. This religious logic
reached a great flowering of acceptance in the decades prior to the
Reformation. It implies that there is no unconditional loving-kindness, no offence without punishment,[6] and no forgiveness without
reparation and atonement. According to this reasoning the relationship between God and humanity is determined by the rules of gift

---

[6] Cf. Arnold Angenendt: "Deus, qui nullum peccatum impunitum dimittit. Ein
'Grundsatz' der mittelalterlichen Bußgeschichte", in: Matthias Lutz-Bachmann (ed.):
Und dennoch ist von Gott zu reden. Festschrift für Herbert Vorgrimler (Freiburg i.Br. – Basel –
Wien, 1994), pp. 142–156.

and return, *do ut des*,[7] sacrifice and absolution, merit and reward, acts and consequences. This in no way excludes the fact that the divine gift of salvation infinitely transcends human atonement and merit; but what is always crucial in this logic is that the person can somehow or other influence the divine reaction, for himself or on behalf of others. By his gifts he puts God in his debt. The Reformation breaks this logic by denying the sinful person any possibility of influencing God's forgiveness and gift of salvation through sacrifice and atonement, satisfaction and merit, and by proclaiming that salvation is totally 'gratis', without any active, voluntary involvement on the human side. In emphasizing that God has given himself for humanity once and for all in the sacrifice of Jesus Christ, the Reformers repudiate the medieval Church as a community of sacrifice and atonement. Their criticism is directed above all against the early capitalist variants of absolution and reward in the shape of indulgences and endowments and consequently against the ideas of a treasury of good works at the disposal of the Church and of Purgatory as a place of punishment and absolution in the hereafter. Jesus Christ as the only valid sacrifice means for them the end of all human sacrifices and all attempts to influence powers in the hereafter by moral, ritual, magical or mystical methods.

With this message the Reformation in its time was in no way a pioneer of the modern age and the modern person. It stood athwart both an archaic and also an early modern piety if we take such as Petrarch, William of Ockham, Erasmus of Rotterdam, Jean Bodin, Michel de Montaigne, Francis Bacon or René Descartes as representative of early modern thinking and modern critique of the Church. Theirs was a culture no longer dominated by the universal authority of the Church. People moved forward to new experiences of the natural world, of earthly causality, religious individuality and human worth. This new kind of critical rationality with its conception of humanity also craved a religion that presupposed a relationship between a person's voluntary morality and his eternal happiness. Here, too, the fundamental religious principles of 'I give so that you give' and divine retribution are still endorsed in principle albeit in a

---

[7] Cf. Marcel Mauss: *Die Gabe. Form und Funktion des Austauschs in archaischen Gesellschaften* (Frankfurt am Main, 3rd edn., 1984); Karl Hoheisel: article "Do ut des", in: *Handbuch religionswissenschaftlicher Grundbegriffe*, vol. 2 (Stuttgart, 1990), pp. 228–230.

philosophically and rationally refined form. Thus the Reformation
with its characteristic configuration of Gospel proclamation, criticism
of authority and program for reform had a curiously old-fashioned
character that was neither medieval nor modern, and a correspondingly
dissonant resonance. It offended basic religious needs of people in
every age, yet found great success, particularly with its message of
justification. In contrast to what was described above as the logic of
divine-human co-operation familiar throughout religious history, the
Reformation developed what could be called an astonishing counter-
logic and an equally astonishing counter-plausibility. For many
contemporaries this lay in the luminous faith in a love which is unconditional from first to last and in the divine majesty of pure giving,
a sovereign grace without any previous obligation. At the same time
this was the plausibility of a message that, as the Reformers' biblical
interpretation tirelessly demonstrated, clearly had every right to appeal
to Jesus and Paul and their 'scandalous' offences against the religious logic of their environment.

But it must also be said that even in the Reformation and in post-
Reformation Protestantism the harsh picture of an angry, avenging
and justly punishing God retained a surprisingly high degree of validity. As in Roman Catholicism it served particularly in interpreting
misfortunes in the world – epidemics, crop failures and the afflictions
of war: Through such collective disasters God punishes the sins of
individual members of the community so that the people must move
him to be merciful through prayer and moral discipline and so ensure
his blessing, the basic requirement of earthly prosperity. According
to the basic trend of Protestant theology a person cannot obtain the
salvation of the soul through moral discipline, but a causal connection can be traced between moral discipline and earthly well-being.
Consequently the ominous workings of demons and witches and the
necessary countermeasures of the purifying witch-hunt find a solid
anchorage in this explanatory model. In many respects the Reformation,
beginning with its theology and sermons, was not a reform of compassion and leniency but one of grave severity and imposed ideals
of discipline and purification.

This raises the question of how strong the core Reformation message of God's unconditional grace and his gift of salvation was and
remained through the history of the Reformation and the differing
branches of Protestantism. Could this unmodern imposition of a radically achievement-free religion on theology, ecclesiastical structuring

and congregational reality hold its own against both the archaic and the perennially modern universal logic of retaliation, acquisition, threat and disciplining pressure? It could – but only in a hotly contested position. Repeated fresh starts and 'reforming rediscoveries' were needed to allow the simple and yet so difficult message of God's perfect loving and giving to be heard in the face of the hardened conceptions of God maintained by contemporaries. Seen in the light of religious history this message was and is absolutely unique. In the face of the ubiquitous ideas of compensation and retaliation it could only achieve the counter-plausibility we have mentioned under the particular living conditions of a highly refined and sensitized religious culture.

VII. *The Reformation as a Continuation of Medieval Trends*

At this stage in my discussion of the Reformation I must make a very important shift in perspective. Up until now I have characterized the Reformation as being first and foremost an epochal break and interruption, as a breach with the system and a dethroning of authority. But now we must also look at its situation within longer-term historical processes of change, for this is just as remarkable. By this I do not mean simply its multiple interconnections in the emergence of the Modern Age and in the phases of change from the 16th to the 18th century but rather its roots in the so-called Middle Ages. Recent research since the '70s has shown that we must understand the Reformation theologically, politically, socially and culturally in the light of the Middle Ages – seeing the medieval period not as a negative background but as a vital source of the Reformation.[8]

An important element in this was a sharpened awareness of the astonishing dynamics of change in the Middle Ages, of its epochal new departures and tension-laden synchronous diversity, to which it

---

[8] In the field of historical theology it was Heiko Augustinus Oberman who opened our eyes to a new, unprejudiced perception of the Late Middle Ages as the source from which the Reformation arose. He showed for example how profoundly Luther's thought was formed by the nominalist *via moderna* and the sharply anti-Pelagian, Augustinian theology of his order. Cf. for instance Oberman: *Werden und Wertung der Reformation. Vom Wegestreit zum Glaubenskampf* (Tübingen, 1977); idem (ed.): *Gregor von Rimini. Werk und Wirkung bis zur Reformation* (Berlin – New York, 1981) [= Spätmittelalter und Reformation 20].

is hard indeed to do justice. In the Middle Ages there were radical cultural and religious breaks which were in their own way just as important as the drastic break in the Age of the Reformation, so that the broad labeling of the epoch as 'Middle Ages' has become more than questionable as a denotation of the centuries between Late Antiquity and the Reformation. The medieval period before the 12th century, prior to the growth of municipal communities, new orders and universities, scholasticism and canon law, of an internalizing and individualizing culture of critical *ratio* and religious feeling, was a completely different era from the medieval period after the 12th century. The same can be said of the radical changes in the 14th century when we consider the rapid decline of the authority of the Papacy and the ecclesiastical hierarchy, the rise of secular control over the power of the clergy, the beginnings of Renaissance culture, the shock of the Black Death and, in nominalism, a new, disturbing awareness of the infinite distance between God and the world and human reason. But we must also take note of the far-reaching changes in the last decades before the Reformation, after the councils of Constance and Basle, in order to understand how significantly the Reformation – from its beginnings in Luther's early theology and in its different main currents – is a continuation of the Middle Ages; or, to be more precise, the richly varied continuation of particular trends in the Middle Ages, while other medieval features were condemned in the strongest possible terms. The Reformation owed its great success to the fact that it was not only a radical break but was also an amplification of changes which had already begun. These changes had been under way for varying lengths of time. We must at least bear in mind such phenomena as the heightened criticism of the Church which was spreading throughout the population. These only come to the fore right at the end of the Middle Ages and are characteristic of the two decades between 1500 and 'Luther's rise to fame'.[9] Thus, for example, his '95 Theses' constitute the climax of a wave of criticism of indulgences from the turn of the century.[10]

---

[9] Cf. Bernd Moeller: "Das Berühmtwerden Luthers", in: *Zeitschrift für Historische Forschung* 15 (1988), pp. 65–92.
[10] Cf. Wilhelm Ernst Winterhager: "Ablaßkritik als Indikator historischen Wandels vor 1517: Ein Beitrag zu Voraussetzungen und Einordnung der Reformation", in: *Archiv für Reformationsgeschichte* 90 (1999), pp. 6–71.

VIII. *Differing Kinds of Continuation of the Middle Ages: Qualitative Leap and Reinforcement or Acceleration*

We have good grounds for saying that all the essential points in the theology, reform program and ecclesiastical change of the Reformation which led to the break with the Roman Church were already prefigured in the Middle Ages. Particular medieval impulses for change were carried farther by the Reformation. To this extent the Reformation belongs in the context of the Late Middle Ages. It does not turn against medieval piety outwardly but inwardly, on the basis of "what the medieval Christian really always knew".[11] To give a theological example: We find already between 1450 and 1520 that some theologians put a strong soteriological emphasis on God's mercy and grace and his saving act in Christ – the late medieval concentration to a kind of *sola misericordia, sola gratia* and *solus Christus*. These theologians tend to maximize the donation of divine mercy, particularly in Christ's Passion, in such a way that the human contribution required is reduced to a minimum. The weak sinner is told: If you cannot feel any true repentance – i.e. any sincere regret – for your sins, then at least feel regret that you cannot feel regret and put your whole trust in the divine mercy, in the infinite merit of Christ's suffering! Hence within the framework of the medieval cultivation of repentance and regret an effective exoneration is offered which entails a minimum of personal sense of pain.[12] Consequently the essential change brought about by the Reformation then lay in the step from that minimum to nothing at all. At the latest by 1518 Luther comes to believe that the forgiveness of sins is in no way dependent on the sinner's repentance but solely on God's mercy and on the faith which lets itself be given this gift of mercy through God's promise of

---

[11] Cf. Bernd Moeller: "Die Rezeption Luthers in der frühen Reformation", in: Berndt Hamm, Bernd Moeller, Dorothea Wendebourg (eds.): *Reformationstheorien. Ein kirchenhistorischer Disput über Einheit und Vielfalt der Reformation* (Göttingen, 1995), pp. 9–29, here 25.

[12] On late medieval 'sola'-thinking and the corresponding formulae see Berndt Hamm: "Von der spätmittelalterlichen reformatio zur Reformation: der Prozeß normativer Zentrierung von Religion und Gesellschaft in Deutschland", in: *Archiv für Reformationsgeschichte* 84 (1993), pp. 7–82, here 36–41; on the program of emotional minimalisation cf. Berndt Hamm: "Wollen und Nicht-Können in der spätmittelalterlichen Bußseelsorge", in: idem, Thomas Lentes (eds.): *Spätmittelalterliche Frömmigkeit zwischen Ideal und Praxis* (Tübingen, 2001) [= Spätmittelalter und Reformation. Neue Reihe 15], pp. 111–146; English translation in chapter 3.

forgiveness.[13] Looking at the situation from the Late Middle Ages
we can almost define Luther's innovation as a logical extension in
the same direction. At the same time, however, I would like to call
it a contingent qualitative leap because Luther totally averts his gaze
from the medieval question of sufficient repentance and makes salvation entirely independent of the proviso of an emotional and active
capacity for repentance on the part of the sinner.

There are great differences in the innovative way in which the
followers of Luther, Zwingli, the Reformation Spiritualists and Baptists
took up and carried on particular medieval trends. How far they
continued or developed them depended to a large extent on their
particular type of Reformation but also on their views of what was
important. I have just used the expression 'qualitative leap' to express
the fact that continuity is combined here with a rupture. In comparison with the considerable potential for criticism in the years
before 1517 we can discern a new quality in the criticism of the
Church and the anticlericalism of the various branches of the Reformation, in their attacks on indulgences, the authority of the Pope,
priestly hierarchy and monastic orders. There was a continuation
and radicalization of particular critical trends which struck at the
roots of the earlier conception of the Church to such an extent that
there was no longer any place for the new critics in the old Church.
In this respect, therefore, the manner in which the medieval criticism was developed led to the break with the medieval Church. On
the other hand, if we look at other Reformation phenomena, we
should lay more stress on the unbroken continuity and consequently
speak of a strengthening or acceleration of particular changes begun
in the Late Middle Ages. I am thinking, for example, of the increasing success of a type of late-medieval theology, very much oriented
towards practical and pastoral concerns, in making an impression on
a vernacular reading-public, particularly among the laity in the cities.

---

[13] Cf. Martin Luther's theses (probably dating from the early summer of 1518)
"Pro veritate inquirenda et timoratis conscientiis consolandis", *WA* 1 (629) 630–633,
for example Thesis 18 (631,23f.): "Super contritionem edificantes remissionem super
arenam, id est super opus hominis, fidem dei edificant" and Theses 8 and 9 (631,
3–6): "Remissio culpe non innititur contritioni peccatoris, nec officio aut potestati
sacerdotis, innititur potius fidei, que est in verbum Christi dicentis: Quodcunque
solveris etc. [Matth. 16, 19]." On this see the interpretation by Oswald Bayer: *Promissio: Geschichte der reformatorischen Wende in Luthers Theologie* (Göttingen, 1971) [= Forschungen zur Kirchen- und Dogmengeschichte 24], pp. 164–202, especially 182–202.

This popularizing movement in the pre-Reformation theology of piety entered into a symbiosis with the new possibilities of dissemination brought about by the printing press and experienced a spectacular extension and acceleration in the mass production of Reformation pamphlets and handbills.

A similar process of continuation and intensification closely connected to the expansion of printed material can be seen in the understanding and use of religious images. In contrast to the sacred religious symbol, whose power to mediate grace was worshipped like the potency of a relic, there came increasingly to the fore in the Late Middle Ages the idea of the intellectually didactic, emotionally evocative image inspiring feelings of reverence and giving moral guidance. In other words, there grew up a tendency to measure the religious worth of an image solely by how far it succeeded in touching people's hearts and moving them to pious deeds. The Reformation enhanced this internalizing, intellectualizing and individualizing dynamic. If it permitted a religious image at all, then only as a medium of an edifying message which mediates religious knowledge and teaches how to act in faith – i.e. as a form of proclamation of the biblical text. What is already there in 15th-century illustrations, adorned with so many inscriptions, was brought to perfection by the Reformation: the image becomes the text. The Reformers, however, did not simply continue this late medieval line but subjected the images to new criteria involving the consistency of image and faith – Luther, as we know, in a different way from Karlstadt, the Upper Germans and the Swiss. Hence the continuity becomes part of a constellation of radical change, extending right up to the literal shattering of the very images that had been objects of piety in the Late Middle Ages.

IX. *The Reformation as a Driving Force of Modernization*

On the basis of the examples of Reformation intensification and acceleration mentioned we can study how and to what extent the Reformation was the cultural avant-garde of its time and how far it was responsible for advancing the long-term processes of the modernization of Europe. In this respect the roots, first shoots and blossoming of the Reformation are inextricably bound up with the educational ideals and critical rational impulses of Renaissance humanism. Many humanists such as Philipp Melanchthon, Martin Bucer or Huldrych Zwingli employed their energies in support of the Reformation, and almost all of the Reformers were fascinated by humanism. The Reformation 'scripture principle' belongs in this connection, with its mobilization of linguistic proficiency in Greek and Hebrew, rational textual criticism, academic education of ministers and the cultivation of literacy in the vernacular among the laity. Already prepared for by the increasing culture of literacy before the Reformation, the new scripture principle was a progressive principle of law and authority in comparison with a foundering culture of rights established by religious custom. Since this also implies that the sole norm of truth is reduced to an ancient source – in the horizon of its interpretation by the early Church Fathers – the humanist understanding of norms also comes into play in the Reformation.

Whichever way one attempts phenomenologically or conceptually to understand the modernizing thrusts running from the Late Middle Ages to the Early Modern Age – as internalization, rationalization (Max Weber), individualization and reinforcement of subjectivism, laicization and secularization, bureaucratization and differentiation of functions, positive re-evaluation of secular work and the practice of a profession, increased investment in schools and education, ethicising of community and social discipline (Gerhard Oestreich), a process of civilization (Norbert Elias), authoritative centralization, disenchantment of the world or christianization of society – the Reformation and the process of confessionalization growing from it must at least be counted among the forces which significantly encouraged these movements so far as they really existed.[14] We cannot make the same claim for modern Roman Catholicism, though we must stress that Roman Catholic confessionalization was also in its own way a force for modernization. Its response to the Reformation, though hostile and itself reforming by centralizing, was considerably influenced by it. In reforming after the Council of Trent Roman Catholicism

---

[14] Cf. on this the summary balance drawn up by Richard van Dülmen: "Reformation und Neuzeit. Ein Versuch", in: *Zeitschrift für Historische Forschung* 14 (1987), pp. 1–25. My qualification "so far as they really existed" expresses my considerable skepticism about the basis in the sources for what we have mentioned as the views and concepts of modernization in contemporary research. Their quotient of construction seems to me very high and their basis in the sources doubtful, but history – regardless of all the remarkable differences between history pursued in proximity to or distance from the sources – cannot in principle be presented in any other way.

also drove forward certain of the late medieval trends which were strengthened and stimulated by the Reformations, e.g. the line of inscription and internalization; but it excluded as heretical other late medieval characteristics which worked on in the Reformation – such as the late medieval criticism of the monarchical authority of the papacy or the sharply intensified Augustinian theology of grace. Consequently we can say that the Reformation was also unintentionally modern in bringing an end to the relatively pluralistic and open Catholicism of the Late Middle Ages and preparing the way for a narrowed, militant Catholicism with its siege mentality.

X. *The Relationship of the Reformation to Emancipative Modernity*

It is remarkable to what extent the modernization of Europe was expedited by the Reformation, not through its own agenda but contrary to or independent of its actual ecclesiastical intentions. This is most obvious when in using the term 'modernization' we do not simply think of the 16th and 17th centuries and the phenomena of confessionalization, early absolutist statehood and the socio-religious disciplining of morals, but select other perspectives relevant to the long period of time from the 14th to the 20th centuries. By this I mean on the one hand long-term processes which were deplored by contemporary critics of all confessions, theologians, lawyers and politicians alike, as symptoms of disintegration (*dissolutio*) and the decline of all good order.[15] These are processes which might be described as pluralistic liberalization, as an opening towards tolerance and freedom from force in religion, as awareness of civil and human rights, as strengthening of republicanism and democratization, of rational understanding and individual civic responsibility, as secularization and the promotion of the natural sciences – in short, as the blossoming of an emancipative Modern Age. To trace their path to the Enlightenment and beyond up to the fundamental crisis of rationality

---

[15] Cf. e.g. Christoph Strohm: "Zur Eigenart der frühen calvinistischen Ethik: Beobachtungen am Beispiel des Calvin-Schülers Lambert Daneau", in: *Archiv für Reformationsgeschichte* 90 (1999), pp. 230–254: here 251 (on Daneau, 1530–1595): "Der Kampf gegen die dissolutio, das Motto 'contre la dissolution de ce temps', das einem seiner Moraltraktate auch ausdrücklich vorangestellt ist, bestimmte das gesamte ethische Werk."

since the end of the 19th century we would have to begin at the latest with the late medieval era of nominalism, humanism and the *devotio moderna*.

There are significant moments in the early Reformation which point in this emancipative direction. Here I shall mention only the leading ideas of a congregational, lay Christianity not dominated by the clergy, of a Christian faith implying immediate social applications and critique of authority or of a Christian community distanced on principle from power, violence and compulsion in matters of belief. Admittedly these features of the Reformation were repressed to the same extent as the rural Reformation was quelled and the Spiritualists or Baptists marginalized in the 'Christian communities' of Europe. But is there not still the specific contribution of Calvinism to the liberal traits in western Europe and North America? Current research into the Early Modern era tends to reject earlier views of a close relationship between the Reformed confession and emancipating modernity. The result of more recent works suggests that if there were in the middle of the 16th century remarkable alliances between particular denominations of Protestantism and a more liberal 'spirit of the Modern Age', the decisive grounds for this are not to be found in the Reformation and a particular denomination which emerged from it – i.e. not, as is often maintained, following Ernst Troeltsch, in the 'nature' of the Reformed tradition of the Zwinglian, Calvinist or German sort.[16] The primary reasons lay rather in contingent historical constellations which favored a factual cooperation of particular Protestant strengths with particular currents of modernity.

Admittedly there are many signs that 'Calvinism' – to use the term taken from the polemical vocabulary of intolerance – was more closely related to the emergence of liberal modernity than was Lutheranism. Its covenant theology offered a basis in principle for the right to resist and the sovereignty of the people while its presbyterian and synodal structure of administration, which from its beginnings in the Reformation remained characteristic of its ecclesiology and practical church order, also served as a model for the

---

[16] Cf. Friedrich Wilhelm Graf, Trutz Rendtorff (eds.): *Ernst Troeltschs Soziallehren. Studien zu ihrer Interpretation* (Gütersloh, 1993), particularly Luise Schorn-Schütte: "Ernst Troeltschs 'Soziallehren' und die gegenwärtige Frühneuzeitforschung. Zur Diskussion um die Bedeutung von Luthertum und Calvinismus für die Entstehung der modernen Welt", pp. 133–151 (with further literature).

development of the institutions of representative democracy. On the whole, however, we must look with the utmost caution on all attempts to trace particular modern traits of the Protestant confessions of the late 16th to the 18th centuries directly back to directions set by the Reformation. The long-term effects of the Reformation should probably be seen principally in a certain ability to internalize and strengthen the conscience and to deepen ethical motivation. It is clear that it was among the Reformed rather than the Lutherans that this took the form of an active shaping of the world, freely interpreting the instructions of the divine law and trusting in the Holy Spirit's power of renewal.[17] But the fact that this genuinely religious energy could on occasion serve the ends of emancipation and eventually could enter into a close association with the modern conception of human rights, particularly in the Anglo-Saxon world, cannot be derived by stringent logic from its origins in the Reformation.

The Reformation was neither the birth of emancipative modernity nor was this its intention, even if later Protestantism would become one of its main supports. But the Reformation de facto fostered and precipitated the emergence of modernity simply by its success in revolting against the authority syndrome of the Roman hierarchy. By unintentionally shattering the unity of the Church the Reformation caused what the critics of modernity mentioned above denounced as its principal evil: *dissolutio* – the disintegration of unified order.

This can be shown briefly by the example of religious tolerance. In the Reformation there were certainly varying ideas as to how much freedom of scope in matters of faith was allowed by evangelical truth, how the relationship should be seen between uncompromising truthfulness and tolerant love and how dyed-in-the-wool heretics or dubious spirits should be treated. We have only to compare the relatively open attitude maintained for a time in Strasbourg with the more rigorous religious policy of Nuremberg. Admittedly Strasbourg's patience also ran out in the case of the Baptists.[18] 'Tolerance' in the

---

[17] I owe this observation to a conversation with my colleague in Bochum, Christoph Strohm. Cf. his article "Calvinismus" in the *Evangelisches Soziallexikon* (Stuttgart, 2001) (with further literature).

[18] On the more patient attitude of the magistracy and the more stringent demands of the preachers in Strasbourg see the good overview of the literature in Matthieu Arnold: "Le rôle des autorités civiles dans la lutte contre les anabaptistes. La conception du Magistrat de Strasbourg et celle de Martin Bucer", in: Anselm Doering-Manteuffel, Kurt Nowak (eds.): *Religionspolitik in Deutschland. Von der Frühen Neuzeit bis*

modern sense – i.e. of a general freedom of worship – did not come
into the perspective of the influential Reformers who cooperated with
the secular authorities. They thought they perceived in dissident
forms of belief the fury of Satan and his hordes who wished to
destroy not only the church of Jesus Christ but all good order in
the world. Since religion constitutes the strongest bond of human
fellowship,[19] a rift in faith – so runs the general axiom – inevitably
leads to the destruction of the political community. Hence the demand
for general tolerance in questions of faith such as was raised initially
by a few Baptists and more clearly by several Spiritualists and non-
conforming humanists[20] was in the view of the magisterial Reformation
a particularly cunning strategy of temptation and destruction on the
part of the devil. The value, honor and dignity deserving unconditional protection were seen only in the divine truth of Holy Scripture,
but not in the human consciences of those of a different creed, and
certainly not of an 'infidel' Jew or Muslim.[21] Truth, not the human
person, was the subject of rights, and persons only to the extent to
which they stand in the truth.

zur Gegenwart, Festschrift für Martin Greschat (Stuttgart, 1999), pp. 11–28; see also Marc
Lienhard: "La liberté de conscience à Strasbourg au XVIe siècle", in: Hans R.
Guggisberg, Frank Lestringant, Jean-Claude Margolin (eds.): *La liberté de conscience
(XVIe–XVIIe siècles)* (Geneva, 1991), pp. 39–54; idem: *Religiöse Toleranz in Straßburg
im 16. Jahrhundert* (Stuttgart, 1991) [= Akademie der Wissenschaften und der Literatur,
Mainz: Abhandlungen der Geistes- und Sozialwissenschaftlichen Klasse 1991, No.
1]; Thomas A. Brady, Jr.: *Zwischen Gott und Mammon. Protestantische Politik und deutsche
Reformation* (Berlin, 1996), especially chs. 4–8, on the Strasbourg councillor Jakob
Sturm.
    [19] On the use of the expression – combining Seneca and Lactantius – "Religio
est vinculum societatis" cf. above, p. 18 n. 50.
    [20] Cf. Lienhard: *Religiöse Toleranz* (as in n. 18); Hans R. Guggisberg: *Religiöse
Toleranz: Dokumente zur Geschichte einer Forderung* (Stuttgart – Bad Cannstatt, 1984);
idem: *Sebastian Castellio 1515–1563. Humanist und Verteidiger der religiösen Toleranz im
konfessionellen Zeitalter* (Göttingen, 1996); also Cary J. Nederman, John Christian Larsen
(eds.): *Difference and Dissent. Theories of Tolerance in Medieval and Early Modern Europe*
(Lanham – New York, 1996), about John of Salisbury, Marsilius of Padua, John
Wyclif, Christine de Pizan, Hans Denck, Sebastian Franck, Samuel Pufendorf and
Benedictus de Spinoza).
    [21] See the collection: *La liberté de conscience* (as in n. 18); also: Silvana Seidel Menchi
(ed.): *Ketzerverfolgung im 16. und frühen 17. Jahrhundert* (Wiesbaden, 1992) [= Wolfenbütteler
Forschungen 51]; Norbert Fischer, Marion Kobelt-Groch (eds.): *Außenseiter zwischen
Mittelalter und Neuzeit, Festschrift für Hans-Jürgen Goertz* (Leiden u.a., 1997) [= Studies
in Medieval and Reformation Thought 56].

Nevertheless the Reformation – against its own intention – considerably facilitated and shaped the emergence of the modern western culture of tolerance. The way in which it set the right of the individual conscience, freed and bound by Holy Scripture, against the traditional Church authority caused the dissolution of ecclesiastical unity into a multitude of forms of worship and churches. But in so doing it paved the way for tolerance – for a pluralizing of Christian perspectives, for a relativizing of the monopoly of truth and for an increasing willingness to allow the conviction of the individual conscience its own value which should be respected and protected. A voice such as that of the Nuremberg abbess, Caritas Pirckheimer, is only conceivable under the changed conditions of the nascent Reformation and the new propagation of "freedom of conscience".[22] In her written petition to the council of the free city in the spring of 1525 she pleads that the nuns of the Order of St. Clare should be allowed to practice their previous form of cloistered life. Even the Turk, she assures the councilors, allows everyone to practice their own form of faith and does not coerce anyone.[23] "It is never right to coerce anyone's faith and conscience since God himself, the Lord of us all, desires that consciences are free and will not force them. Hence it is not proper for any person to bind them and imprison them."[24] By this line of reasoning respect for religious freedom of conscience must result in a tolerant religious policy.

XI. *The Relationship of the Reformation to Repressive Modernity*

The long-term effects of the Reformation, however, promoted the modernization of Europe up until the 20th century in quite another respect, not in the sense of an individual, liberal, secularizing and emancipating culture of tolerance but in the competing sense of a

---

[22] Although there are at least two earlier instances from the 6th and 12th centuries, the concept of "freedom of conscience"/"libertas conscientiae" is a discovery of Luther's dating from 1521 and became through him a theme in the western world. Cf. Gerhard Ebeling: *Lutherstudien*, vol. 3 (Tübingen, 1985), pp. 108–125 and 385–389, especially 385; Berndt Hamm: *Zwinglis Reformation der Freiheit* (Neukirchen – Vluyn, 1988), p. 64, n. 286.

[23] Josef Pfanner (ed.): *Die "Denkwürdigkeiten" der Caritas Pirckheimer (aus den Jahren 1524–1528)* (Landshut, 1962) [= Caritas Pirckheimer-Quellensammlung 2], p. 48, 5f.: "lest doch der dürck yderman in seinem gelauben und nottet nymant".

[24] Ibid., p. 48, 8–12.

religiously warranted modernity of repression and authoritarian standardization which opposed respect for individual human dignity and
eventually developed totalitarian traits. Here, too, Protestantism could
contribute its religious potential of internalization, its biblical-theo-
logical warrant and its moral discipline. It can hardly be doubted
that in so doing Protestantism drew on the sources of the Reformation
and confessionalization. But it is not easy to answer the question
how far support for an anti-emancipatory, repressive modernity grew
out of genuine impulses, tendencies and intentions of the Reformation.
This much we can say, even apart from the fervent opposition of
the Reformers to early modern demands for tolerance: The Protestant
rejection of the Roman Catholic polarities of sacred and profane,
priests and laity, unmarried and married, church and state led early
Protestantism – and by no means only the Lutherans – in the age
of the Reformation to claim for certain natural and historical forms
of life the solemn dignity of being willed by the divine Creator and
consequently to sanction them religiously as 'ranks' and 'orders' established by God. Initially they were thinking here of marriage and the
civil authorities – i.e. on the one hand the binding obligation of the
individual to the only legitimate way of life, to marriage, physical
motherhood and natural family – in sharp contrast to voluntary
celibacy, the idea of spiritual motherhood and the family of the cloister[25] – on the other, the equally rigid bond of obedience owed by
subjects to the will of the civil authorities in temporal matters.
Consequently in 1528 the Nuremberg council clerk mentioned above,
Lazarus Spengler, a faithful follower of Luther, formulated the opinion that in areas where the Bible neither commands nor forbids –
e.g. in particular matters relating to marriage – the decrees of the
secular authorities should have the force of "divine laws and commandments".[26] In this Spengler represents a position which was very

---

[25] On this conflict, especially on the confessional antinomy between biologically
prescribed motherhood and the picture of the abbess as spiritual mother as also
between the natural family and the monastic family (as being "against the divine
order, yea against nature") cf. Nadja Bennewitz: "Handlungsmöglichkeiten und
begrenzte Mitwirkung: die Beteiligung von Frauen an der reformatorischen Bewegung
in Nürnberg", in: *Zeitschrift für bayerische Kirchengeschichte* 68 (1999), pp. 21–46 (quote
on p. 39); see too Petra Seegets: "Professionelles Christentum und allgemeines
Priestertum – Überlegungen zum reformatorischen Frauenbild", in: Heidemarie
Wüst, Jutta Jahn (eds.): *Frauen der Reformation* (Wittenberg, 1999) [= Tagungstexte
der Evang. Akademie Sachsen 5], pp. 167–180.
[26] Cf. *Lazarus Spengler Schriften*, vol. 2, ed. Berndt Hamm, Wolfgang Huber, Gudrun

widespread in the magisterial Reformation: the sacral upgrading of patriarchal authority in the political community analogous to the 'holy' authority of the head of the household in the family.

Here we can observe the obverse of Protestant desacralization and profanization in a tendency to allow a massive sacralization and religious over-legitimation of earthly, historical instances to enter by the back door of a theology of creation brought to bear upon the state of humanity after the Fall. Hence it provides an ideal partner for such modern syntheses as blend secular culture, politics or economy with religion. The corresponding lines lead, for example, to the educational religion of the time of Goethe and Schleiermacher or to the nationalist and militarist religiosity and the popular folk religion of the 19th and 20th centuries. This exaggerated religious adulation of nature and of what history has brought forth certainly also has its roots in the Reformation. At least one cannot generally deny an effective historical connection between particular Reformation impulses, tendencies and intentions and these subsequent syntheses of God and the world. Admittedly there were also protests – and not only from Karl Barth – against this modern secular piety precisely in the name of the Reformation and its belief in God's utter transcendence.[27] And we can also say with a certain clarity of distinction that the original evangelical vision of the sanctifying impulses of faith in all areas of the world has in principle nothing to do with a piety aiming to transfigure the world or a theological legitimization of oppressive use of power. On the contrary: the sanctifying movement of love in the sense of the early Reformation must be understood as a critical counterweight to any repressive patronization of the faithful, exposing so-called 'divine right' as human right and thus freeing humanity from a constricting religious justification of particular ways of life.

Litz, (Gütersloh, 1999) [= Quellen und Forschungen zur Reformationgeschichte 70], pp. 354,6 and 355,4: "das solchs gottliche gepott und bevelch sein" (Nr. 84: Gutachten zur Bestrafung Hans Hühnerkopfs, Sept. 1528). Spengler here quotes verbally from Melanchthons "Articuli de quibus egerunt per visitatores in regione Saxoniae" (1527): *Corpus Reformatorum* 26, col. 17 (art. "De magistratibus").

[27] Thus even earlier the founder of Dutch neo-Calvinism Abraham Kuyper, e.g. in his rector's address: *De verflauwing der grenzen. Rede bij de overdracht van het rectoraat aan de Vrije Universiteit op 20 october 1892 gehouden* (Amsterdam, 1892); German translation: *Die Verwischung der Grenzen* (Leipzig, 1898). Cf. on this Cornelis Augustijn, Jasper Vree: *Abraham Kuyper: vast en veranderlijk. De ontwikkeling van zijn denken* (Zoetermeer, 1998).

XII. *Summary: The Reformation as Engine and Interruption of Modernity*

In summing up I should like to record that we have won a many-sided – and ambivalent – picture of the place of the Reformation in the second Christian millennium. *On the one hand*: we see it as an active factor of continuation, reinforcement and acceleration interwoven in long-term processes of modernization. I emphasized that the nature of change in this modern age imprinted by the Reformation is by no means simply to be understood in the sense of the ideals of the Enlightenment or an increasing responsibility on the part of the individual. It should also be seen in the sense of a contrary, enslaving modernity for which concepts such as 'human rights' and 'human dignity' represent non-values. I find it particularly important that we do not imagine that the long-term, far-reaching dynamics of change which played a leading role in the Reformation had their genesis in the early 16th century, but that we recognize that they are anchored in the Middle Ages, in part already in the 11th and 12th centuries. But I also think it important to observe how much of the actual long-term effect of the Reformation was not intended by its spokesmen and their followers. Admittedly this does not mean that a substantial connection of cause and effect cannot exist between such unintended consequences and the genuine character of the Reformation. One could demonstrate this complicated co-existence of "not really meant like that" and yet caused or co-created by the example of the historical coherence between Christian hatred of the Jews in the Late Middle Ages and the Reformation – particularly Luther's polemics against the Jews – and modern Protestant anti-Semitism.

On the other hand: we can see the Reformation as a drastic interruption, as a kind of break in the system, which likewise appears as much un-modern as un-archaic when compared with predominant trends in the Middle Ages and modern times. I have tried to show that the groundwork for this break was to a very large extent also laid in particular trends in medieval theology and piety. I do believe, however, that the Reformation was dominated by an overall constellation of radical change in which these medieval trends took on a new complexion. I detected the disconnecting nature of the Reformation above all in a new disjunctive understanding of the relationship between God and the world, combined with a different understanding of holiness, and in a basic posture of faith which opposed on principle the historical religious logic based on giving and taking, retaliation and punishment, sacrifice and atonement. We can only do justice to the Reformation if we take this two-sidedness seriously – its role both as an advance guard of modernity and as a counterbalance to it. Its historical dynamic and its success lay in the combination of the two.

XIII. *The Prospect: The Significance of the Reformation for the Future of Church and Society*

What, however, does the legacy of the Reformation hold out for the future? Here too, my conclusion on the basis of historical analysis has two sides. The Reformation has fulfilled but probably also exhausted its former role as a driving force of modern culture – in both the positive and the negative sense. This statement should not be misunderstood. The present-day churches which grew out of the Reformation and their theological faculties are of course still among the forces both shaping our culture and depending upon it. It is essential to their importance in society that they keep abreast of the times culturally, are intellectually equipped for dialogue with the challenging ideas of the future and strengthen particular energies required by a humane culture. But this can hardly be the conclusive reason for their significance in the future. Our secularized culture and religiosity, long since detached from the legitimating structure of confessional Christianity, no longer require recognition and reinforcement from the Church. In this situation the eccentric position of the Reformation athwart both the Middle Ages and modern times could at the same time signal the chance for a lively future for the churches of the Reformation. What was then in the 16th century highly innovative but strangely un-modern has presumably also escaped being overtaken by modernity. From the point of view of Protestantism today this would mean: what modern society needs is intervention on the part of the Church which would realize afresh the Reformation's primal Protestant witness to the capacity of the biblical witness to interrupt and contradict. Politics, industry, the media, science, education, the arts, sport and the rest need to be confronted by a Christian faith which, in the course of a critical continuing and universalizing of the Reformation, challenges what is largely an extremely unfree, shallow and covertly primitive logic of modernization. Only by so doing will it expose the future of the humane. The Reformation was not a movement for human dignity. But it made possible grounds for human dignity which remain valid even when people have the experience, both radical and incapable of being mastered rationally, of their own lack of dignity and worth. That human dignity is inalienable stands in Article 1 of the Constitution of the Federal Republic of Germany. But how do we deal with the real experience of infringement, degradation and worthlessness of people, with their ruined image of God and their bestiality? Anyone who learns from the Reformation and transposes it to a new time can say to future generations that the dignity of human beings and all creatures does not rest, closed and disposable, in themselves, but exists thanks to the universal and unconditional promise of God – a promise not of subordinating control but of life-giving friendship: "The Kingdom of God" as "The Kingdom of Friendship".[28] The whole potential of an alternative ethics is implicit in this perspective of the Reformation's *extra nos*.

With that I have returned to the question I asked at the beginning about the relevance of the Reformation. From the historical observation of how the Reformation in the 16th century was innovative in a way fundamentally different from the other innovations of its time, we have the chance to discern that it remains present as an operative force in the 21st century too – not simply as a venerable component of our cultural memory but above all as a force of critical confrontation with the culture prevalent at any one time. It is precisely in this way that the Christian faith can give shaping and transforming momentum to contemporary culture.[29]

---

[28] Cf. Walter Sparn: "Reich Gottes: Reich der Freundschaft. Für eine trinitarische Bestimmung des Begriffs der Gottesherrschaft", in: *Marburger Jahrbuch Theologie* 11 (1999), pp. 31–61.

[29] Cf. *Gestaltung und Kritik. Zum Verhältnis von Protestantismus und Kultur*, published by the Kirchenamt der Evangelischen Kirche in Deutschland (EKD) and the Geschäftsstelle der Vereinigung Evangelischer Freikirchen (VEF), (Hannover – Frankfurt am Main, 1999) [= EKD-Texte 64].

INDEX OF PERSONS AND PLACES

INDEX OF SUBJECTS

Studies in the History
of Christian Thought

EDITED BY HEIKO A. OBERMAN

46. GARSTEIN, O. *Rome and the Counter-Reformation in Scandinavia*. 1553-1622. 1992
47. GARSTEIN, O. *Rome and the Counter-Reformation in Scandinavia*. 1622-1656. 1992
48. PERRONE COMPAGNI, V. (ed.). *Cornelius Agrippa, De occulta philosophia Libri tres*. 1992
49. MARTIN, D. D. *Fifteenth-Century Carthusian Reform*. The World of Nicholas Kempf. 1992
50. HOENEN, M. J. F. M. *Marsilius of Inghen*. Divine Knowledge in Late Medieval Thought. 1993
51. O'MALLEY, J. W., IZBICKI, T. M. and CHRISTIANSON, G. (eds.). *Humanity and Divinity in Renaissance and Reformation*. Essays in Honor of Charles Trinkaus. 1993
52. REEVE, A. (ed.) and SCREECH, M. A. (introd.). *Erasmus' Annotations on the New Testament*. Galatians to the Apocalypse. 1993
53. STUMP, Ph. H. *The Reforms of the Council of Constance (1414-1418)*. 1994
54. GIAKALIS, A. *Images of the Divine*. The Theology of Icons at the Seventh Ecumenical Council. With a Foreword by Henry Chadwick. 1994
55. NELLEN, H. J. M. and RABBIE, E. (eds.). *Hugo Grotius – Theologian*. Essays in Honour of G. H. M. Posthumus Meyjes. 1994
56. TRIGG, J. D. *Baptism in the Theology of Martin Luther*. 1994
57. JANSE, W. *Albert Hardenberg als Theologe*. Profil eines Bucer-Schülers. 1994
59. SCHOOR, R.J.M. van de. *The Irenical Theology of Théophile Brachet de La Milletière (1588-1665)*. 1995
60. STREHLE, S. *The Catholic Roots of the Protestant Gospel*. Encounter between the Middle Ages and the Reformation. 1995
61. BROWN, M.L. *Donne and the Politics of Conscience in Early Modern England*. 1995
62. SCREECH, M.A. (ed.). *Richard Mocket, Warden of All Souls College, Oxford, Doctrina et Politia Ecclesiae Anglicanae*. An Anglican Summa. Facsimile with Variants of the Text of 1617. Edited with an Introduction. 1995
63. SNOEK, G.J.C. *Medieval Piety from Relics to the Eucharist*. A Process of Mutual Interaction. 1995
64. PIXTON, P.B. *The German Episcopacy and the Implementation of the Decrees of the Fourth Lateran Council, 1216-1245*. Watchmen on the Tower. 1995
65. DOLNIKOWSKI, E.W. *Thomas Bradwardine: A View of Time and a Vision of Eternity in Fourteenth-Century Thought*. 1995
66. RABBIE, E. (ed.). *Hugo Grotius, Ordinum Hollandiae ac Westfrisiae Pietas (1613)*. Critical Edition with Translation and Commentary. 1995
67. HIRSH, J. C. *The Boundaries of Faith*. The Development and Transmission of Medieval Spirituality. 1996
68. BURNETT, S.G. *From Christian Hebraism to Jewish Studies*. Johannes Buxtorf (1564-1629) and Hebrew Learning in the Seventeenth Century. 1996
69. BOLAND O.P., V. *Ideas in God according to Saint Thomas Aquinas*. Sources and Synthesis. 1996
70. LANGE, M.E. *Telling Tears in the English Renaissance*. 1996
71. CHRISTIANSON, G. and T.M. IZBICKI (eds.). *Nicholas of Cusa on Christ and the Church*. Essays in Memory of Chandler McCuskey Brooks for the American Cusanus Society. 1996
72. MALI, A. *Mystic in the New World*. Marie de l'Incarnation (1599-1672). 1996
73. VISSER, D. *Apocalypse as Utopian Expectation (800-1500)*. The Apocalypse Commentary of Berengaudus of Ferrières and the Relationship between Exegesis, Liturgy and Iconography. 1996
74. O'ROURKE BOYLE, M. *Divine Domesticity*. Augustine of Thagaste to Teresa of Avila. 1997
75. PFIZENMAIER, T.C. *The Trinitarian Theology of Dr. Samuel Clarke (1675-1729)*. Context, Sources, and Controversy. 1997
76. BERKVENS-STEVELINCK, C., J. ISRAEL and G.H.M. POSTHUMUS MEYJES (eds.). *The Emergence of Tolerance in the Dutch Republic*. 1997
77. HAYKIN, M.A.G. (ed.). *The Life and Thought of John Gill (1697-1771)*. A Tercentennial Appreciation. 1997
78. KAISER, C.B. *Creational Theology and the History of Physical Science*. The Creationist Tradition from Basil to Bohr. 1997
79. LEES, J.T. *Anselm of Havelberg*. Deeds into Words in the Twelfth Century. 1997
80. WINTER, J.M. van. *Sources Concerning the Hospitallers of St John in the Netherlands, 14th-18th Centuries*. 1998

81. TIERNEY, B. *Foundations of the Conciliar Theory*. The Contribution of the Medieval Canonists from Gratian to the Great Schism. Enlarged New Edition. 1998

82. MIERNOWSKI, J. *Le Dieu Néant*. Théologies négatives à l'aube des temps modernes. 1998

83. HALVERSON, J.L. *Peter Aureol on Predestination*. A Challenge to Late Medieval Thought. 1998.

84. HOULISTON, V. (ed.). *Robert Persons, S.J.: The Christian Directory (1582)*. The First Booke of the Christian Exercise, appertayning to Resolution. 1998

85. GRELL, O.P. (ed.). *Paracelsus*. The Man and His Reputation, His Ideas and Their Transformation. 1998

86. MAZZOLA, E. *The Pathology of the English Renaissance*. Sacred Remains and Holy Ghosts. 1998.

87. 88. MARSILIUS VON INGHEN. *Quaestiones super quattuor libros sententiarum*. Super Primum. Bearbeitet von M. Santos Noya. 2 Bände. I. Quaestiones 1-7. II. Quaestiones 8-21. 2000

89. FAUPEL-DREVS, K. *Vom rechten Gebrauch der Bilder im liturgischen Raum*. Mittelalterliche Funktionsbestimmungen bildender Kunst im *Rationale divinorum officiorum* des Durandus von Mende (1230/1-1296). 1999

90. KREY, P.D.W. and SMITH, L. (eds.). *Nicholas of Lyra*. the Senses of Scripture. 2000

92. OAKLEY, F. *Politics and Eternity*. Studies in the History of Medieval and Early-Modern Political Thought. 1999

93. PRYDS, D. *The Politics of Preaching*. Robert of Naples (1309-1343) and his Sermons. 2000

94. POSTHUMUS MEYJES, G.H.M. *Jean Gerson – Apostle of Unity*. His Church Politics and Ecclesiology. Translated by J.C. Grayson. 1999

95. BERG, J. VAN DEN. *Religious Currents and Cross-Currents*. Essays on Early Modern Protestantism and the Protestant Enlightenment. Edited by J. de Bruijn, P. Holtrop, and E. van der Wall. 1999

96. IZBICKI, T.M. and BELLITTO, C.M. (eds.). *Reform and Renewal in the Middle Ages and the Renaissance*. Studies in Honor of Louis Pascoe, S. J. 2000

97. KELLY, D. *The Conspiracy of Allusion*. Description, Rewriting, and Authorship from Macrobius to Medieval Romance. 1999

98. MARRONE, S.P. *The Light of Thy Countenance*. Science and Knowledge of God in the Thirteenth Century. 2 volumes. 1. A Doctrine of Divine Illumination. 2. God at the Core of Cognition. 2001

99. HOWSON, B.H. *Erroneous and Schismatical Opinions*. The Question of Orthodoxy regarding the Theology of Hanserd Knollys (c. 1599-169)). 2001

100. ASSELT, W.J. VAN. *The Federal Theology of Johannes Cocceius (1603-1669)*. 2001

101. CELENZA, C.S. *Piety and Pythagoras in Renaissance Florence the* Symbolum Nesianum. 2001

102. DAM, H.-J. VAN (ed.), *Hugo Grotius, De imperio summarum potestatum circa sacra*. Critical Edition with Introduction, English translation and Commentary. 2 volumes. 2001

103. BAGGE, S. *Kings, Politics, and the Right Order of the World in German Historiography c. 950-1150*. 2002

104. STEIGER, J.A. *Fünf Zentralthemen der Theologie Luthers und seiner Erben*. Communicatio – Imago – Figura – Maria – Exempla. Mit Edition zweier christologischer Frühschriften Johann Gerhards. 2002

105. IZBICKI T.M. and BELLITTO C.M. (eds.). *Nicholas of Cusa and his Age: Intellect and Spirituality*. Essays Dedicated to the Memory of F. Edward Cranz, Thomas P. McTighe and Charles Trinkaus. 2002

106. HASCHER-BURGER, U. *Gesungene Innigkeit*. Studien zu einer Musikhandschrift der Devotio moderna (Utrecht, Universiteitsbibliotheek, MS 16 H 94, olim B 113). Mit einer Edition der Gesänge. 2002

107. BOLLIGER, D. *Infiniti Contemplatio*. Grundzüge der Scotus- und Scotismusrezeption im Werk Huldrych Zwinglis. 2003

108. CLARK, F. *The 'Gregorian'* Dialogues *and the Origins of Benedictine Monasticism*. 2002

109. ELM, E. *Die Macht der Weisheit*. Das Bild des Bischofs in der *Vita Augustini* des Possidius und andere spätantiken und frühmittelalterlichen Bischofsviten. 2003

110. BAST, R.J. (ed.). *The Reformation of Faith in the Context of Late Medieval Theology and Piety*. Essays by Berndt Hamm. 2004.

111. HEERING, J.-P. (ed.). *Hugo Grotius as Apologist for the Christian Religion*. A Study of his Work *De Veritate Religionis Christianae* (1640). Translated by J.C. Grayson. 2004.